A GUIDE TO THE MERCHANT SHIPPING ACTS

VOLUME ONE

A GUIDE TO THE MERCHANT SHIPPING ACTS

VOLUME ONE

BY

L. F. H. STANTON
F.C.I.T.

GLASGOW
BROWN, SON & FERGUSON, LTD.
52 DARNLEY STREET, G41 2SG

First Edition - - 1976

ISBN 0 85174 258 0

Printed and Made in Great Britain

FOREWORD

IT goes without saying that the writing of such a tome as *A Guide to the Merchant Shipping Acts* is a somewhat perilous task. Firstly, because one is always conscious that all has been said before, and conjoined with this, the real necessity of presenting knowledge in an easily-readable manner, and still to maintain the scholarship that such a work merits.

I owe great debts to the many generations of scholars whose endeavours have laid the foundations on which this edition is based.

I am aware of my special obligations in this respect, and acknowledge unreservedly the assistance I have received from past authors in this fascinating subject, a subject which is based in antiquity, and yet through its diverse branches, flourishes anew in the fullness of time.

I owe special thanks to two persons, without whose assistance I could not have compiled the work. One, Alfred C. Hedges, Esq., one-time Librarian and Curator to the Great Yarmouth Borough Council, for his meticulous proof-reading, and the other, Frederick J. G. Gregory, Esq., who besides interpreting my spasmodic handwriting, took upon himself, amongst other things, the compilation of the various indices, a most onerous task.

Great Yarmouth, 1976. L.F.H.S.

PREFACE

A GUIDE TO THE MERCHANT SHIPPING ACTS
HISTORICAL PROSPECTUS

THE year 1660 saw the beginning of a code of shipping law in this country known as the Navigation Acts. They were mainly concerned with the restriction of seaborne commerce to ships owned by British subjects and were brought into being by the then economic policy of this country. The building of British ships for British owners was restricted to British and Dominion builders, although an exception was made in respect to vessels taken as prize in war. One of the most important principles contained in the Navigation Laws was the obvious compulsory registration of British ships, which, with certain modifications remains to this day. Apart from these laws, legislation was in the main spasmodic and fragmentary. In fact, apart from being the core of legislation as we know it today, little resemblance is seen.

The early part of the nineteenth century saw the rise of British Commercial supremacy and the corollary of this development was the desire on the part of British shipowners, supported by the rising industrialists, for these restrictive protection laws to be repealed. As the result of pressure by these individuals (who regarded FREE TRADE as absolutely necessary for the economic advancement of an island kingdom) the laws were in 1849 repealed and the ports of Great Britain were opened to the vessels of all nations that granted British vessels reciprocal rights.

The year 1850 saw, with the enactment of the Mercantile Marine Act of that year, the establishment of the first comprehensive system for the regulation of matters relating to the Merchant Service, and for the first time, brought the responsibilities of the Mercantile Marine under the aegis of the Board of Trade. By 1854 there were 48 different Acts or part of Acts in being for the general regulation of the Mercantile Service. It was clear that the time had arrived for these laws to be consolidated into a single Act, and this was effected by the Merchant Shipping Act of 1854.

The growth of world commerce, aided by the industrial revolution, now in full swing, continued its upward trend, with the British Merchant Service playing a predominant and vital part. This of necessity brought about amendments and changes in the law and during the next 40 years, a further 27 Acts were entered in the Statute Book. The most important provisions of these were:—

1862—Introduction of certificate of competency for engineers. Regulations for Preventing Collisions at Sea drafted in modern form and provisions made for their future modification by Orders in Council.
The commencement of International application of certain provisions of the Acts.
1876—Commencement of compulsory marking of Load-lines on vessels.
(The result of Samuel Plimsoll's efforts.)
1880—The prevention of Grain cargoes from shifting.
1889—Direct representation given to Pilots and Shipowners on Pilotage Authorities.
1890—Position of Load-line to be ascertained in accordance with official Tables.

The result of all these modifications and amendments led to the great Consolidation Act of 1894, which still remains the principal Act. From 1894 to the present day, numerous Acts amending the principal Act, have come into being and it is held by many authorities that the time is not too distant when the laws relating to merchant shipping will have to be further consolidated.

The Acts from 1894 to 1964 which have affected the Principal Act or are intimately concerned with the Merchant Shipping Acts are as follows:—

1897—Merchant Shipping Act 1897.
(Extension of powers of detention for under-manning.)
1898—Merchant Shipping (Mercantile Marine Fund) Act 1898.
(Payment of certain expenses and levying of Light Dues.)
Merchant Shipping (Liability of Shipowners) Act 1898. (Repealed 1958.)
1900—Merchant Shipping (Liability of Shipowners and Others) Act 1900—(Section 1 repealed 1958.)
1906—Merchant Shipping Act 1906.
(Numerous amendments of the Principal Act.)
1907—Merchant Shipping Act 1907.
(Tonnage deduction.)
1911—Merchant Shipping (Stevedores and Trimmers) Act 1911.
(Repealed.)
1911—Merchant Shipping Act 1911.
Jurisdiction to British Courts in foreign countries.)
1911—Maritime Conventions Act 1911.
1913—Pilotage Act 1913.

1914—Merchant Shipping (Certificates) Act 1914.
(Amendment of Law relating to Examinations.)

1919—Merchant Shipping (Wireless Telegraphy) Act 1919.
Repealed by the Merchant Shipping (Safety Convention) 1949.

1920—Merchant Shipping (Amendment) Act 1920.
(General Lighthouse Fund.)
Merchant Shipping (Scottish Fishing-Boats) Act 1920.
(Extension of Part 10 of Principal Act.)

1921—Merchant Shipping Act 1921.
(Amendments to Merchant Shipping Acts 1894–1920 in respect of Barges, Lighters, etc.)

1923—Fees (Increase) Act, 1923.
Merchant Shipping Acts (Amendment) Act 1923.
(Medical Expenses.)

1925—Merchant Shipping (Equivalent Provisions) Act 1925.
(Exception for certain vessels from provisions of the Merchant Shipping Acts.)
Merchant Shipping (International Labour Conventions) Act 1925.

1928—Merchant Shipping (Line-Throwing Appliance) Act 1928.
Repealed by the Merchant Shipping (Safety conventions) Act 1949.

1932—Merchant Shipping (Safety and Load-Line Conventions) Act 1932.

1936—Pilotage Authorities (Limitation of Liability) Act 1936.

1937—Merchant Shipping Act, 1937.
(Load-Lines and Fishing-Vessels.)
Merchant Shipping (Superannuation Contributions) Act 1937.

1938—Sea-Fish Industry Act 1938
(Amendment of Part X of Merchant Shipping Act 1894.)

1939—Ships and Aircraft (Transfer Destruction) Act 1939.
Repealed by the Emergency Laws (Repeal) Act 1959.

1940—Merchant Shipping (Salvage) Act 1940.
Repealed by the Crown Proceedings Act 1947.

1947—Crown Proceedings Act 1947.
(H.M. ships put in the same position as private individuals.)

1948—Merchant Shipping Act 1948.
(Amendment of Merchant Shipping Act from the Seattle Convention 1946.

1949—Merchant Shipping (Safety Convention) Act 1949.

1950 Merchant Shipping Act 1950.
(Provisions for Crew Accommodation in Fishing-Boats.)

1952—Merchant Shipping Acts 1952.
(Exemptions as to Crew Accommodation.)

1954—Merchant Shipping Act 1954.
(Amendments of law relating to deductions for measurement in small vessels.)

1958—Merchant Shipping (Liability of Shipowners and Others) Act 1958.

1960—Merchant Shipping (Ministry Lighthouse) Act 1960
(Transference of Lighthouse funds to Government of India.)

1961—North Atlantic Shipping Act 1961.

1963—Oil in Navigable Waters Act 1963.

1965—Merchant Shipping Act 1965.

1967—Load-Lines Act 1970.

1970—Merchant Shipping Act 1970.

1975—Merchant Shipping Act 1974.

The Acts have brought in their wakes numerous Rules and Orders which are referred to in the text.

It can be seen that over the years, Merchant Shipping legislation has increased, not only in substance, but also in territorial application. Numerous International Conventions have made their contributions and with few exceptions, the laws relating to the safety and general wellbeing of the seafarer have been accepted by all maritime nations.

Introduction—The Principal Act of 1894 is divided into fourteen parts as follows:—

PART I.	Registry.
PART II	Masters and Seamen.
PART III.	Passenger and Emigrant ships.
PART IV.	Fishing-Boats.
PART V.	Safety.
PART VI.	Special Shipping Enquiries and Courts.
PART VII.	Delivery of Goods.
PART VIII.	Liability of Shipowner.
PART IX.	Wreck and Salvage.
PART X.	Pilotage (Repealed by the Pilotage Act 1913).
PART XI.	Lighthouses.
PART XII.	Mercantile Marine Fund.
PART XIII.	Legal Proceedings.
PART XIV.	Supplemental.

The Ministry Responsible—The general superintendence of merchant shipping and seamen was entrusted under the Merchant

Shipping Act 1894 to a government department known as the Board of Trade. Throughout the intervening years, as a result of government policy and extraneous difficulties brought into being by the Second World War the control and superintendence has been successively transferred and vested in the following bodies:—

1939—Ministry of Shipping.
1941—Ministry of War Transport.
1946—Ministry of Transport.
1953—Ministry of Transport and Civil Aviation.
1959—Ministry of Transport.

In 1965, the Transfer of Functions (Shipping and Constructions of Ships) Order 1965, provided for the functions exercisable by the Ministry of Transport to be transferred to the Board of Trade with the exception of the provisions of section 2 (*b*) of the Merchant Shipping (Liability of Shipowners and Others) Act 1958 and as respects functions under section 80 of the Merchant Shipping Act 1906, in relation to government ships in the service of the Ministry of Transport.

In 1970, the Board of Trade was merged into a new Department, called the Department of Trade and Industry. This was effected on the 20th of October, 1970, by the Secretary of State for Trade and Industry Order 1970, Statutory Instrument 1537/1970.

CONTENTS

PAGE

Part Six—Special Shipping Enquiries and Courts:

Part Seven—Delivery of Goods and Lien for Freight:

Part Eight—Limitation of Liability:

Part Nine—Wreck and Salvage:

TABLE OF CASES CITED

PAGE

The Acrux 1962 – – – – – – – – – – 31
The Admiralty Commissioners *v. The Valverda* 1938 – – – – 302
The Adriatic – – – – – – – – – – – 140
The Aeolius 1873 – – – – – – – – – – 289
The Aglaia 1886 – – – – – – – – – – 289
The Aid 1822 – – – – – – – – – – – 286
The Albion 1953 – – – – – – – – – – 136
The Alde 1926 – – – – – – – – – – 221
The Amalia 1863 – – – – – – – – – – 226
The America and *The Syria* 1874 – – – – – – – 221
Anchor Line (Henderson Bros. Ltd.) *v.* Dundee Harbour Trustees 1922 280
The Andalania 1886 – – – – – – – – – 320
The Andrew Wilson 1863 – – – – – – – – 293, 295
The Annandale 1877 – – – – – – – – – 58
The Annie 1886 – – – – – – – – – – 287
The Anonity 1961 – – – – – – – – – – 220
The Apollo 1824 – – – – – – – – – – 8
The Aquila 1798 – – – – – – – – – – 265
The Arabert 1961 – – – – – – – – – – 223
The Arizona 1880 – – – – – – – – – 177, 178
Arkle *v.* Lienzell 1858 – – – – – – – – – 16
The Athelvictor 1946 – – – – – – – – – 221
The Australia 1859 – – – – – – – – – – 26

Baithyany *v.* Bouch 1881 – – – – – – – – – 24
Barclay *v.* Poole 1907 – – – – – – – – – 50
Barraclough *v.* Brown 1897 – – – – – – – – 280
Barras *v.* Aberdeen Fishing Co. 1933 – – – – – – 87
Beaverford *v. The Kafiristan* 1938 – – – – – – – 139
Beauchamp *v.* Turrel 1952 – – – – – – – – 220
The Bedeburn 1914 – – – – – – – – – – 289
Behnke *v.* Bede Shipping Co. 1927 – – – – – – – 24
The Benwell Tower 1895 – – – – – – – – 32, 34
Bell *v.* Bank of London 1858 – – – – – – – 32, 44
Bell *v.* Blythe 1868 – – – – – – – – – – 33
Benyon *v.* Cresswell 1848 – – – – – – – – 4, 24
The Bernina 1886 – – – – – – – – – – 221
The Bertie 1886 – – – – – – – – – – 302
Black *v.* Williams 1895 – – – – – – – – 33, 51
The Blanche 1904 – – – – – – – – – – 225
Bly *v.* Simpson, *The Fusilier* 1865 – – – – – – – 286
Board of Trade *v.* Leith Local Marine Board 1896 – – – – – 176

PAGE

Daimler Co. Ltd. *v.* Continental Tyre & Rubber Co. Ltd. 1916 – – 3
De Mattos *v.* Gibson 1858 – – – – – – – – 35
Dennis *v.* Cork S.S. Co. 1913 – – – – – – – – 200
Dickinson *v.* Kitchen 1858 – – – – – – – – 34
The Dione 1885 – – – – – – – – – 223
Dixon *v.* Colecraft 1802 – – – – – – – – – 162
Dixon *v.* Farrer 1886 – – – – – – – – – 162
Dormant *v.* Furness Railway Co. 1883 – – – – – – 280
The Douglas 1882 – – – – – – – – – – 279
The Dowthorpe 1843 – – – – – – – – – 33
The Driade 1959 – – – – – – – – – – 289
Dudgeon *v.* Pembroke 1874 – – – – – – – – 97

The Ella 1915 – – – – – – – – – – 279
Ellerman Lines Ltd. *v.* Murray 1931 – – – – – – – 86
Elliot Steam Co. *v.* Admiralty Commissioners 1921 – – – – 302
The Emmy Haase 1884 – – – – – – – – – 140
The Empire Antelope 1943 – – – – – – – – 179
The Empire Jamaica 1957 – – – – – – – – 220
The Energie 1875 – – – – – – – – – – 204
The Englishman 1894 – – – – – – – – – 221
The Enterprise 1912 – – – – – – – – – 135
European & Australian Royal Mail Co. *v.* P. & O. Steam Nav. Co. 1886 24
European & Australian Royal Mail Co. *v.* Royal Mail Steam Packet Co. 1858 – – – – – – – – – – – 35
Ex *Parte Minto* 1877 – – – – – – – – – 174
Ex *Parte Storey* 1878 – – – – – – – – – 177

The Famenotle 1882 – – – – – – – – – 178
The Fanny 1912 – – – – – – – – – – 219
The F. D. Lambert 1917 – – – – – – – – – 265
Foong Tai & Co. *v.* Buolleister & Co. 1908 – – – – – 51
The Five Steel Barges 1890 – – – – – – – – 286
The Frances 1829 – – – – – – – – – – 16
Frazer *v.* Cuthbertson 1880 – – – – – – – – 7, 52
The Freden 1950 – – – – – – – – – – 237
The Frederick 1838 – – – – – – – – – 224, 289
The Fulham 1898 – – – – 171, 191, 266, 271, 273, 283, 288, 298
The Fusilier 1865 – – – – – – – – – – 287

The Gee Whizz 1951 – – – – – – – – – 389
The Generous 1868 – – – – – – – – – 293, 295
The Genessee 1848 – – – – – – – – – – 265
Genochio *v.* Steward 1907 – – – – – – – – 147
The Gertrude 1861 – – – – – – – – – – 265
Gibson *v.* Inso 1847 – – – – – – – – – 17
The Glengyle 1889 – – – – – – – – – – 295
The Glenmorven 1913 – – – – – – – – – 289

PAGE

Glyn, Mills & Co. *v.* East & West India Dock Co. 1882 – – – 201
The Golden Sea 1882 – – – – – – – – – 177
Goss *v.* Quinton 1842 – – – – – – – – – 13
Graham *v.* Duncan 1950 – – – – – – – – – 96
Great Western Rail Co. *v.* Kassos Steam Navigation Co. 1930 – – 67

Hannibal v. The Queen 1867 – – – – – – – – 139
The Hans Hoth 1952 – – – – – – – – – 219
The Harlow 1922 – – – – – – – – – 221, 388
The Harriet 1857 – – – – – – – – – – 295
The Harrington 1888 – – – – – – – – – 280
Hart *v.* Hudson Bros. Ltd. 1928 – – – – – – – 243
The Henry 1851 – – – – – – – – – – 295
The Henry Coxon 1878 – – – – – – – – – 172
The Hereward 1895 – – – – – – – – – 8
Hick *v.* Rodocanachi 1891 – – – – – – – – 199
The Hildina 1957 – – – – – – – – – – 219
Hill *v.* Audus 1855 – – – – – – – – – 225, 226
Hook *v.* Consolidated Fisheries Ltd. 1953 – – – – – – 220
The Humorous 1895 – – – – – – – – – 24
Hutton *v.* Ras S.S. Co. 1907 – – – – – – – – 189

The Ida 1866 – – – – – – – – – – – 182
The Inisfallen 1866 – – – – – – – – – – 32
The Inventor 1905 – – – – – – – – – – 225

The Jassy 1906 – – – – – – – – – – 290
The Johannes 1860 – – – – – – – – – – 286
The John Ormston 1881 – – – – – – – – – 223
Jorgensen *v.* Neptune Steam Fishing Co. Ltd. 1902 – – – – 287

The Karo 1887 – – – – – – – – – – 167
Keith *v.* Burrows 1877 – – – – – – – – – 34
The Kestrel 1881 – – – – – – – – – 177, 182
The Kingalock 1854 – – – – – – – – – 295
Kinley *v.* Sierra Nevada 1924 – – – – – – – – 389
The Kirkness 1957 – – – – – – – – – 223, 250
The Kronprinz Olaf 1921 – – – – – – – – – 228

The Lady Gwendoline 1964 – – – – – – – – 220
The Lady Katherine Barham 1961 – – – – – – – 298
Larsen *v.* Hart 1900 – – – – – – – – – 275
Lawther *v.* Belfast Harbour Commissioners 1864 – – – – 200
Lennards Carrying Co. *v.* Asiatic Petroleum Co. 1915 – – 214, 219, 220
The Leoborg (No. 2) 1964 – – – – – – – – 34
The Leon Bluhm 1915 – – – – – – – – – 289
The Liffey 1887 – – – – – – – – – – 272
Lewis *v.* Gray 1876 – – – – – – – – – 162

PAGE
Patersons Steamships Ltd. *v.* Canadian Co-operative Wheat Producers Ltd. 1934 – – – – – – – – – – 220
Phillips *v.* Parnaby 1934 – – – – – – – – – 243
The Polzeath 1916 – – – – – – – – – – 3
The Port Hunter 1910 – – – – – – – – – 295
The Porto Alexandre 1920 – – – – – – – – 290
The Princess Victoria 1953 – – – – – – 175, 177, 182

The Queen 1869 – – – – – – – – – – 139

R. *v.* Two Casks of Tallow 1837 – – – – – – – 265
R. *v.* Lopez 1858 – – – – – – – – – – 351
R. *v.* Satter 1858 – – – – – – – – – – 351
R. *v.* Bjornsen – – – – – – – – – – 2, 15
R. *v.* Collinbridge 1864 – – – – – – – – – 179
R. *v.* 49 Cases of Brandy 1836 – – – – – – – – 265
R. *v.* Tomlinson 1866 – – – – – – – – – 179
R. *v.* Stewart 1899 – – – – – – – – – – 84
The Radiant 1958 – – – – – – – – – – 220
The Rajah 1872 – – – – – – – – – – 222
Rankine *v.* Raschen 1887 – – – – – – – – 228
The Rapid 1938 – – – – – – – – – – 302
The Recepta 1889 – – – – – – – – – 63, 224
Red 'R' S.S. Co. *v.* Allatine 1908 – – – – – – – 202
The Rempor 1883 – – – – – – – – – – 286
Richmond Hill S.S. Co. *v.* Trinity House 1896 – – – – – 67
The Rijnstroon 1889 – – – – – – – – – 226
The Rose 1873 – – – – – – – – – – 33
The Rosslyn 1904 – – – – – – – – – – 224
The Royal Star 1928 – – – – – – – – – 185
The Ruapeha 1927 – – – – – – – – – – 232
The Ruapeha (No. 2) 1929 – – – – – – – – 232
The Ruby 1900 – – – – – – – – – – 35

The St. Olaf 1876 – – – – – – – – – – 17
The St. Tudno 1916 – – – – – – – – – – 3
Salmon & Woods Ex Partegould 1885 – – – – – – – 24
The Salt Union *v.* Wood 1893 – – – – – – – 106, 149, 151
Sapp *v.* Bono 1887 – – – – – – – – – – 24
The San Onofre 1922 – – – – – – – – – 139
The Saratoga 1861 – – – – – – – – – – 289
The Sarden 1861 – – – – – – – – – – 302
The Satanita 1897 – – – – – – – – – – 218
Scheiber *v.* Furness 1893 – – – – – – – – – 110
The Schwan 1882 – – – – – – – – – – 222
The Sceptre 1876 – – – – – – – – – – 58
The Scotia 1903 – – – – – – – – – – 287

PAGE
The Seistan 1959 – – – – – – – – – 175, 182
Sheppey & Chemical Works *v.* The Conservators of River Medway 1926 280
The Sisters 1875 – – – – – – – – – – 226
Smitten *v.* Orient Steam Navigation Co. 1907 – – – – – 214
Smith *v.* Kirby 1875 – – – – – – – – – 219
The Snark 1900 – – – – – – – – – – 279
The Sophie 1841 – – – – – – – – – – 265
Stapleton *v.* Haymen 1864 – – – – – – – – 26
Steele *v.* Lester & Lilee 1877 – – – – – – – – 110
The Stella 1900 – – – – – – – – – 221, 222
The Stonedale No. 1 1956 – – – – – – – 222, 250
The Stonedale No. 4 1956 – – – – – – – – 222
The Stranna 1938 – – – – – – – – – – 157
Summers *v.* Buchan 1891 – – – – – – – – – 237
The Spirit of the Ocean – – – – – – – – – 226

The Teal 1949 – – – – – – – – – – 226
The Terneuzen 1938 – – – – – – – – – 86
The Thames 1940 – – – – – – – – – 219, 236
Thomas *v.* Farrer 1882 – – – – – – – – – 162
The Thuringia 1872 – – – – – – – – – – 162
Trinity House *v.* Maritime Salvors Ltd. 1923 – – – – 280, 281
The Truculent 1952 – – – – – – – – – 220, 260
The Two Ellens 1871 – – – – – – – – – 36
Tyne Improvement Commissioners *v.* The Armement S/A *The Brabo* 1949 280

The Ulysses 1888 – – – – – – – – – – 302
Union Bank of London *v.* Lenanton 1879 per Bramwell L. J. – – 3, 24
Utopia (Owners) *v.* *Primula* (Owners) *The Utopia* 1893 – – – 279

The Venture 1908 – – – – – – – – – – 51
The Victoria 1888 – – – – – – – – – – 227
The Vigilant 1921 – – – – – – – – – – 220
Virginia Carolina Chemical Co. *v.* Norfolk & North American S.S. Co. 1912 – – – – – – – – – – – 213

Waddle *v.* Wallsend Shipping Co. Ltd. 1852 – – – – – 158
The Warkworth 1884 – – – – – – – – 219, 220
Watson *v.* B.O.T. 1884 – – – – – – – – – 178
The Western Ocean 1870 – – – – – – – – – 34
The Westbourne 1889 – – – – – – – – 289, 295
The White Star Line *v.* Cometford 1931 – – – – – – 86
White & Co. *v.* Furness Withy & Co. 1895 – – – – – 203
Wiley *v.* Cranford 1861 – – – – – – – – – 17
Wheeler *v.* London & Rochester Trading Co. 1957 – – – – 225
Williams *v.* Allsop 1861 – – – – – – – – 33, 35
The Willem III 1871 – – – – – – – – 286, 287
The William & John 1863 – – – – – – – – 293

	PAGE
The Wills, No. 66 1914	22
Woods *v.* Russel 1822	13
The Wousung 1876	303
The Yarmouth 1909	371
The Yolande Barbara 1961	32
Young *v.* Docherty 1929	96
Young *v.* Scotia 1903	136
The Zeta 1875	265, 272

A GUIDE TO THE MERCHANT SHIPPING ACTS

An Act to consolidate Enactments relating to Merchant Shipping. [25th August 1894.]

A.D. 1894.

BE it enacted by the Queen's most Excellent Majesty, by and with the advice and consent of the Lords Spiritual and Temporal, and Commons, in this present Parliament assembled, and by the authority of the same, as follows:

PART I

REGISTRY

Qualification for owning British Ships

Qualification for owning British ship.

1 A ship shall not be deemed to be a British ship unless owned wholly by persons of the following description (in this Act referred to as persons qualified to be owners of British ships); namely—

(*a*) Natural-born British subjects;

(*b*) Persons naturalised by or in pursuance of an Act of Parliament of the United Kingdom, or by or in pursuance of an Act or ordinance of the proper legislative authority in a British possession;

(*c*) Persons made denizens by letters of denization; and

(*d*) Bodies corporate established under and subject to the laws of some part of Her Majesty's dominions and having their principal place of business in those dominions:

Provided that any person who either—

(i) being a natural-born British subject has taken the oath of allegiance to a foreign sovereign or state or has otherwise become a citizen or subject of a foreign state; or

(ii) has been naturalised or made a denizen as aforesaid;

Qualification for owning British ship.

shall not be qualified to be owner of a British ship unless, after taking the said oath, or becoming a citizen or subject of a foreign state, or on or after being naturalised or made denizen as aforesaid, he has taken the oath of allegiance to Her Majesty the Queen, and is during the time he is owner of the ship either resident in Her Majesty's dominions, or partner in a firm actually carrying on business in Her Majesty's dominions.

COMMENTS.

The words underlined were repealed by the British Nationality Act, 1948, section 31 and the Fourth schedule, part 1, with effect from 1st January 1949.

British Subjects.

The term British Subject retained in this section is now defined as a result of the British Nationality Act, 1948 as:—

(*a*) Citizens of the United Kingdom and Colonies;

(*b*) Citizens of the Commonwealth countries;

(*c*) Certain citizens of the Republic of Ireland;

(*d*) British subjects whose citizenship had not been ascertained at the commencement of the British Nationality Act, 1948.

British Ship.

This term is not defined in the Act. It would appear, however, that 'unless a ship be employed under letters of marque of Government which make her become a ship of the Government . . . the nationality of a ship depends upon her ownership and upon that alone'—Chartered Mercantile Bank of India *v.* Netherlands India Steam Navigation Company 1883 *per* Brett L. J.

A British Certificate of Registry is normally evidence that the vessel is a British ship, but if it is proved that the owner is in fact an alien then this presumption is rebutted, R. *v.* Bjornsen 1865. If a vessel is not registered as a British ship, when required by the Act to be so registered, then she will not be registered as a British ship and thus will not be entitled to the benefits of such registration. She may still incur certain of the liabilities of being a British ship.

See section 2 for the obligation to register.

See section 70 as to penalty for concealment of British or assumption of foreign character.

See section 72 as to being recognised as British.

In Mortimer *v.* Vlisker 1914, where a vessel was not registered in accordance with the requirements of the Act, it was held not to be a ship registered in the United Kingdom or any other British ship within the meaning of the now repealed Workmen's Compensation Acts. It would appear that the decision is applicable to the determination as to whether a vessel is an 'injured person' under the National Insurance (Industrial Injuries) Acts, 1946–1963.

Bodies Corporate.

A corporation may be qualified to own a British ship, although the nationality of some of the individual shareholders are foreigners, R. *v.* Arnaud 1846.

In the question of prize, nationality may be material. The *St. Tudno* 1916.

The general position as to companies incorporated in England, but controlled by aliens is explained in Daimler Co. Ltd. *v.* Continental Tyre & Rubber Co. (Great Britain) Ltd. 1916. For the purpose of this Act, the yardstick would appear to be the locality of the control of this business.

In the *Polzeath* 1916, where the vessel was owned by a company registered in the United Kingdom, it was shown that the effective control of the business was centred in Hamburg, Germany. Accordingly therefore, the ship was forfeit to the Crown.

Obligation to register British Ships

2 (1) Every British ship shall, unless exempted from registry, be registered under this Act. Obligation to register British ships.

(2) If a ship required by this Act to be registered is not registered under this Act she shall not be recognised as a British ship.

(3) A ship required by this Act to be registered may be detained until the master of the ship, if so required, produces the certificate of the registry of the ship.

COMMENTS.

There is no penalty for not registering but the consequence of non-registration is that the owner does not get the benefits of his British ownership. Union Bank of London *v.* Lenanton 1879 *per* Bramwell, L.J.

See section 72 as to the liability of ships not registered as British under the Mercantile Shipping (Liability of Shipowners and others) Act, 1958, section 4 (2) the fact of non-registration does not affect the right of any British ship to limit liability. Under the Merchant Shipping Act 1906, the Commissioners of Customs may call for proof of title if there is doubt as to the title of a ship registered as a British ship.

⚓ ⚓ ⚓ ⚓

Exemptions from registry.

3 The following ships are exempted from registry under this Act:—

(1) Ships not exceeding fifteen tons burden employed solely in navigation on the rivers or coasts of the United Kingdom, or on the rivers or coasts of some British possession within which the managing owners of the ships are resident;

(2) Ships not exceeding thirty tons burden and not having a whole or fixed deck, and employed solely in fishing or trading coastwise on the shores of Newfoundland or parts adjacent thereto, or in the Gulf of Saint Lawrence, or on such portions of the coasts of Canada as lie bordering on that gulf.

COMMENTS.

Tons Burden.

This means the net registered tonnage (*see* sections 77–79 as amended) and not the gross tonnage. The *Brunel* 1900.

General.

Where registration was unnecessary, but had actually been registered, then the vessel may be transferred without a registered bill of sale. Bengin *v.* Cresswell 1848.

United Kingdom.

For the purpose of this section the expression 'United Kingdom' includes the Republic of Ireland. Unless the term 'United Kingdom' is expressly or implicitly extended by the enactment in which it occurs, the Channel Islands and the Isle of Man are excluded.

British Possession.

This is defined by the Interpretation Act 1889 as 'any part of Her Majesty's dominions exclusive of the United Kingdom the position of British possessions to alter the provisions of the Act is contained in sections 735 and 736 of this Act'.

Her Majesty's Vessels.

These are exempt from registration, *see* section 741, with the exception of those government vessels which are registrable under section 80 of the Merchant Shipping Act 1906.

⚓ ⚓ ⚓ ⚓

Procedure for Registration

4 (1) The following persons shall be registrars of British ships:— Registrars of British ships.

(*a*) At any port in the United Kingdom, or Isle of Man, approved by the Commissioners of Customs for the registry of ships, the chief officer of customs;

(*b*) In Guernsey and Jersey, the chief officers of customs together with the governor;

(*c*) In Malta and Gibraltar, the governor;

(*d*) At Calcutta, Madras, and Bombay, the port officer;

(*e*) At any other port in any British possession approved by the governor of the possession for the registry of ships, the chief officer of customs, or, if there is no such officer there resident, the governor of the possession in which the port is situate, or any officer appointed for the purpose by the governor;

(*f*) At a port of registry established by Order in Council under this Act, persons of the description in that behalf declared by the Order.

(2) Notwithstanding anything in this section Her Majesty may by Order in Council declare, with respect to any British possession named in the Order, not being the Channel Islands or the Isle of Man, the description of persons who are to be registrars of British ships in that possession.

(3) A registrar shall not be liable to damages or otherwise for any loss accruing to any person by reason of any act done or default made by him in his character of registrar, unless the same has happened through his neglect or wilful act.

COMMENTS.

British Ships.

See section 1.

United Kingdom.

See section 3.

British Possession.

See section 3.

Chief Offices of Customs.

See section 742.

Commissioners of Customs, now the Commissioners of Customs and Excise.

See the Customs and Excise Act 1952, section 318.

Orders under Sub-section 2.

Various officials have been appointed as registrars in Singapore, Penang and Malasia; Gibraltar, Tasmania, by orders in Council. It would appear that instituted registrars in Burma and India have been altered by the Burma Independence Act 1947, and the India Independence Act of the same year.

⚓ ⚓ ⚓ ⚓

Register book. **5** Every registrar of British ships shall keep a book to be called the register book, and entries in that book shall be made in accordance with the following provisions:—

(i) The property in a ship shall be divided into sixty-four shares:

(ii) Subject to the provisions of this Act with respect to joint owners or owners by transmission, not more than sixty-four individuals shall be entitled to be registered at the same time as owners of any one ship; but this rule shall not affect the beneficial title of any number of persons or of any company represented by or claiming under or through any registered owner or joint owner:

(ii) A person shall not be entitled to be registered as owner of a fractional part of a share in a ship; but any number of persons not exceeding five may be registered as joint owners of a ship or of any share or shares therein:

(iv) Joint owners shall be considered as constituting one person only as regards the persons entitled to be registered, and shall not be entitled to dispose in severalty of any interest in a ship, or in any share therein in respect of which they are registered:

(v) A corporation may be registered as owner by its corporate name.

COMMENTS.

Register Book.

This book is admissable in evidence and may be inspected on payment of a fee. *See* section 64.

A mortgage of a ship or share must be recorded in this book. *See* section 31.

Particulars on application for certificate of mortgage and sale must be entered. *See* section 40.

For declaration of Ownership on registry. *See* section 9.

Entry of particulars in the register book. *See* section 11.

A notice of trust cannot be entered. *See* section 56.

Beneficial Title and Interests.

See sections 56 to 58, which include the power of registered owner to dispose of the ship or share.

Transmission of Property.

See section 27.

Liability as Between Part Owners.

Persons owning shares in a ship fall into these two broadly defined classes. They may be:

(1) Joint owners who own the ship or share jointly, but with unity of title, and:

(2) Co-owners who own distinct shares in the ship with an undivided interest in the whole. These are tenents in common with each other in respect of their shares. It is usual for the relations of the co-owners to be regulated by express agreement and this authority is frequently delegated to one of their number who is known as the managing owner. This term which is not defined in the Merchant Shipping Act 1894, is a commercial and not a legal expression. Frazer *v.* Cuthbertson 1880 *per* Bowen J.

A person who is not a part owner may assume the functions of a managing owner and is known as a ship's husband.

The Employment of a Ship.

In principle, the control and employment of the ship lies with the desire of the majority owners. In the event of there being a dissenting minority, it is allowable for the majority owners to pursue the voyage, but in this event, the minority owners are excluded from any share in the profit and loss, and in any case before the majority owners are allowed to proceed, they are compelled to give security upon the safe return of the vessel. The *Apollo* 1824.

The amount of security given must bear the same relation to the value of the vessel as the number of shares held by the minority holders to the total number of shares in the ship. The *Candur* 1898.

The Sale of the Ship.

The broad principle of English Law has been enunciated in that the will of the majority will prevail as long as the interests of the dissentient minority can be protected.

Thus, in certain cases the court will order that a ship be sold, but even in the event of the majority owners so desiring, a strong case must be made out. In a proper case, the power of sale will be exercised at the instance of the minority owners. The *Hereward* 1895.

⚓ ⚓ ⚓ ⚓

Survey and measurement of ship.

6 Every British ship shall before registry be surveyed by a surveyor of ships and her tonnage ascertained in accordance with the tonnage regulations of this Act, and the surveyor shall grant his certificate specifying the ship's tonnage and build, and such other particulars descriptive of the identity of the ship as may for the time being be required by the Board of Trade, and such certificate shall be delivered to the registrar before registry.

COMMENTS.

Surveyors.

For the appointment and powers of surveyors, *see* sections 724–727 and the Merchant Shipping Act 1906, section 75.

Tonnage Regulations.

For details, *see* sections 77–81.

The Merchant Shipping Act 1906, section 54.

The Merchant Shipping Act 1907, section 1.

When such tonnage is ascertained and registered, it is deemed to be the tonnage of the ship, unless there is an alteration in the form or capacity of the ship or the discovery of an error in assessment, section 82.

The form of certificate is seen in section 65 and is retained by the registrars in the registry of the ship, section 12.

British Ship.

See comments to section 1.

⚓ ⚓ ⚓ ⚓

7 (1) Every British ship shall before registry be marked permanently and conspicuously to the satisfaction of the Board of Trade as follows— Marking of ship.

(*a*) Her name shall be marked on each of her bows, and her name and the name of her port of registry must be marked on her stern, on a dark ground in white or yellow letters, or on a light ground in black letters, such letters to be of a length not less than four inches, and of proportionate breadth:

(*b*) Her official number and the number denoting her registered tonnage shall be cut in on her main beam:

(*c*) A scale of feet denoting her draught of water shall be marked on each side of her stem and of her stern post in Roman capital letters or in figures, not less than six inches in length, the lower line of such letters or figures to coincide with the draught line denoted thereby, and those letters and figures must be marked by being cut in and painted white or yellow on a dark ground, or in such other way as the Board of Trade approve.

(2) The Board of Trade may exempt any class of ships from all or any of the requirements of this section, and a fishing-boat entered in the fishing-boat register, and lettered and numbered in pursuance of the Fourth Part of this Act, need not have her name and port of registry marked under this section.

(3) If the scale of feet showing the ship's draught of water is in any respect inaccurate, so as to be likely to mislead, the owner of the ship shall be liable to a fine not exceeding one hundred pounds.

(4) The marks required by this section shall be permanently continued, and no alteration shall be made therein, except in the event of any of the particulars thereby denoted being altered in the manner provided by this Act.

(5) If an owner or master of a British ship neglects to cause his ship to be marked as required by this section, or to keep her so marked, or if any person conceals, removes, alters, defaces, or obliterates or suffers any person under his control to conceal, remove, alter, deface, or obliterate any of the said marks, except in the event aforesaid, or except for the purpose of escaping capture by an enemy, that owner, master, or person shall for each offence be liable to a fine not exceeding one hundred pounds, and on a certificate from a surveyor of ships, or Board of Trade inspector under this Act, that a ship is insufficiently or inaccurately marked the ship may be detained until the insufficiency or inaccuracy has been remedied.

COMMENTS.

British Ship.

See section 1 and comments thereto.

Name.

For details of material regarding names, *see* section 47, and the Merchant Shipping Act 1906, section 50.

Registered Tonnage.

See section 77 as to how ascertained.

Port of Registry.

See section 13 for details and in the event of change, *See* section 53.

Draught.

To be recorded and forwarded, as *per* section 436.

Surveyor.

See sections 724–727.

Inspector.

See sections 728–730.

To Enforce Detention.

See section 692.

⚓ ⚓ ⚓ ⚓

Application for registry.

8 An application for registry of a ship shall be made in the case of individuals by the person requiring to be registered as owner, or by some one or more of the persons so requiring if more than one, or by his or their agent, and in the case of corporations by their agent, and the authority of the agent shall be testified by writing, if appointed by individuals, under the hands of the appointors, and, if appointed by a corporation, under the common seal of that corporation.

COMMENTS.

Section 2 relates to the obligation to register British ships.

Section 5 as to registration of owners.

Section 60 as to the power of the registrar to deal with any evidence.

9 A person shall not be entitled to be registered as owner of a ship or of a share therein until he, or in the case of a corporation the person authorised by this Act to make declarations on behalf of the corporation, has made and signed a declaration of ownership, referring to the ship as described in the certificate of the surveyor, and containing the following particulars:— **Declaration of ownership on registry.**

(i) A statement of his qualification to own a British ship, or in the case of a corporation, of such circumstances of the constitution and business thereof as prove it to be qualified to own a British ship:

(ii) A statement of the time when and the place where the ship was built, or, if the ship is foreign built, and the time and place of building unknown, a statement that she is foreign built, and that the declarant does not know the time or place of her building; and, in addition thereto, in the case of a foreign ship, a statement of her foreign name, or, in the case of a ship condemned, a statement of the time, place and court at and by which she was condemned:

(iii) A statement of the name of the master:

(iv) A statement of the number of shares in the ship of which he or the corporation, as the case may be, is entitled to be registered as owner:

(v) A declaration that, to the best of his knowledge and belief, no unqualified person or body of persons is entitled as owner to any legal or beneficial interest in the ship or any share therein.

COMMENTS.

Declaration of Ownership.

This is retained by the registrar on registration. *See* section 12.

Change of Ownership.
Must be endorsed on the certificate of registry. *See* section 20.

Procedure for Registry Anew.
See section 51.

Declaration by Incapacitated Persons.
See section 55.

Power of Registrar to Dispense with Declarations.
See section 60.

Mode of Making Declarations and Persons Authorised.
See section 61.

Admissibility of Declarations in Evidence.
See section 64.

Prescribed Forms.
See section 65.

Qualification to Own British Ship.
See section 1.

Shares in the Ship.
See section 5.

Beneficial Interest.
See section 57.

⚓ ⚓ ⚓ ⚓

Evidence on first registry.

10 (1) On the first registry of a ship the following evidence shall be produced in addition to the declaration of ownership:—

(*a*) In the case of a British-built ship, a builder's certificate, that is to say, a certificate signed by the builder of the ship, and containing a true account of the proper denomination and of the tonnage of the ship, as estimated by him, and of the time when and the place where she was built, and of the name of the person (if any) on whose account the ship was built, and if there has been any sale, the bill of sale under which the ship, or a share therein, has become vested in the applicant for registry:

(*b*) In the case of a foreign-built ship, the same evidence as in the case of a British-built ship, unless the declarant who makes the declaration of ownership declares that the time and place of her building are unknown to him, or that the builder's certificate cannot be procured, in which case there shall be required only the bill of sale under which the ship, or a share therein, became vested in the applicant for registry:

(*c*) In the case of a ship condemned by any competent court, an official copy of the condemnation.

(2) The builder shall grant the certificate required by this section, and such person as the Commissioners of Customs recognise as carrying on the business of the builder of a ship, shall be included, for the purposes of this section, in the expression 'builder of the ship'.

(3) If the person granting a builder's certificate under this section wilfully makes a false statement in that certificate he shall for each offence be liable to a fine not exceeding one hundred pounds.

COMMENTS.

Power of Registrar to Dispose with Declaration and Evidence.
See section 60.

Declaration of Ownership.
See section 9.

Builder's Certificate.
This may be given before the ship is complete. Woods *v.* Russell 1822. Goss *v.* Quinton 1842.
See section 12 regarding retention by registrar.

Fines.
See section 680.

11 As soon as the requirements of this Act preliminary to registry have been complied with the registrar shall enter in the register book the following particulars respecting the ship:— Entry of particulars in register book.

(*a*) The name of the ship and the name of the port to which she belongs:

(*b*) The details comprised in the surveyor's certificate:

(*c*) The particulars respecting her origin stated in the declaration of ownership: and (*d*) The name and description of her registered owner or owners, and if there are more owners than one, the proportions in which they are interested in her.

COMMENTS.

Register Book.

Entries to be made in accordance with provisions in section 5.

Certificate of Registry.

Contains the same particulars as the register book. *See* section 14·

Registry of Alterations.

See section 48.

Entitlement to Copy of Particulars.

See section 695.

Name.

For rules as to name, *see* section 47, and Merchant Shipping Act 1906, section 50 and regulations made thereunder.

Home Port.

The port at which registered is the port to which she belongs. *See* section 13.

Declaration of Ownership.

See section 9.

Change of Ownership.

See section 20.

Surveyor's Certificate.

See section 6.

Documents to be retained by registrar.

12 On the registry of a ship the registrar shall retain in his possession the following documents; namely, the surveyor's certificate, the builder's certificate, any bill of sale of the ship previously made, the copy of the condemnation (if any), and all declarations of ownership.

COMMENTS.

Declaration of Ownership.

See section 9.

Builder's Certificate.

See section 10.

Surveyor's Certificate.

See section 6.

⚓ ⚓ ⚓ ⚓

13 The port at which a British ship is registered for the time being shall be deemed her port of registry and the port to which she belongs. Port of registry.

COMMENTS.

The port of registry may be transferred to another. *See* section 53.

⚓ ⚓ ⚓ ⚓

Certificate of Registry

14 On completion of the registry of a ship, the registrar shall grant a certificate of registry comprising the particulars respecting her entered in the register book, with the name of her master. Certificate of registry.

COMMENTS.

Form of Certificate.

For provisions *see* section 65.

Admissibility in Evidence.

See section 64.

The certificate of registry is *prima facie* evidence that the ship is British. R. *v.* Bjornsen 1865.

Terminable Certificates.

May be granted for small ships in the colonies. *See* section 90.

Alterations.

See section 49.

Provisional Certificates.

See section 50.

Particulars in Register Book.

See section 11.

⚓ ⚓ ⚓ ⚓

15 (1) The certificate of registry shall be used only for the lawful navigation of the ship, and shall not be subject to detention by reason of any title, lien, charge, or interest Custody of certificate.

whatever had or claimed by any owner, mortgagee, or other person to, on, or in the ship.

(2) If any person, whether interested in the ship or not, refuses on request to deliver up the certificate of registry when in his possession or under his control to the person entitled to the custody thereof for the purposes of the lawful navigation of the ship, or to any registrar, officer of customs, or other person entitled by law to require such delivery, any justice by warrant under his hand and seal, or any court capable of taking cognizance of the matter, may summon the person so refusing to appear before such justice or court, and to be examined touching such refusal, and unless it is proved to the satisfaction of such justice or court that there was reasonable cause for such refusal, the offender shall be liable to a fine not exceeding one hundred pounds, but if it is shown to such justice or court that the certificate is lost, the person summoned shall be discharged, and the justice or court shall certify that the certificate of registry is lost.

(3) If the person so refusing is proved to have absconded so that the warrant of a justice or process of a court cannot be served on him, or if he persists in not delivering up the certificate, the justice or court shall certify the fact, and the same proceedings may then be taken as in the case of a certificate mislaid, lost, or destroyed, or as near thereto as circumstances permit.

COMMENTS.

Fines.

For recovery *see* sections 680–682.

Lost Certificate.

See section 18.

Various.

For an instance where the master's action in withholding the certificate from the managing owner was held to be reasonable, *see* Arkle *v.* Lienzell 1858.

An instance where conviction was obtained for detaining certificate is contained in R. *v.* Walsh 1834.

It would appear that the High Court has independent jurisdiction in respect of this section, but will only order the delivery of a certificate to those holding a clear title to it. The *Frances* 1820.

In the *Celtic King* 1894, the court ordered the delivery of certificate to a purchaser from a mortgagee, where the mortgagor had placed the certificate in the hands of other persons without notice to the mortgagees.

Where a master who was also the sole owner pledged the certificate it was held that he was entitled to recover it for the purpose of Navigation. Wiley *v.* Cranford 1861.

A master who has been wrongfully dismissed has no lien upon the certificate for wages or disbursements. Gibson *v.* Inso 1847.

A master has no lien upon the certificate in the case of wrongful dismissal by the managing owners.

This is applicable whether he is co-owner or not. The *St. Olaf* 1876.

⚓ ⚓ ⚓ ⚓

16 If the master or owner of a ship uses or attempts to use for her navigation a certificate of registry not legally granted in respect of the ship, he shall, in respect of each offence, be guilty of a misdemeanor, and the ship shall be subject to forfeiture under this Act. Penalty for use of improper certificate.

COMMENTS.

Misdemeanours.

See section 680.

Forfeiture.

See section 76.

Master.

Definition—*See* section 742.

⚓ ⚓ ⚓ ⚓

17 The registrar of the port of registry of a ship may, with the approval of the Commissioners of Customs, and on the delivery up to him of the certificate of registry of a ship, grant a new certificate in lieu thereof. Power to grant new certificate.

COMMENTS.

Commissioners of Customs.

Now the Commissioners of Customs and Excise.

⚓ ⚓ ⚓ ⚓

18 (1) In the event of the certificate of registry of a ship being mislaid, lost, or destroyed, the registrar of her port of registry shall grant a new certificate of registry in lieu of her original certificate. Provision for loss of certificate.

(2) If the port (having a British registrar or consular officer) at which the ship is at the time of the event, or first arrives after the event—

(*a*) is not in the United Kingdom, where the ship is registered in the United Kingdom; or,

(*b*) is not in the British possession in which the ship is registered; or,

(*c*) where the ship is registered at a port of registry established by Order in Council under this Act, is not that port;

then the master of the ship, or some other person having knowledge of the facts of the case, shall make a declaration stating the facts of the case, and the names and descriptions of the registered owners of such ship to the best of the declarant's knowledge and belief, and the registrar or consular officer, as the case may be, shall thereupon grant a provisional certificate, containing a statement of the circumstances under which it is granted.

(3) The provisional certificate shall within ten days after the first subsequent arrival of the ship at her port of discharge in the United Kingdom, where she is registered in the United Kingdom, or in the British possession in which she is registered, or where she is registered at a port of registry established by Order in Council under this Act at that port, be delivered up to the registrar of her port of registry, and the registrar shall thereupon grant the new certificate of registry; and if the master without reasonable cause fails to deliver up the provisional certificate within the ten days aforesaid, he shall be liable to a fine not exceeding fifty pounds.

COMMENTS.

Port of Registry Established by Order in Council.

See section 88.

Fine, as to Recovery and Summary Prosecution.

See sections 680–682.

⚓ ⚓ ⚓ ⚓

Endorsement of change of master on certificate.

19 Where the master of a registered British ship is changed, each of the following persons; (that is to say),

(*a*) if the change is made in consequence of the sentence of a naval court, the presiding officer of that court; and (*b*) if the change is made in consequence of the removal of the master by a court under Part VI of this Act, the proper officer of that court; and

(*c*) if the change occurs from any other cause, the registrar, or if there is none the British consular officer, at the port where the change occurs,

shall endorse and sign on the certificate of registry a memorandum of the change, and shall forthwith report the change to the Registrar-General of Shipping and Seamen; and any officer of customs at any port in Her Majesty's dominions may refuse to admit any person to do any act there as master of a British ship unless his name is inserted in or endorsed on her certificate of registry as her last appointed master.

COMMENTS.

Endorsement on Certificate.

Endorsement is admissible in evidence. *See* sections 64 and 695.

Naval Courts.

For power of naval court to remove master, *see* section 483.

Admiralty Court.

For power to remove master, *see* section 472.

Registrar-General of Shipping and Seamen.

As to appointment, *see* section 251.

Repeal.

Words underlined from "each" to "cause" repealed. Schedule 5 M.S.A. 1970, when authorised by statutory instrument.

20 (1) Whenever a change occurs in the registered ownership of a ship, the change of ownership shall be endorsed on her certificate of registry either by the registrar of the ship's port of registry, or by the registrar of any port at which the ship arrives who has been advised of the change by the registrar of the ship's port of registry. Endorsement of change of ownership.

(2) The master shall, for the purpose of such endorsement by the registrar of the ship's port of registry, deliver the certificate of registry to the registrar, forthwith after the change if the change occurs when the ship is at her port of registry, and if it occurs during her absence from that port and the endorsement under this section is not made before her return then upon her first return to that port.

(3) The registrar of any port, not being the ship's port of registry, who is required to make an endorsement under this section may for that purpose require the master of the ship to deliver to him the ship's certificate of registry, so that the ship be not thereby detained, and the master shall deliver the same accordingly.

(4) If the master fails to deliver to the registrar the certificate of registry as required by this section he shall, for each offence, be liable to a fine not exceeding one hundred pounds.

COMMENTS.

Endorsement.

Admissible in evidence. *See* sections 64 and 695.

Registration Anew.

See section 51.

⚓ ⚓ ⚓ ⚓

Delivery up of certificate of ship lost or ceasing to be British owned.

21 (1) In the event of a registered ship being either actually or constructively lost, taken by the enemy, burnt, or broken up, or ceasing by reason of a transfer to persons not qualified to be owners of British ships, or otherwise, to be a British ship, every owner of the ship or any share in the ship shall, immediately on obtaining knowledge of the event, if no notice thereof has already been given to the registrar, give notice thereof to the registrar at her port of registry, and that registrar shall make an entry thereof in the register book.

(2) In any such case, except where the ship's certificate of registry is lost or destroyed, the master of the ship shall, if the event occurs in port immediately, but if it occurs elsewhere then within ten days after his arrival in port, deliver the certificate to the registrar, or, if there is none, to the British consular officer there, and the registrar, if he is not himself the registrar of her port of registry, or the British consular officer, shall forthwith forward the certificate delivered to him to the registrar of her port of registry.

(3) If any such owner or master fails, without reasonable cause, to comply with this section, he shall for each offence be liable to a fine not exceeding one hundred pounds.

COMMENTS.

By the Merchant Shipping Act 1906, section 52, sub-section 1, the following is to be read in sub-section 1 above, as if it were inserted as to follow on from '. . . thereof in the register book . . .'—and the registry of the ship in that book shall be considered as closed except so far as relates to any unsatisfied mortgages or existing certificates of mortgage entered therein.

Constructively Lost.

The term 'Constructively lost' has no meaning except as defined in marine insurance, for which *see* the Marine Insurance Act 1906, section 60. However, it was held in Manchester Ship Canal Co. *v.* Hislock 1914, per Swinfen Eady L.J., that a constructive total loss within the definition of section 60 of the Marine Insurance Act 1906 is constructively lost within the meaning of this section.

Transfer to Persons not Qualified to be Owners of a British Ship.

It would appear that any effective form to transfer property will suffice, where the purchaser is not qualified to be an owner of a British ship.

The usual procedure is, however, for the owner to execute a statutory bill of sale (*see* section 24) and to give the required notice to the registrar. The registrar then closes the registry (subject to unsatisfied mortgages for which *see* section 52) the registrar, will, if required, give a suitably endorsed certificate to the purchaser.

In the event of a transfer to a person not qualified to be the owner of a British ship, which takes place within the country of the port of registry the notice required under this section, i.e. section 21, is sufficient to close the register and there is no need to produce the bill of sale or other instrument of transfer.

In the event, however, of the transfer taking place outside the country of port of registry an acceptable bill of sale must be produced to the registrar or British Consular officer together with the certificate of sale and certificate of registry. For rules dealing with certificate of sale *see* section 44: *Re-registration of Abandoned Ships*. *See* section 54.

⚓ ⚓ ⚓ ⚓

Provisional certificate for ships becoming British owned abroad.

22 (1) If at a port not within Her Majesty's dominions and not being a port of registry established by Order in Council under this Act, a ship becomes the property of persons qualified to own a British ship, the British consular officer there may grant to her master, on his application, a provisional certificate, stating—

(*a*) the name of the ship;

(*b*) the time and place of her purchase, and the names of her purchasers;

(*c*) the name of her master; and

(*d*) the best particulars respecting her tonnage, build, and description which he is able to obtain;

and shall forward a copy of the certificate at the first convenient opportunity to the Registrar-General of Shipping and Seamen.

(2) Such a provisional certificate shall have the effect of a certificate of registry until the expiration of six months from its date, or until the ship's arrival at a port where there is a registrar (whichever first happens), and on either of those events happening shall cease to have effect.

COMMENTS.

Provisional Certificate.

See section 65 as to form of certificate.

Port of Registry.

See section 88.

Master—Definition of:

See section 742.

Consular Officer—Definition of:

See section 742.

⚓ ⚓ ⚓ ⚓

Temporary passes in lieu of certificates of registry.

23 Where it appears to the Commissioners of Customs, or to the governor of a British possession, that by reason of special circumstances it would be desirable that permission should be granted to any British ship to pass, without being previously registered, from any port in Her Majesty's dominions, to any other port within Her Majesty's dominions, the Commissioners or the governor may grant a pass accordingly, and that pass shall, for the time and within the limits therein mentioned, have the same effect as a certificate of registry.

COMMENTS.

Unregistered Vessel Under Pass.

An unregistered vessel sailing in her prescribed voyage under a pass granted under the provisions of this section is in the same position as if registered. In The Wills No. 66 1914, it was held that she was entitled to limit her liability as a result of collision.

Under the Merchant Shipping (Safety of Shipowners and Others) Act 1958, the right to limit liability now extends to British ships not yet registered.

Commissioners of Customs.

See section 4.

British Possession.

See section 3.

British Ship.

See section 1.

Transfers and Transmissions

24 (1) A registered ship or a share therein (when disposed of to a person qualified to own a British ship) shall be transferred by bill of sale. Transfer of ships or shares.

(2) The bill of sale shall contain such description of the ship as is contained in the surveyor's certificate, or some other description sufficient to identify the ship to the satisfaction of the registrar, and shall be in the form marked A in the first part of the First Schedule to this Act, or as near thereto as circumstances permit, and shall be executed by the transferor in the presence of, and be attested by, a witness or witnesses.

COMMENTS.

Emergency Provisions.

The Ships and Aircraft (Transfer Restriction) Act 1939 was passed immeidately prior to the outbreak of hostilities in 1939, to prevent British ships or British-registered ships from passing into enemy or neutral hands. By the provisions of the Emergency Laws (Repeal) Act 1959 the Ships and Aircraft (Transfer Restriction) Act 1939 has expired as from the 31st December 1964, 'except as respect things previously done or omitted to be done', and section 13 (2) has been repealed.

However, in the rapidly changing conditions which exist in the world it is recommended that the Board of Trade be consulted in the event of transfer of property to persons not qualified to own a British ship.

Bill of Sale.

By the Bills of Sale Act 1878, section 4, an assignment of any ship or vessel or any share thereof is not included in the definition of 'bill of sale' under that section.

This section, i.e. section 24 of the Merchant Shipping Act 1894, provides an exception in that a registered ship may only be transferred to a person qualified to own a British ship by bill of sale. Accordingly, therefore, where registration is unnecessary the bill of sale procedure does not apply. Sapp *v.* Bono 1887. In this case, it was held that a dumb barge propelled by oars was not a ship as defined by the Merchant Shipping Act 1854 or 1894. It was, however, held to be a vessel within the Bills of Sale Acts and therefore transferable without registration. However the meanings of ship or vessel have been extended by the Merchant Shipping Act 1921, section 1.

Furthermore, transfer by bill of sale is not required in the case of a ship which had in fact been registered although not required to do so. Benyon *v.* Cresswell 1848.

Transfer by bill of sale is not required in the case of a ship which from long and continued use as a coal hulk, had ceased to rank as a ship. European & Australian Royal Mail Co. *v.* P. & O. Steam Navigation Co. 1866. When a ship was not British within the statutory meaning, a bill of sale was held not to be necessary. Union Bank of London *v.* Lenanton 1878.

Transfer of Ship.

A ship comes within the meaning of 'goods' as contained in section 62 of the Sale of Goods Act 1893, and accordingly therefore, the court may order specific performance of such a contract in appropriate cases. Behnke *v.* Bede Shipping Co. 1927.

It is usually understood that all gear on board necessary for the prosecution of the voyage passes within the sale of the ship. Coltman *v.* Chamberlain 1890. Gear must be actually appropriated to the mortgaged ship. Salmon & Woods, ex Partegould 1885.

It has been held that the mere marking of gear with the particulars of a ship is not sufficient evidence of appropriation to that ship. The *Humourous*, the *Mabel Vera* 1933.

A declaration of transfer must be made. *See* section 25.

See section 26 re details of registration of transfers and entering of bill of sale in the register book.

The requirements in sub-section 2 relate to the actual instrument of transfer, and a mere agreement to transfer a ship need not be registered. Baithyany *v.* Bouch 1881. *See* section 65 for the form of document. Proof of attestation is not required, *see* section 694. Upon registration, the bill of sale is retained by the registrar.

Registered Ship or Share.

The obligation to register is contained in section 2 and this brings them within this section. *See* section 3 as regards ships exempted from registry under this Act, and therefore exempted from this section.

Section 39 contains the provisions for power of sale, out of the country in which the port of registry is situated.

Repeal.

Worlds underlined from 'and shall be in' to 'permit' repealed. M.S.A. 1965, Schedule 2.

⚓ ⚓ ⚓ ⚓

25 Where a registered ship or a share therein is transferred, the transferee shall not be entitled to be registered as owner thereof until he, or, in the case of a corporation, the person authorised by this Act to make declarations on behalf of the corporation, has made and signed a declaration (in this Act called a declaration of transfer) referring to the ship, and containing— **Declaration of transfer.**

(*a*) a statement of the qualification of the transferee to own a British ship, or if the transferee is a corporation, of such circumstances of the constitution and business thereof as prove it to be qualified to own a British ship; and

(*b*) a declaration that, to the best of his knowledge and belief, no unqualified person or body of persons is entitled as owner to any legal or beneficial interest in the ship or any share therein.

COMMENTS.

Beneficial Interest.

See section 57.

Qualification to Own a British Ship.

See section 1.

Corporation.

As to persons authorised to make declarations, *see* section 61.

Declarations (*Generally*).

Admissibility in evidence, *see* section 64. Declarations to be retained by registrar. *See* section 12.

As to false declarations, *see* section 64, Power of registrar to dispose with declarations. *See* section 60.

⚓ ⚓ ⚓ ⚓

26 (1) Every bill of sale for the transfer of a registered ship or of a share therein, when duly executed, shall be produced to the registrar of her port of registry, with the declaration of transfer, and the registrar shall thereupon **Registry of transfer.**

enter in the register book the name of the transferee as owner of the ship or share, and shall endorse on the bill of sale the fact of that entry having been made, with the day and hour thereof.

(2) Bills of sale of a ship or of a share therein shall be entered in the register book in the order of their production to the registrar.

COMMENTS.

The property in the ship passes as between the seller and his assignees, and the purchaser, by a bill of sale, although the transfer is not registered. Stapleton *v*. Haymen 1864.

Non-registration of a bill of sale by a purchaser, does not affect the title of a subsequent bona fide purchaser. The *Australia* 1859. The duty to register a transfer rests with the purchaser.

Declaration of Transfer.

See section 25.

Register Book.

See section 12 regarding retainment by registrar of bill of sale.

⚓ ⚓ ⚓ ⚓

Transmission of property in ship on death, bankruptcy, marriage, &c.

27 (1) Where the property in a registered ship or share therein is transmitted to a person qualified to own a British ship on the marriage, death, or bankruptcy of any registered owner, or by any lawful means other than by a transfer under this Act—

(*a*) That person shall authenticate the transmission by making and signing a declaration (in this Act called a declaration of transmission) identifying the ship and containing the several statements herein-before required to be contained in a declaration of transfer, or as near thereto as circumstances admit, and also a statement of the manner in which and the person to whom the property has been transmitted.

(*b*) If the transmission takes place by virtue of marriage, the declaration shall be accompanied by a copy of the register of the marriage, or other legal evidence of the celebration thereof, and shall declare the identity of the female owner.

(*c*) If the transmission is consequent on bankruptcy, the declaration of transmission shall be accompanied by such evidence as is for the time being receivable in courts of justice as proof of the title of persons claiming under a bankruptcy.

(*d*) If the transmission is consequent on death, the declaration of transmission shall be accompanied by the instrument of representation, or an official extract therefrom.

(2) The registrar, on receipt of the declaration of transmission so accompanied, shall enter in the register book the name of the person entitled under the transmission as owner of the ship or share the property in which has been transmitted, and, where there is more than one such person, shall enter the names of all those persons, but those persons, however numerous, shall, for the purpose of the provision of this Act with respect to the number of persons entitled to be registered as owners, be considered as one person.

COMMENTS.

Persons Qualified to Own British Ship.

See section 1.

For Transmissions to Unqualified Persons.

See section 28.

Transmission.

The term given to involuntary transfer of property as a result of death, marriage, and bankruptcy as opposed to a voluntary acquisition of a vessel by purchase.

NOTE:—It would appear that marriage by itself can no longer bring about transmission in a ship. This, of course, in most cases is mostly academic, as ships are now usually owned by the limited companies.

Transfer of Ship or Sale by Order of Court.

See section 29.

The words '. . . by any lawful means other than by a transfer under this Act . . .' only apply to an operation of law unconnected with any direct act of the party to whom the ship is transmitted. Therefore, a sale by limitation by order of a court is not a transmission by any lawful means. In Chasteauneuf *v.* Capeyron 1882, it was held that the registrar acted correctly in refusing to register such a transfer in the absence of conveyance by bill of sale.

Bankruptcy.

When a trustee is appointed, the bankrupt's property passes and vests in the trustee. Bankruptcy Act 1914, Section 53.

Representation.

See section 742 for definition.

Persons Entitled to be Registered as Owners.

Not more than 64 persons are entitled to be registered as owners. *See* section 5.

⚓ ⚓ ⚓ ⚓

Order for sale on transmission to unqualified person.

28 (1) Where the property in a registered ship or share therein is transmitted on marriage, death, bankruptcy, or otherwise to a person not qualified to own a British ship, then—

if the ship is registered in England or Ireland, the High Court; or

if the ship is registered in Scotland, the Court of Session; or

if the ship is registered in any British possesion, the court having the principal civil jurisdiction in that possession; or

if the ship is registered in a port of registry established by Order in Council under this Act, the British court having the principal civil jurisdiction there;

may on application by or on behalf of the unqualified person, order a sale of the property so transmitted, and direct that the proceeds of the sale, after deducting the expenses thereof, be paid to the person entitled under such transmission or otherwise as the court direct.

(2) The court may require any evidence in support of the application they think requisite, and may make the order on any terms and conditions they think just, or may refuse to make the order, and generally may act in the case as the justice of the case requires.

(3) Every such application for sale must be made within four weeks after the occurrence of the event on which the transmission has taken place, or within such further time (not exceeding in the whole one year from the date of the occurrence) as the court allow.

(4) If such an application is not made within the time aforesaid, or if the court refuse an order for sale, the ship or share transmitted shall thereupon be subject to forfeiture under this Act.

COMMENTS.

Person Not Qualified to Own a British Ship.

See section 1 for persons qualified to own a British ship.

High Court.

Admiralty jurisdiction of the High Court was re-enacted in the Supreme Court of Judicature (Consolidation) Act 1925. The jurisdiction under this section as well as sections 30 and 504 are not assigned solely to the Probate, Divorce and Admiralty Division. The Admiralty jurisdiction of the High Court is now to be found in the Administration of Justice Act 1956.

Ireland.

Means Northern Ireland only.

Port of Registry Established by Order in Council.

See section 88.

British Possession.

See section 3.

Sale of Property Transmitted.

The court may order a particular sale, or a sale generally. The *Santon* 1878.

Forfeiture.

Sub-section (4) of this section outlines the circumstances under which a ship is liable to forfeiture in accord with this section.

Under such circumstances, however, the Crown does not usually enforce the forfeiture as to the proceeds, but hands the net amount over to the foreigner. The *Millicent* 1891.

⚓ ⚓ ⚓ ⚓

29 Where any court, whether under the preceding sections of this Act or otherwise, order the sale of any ship or share therein, the order of the court shall contain a declaration vesting in some person named by the court the right to transfer that ship or share, and that person shall thereupon be entitled to transfer the ship or share in the same manner and to the same extent as if he were the registered owner thereof; and every registrar shall obey the requisition of the person so named in respect of any transfer to the same extent as if such person were the registered owner.

Transfer of ship or sale by order of court.

COMMENTS.

This section allows a sale by order of the court to give to the purchaser a clean title against all the world, and allows the duty of every registrar to obey the requisition of the person so named as if he were the registered owner.

⚓ ⚓ ⚓ ⚓

Power of court to prohibit transfer.

30 Each of the following courts; namely—

(*a*) in England or Ireland the High Court,

(*b*) in Scotland the Court of Session,

(*c*) in any British possession the court having the principal civil jurisdiction in that possession; and

(*d*) in the case of a port of registry established by Order in Council under this Act, the British court having the principal civil jurisdiction there,

may, if the court think fit (without prejudice to the exercise of any other power of the court), on the application of any interested person make an order prohibiting for a time specified any dealing with a ship or any share therein, and the court may make the order on any terms or conditions they think just, or may refuse to make the order, or may discharge the order when made, with or without costs, and generally may act in the case as the justice of the case requires; and every registrar, without being made a party to the proceeding, shall on being served with the order or an official copy thereof obey the same.

COMMENTS.

High Court in England.

An application under this section may be made by summons or otherwise, and either *ex parte* or upon service of notice on any person as the court may direct. *See* also comment under section 28.

High Court of Ireland.

Now the High Court of Northern Ireland.

British Possession.

See comments to section 3.

Port of Registry Established by Order in Council.

See section 88.

General Principles.

Due to the peculiar and in many ways unsatisfactory security, afforded by a ship the Merchant Shipping Acts have established a system of mortgaging, not only to protect the lender, i.e. the mortgagee, but also to afford to the borrower, i.e. the mortgagor, the facility of remaining in possession of the ship or shares therein. The sections 31 to 46 of this Act show how the law has been exacted to protect not only the borrower and lender, but the rights of third parties as well.

It is well to note that registration of a mortgage is not essential, to its validity, even in respect of a British Registered ship. The Companies

Act 1948, does, however, contain provisions as to the registration of mortgages and it would be well to consult this Act if involved either as a mortgagee or mortgagor.

The Administration of Justice Act 1956 enacts amongst other things, that the Admiralty jurisdiction of the High Court in England has been extended to include '. . . any claim in respect of a mortgage of or charge on a ship or any share therein . . .' In section 8, sub-section 1 of the same Act, the term 'ship' includes any description of vessel used in navigation. One of the main changes in the law is to provide jurisdiction in Admiralty in respect of not only registered mortgages but unregistered ones as well.

Included in the comments to section 29 of the Merchant Shipping Act 1894, is the statement that '. . . A sale by order of the court gives to the purchaser a clean title against all the world . . .' and in respect of mortgages, they are not open to proceed subsequently against the ship for any balance of cash due to them under a mortgage which existed before the sale. The *Acrux* 1962.

Mortgages

31 (1) A registered ship or a share therein may be made a security for a loan or other valuable consideration, and the instrument creating the security (in this Act called a mortgage) shall be in the form marked B in the first part of the First Schedule to this Act, or as near thereto as circumstances permit, and on the production of such instrument the registrar of the ship's port of registry shall record it in the register book. **Mortgage of ship or share.**

(2) Mortgages shall be recorded by the registrar in the order in time in which they are produced to him for that purpose, and the registrar shall by memorandum under his hand notify on each mortgage that it has been recorded by him, stating the day and hour of that record.

COMMENTS.

Obligation to register British ships. *See* section 2.

Ships exempted from registry. *See* section 3.

Property in a ship divided into 64 shares. *See* section 5.

Necessary gear and appurtenances. *See* comments to section 24.

Mortgage.

This section specifically states the form in which the mortgage shall be created, i.e. the form marked 'B' in the first part of the first schedule to this act. It would be miraculous indeed if such a prescribed form took into its confines the whole gamut of human relationship and business activities, besides the safeguarding of interests involved.

Accordingly, therefore, it is usual for the details of such a mortgage to be contained in a separate deed or covenant. The terms of such an agreement are, of course, boundless, but most include the agreement of the mortgagee to exercise his powers, unless the mortgagor defaults in perhaps the payment of interest or insurance. Other matters commonly found in such a deed of covenant are the details of the repayment of the principle, provisions as to entry into a Protection and Indemnity Club or possibly a Freight or Demurrage Association, adherence to statutory regulations and the limiting of the employment of the vessel generally and territorially. Indeed, the court will take into account all relevant arrangements between the parties. The *Innisfallen* 1866. (Decided under the M.S.A. 1862), the *Cathcart* 1867. (Decided under the M.S.A. 1862). The *Benwell Tower* 1895.

The Importance of Registration.

To the outside world, the shipowner appears to be the undisputed, unrestricted owner of the ship and thus enjoys the facilities of extended credit. The mortgagee, although the owner of a valid mortgage, between himself and the shipowner is not protected against the possibility of the shipowner obtaining further advances on the security of the vessel, as indeed, subsequent lenders would have no knowledge of prior mortgage commitments. The method brought into being by the M.S.A. allows the mortgage to be registered, and by this very act of registration the existence of a mortgage to possible future lenders, and in addition as from the date of registration of the mortgage document, the lender is secured as against later executed and registered mortgages as well as against his trustee in bankruptcy.

If the mortgage is not registered in accordance with the provisions of this section, it ranks only as an equitable charge. Details as to the enforcement of such charges are contained in section 57 of the Act, while attention is again drawn to the necessity of compliance with the provisions of the Companies Act 1948. The court has the power to order the details of the registration of an invalid mortgage to be expunged from the register. Brond *v.* Broomhall 1906, Burgess *v.* Constantine 1908. The court has power to order that the details of the mortgage in the register be expunged after the mortgage has been redeemed. The *Yolanda Barbara* 1961.

A mistake in the name of the vessel will not invalidate a mortgage if the identity of the vessel is established. Bell *v.* Bank of London 1858.

32 Where a registered mortgage is discharged, the registrar shall, on the production of the mortgage deed, with a receipt for the mortgage money endorsed thereon, duly signed and attested, make an entry in the register book to the effect that the mortgage has been discharged, and on that entry being made the estate (if any) which passed to the mortgagee shall vest in the person in whom (having regard to intervening acts and circumstances, if any), it would have vested if the mortgage had not been made.

Entry of discharge of mortgage.

COMMENTS.

Discharge of the Mortgage.

The registrar has no power to erase an entry of a mortgage upon its discharge. Chasteauneuf *v.* Capeyron 1882, but see comments to section 31 as to the power of court to expunge entries of invalid mortgages and the power of the court to expunge the mortgage entry after redemption.

The entry of a discharge of the mortgage, by the registrar discharges the mortgage, and if given in mistake cannot be revived by a memorandum on the register. Bell *v.* Blyth 1868. The question of priorities was involved in this case.

Where, however, a receipt has been endorsed on the mortgage by mistake, the court will set aside the endorsement. The *Rose* 1873. In this case, however, there was no question of priorities.

33 If there are more mortgages than one registered in respect of the same ship or share, the mortgagees shall, notwithstanding any express, implied, or constructive notice, be entitled in priority one over the other, according to the date at which each mortgage is recorded in the register book and not according to the date of each mortgage itself.

Priority of mortgages.

COMMENTS.

The rights of a registered mortgagee stand in priority to those of an un-registered mortgagee even though the date of the registered mortgage is later than the unregistered mortgage. Coombes *v.* Mansfield 1855.

This is so even if the existence of the unregistered mortgage was known to the registered mortgagee when he took up the mortgage. Black *v.* Williams 1895. The rights of mortgagees are postponed to those of persons holding possessory liens. Williams *v.* Allsup 1861.

They are also postponed to persons in possession of a maritime lien. The *Dowthorpe* 1843. There are, however, circumstances where the priorities between registered mortgages do not depend upon the actual dates of registration and in such cases this section does not apply. For example, a first mortgagee, whose mortgage covers future advances, is not able to claim over a subsequent mortgagee the benefit of any advances made after receiving notice of the subsequent mortgage. The *Bennel Tower* 1895.

In the event of a first mortgagee entering into a subsequent mortgage agreement in a separate unregistered instrument, his rights under his unregistered mortgage will be postponed to the rights of a second-registered mortgagee even though the second-registered mortgagee had knowledge of the prior unregistered mortgage by the first-registered mortgagee. Parr *v.* Applebee 1855.

In the event of a second mortgagee unsuccessfully disputing the valid claims of the first mortgagee, he will be responsible for the costs arising out of the dispute. The *Western Ocean* 1870.

⚓ ⚓ ⚓ ⚓

Mortgagee not treated as owner.

34 Except as far as may be necessary for making a mortgaged ship or share available as a security for the mortgage debt, the mortgagee shall not by reason of the mortgage be deemed the owner of the ship or share, nor shall the mortgagor be deemed to have ceased to be owner thereof.

COMMENTS.

Generally speaking, the mortgager in possession retains all rights and powers of ownership and the contracts he may make with regard to the ship are valid, provided that his dealings do not impair the security. Collins *v.* Lamport 1864.

Until the mortgagee takes possession the mortgagor remains the dominus in respect of everything connected with the employment of the ship. Keith *v.* Burrows 1877. The mortgagee is protected from liabilities connected with the employment of the ship. Dickinson *v.* Kitchen 1858.

An admirable summary of the principal cases dealing with the rights and liabilities of mortgager and mortgagee is contained in *Temperley*, Volume II. The M.S.A. *British Shipping Laws*, paragraphs 69–76 inclusive.

It should be noticed in addition that the question whether or not a claim brought under the Administration of Justice Act 1956, for wages earned on board a sister ship, has priority over the mortgage of the ship against which the claim was brought was raised, but was not decided on. The *Leoborg* (No. 2) 1964.

⚓ ⚓ ⚓ ⚓

35 Every registered mortgagee shall have power absolutely to dispose of the ship or share in respect of which he is registered, and to give effectual receipts for the purchase money; but where there are more persons than one registered as mortgagees of the same ship or share, a subsequent mortgagee shall not, except under the order of a court of competent jurisdiction, sell the ship or share without the concurrence of every prior mortgagee. Mortgagee to have power of sale.

COMMENTS.

The power of the mortgagee to sell the ship is invariably contained in a separate deed or agreement. (*See* comment to section 31.) Resulting from this, the power of sale does vary in accordance with the interpretation of the various provisions of such deed or conventions. In European and Australian Royal Mail Co. *v.* Royal Mail Steam Packet Co. 1858, it was held that a mortgagee in possession was not bound to sell the ship. The vessel may, however, be employed in such a way so that her value is not impaired, and in any event he must not dispose of her disadvantageously.

In the position where the vessel is under a restrictive covenant, such as a hire charter, *see* De Mattos *v.* Gibson 1858 and the *Lord Strathcona* 1925.

Court of Competent Jurisdiction.

See the Administration of Justice Act 1956, section 1.

36 A registered mortgage of a ship or share shall not be affected by any act of bankruptcy committed by the mortgagor after the date of the record of the mortgage, notwithstanding that the mortgagor at the commencement of his bankruptcy had the ship or share in his possession, order, or disposition, or was reputed owner thereof, and the mortgage shall be preferred to any right, claim, or interest therein of the other creditors of the bankrupt or any trustee or assignee on their behalf. Mortgage not affected by bankruptcy.

COMMENTS.

The rights of a mortgagee are not affected by the bankruptcy of the mortgager, committed after the date of the mortgage. Also, as long as the mortgagee had no notice of the act of bankruptcy, committed before the date of the mortgage the rights of the mortgagee remain unimpaired. The *Ruby* 1900.

It has been submitted but not decided that this is the case in respect of all mortgages, registered or unregistered.

Transfer of mortgages.

37 A registered mortgage of a ship or share may be transferred to any person, and the instrument effecting the transfer shall be in the form marked C in the first part of the First Schedule to this Act, or as near thereto as circumstances permit, and on the production of such instrument the registrar shall record it by entering in the register book the name of the transferee as mortgagee of the ship or share, and shall by memorandum under his hand notify on the instrument of transfer that it has been recorded by him, stating the day and hour of the record.

COMMENTS.

In the event of a mortgage being transferred, the rights as between the transferor and the transferee take effect as from the execution of the transfer and not from the date and time of the registration. The *Two Ellens* 1871.

Transmission of interest in mortgage by death, bankruptcy, marriage, &c.

38 (1) Where the interest of a mortgagee in a ship or share is transmitted on marriage, death, or bankruptcy, or by any lawful means, other than by a transfer under this Act, the transmission shall be authenticated by a declaration of the person to whom the interest is transmitted, containing a statement of the manner in which and the person to whom the property has been transmitted, and shall be accompanied by the like evidence as is by this Act required in case of a corresponding transmission of the ownership of a ship or share.

(2) The registrar on the receipt of the declaration, and the production of the evidence aforesaid, shall enter the name of the person entitled under the transmission in the register book as mortgagee of the ship or share.

COMMENTS.

Transfer.

See section 27 and comments thereto.

Transmission by Marriage.

In accordance with the Law Reform (Married Women and Tortfeasors) Act 1935, section 2, marriage by itself can no longer cause a transmission of property. In other words, all property belonging to a woman at the time of her marriage belongs to her as if she were a single woman.

Declarations.

Power of registrar to dispense with declarations. *See* section 60.
Mode of making declarations. *See* section 61.
Admissibility in evidence. *See* section 64.
False declarations. *See* section 67.

Certificate of Mortgage and Sale

39 A registered owner, if desirous of disposing by way of mortgage or sale of the ship or share in respect of which he is registered at any place out of the country in which the port of registry of the ship is situate, may apply to the registrar, and the registrar shall thereupon enable him to do so by granting a certificate of mortgage or a certificate of sale. Powers of mortgage and sale.

COMMENTS.

Port of Registry.
See section 13.

Registered Owner.
See section 9.

Mortgages.
See sections 31–38.

Transfer of Sale.
See sections 24–30.

40 Before a certificate of mortgage or sale is granted, the applicant shall state to the registrar, and the registrar shall enter in the register book, the following particulars; (that is to say,) Requisites for certificates of mortgage and sale.

(i) the name of the person by whom the power mentioned in the certificate is to be exercised, and in the case of a mortgage the maximum amount of charge to be created, if it is intended to fix any such maximum, and in the case of a sale the minimum price at which a sale is to be made, if it is intended to fix any such minimum:

(ii) the place where the power is to be exercised, or if no place is specified, a declaration that it may be exercised anywhere, subject to the provisions of this Act:

(iii) the limit of time within which the power may be exercised.

COMMENTS.

Certificate of Mortgage.

General.

Certificate of Sale.

Section 39–46 (inc.) refer.

⚓ ⚓ ⚓ ⚓

Restrictions on certificates of mortgage and sale.

41 A certificate of mortgage or sale shall not be granted so as to authorise any mortgage or sale to be made—

If the port of registry of the ship is situate in the United Kingdom, at any place within the United Kingdom; or

If the port of registry is situate within a British possession, at any place within the same British possession; or

If the port of registry is established by Order in Council under this Act, at that port, or within such adjoining area as is specified in the order; or

By any person not named in the certificate.

COMMENTS.

Port of Registry Established by Order in Council.

See section 88 and comments thereto.

⚓ ⚓ ⚓ ⚓

Contents of certificates of mortgage and sale.

42 A certificate of mortgage and a certificate of sale shall contain a statement of the several particulars by this Act directed to be entered in the register book on the application for the certificate, and in addition thereto an enumeration of any registered mortgages or certificates of mortgage or sale affecting the ship or share in respect of which the certificate is given.

COMMENTS.

Particulars to be Entered.

See section 40.

Registration of Mortgages.

See section 31.

⚓ ⚓ ⚓ ⚓

43 The following rules shall be observed as to certificates of mortgage:—

(1) The power shall be exercised in conformity with the directions contained in the certificate:

(2) Every mortgage made thereunder shall be registered by the endorsement of a record thereof on the certificate by a registrar or British consular officer:

(3) A mortgage made in good faith thereunder shall not be impeached by reason of the person by whom the power was given dying before the making of the mortgage:

(4) Whenever the certificate contains a specification of the place at which, and a limit of time not exceeding twelve months within which, the power is to be exercised, a mortgage made in good faith to a mortgagee without notice shall not be impeached by reason of the bankruptcy of the person by whom the power was given:

(5) Every mortgage which is so registered as aforesaid on the certificate shall have priority over all mortgages of the same ship or share created subsequently to the date of the entry of the certificate in the register book; and, if there are more mortgages than one so registered, the respective mortgagees claiming thereunder shall, notwithstanding any express, implied, or constructive notice, be entitled one before the other according to the date at which each mortgage is registered on the certificate, and not according to the date of the mortgage:

(6) Subject to the foregoing rules, every mortgagee whose mortgage is registered on the certificate shall have the same right and powers and be subject to the same liabilities as he would have had and been subject to if his mortgage had been registered in the register book instead of on the certificate:

(7) The discharge of any mortgage so registered on the certificate may be endorsed on the certificate by any registrar or British consular officer, on the production of such evidence as is by this Act required to be produced to the registrar on the entry of the discharge of a mortgage in the register book; and on that endorsement being made, the interest, if any, which passed to the mortgagee shall vest in the same person

or persons in whom it would (having regard to intervening acts and circumstances, if any), have vested, if the mortgage had not been made:

(8) On the delivery of any certificate of mortgage to the registrar by whom it was granted, he shall, after recording in the register book, in such manner as to preserve its priority, any unsatisfied mortgage registered thereon, cancel the certificate, and enter the fact of the cancellation in the register book; and every certificate so cancelled shall be void to all intents.

COMMENTS.

Priority of Mortgages.

See section 33 and comments thereto.

Powers and Rights of Mortgagees.

See sections 33–37 inclusive.

Entry of Discharge of Mortgage.

See section 32.

Rules as to certificates of sale.

44 The following rules shall be observed as to certificates of sale:—

(1) A certificate of sale shall not be granted except for the sale of an entire ship:

(2) The power shall be exercised in conformity with the directions contained in the certificate:

(3) A sale made in good faith thereunder to a purchaser for valuable consideration shall not be impeached by reason of the person by whom the power was given dying before the making of such sale:

(4) Whenever the certificate contains a specification of the place at which, and a limit of time not exceeding twelve months within which, the power is to be exercised, a sale made in good faith to a purchaser for valuable consideration without notice shall not be impeached by reason of the bankruptcy of the person by whom the power was given:

(5) A transfer made to a person qualified to be the owner of a British ship shall be by a bill of sale in accordance with this Act:

(6) If the ship is sold to a person qualified to be the owner of a British ship the ship shall be registered anew; but

notice of all mortgages enumerated on the certificate of sale shall be entered in the register book:

(7) Before registry anew there shall be produced to the registrar required to make the same the bill of sale by which the ship is transferred, the certificate of sale, and the certificate of registry of such ship:

(8) The last-mentioned registrar shall retain the certificates of sale and registry, and after having endorsed on both of those instruments an entry of the fact of a sale having taken place, shall forward them to the registrar of the port appearing thereon to be the former port of registry of the ship, and the last-mentioned registrar shall thereupon make a memorandum of the sale in his register book and the registry of the ship in that book shall be considered as closed, except as far as relates to any unsatisfied mortgages or existing certificates of mortgage entered therein:

(9) On such registry anew the description of the ship contained in her original certificate of registry may be transferred to the new register book, without her being re-surveyed, and the declaration to be made by the purchaser shall be the same as would be required to be made by an ordinary transferee:

(10) If the ship is sold to a person not qualified to be the owner of a British ship, the bill of sale by which the ship is transferred, the certificate of sale, and the certificate of registry shall be produced to a registrar or British consular officer, and that registrar or officer shall retain the certificates of sale and registry, and, having endorsed thereon the fact of that ship having been sold to a person not qualified to be the owner of a British ship, shall forward the certificates to the registrar of the port appearing on the certificate of registry to be the port of registry of that ship; and that registrar shall thereupon make a memorandum of the sale in his register book, and the registry of the ship in that book shall be considered as closed, except so far as relates to any unsatisfied mortgages or existing certificates of mortgage entered therein:

(11) If, on a sale being made to a person not qualified to be the owner of a British ship, default is made in the production of such certificates as are mentioned in the last rule, that person shall be considered by British law as having acquired no title to or interest in the

ship; and further, the person upon whose application the certificate of sale was granted, and the person exercising the power, shall each be liable to a fine not exceeding one hundred pounds:

(12) If no sale is made in conformity with the certificate of sale, that certificate shall be delivered to the registrar by whom the same was granted; and he shall thereupon cancel it and enter the fact of the cancellation in the register book; and every certificate so cancelled shall be void for all intents and purposes.

COMMENTS.

Directions contained in the Certificate.

Where a bill of sale appeared as if it were made out in conformity with the certificate, but in fact was not so, it was held that the registry of the sale was void. Orr *v.* Dickinson 1859.

Qualification of Ownership.

See section 1.

Transfer by Bill of Sale.

See section 24.

Registered Anew.

See section 52.

Enforcement of Unsatisfied Mortgage.

See section 52, sub-section 2 of the Merchant Shipping Act 1906 as to any unsatisfied registered mortgage being enforced by the court, notwithstanding the transfer, under sub-section 10 of this section.

Bill of Sale.

See section 24.

Recovery of Fines.

See section 680.

⚓ ⚓ ⚓ ⚓

Power of Commissioners of Customs in case of loss of certificate of mortgage or sale.

45 On proof at any time to the satisfaction of the Commissioners of Customs that a certificate of mortgage or sale is lost or destroyed, or so obliterated as to be useless, and that the powers thereby given have never been exercised, or if they have been exercised, then on proof of the several matters and things that have been done thereunder, the registrar may, with the sanction of the Commissioners, as circumstances require, either issue a new certificate, or direct such entries to be made in the register books, or such other things to be done, as might have been made or done if the loss, destruction, or obliteration had not taken place.

46 (1) The registered owner of any ship or share therein in respect of which a certificate of mortgage or sale has been granted, specifying the places where the power thereby given is to be exercised, may, by an instrument under his hand, authorise the registrar by whom the certificate was granted to give notice to the registrar or British consular officer at every such place that the certificate is revoked.

Revocation of certificates of mortgage and sale.

(2) Notice shall thereupon be given accordingly and shall be recorded by the registrar or British consular officer receiving it, and after it is recorded the certificate shall be deemed to be revoked and of no effect so far as respects any mortgage or sale to be thereafter made at that place.

(3) The notice after it has been recorded shall be exhibited to every person applying for the purpose of effecting or obtaining a mortgage or transfer under the certificate.

(4) A registrar or British consular officer on recording any such notice shall state to the registrar by whom the certificate was granted whether any previous exercise of the power to which such certificate refers has taken place.

COMMENTS.

Form of Revocation.

See section 65 and part 11 of Schedule 1.

Name of Ship

47 (1) A ship shall not be described by any name other than that by which she is for the time being registered.

Rules as to name of ship.

(2) A change shall not be made in the name of a ship without the previous written permission of the Board of Trade.

(3) Application for that permission shall be in writing, and if the Board are of opinion that the application is reasonable they may entertain it, and thereupon require notice thereof to be published in such form and manner as they think fit.

(4) On permission being granted to change the name, the ship's name shall forthwith be altered in the register book, in the ship's certificate of registry, and on her bows and stern.

(5) If it is shown to the satisfaction of the Board of Trade that the name of any ship has been changed without their permission they shall direct that her name be altered into that which she bore before the change, and the name shall be altered in the register book, in the ship's certificate of registry, and on her bows and stern accordingly.

(6) Where a ship having once been registered has ceased to be so registered no person unless ignorant of the previous registry (proof whereof shall lie on him) shall apply to register, and no registrar shall knowingly register, the ship, except by the name by which she was previously registered, unless with the previous written permission of the Board of Trade.

(7) Where a foreign ship, not having at any previous time been registered as a British ship, becomes a British ship, no person shall apply to register, and no registrar shall knowingly register, the ship, except by the name which she bore as a foreign ship immediately before becoming a British ship, unless with the previous written permission of the Board of Trade.

(8) If any person acts, or suffers any person under his control to act, in contravention of this section, or omits to do, or suffers any person under his control to omit to do, anything required by this section, he shall for each offence be liable to a fine not exceeding one hundred pounds, and (except in the case of an application being made under the section with respect to a foreign ship which not having at any previous time been registered as a British ship has become a British ship) the ship may be detained until this section is complied with.

COMMENTS.

Regulations as to Ships' Names.

See Merchant Shipping Act 1906, section 50. Name must be marked on the ship, *see* section 7. Name to be entered in register book, *see* section 11.

Instance of the effect of mistaken name, *see* comments to section 31 where Bell *v.* Bank of London acted.

Enforcement of Detention.

See section 692.

Recovery of Fines.

See section 680.

British Ship.

See section 1.

48 (1) When a registered ship is so altered as not to correspond with the particulars relating to her tonnage or description contained in the register book, then, if the alteration is made at any port having a registrar, that registrar, or, if it is made elsewhere, the registrar of the first port having a registrar at which the ship arrives after the alteration, shall, on application being made to him, and on receipt of a certificate from the proper surveyor stating the particulars of the alteration, either cause the alteration to be registered, or direct that the ship be registered anew. Registry of alterations, registry anew, and transfer of registry.

(2) On failure to register anew a ship or to register an alteration of a ship so altered as aforesaid, that ship shall be deemed not duly registered, and shall not be recognised as a British ship.

COMMENTS.

Sub-section 2 was substituted by section 53 of the Merchant Shipping Act 1906.

Register Book.

For entry of particulars *see* section 11.

Proper Surveyor.

Consult section 6.

Registry Anew.

See sections 50, 51, and 52.

Summary Procedure.

See sections 680 to 687, including fines.

⚓ ⚓ ⚓ ⚓

49 (1) For the purpose of the registry of an alteration in a ship, the ship's certificate of registry shall be produced to the registrar, and the registrar shall, in his discretion, either retain the certificate of registry and grant a new certificate of registry containing a description of the ship as altered, or endorse and sign on the existing certificate a memorandum of the alteration. Regulations for registry of alteration.

(2) The particulars of the alteration so made, and the fact of the new certificate having been granted, or endorsement having been made, shall be entered by the registrar of the ship's port of registry in his register book; and for that purpose the registrar to whom the application for the registry of the alteration has been made (if he is not the registrar of the ship's port of registry), shall forthwith report to the last-mentioned registrar the particulars and facts as aforesaid,

accompanied, where a new certificate of registry has been granted, by the old certificate of registry.

COMMENTS.

Certificate of Registry.

Consult section 14.

Port of Registration.

Consult section 13.

⚓ ⚓ ⚓ ⚓

Provisional certificate and endorsement.

50 (1) Where any registrar, not being the registrar of the ship's port of registry, on an application as to an alteration in a ship directs the ship to be registered anew, he shall either grant a provisional certificate, describing the ship as altered, or provisionally endorse the particulars of the alteration on the existing certificate.

(2) Every such provisional certificate or certificate provisionally endorsed, shall within ten days after the first subsequent arrival of the ship at her port of discharge in the United Kingdom, if she is registered in the United Kingdom, or, if she is registered in a British possession, at her port of discharge in that British possession, or, if she is registered at a port of registry established by Order in Council under this Act, at that port, be delivered up to the registrar thereof, and that registrar shall cause the ship to be registered anew.

(3) The registrar granting a provisional certificate under this section, or provisionally endorsing a certificate, shall add to the certificate or endorsement a statement that the same is made provisionally, and shall send a report of the particulars of the case to the registrar of the ship's port of registry, containing a similar statement as the certificate or endorsement.

COMMENTS.

Foreign Ports of Registry.

Consult section 88.

Term of Certificate.

See section 65 and part 11 of section 1.

Granting of Certificate.

See section 14.

United Kingdom.

See comments to section 3.

British Possession.

See comments to section 3.

⚓ ⚓ ⚓ ⚓

51 Where the ownership of any ship is changed, the registrar of the port at which the ship is registered may, on the application of the owners of the ship register the ship anew, although registration anew is not required under this Act. Registry anew on change of ownership.

COMMENTS.

Change of Ownership.

See section 20, regarding endorsement on the ship's certificate of Registry.

Registry Anew.

See section 44, sub-section 6.

⚓ ⚓ ⚓ ⚓

52 (1) Where a ship is to be registered anew, the registrar shall proceed as in the case of first registry, and on the delivery up to him of the existing certificate of registry, and on the other requisites to registry, or in the case of a change of ownership such of them as he thinks material, being duly complied with, shall make such registry anew, and grant a certificate thereof. Procedure for registry anew.

(2) When a ship is registered anew, her former register shall be considered as closed, except so far as relates to any unsatisfied mortgage or existing certificates of sale or mortgage entered thereon, but the names of all persons appearing on the former register to be interested in the ship, as owners or mortgagees shall be entered on the new register, and the registry anew shall not in any way affect the rights of any of those persons.

COMMENTS.

First Registry.

See sections 10 to 12.

⚓ ⚓ ⚓ ⚓

53 (1) The registry of any ship may be transferred from one port to another on the application to the registrar of the existing port of registry of the ship made by declaration in writing of all persons appearing on the register to be Transfer of registry.

interested therein as owners or mortgagees, but that transfer shall not in any way affect the rights of those persons or any of them, and those rights shall in all respects continue in the same manner as if no such transfer had been effected.

(2) On any such application the registrar shall transmit notice thereof to the registrar of the intended port of registry with a copy of all particulars relating to the ship, and the names of all persons appearing on the register to be interested therein as owners or mortgagees.

(3) The ship's certificate of registry shall be delivered up to the registrar either of the existing or intended port of registry, and, if delivered up to the former, shall be transmitted to the registrar of the intended port of registry.

(4) On the receipt of the above documents the registrar of the intended port of registry shall enter in his register book all the particulars and names so transmitted as aforesaid, and grant a fresh certificate of registry, and thenceforth such ship shall be considered as registered at the new port of registry, and the name of the ship's new port of registry shall be substituted for the name of her former port of registry on the ship's stern.

COMMENTS.

Port of Registry.

See section 13.

Certificate of Registry.

See section 14.

⚓ ⚓ ⚓ ⚓

Restrictions on re-registration of abandoned ships.

54 Where a ship has ceased to be registered as a British ship by reason of having been wrecked or abandoned, or for any reason other than capture by the enemy or transferred to a person not qualified to own a British ship, the ship shall not be re-registered until she has, at the expense of the applicant for registration, been surveyed by a surveyor of ships and certified by him to be seaworthy.

COMMENTS.

Delivery Up of Certificate.

This is required in the case of a ship lost, or ceasing to be British-owned. *See* section 21.

Granting of New Certificate.

See section 17.

Qualification for Ownership.

See section 1.

Appointment of Surveyors.

See section 724.

Incapacitated Persons

55 (1) Where by reason of infancy, lunacy, or any other cause any person interested in any ship or any share therein, is incapable of making any declaration or doing anything required or permitted by this Act to be made or done in connexion with the registry of the ship or share, the guardian or committee, if any, of that person, or, if there is none, any person appointed on application made on behalf of the incapable person, or of any other person interested, by any court or judge having jurisdiction in respect of the property of incapable persons, may make such declaration or a declaration as nearly corresponding thereto as circumstances permit, and do such act or thing in the name and on behalf of the incapable person; and all acts done by the substitute shall be as effectual as if done by the person for whom he is substituted.

Provision for cases of infancy or other incapacity.

(2) The Trustee Act, 1850, and the Acts amending the same, shall, so far as regards the court exercising jurisdiction in lunacy in Ireland, apply to shares in ships registered under this Act as if they were stock as defined by that Act.

COMMENTS.

In respect of sub-section 1 consult the Mental Health Act, 1959, part VIII; *see* also section 121 and schedule V.

The Guardian of an infant-registered owner has not the power under this section to sell or mortgage a ship. Michael *v.* Fripp 1868. In this case, it was stated that (per Malins V.C.) . . , 'the words evidently go to the minor unimportant acts falling far short of an absolute disposition of the thing which is to be protected and taken care of', . . .

Power to Dispense with Declaration.

See section 60.

Section 2: The Trustees Act, 1850. *See* now the Trustee Act, 1925, section 51.

Trusts and Equitable Rights

Notice of trusts not received.

56 No notice of any trust, express, implied, or constructive, shall be entered in the register book or be receivable by the registrar, and, subject to any right and powers appearing by the register book to be vested in any other person, the registered owner of a ship or of a share therein shall have power absolutely to dispose in manner in this Act provided of the ship or share, and to give effectual receipts for any money paid or advanced by way of consideration.

COMMENTS.

A registered owner who is a trustee is unable to create a mortgage which would stand against the beneficial owner except in accordance with the registration procedure under this Act. Burgis *v.* Constantine 1905.

By this section, the right is given to the registered owner to give 'effectual receipts' for the purchase money, and arising therefrom, it allows him to enter into a contract to have the purchase money dealt with in accordance with the terms of such contract, and this takes presidence over a prior unregistered mortgage. Barclay *v.* Poole 1907.

Equities not excluded by Act.

57 The expression "beneficial interest", where used in this Part of this Act, includes interests arising under contract and other equitable interests; and the intention of this Act is, that without prejudice to the provisions of this Act for preventing notice of trusts from being entered in the register book or received by the registrar, and without prejudice to the powers of disposition and of giving receipts conferred by this Act on registered owners and mortgagees, and without prejudice to the provisions of this Act relating to the exclusion of unqualified persons from the ownership of British ships, interests arising under contract or other equitable interests may be enforced by or against owners and mortgagees of ships in respect of their interest therein in the same manner as in respect of any other personal property.

COMMENTS.

Beneficial Interests.

The use of this expression and similar expressions are also contained in sections 5, 9, 58 and 71.

Qualification for Owning a British Ship.

See section 1.

Powers of Mortgages and Owners to Sell.

See sections 35 and 56.

Trusts.

Notice of trusts is not received by the registrar.

General.

Prior to the Merchant Shipping Amendment Act 1862, section 3 (now repealed and re-enacted in this section) were not enforceable. Equitable interests are now recognised, but a properly executed and registered legal mortgage has priority. Black *v.* Williams 1895.

Under the old registry Acts, the court could not enforce the resulting trust where a vessel was paid for by two persons and registered in the name of one. The court has now power, under this section, to enforce the trust. *The Venture* 1908.

In Foong Tai & Co. *v.* Buolleister & Co. 1908, it was held that such a trust will not take priority over a claim for necessaries pledged on the credit of the ship.

⚓ ⚓ ⚓ ⚓

Liability of Beneficial Owner

58 Where any person is beneficially interested, otherwise than by way of mortgage, in any ship or share in a ship registered in the name of some other person as owner, the person so interested shall, as well as the registered owner, be subject to all pecuniary penalties imposed by this or any other Act on the owners of ships or shares therein, so nevertheless that proceedings may be taken for the enforcement of any such penalties against both or either of the aforesaid parties, with or without joining the other of them. Liability of owners.

COMMENTS.

Position of Mortgagee.

A mortgagee is not normally deemed the owner. But, by entering into possession, he may incur the liabilities of an owner. *See* section 34, and comments thereto.

⚓ ⚓ ⚓ ⚓

Managing Owner

59 (1) The name and address of the managing owner for the time being of every ship registered at a port in the United Kingdom shall be registered at the custom house of that port. Ship's managing owner or manager to be registered.

(2) Where there is not a managing owner there shall be so registered the name of the ship's husband or other person to whom the management of the ship is entrusted by or on behalf of the owner; and any person whose name is so registered shall, for the purposes of this Act, be under the same obligations, and subject to the same liabilities, as if he were the managing owner.

(3) If default is made in complying with this section the owner shall be liable, or if there are more owners than one each owner shall be liable in proportion to his interest in the ship, to a fine not exceeding in the whole one hundred pounds each time the ship leaves any port in the United Kingdom.

COMMENTS.

The term 'managing owner' is not defined in this Act. For the general position in regard to his authority *see* Frazer *v.* Cuthbertson 1880, where the position was clearly enunciated by Bowen L.J. 'It is a commercial and not a legal expression . . . There is no magic in the term managing owner which creates him a plenipotentiary for those owners whose agent he is not in fact.'

He must give notice to the Minister of Transport of loss of vessel. *See* section 426. Section 696 gives details as to service of documents on the managing owner.

A person who is not a part owner may exercise the function of such a person, but he is then known as a 'ship's husband'.

United Kingdom.

For meaning, *see* section 3.

⚓ ⚓ ⚓ ⚓

Declarations, Inspection of Register, and Fees

Power of registrar to dispense with declarations and other evidence.

60 When, under this Part of this Act, any person is required to make a declaration on behalf of himself or of any corporation, or any evidence is required to be produced to the registrar, and it is shown to the satisfaction of the registrar that from any reasonable cause that person is unable to make the declaration, or that the evidence cannot be produced, the registrar may, with the approval of the Commissioners of Customs, and on the production of such other evidence, and subject to such terms as they may think fit, dispense with the declaration or evidence.

COMMENTS.

Declarations on behalf of incapacitated persons. *See* section 55.

⚓ ⚓ ⚓ ⚓

61 (1) Declarations required by this Part of this Act shall be made before a registrar of British ships, or a justice of the peace, or a commissioner for oaths, or a British consular officer. Mode of making declarations.

(2) Declarations required by this Part of this Act may be made on behalf of a corporation by the secretary or any other officer of the corporation authorised by them for the purpose.

COMMENTS.

False Declarations.

See section 67.

Registration of British Ships.

See section 4.

Consular Offices.

See section 742.

62 All fees authorised to be taken under this Part of this Act, shall, except where otherwise in this Act provided, if taken in any part of the United Kingdom, be applied in payment of the general expenses of carrying into effect this Part of this Act, or otherwise as the Treasury may direct; if taken in a British possession, be disposed of in such way as the executive Government of the possession direct; and if taken at any port of registry established by Order in Council under this Act, be disposed of as Her Majesty in Council directs. Application of fees.

COMMENTS.

Port of Registry.

See section 88.

Returns, Evidence, and Forms

63 (1) Every registrar in the United Kingdom shall at the expiration of every month, and every other registrar at such times as may be fixed by the Registrar-General of Shipping and Seamen, transmit to him a full return, in such form as the said Registrar-General may direct, of all registries, transfers, transmissions, mortgages, and other dealings with ships which have been registered by or communicated to him in his character of registrar, and of the names of the persons Returns to be made by registrars.

concerned in the same, and of such other particulars as may be directed by the said Registrar-General.

(2) Every registrar at a port in the United Kingdom shall on or before the first day of February and the first day of August in every year transmit to the Registrar-General of Shipping and Seamen a list of all ships registered at that port, and also of all ships whose registers have been transferred or cancelled at that port since the last preceding return.

COMMENTS.

Registrar—General.

For appointment *see* section 251.

⚓ ⚓ ⚓ ⚓

Evidence of register book certificate of registry, and other documents.

64 (1) A person, on payment of a fee not exceeding one shilling, to be fixed by the Commissioners of Customs, may on application to the registrar at a reasonable time during the hours of his official attendance, inspect any register book.

(2) The following documents shall be admissible in evidence in manner provided by this Act; namely:—

(*a*) Any register book under this Part of this Act on its production from the custody of the registrar or other person having the lawful custody thereof;

(*b*) A certificate of registry under this Act purporting to be signed by the registrar or other proper officer;

(*c*) An endorsement on a certificate of registry purporting to be signed by the registrar or other proper officer;

(*d*) Every declaration made in pursuance of this Part of this Act in respect of a British ship.

(3) A copy or transcript of the register of British ships kept by the Registrar-General of Shipping and Seamen under the direction of the Board of Trade shall be admissible in evidence in manner provided by this Act, and have the same effect to all intents as the original register of which it is a copy or transcript.

COMMENTS.

The fee of one shilling underlined in the section was subsequently amended by the Fees Increase Act, 1923, and in turn was repealed by the Merchant Shipping (Safety Convention) Act, 1949, section 37, subsection 5 and schedule 111 of that Act. The regulations at present in force and since the 1st May 1971, under this section and other sections of the Merchant Shipping Acts are the Merchant Shipping (Fees) Regulations 1971, which replace all such previous regulations. The fee for each inspection of the register book, in accordance with this section is now £0·65.

Inspection of Register Book.

Where a shipwright effects repairs to a vessel upon instructions from the mortgagor (with the implied authority of the mortgagee), the shipwrights' lien against the mortgagee is not lost because of failure to inspect the register, as to the existence of a mortgage.

The provision is merely permissive and not obligatory. Williams *v* Allsop 1861.

Admissibility of Documents in Evidence.

See sections 694, 695, and sections 719 to 721.

⚓ ⚓ ⚓ ⚓

65 (1) The several instruments and documents specified in the second part of the First Schedule to this Act shall be in the form prescribed by the Commissioners of Customs, with the consent of the Board of Trade, or as near thereto as circumstances permit; and the Commissioners of Customs may, with the consent of the Board of Trade, make such alterations in the forms so prescribed, and also in the forms set out in the first part of the said schedule, as they may deem requisite. Forms of documents, and instructions as to registry.

(2) A registrar shall not be required without the special direction of the Commissioners of Customs to receive and enter in the register book any bill of sale, mortgage, or other instrument for the disposal or transfer of any ship or share, or any interest therein, which is made in any form other than that for the time being required under this Part of this Act, or which contains any particulars other than those contained in such form; but the said Commissioners shall, before altering the forms, give such public notice thereof as may be necessary in order to prevent inconvenience.

(3) The Commissioners of Customs shall cause the said forms to be supplied to all registrars under this Act for distribution to persons requiring to use the same, either free of charge, or at such moderate prices as they may direct.

(4) The Commissioners of Customs, with the consent of the Board of Trade, may also, for carrying into effect this Part of this Act, give such instructions to their officers as to the manner of making entries in the register book, as to the execution and attestation of powers of attorney, as to any

evidence required for identifying any person, as to the referring to themselves of any question involving doubt or difficulty, and generally as to any act or thing to be done in pursuance of this Part of this Act, as they think fit.

COMMENTS.

Exemptions from Stamp Duty.

See section 721.

Forgery and False Declarations

Forgery of documents.

66 If any person forges, or fraudulently alters, or assists in forging or fraudulently altering, or procures to be forged or fraudulently altered, any of the following documents, namely, any register book, builder's certificate, surveyor's certificate, certificate of registry, declaration bill of sale, instrument of mortgage, or certificate of mortgage or sale under this Part of this Act, or any entry or endorsement required by this Part of this Act to be made in or on any of those documents, that person shall in respect of each offence be guilty of felony.

COMMENTS.

Forgery of the documents listed in this section, if committed with intent to defraud or deceive is punishable. *See* the forgery Act 1913, section 3, sub-section 3.

False declarations.

67 (1) If any person in the case of any declaration made in the presence of or produced to a registrar under this Part of this Act, or in any document or other evidence produced to such registrar—

(i) wilfully makes, or assists in making, or procures to be made any false statement concerning the title to or ownership of, or the interest existing in any ship, or any share in a ship; or

(ii) utters, produces, or makes use of any declaration or document containing any such false statement knowing the same to be false,

he shall in respect of each offence be guilty of a misdemeanor.

(2) If any person wilfully makes a false declaration touching the qualification of himself or of any other person or of any corporation to own a British ship or any share therein, he shall for each offence be guilty of a misdemeanor,

and that ship or share shall be subject to forfeiture under this Act, to the extent of the interest therein of the declarant, and also, unless it is proved that the declaration was made without authority, of any person or corporation on behalf of whom the declaration is made.

COMMENTS.

Misdemeanor.

Prosecution of etc., *see* section 680.

Proceedings of Forfeiture.

See section 76.

⚓ ⚓ ⚓ ⚓

National Character and Flag

National character of ship to be declared before clearance.

68 (1) An officer of customs shall not grant a clearance or transire for any ship until the master of such ship has declared to that officer the name of the nation to which he claims that she belongs, and that officer shall thereupon inscribe that name on the clearance or transire.

(2) If a ship attempts to proceed to sea without such clearance or transire, she may be detained until the declaration is made.

COMMENTS.

Provisions as to Detention.

See section 692.

Procedure on Clearance.

See section 128 of the Customs Consolidation Act 1876.

⚓ ⚓ ⚓ ⚓

Penalty for unduly assuming British character.

69 (1) If a person uses the British flag and assumes the British national character on board a ship owned in whole or in part by any persons not qualified to own a British ship, for the purpose of making the ship appear to be a British ship, the ship shall be subject to forfeiture under this Act, unless the assumption has been made for the purpose of escaping capture by an enemy or by a foreign ship of war in the exercise of some belligerent right.

(2) In any proceeding for enforcing any such forfeiture the burden of proving a title to use the British flag and assume

the British national character shall lie upon the person using and assuming the same.

COMMENTS.

Qualification for Ownership.

See section 1.

Proceedings in Forfeiture.

See section 76.

Penalty for concealment of British or assumption of foreign character.

70 If the master or owner of a British ship does anything or permits anything to be done, or carries or permits to be carried any papers or documents, with intent to conceal the British character of the ship from any person entitled by British law to inquire into the same, or with intent to assume a foreign character, or with intent to deceive any person so entitled as aforesaid, the ship shall be subject to forfeiture under this Act; and the master, if he commits or is privy to the commission of the offence, shall in respect of each offence be guilty of a misdemeanor.

COMMENTS.

British Ship.

See section 1.

Proceedings in Forfeiture.

See section 76, the Merchant Shipping Act 1854, section 103, subsection 1, now repealed provided . . . 'that a ship . . . shall be forfeited'. It was held that under these words, the court had no option but to order forfeiture, even though the ship in question had passed into the hands of a bona fide purchaser without notice. *The Annandale* 1877.

In this Act, i.e. the Merchant Shipping Act 1894, section 70, the words 'subject to forfeiture' have been substituted for 'shall be forfeit', and some doubts have been cast as to whether the language of the present Act permits an option by the court. This was considered in *The Maori King* 1909 when it was held that no option was conferred.

For an instance where a ship was forfeited under this section *see The Sceptre* 1876.

Prosecution of Misdemeanours.

See section 680.

71 If an unqualified person acquires as owner, otherwise than by such transmission as herein-before provided for, any interest, either legal or beneficial, in a ship using a British flag and assuming the British character, that interest shall be subject to forfeiture under this Act.

Penalty for acquiring ownership if unqualified.

COMMENTS.

Qualification for Ownership.

See section 1.

Provisions Regulating Transmission.

See sections 27 and 28.

Beneficial Interest.

For meaning *see* section 57.

Procedure on Forfeiture.

See section 76.

General.

In accord with the Merchant Shipping Act 1906, section 51, the Commissioners of Customs and Excise can call for proof of title at any time.

⚓ ⚓ ⚓ ⚓

72 Where it is declared by this Act that a British ship shall not be recognised as a British ship, that ship shall not be entitled to any benefits, privileges, advantages, or protection usually enjoyed by British ships nor to use the British flag or assume the British national character, but so far as regards the payment of dues, the liability to fines and forfeiture, and the punishment of offences committed on board such ship, or by any persons belonging to her, such ship shall be dealt with in the same manner in all respects as if she were a recognised British ship.

Liabilities of ships not recognised as British.

COMMENTS.

Qualifications for Ownership of British Ship.

See section 1.

Obligation to Register.

See section 2.

Exemption from Registration.

See section 3.

Limitation of Liability.

This has been extended to cover the period from launching to registration. *See* Merchant Shipping (Liability) (of shipping and Others) Act 1958, section 4.

Application of Part II of this Act to an Unregistered British Ship.

See section 266.

Jurisdiction of Naval Courts Over Unregistered British Ships.

See section 486.

⚓ ⚓ ⚓ ⚓

National colours for ships, and penalty on carrying improper colours.

73 (1) The red ensign usually worn by merchant ships, without any defacement or modification whatsoever, is hereby declared to be the proper national colours for all ships and boats belonging to any British subject, except in the case of Her Majesty's ships or boats, or in the case of any other ship or boat for the time being allowed to wear any other national colours in pursuance of a warrant from Her Majesty or from the Admiralty.

(2) If any distinctive national colours, except such red ensign or except the Union Jack with a white border, or if any colours usually worn by Her Majesty's ships or resembling those of Her Majesty, or if the pendant usually carried by Her Majesty's ships or any pendant resembling that pendant, are or is hoisted on board any ship or boat belonging to any British subject without warrant from Her Majesty or from the Admiralty, the master of the ship or boat, or the owner thereof, if on board the same, and every other person hoisting the colours or pendant, shall for each offence incur a fine not exceeding five hundred pounds.

(3) Any commissioned officer on full pay in the military or naval service of Her Majesty, or any officer of customs in Her Majesty's dominions, or any British consular officer, may board any ship or boat on which any colours or pendants are hoisted contrary to this Act, and seize and take away the colours or pendant, and the colours or pendant shall be forfeited to Her Majesty.

(4) A fine under this section may be recovered with costs in the High Court in England or Ireland, or in the Court of Session in Scotland, or in any Colonial Court of Admiralty or Vice-Admiralty Court within Her Majesty's dominions.

(5) Any offence mentioned in this section may also be prosecuted, and the fine for it recovered, summarily, provided that:—

(*a*) where any such offence is prosecuted summarily, the court imposing the fine shall not impose a higher fine than one hundred pounds; and

(*b*) nothing in this section shall authorise the imposition of more than one fine in respect of the same offence.

COMMENTS.

Under certain circumstances, British Merchant ships and fishing-vessels are allowed to wear the Blue Ensign by Admiralty warrant. For details *see* Queen's Regulations and Admiralty Instructions as published from time to time by H.M. Stationery Office.

Union Jack with White Border.

This flag colloquially known as the 'Pilot Jack' may be displayed as a signal for a pilot. *See* section 45 of the Pilotage Act 1913, and Order in Council (S.R. & O. 1933, No. 976) made under the provisions of the Act in respect of pilot signals.

Colours Forfeited.

See section 76.

74 (1) A ship belonging to a British subject shall hoist the proper national colours— Penalty on ship not showing colours.

(*a*) on a signal being made to her by one of Her Majesty's ships (including any vessel under the command of an officer of Her Majesty's navy on full pay), and

(*b*) on entering or leaving any foreign port, and

(*c*) if of fifty tons gross tonnage or upwards, on entering or leaving any British port.

(2) If default is made on board any such ship in complying with this section, the master of the ship shall for each offence be liable to a fine not exceeding one hundred pounds.

(3) This section shall not apply to a fishing-boat duly entered in the fishing-boat register and lettered and numbered as required by the Fourth Part of this Act.

75 The provisions of this Act with respect to colours worn by merchant ships shall not affect any other power of the Admiralty in relation thereto. Saving for Admiralty.

COMMENTS.

For powers of the Admiralty *see* Queen's Regulations and Admiralty Instructions.

⚓ ⚓ ⚓ ⚓

Forfeiture of Ship

Proceedings on forfeiture of ship.

76 (1) Where any ship has either wholly or as to any share therein become subject to forfeiture under this Part of this Act,

(*a*) any commissioned officer on full pay in the military or naval service of Her Majesty;

(*b*) any officer of customs in Her Majesty's dominions; or

(*c*) any British consular officer,

may seize and detain the ship, and bring her for adjudication before the High Court in England or Ireland, or before the Court of Session in Scotland, and elsewhere before any colonial Court of Admiralty or Vice-Admiralty Court in Her Majesty's dominions, and the court may thereupon adjudge the ship with her tackle, apparel, and furniture to be forfeited to Her Majesty, and make such order in the case as to the court seems just, and may award to the officer bringing in the ship for adjudication such portion of the proceeds of the sale of the ship, or any share therein, as the court think fit.

(2) Any such officer as in this section mentioned shall not be responsible either civilly or criminally to any person whomsoever in respect of any such seizure or detention as aforesaid, notwithstanding that the ship has not been brought in for adjudication, or if so brought in is declared not liable to forfeiture, if it is shown to the satisfaction of the court before whom any trial relating to such ship or such seizure or detention is held that there were reasonable grounds for such seizure or detention; but if no such grounds are shown the court may award costs and damages to any party aggrieved, and make such other order in the premises as the court thinks just.

Section 77. Repealed Merchant Shipping Act 1965, schedule 2.

Section 78. Repealed Merchant Shipping Act 1965, schedule 2.

Section 79. Repealed Merchant Shipping Act 1965, schedule 2.

Section 80. Repealed Merchant Shipping Act 1965, schedule 2.

Section 81. Repealed Merchant Shipping Act 1965, schedule 2.

COMMENTS.

Subject to Forfeiture.

See comments to section 71.

Extension of Jurisdiction.

The Merchant Shipping Act 1911, section 1, extends the jurisdiction of this section to certain British courts in foreign countries.

Application of This Section.

This section has been adopted under various other statutes, viz. Seal Fisheries (North Pacific) Act 1912, section 3, sub-section 2. Treaties of Washington Act 1922, section 2, sub-section 5.

Enforcement of Detention.

See section 692.

Colonial Court of Admiralty: Vice-Admiralty Court.

For jurisdiction of these courts *see* Colonial Courts of Admiralty Act, 1890, sections 2 and 9.

82 Whenever the tonnage of any ship has been ascertained and registered in accordance with the tonnage regulations of this Act, the same shall thenceforth be deemed to be the tonnage of the ship, and shall be repeated in every subsequent registry thereof, unless any alteration is made in the form or capacity of the ship, or unless it is discovered that the tonnage of the ship has been erroneously computed; and in either of those cases the ship shall be re-measured, and her tonnage determined and registered according to the tonnage regulations of this Act.

Tonnage once ascertained to be the tonnage of ship.

COMMENTS.

In an action of limitation of liability, evidence to show that the registered tonnage of the plaintiffs' ship was not the correct tonnage was held admissible. *The Recepta*, 1889.

Tonnage Regulations of this Act.

See section 77.

83 Such fees as the Board of Trade determine shall be paid in respect of the measurement of a ship's tonnage not exceeding those specified in the Third Schedule to this Act, and those fees shall be paid into the Mercantile Marine Fund.

Fees for measurement.

COMMENTS.

The words underlined were repealed by section 37, sub-section 5, and the Third Schedule of the Merchant Shipping (Safety Convention) Act 1949.

The Fees at present in force are contained in Statutory Instrument 1971, No. 643, The Merchant Shipping (Fees) Regulations 1971, as amended. The Merchant Shipping (Fees) (Amendment No. 2) Regulations 1971.

Mercantile Marine Fund.

Fees are now paid into the Exchequer. *See* the Merchant Shipping (Mercantile Marine Fund) Act 1898, section 1.

⚓ ⚓ ⚓ ⚓

Tonnage of ships of foreign countries adopting tonnage regulations.

84 (1) Whenever it appears to Her Majesty the Queen in Council that the tonnage regulations of this Act have been adopted by any foreign country, and are in force there, Her Majesty in Council may order that the ships of that country shall, without being re-measured in Her Majesty's dominions, be deemed to be of the tonnage denoted in their certificates of registry or other national papers, in the same manner, to the same extent, and for the same purposes as the tonnage denoted in the certificate of registry of a British ship is deemed to be the tonnage of that ship*

*Amended by Merchant Shipping Act 1965.
Schedule 1.
'and any space shown by the certificate of registry, or other national papers of any such ship as deducted from the tonnage shall, where a similar deduction in the case of a British ship depends on compliance with any conditions or on the compliance being evidenced in any manner, be deemed to comply with those conditions, and to be so evidenced, unless a surveyor of ships certifies to the Board of Trade that the construction and the equipment of the ship as respects that space do not come up to the standard which would be required if the ship were a British ship registered in the United Kingdom'.
N.B.—This in turn repealed section 55 of the 1906 Act.

(2) Her Majesty in Council may limit the time during which the Order is to remain in operation, and make the Order subject to such conditions and qualifications (if any) as Her Majesty may deem expedient, and the operation of the Order shall be limited and modified accordingly.

(3) If it is made to appear to Her Majesty that the tonnage of any foreign ship, as measured by the rules of the country to which she belongs, materially differs from that which would be her tonnage if measured under this Act, Her Majesty in Council may order that, notwithstanding any

Order in Council for the time being in force under this section, any of the ships of that country may, for all or any of the purposes of this Act, be re-measured in accordance with this Act.

COMMENTS.

In relation to a ship of any foreign country, being a ship to which regulations made under the Merchant Shipping Act 1948, section 1 would apply, if she were a British ship, and also registered in the United Kingdom, sub-section 1, has effect as if for the first group of words underlined, that is 'shall be . . . ships', there were substituted the words 'shall be deemed to have been specified in a certificate issued under the Merchant Shipping Act 1948, and to comply with regulations made under section 1 of that Act' and for the second group of words underlined, that is 'the standard . . . ship' there were substituted the words 'the standard which would be required under or for the purposes of those regulations if she were a British ship registered in the United Kingdom';

Consult the Merchant Shipping Act 1948, section 4, sub-section 2 and also the Merchant Shipping (Crew Accommodation) Regulations 1953 (S.I. 1953, No. 1036) (as amended by the Merchant Shipping (Crew Accommodation) (Amendment) Regulations 1954, S.I. 1954, No. 1660 and the Merchant Shipping (Crew Accommodation) (Amendment) Regulations 1961, S.I. 1961, No. 393.

Surveyor of Ships.
For powers of surveyors of ships *see* section 725.

Tonnage Regulations.
See section 77.

Countries in Respect of which Orders Have Been Made.

	Year		*Year*
Austria–Hungary	1871	Japan – –	1923
Belgium – –	1884	Latvia – –	1927
Denmark – –	1895	Netherlands –	1888
Egypt – –	1939	Norway – –	1894
Estonia – –	1926	Poland – –	1935
France – –	1904	Portugal – –	1926
Free city of Danzig	1936	Russia & Finland	1880
Germany – –	1896	Spain – –	1911
Greece – –	1927	Sweden – –	1882
Iceland – –	1925	U.S.A. – –	1895
Italy – – –	1906		

For provisions as to Orders in Council *see* section 738 and for the saving of Orders in Council made before 1895, *see* section 745.

Amendment.

See above, immediately following this section Merchant Shipping Act 1965.

⚓ ⚓ ⚓ ⚓

Space occupied by deck cargo to be liable to dues.

85 (1) If any ship, British or foreign, other than a home trade ship as defined by this Act, carries as deck cargo, that it to say, in any uncovered space upon deck, or in any covered space not included in the cubical contents forming the ship's registered tonnage,* timber, stores, or other goods, all dues payable on the ship's tonnage shall be payable as if there were added to the ship's registered tonnage the tonnage of the space occupied by those goods at the time at which the dues become payable.

(2) The space so occupied shall be deemed to be the space limited by the area occupied by the goods and by straight lines enclosing a rectangular space sufficient to include the goods.

(3) The tonnage of the space shall be ascertained by an officer of the Board of Trade or of Customs in manner directed† as to the measurement of poops or other closed-in spaces by Rule I in the Second Schedule to this Act, and when so ascertained shall be entered by him in the ship's official log-book, and also in a memorandum which he shall deliver to the master, and the master shall, when the said dues are demanded, produce that memorandum in like manner as if it were the certificate of registry, or, in the case of a foreign ship, the document equivalent to a certificate of registry, and in default shall be liable to the same penalty as if he had failed to produce the said certificate or document.

(4) Nothing in this section shall apply to any ship employed exclusively in trading or going from place to place in any river or inland water of which the whole or part is in any British possession, or to deck cargo carried by a ship while engaged in the coasting trade of any British possession.

*Amended by Merchant Shipping Act 1965.
Schedule 1.
'And not exempted by regulations under The Merchant Shipping Act 1965.'

†UNDERLINED:—amended by Merchant Shipping Act 1965.
Schedule 1.
'In accordance with regulations made under the Merchant Shipping Act 1965.'

COMMENTS.

Home-Trade Ship, Definition of.

A Home-Trade ship includes every ship employed in trading or going within the limits of the United Kingdom, the Channel Islands, and the Isle of Man and the Continent of Europe between the River Elbe and Brest inclusive.

It should be noted that the term 'United Kingdom' in this definition includes the Republic of Ireland.

Stores or Other Goods.

Bunker coal carried in an uncovered space or deck for use on voyage is included in the term. Cairn Line *v.* Trinity House 1908.

In Richmond Hill S.S. Co. *v.* Trinity House 1896, it was held that the term '. . . other goods' included horses and cattle.

Officer of Customs and Measurement.

This must be carried out in accordance with the Act. It was held in Great Western Rail Co. *v.* Kassos Steam Navigation Co. 1930, that a memorandum by an officer of customs that the proper measurements has been made is of no effect, if that measurement had in fact been made by some other method.

Repeal.

Words underlined from 'in' to 'also' repealed. Schedule 5. Merchant Shipping Act 1970 as from 1st January 1973.

Merchant Shipping Act 1970
(Commencement No. 1) Order 1972

Amendment.

See above immediately following this section. Merchant Shipping Act 1965.

⚓ ⚓ ⚓ ⚓

86 All duties in relation to the survey and measurement of ships shall be performed by surveyors of ships under this Act in accordance with regulations made by the Board of Trade.

Surveyors and Regulations for measurement of ships.

COMMENTS.

The regulations under this section are contained in the Instructions to Surveyors, issued by the Board of Trade.

⚓ ⚓ ⚓ ⚓

87 Any persons having power to levy tonnage rates on ships may, if they think fit, with the consent of the Board of Trade, levy those tonnage rates upon the registered tonnage of

Levy of tonnage rates under local Acts on the registered tonnage.

the ships as determined by the tonnage regulations of this Act, notwithstanding that any local Act under which those rates are levied provides for levying the same upon some different system of tonnage measurement.

COMMENTS.

Consult section 77 for the tonnage regulations of this Act.

Ports of Registry in Place under Foreign Jurisdiction Act

Foreign ports of registry. 53 & 54 Vict. c. 37.

88 Where, in accordance with the Foreign Jurisdiction Act, 1890, Her Majesty exercises jurisdiction within any port, it shall be lawful for Her Majesty, by Order in Council to declare that port a port of registry, and by the same or any subsequent Order in Council to declare the description of persons who are to be registrars of British ships at that port of registry, and to make regulations with respect to the registry of British ships thereat.

COMMENTS.

British Ships.

See comments to section 1.

Orders Under this Section.

British Solomon Isles Maritime Order in Council 1912, S.R. No. 1912, No. 1862 as amended by S.I. 1948, No. 2063. This substituted Honiara for Tulagi as a port of registry. Port of Vila, New Hebrides S.R. & O. 1917, No. 1018. Port of Mombassa S.R. & O. 1926, No. 825, as amended by S.I. 1961, No. 2322.

Port of Zanzibar S.R. & O. 1926, No. 826.

Fort Johnston (Nyasaland) S.I. 1952, No. 1863.

Registry in Colonies

Powers of governors in colonies.

89 In every British possession the governor of the possession shall occupy the place of the Commissioners of Customs with regard to the performance of anything relating to the registry of a ship or of any interest in a ship registered in that possession, and shall have power to approve a port within the possession for the registry of ships.

COMMENTS.

Commissioners of Customs.

Now the Commissioners of Customs & Excise.

Appointment of Surveyors of Ships.

Consult section 727.

General.

It would appear that some doubt existed whether certain powers, transferred since 1854 from the Commissioners of Customs and Excise to the Board of Trade/Minister of Transport, were still enjoyed by governors of colonies.

It has been stated that under the present section such powers are not conferred on governors.

⚓ ⚓ ⚓ ⚓

90 (1) The governor of a British possession may, with the approval of a Secretary of State, make regulations providing that, on an application for the registry under this Act in that possession of any ship which does not exceed sixty tons burden, the registrar may grant, in lieu of a certificate of registry as required by this Act, a certificate of registry to be terminable at the end of six months or any longer period from the granting thereof, and all certificates of registry granted under any such regulations shall be in such form and have effect subject to such conditions as the regulations provide.

Terminable certificates of registry for small ships in colonies.

(2) Any ship to which a certificate is granted under any such regulations shall, while that certificate is in force, and in relation to all things done or omitted during that period, be deemed to be a registered British ship.

COMMENTS.

British Possession.

Consult section 3.

Tons Burden.

In reference to registration this term means net registered tonnage and not gross tonnage. *The Brunel* 1900.

British Ship.

Consult section 1 and for liabilities of ships not recognised as British consult section 72.

⚓ ⚓ ⚓ ⚓

Application of Part I

91 This Part of this Act shall apply to the whole of Her Majesty's dominions, and to all places where Her Majesty has jurisdiction.

Application of Part I.

COMMENTS.

Consult sections 735 and 736 for power of legislation to alter provisions of this Act, and for the regulation of the coasting trade.

M.S.A. 1894

PART II

MASTERS AND SEAMEN

F

PART II

MASTERS AND SEAMEN

GENERAL NOTES AND COMMENTS

British Seamen's Cards.

These cards fulfil the purpose of the Seafarers' Identity Documents Convention, 1958, in relation to seafarers' identity documents. *Consult*: British Seamen's Cards Order 1960, No. 967, as amended by the British Seamen's Cards (Amendment) Order 1962, No. 1324; The British Seamen's Cards (Amendment) Order 1964, No. 1059; The British Seamen's Card (Amendment) Order 1967, No. 1610.

Restriction on Employment of Aliens.

Consult generally the Aliens Restriction (Amendment) Act 1919. Under this Act no alien shall act as master, chief officer or chief engineer of a British ship registered in the United Kingdom, except in the case of a ship or boat employed habitually in voyages between ports outside the United Kingdom.

Provided that this prohibition shall not apply to any alien who has acted as master, chief officer or chief engineer of a British ship, or as a skipper or second hand of a British fishing-boat, at any time during the war, and is certified by the Admiralty to have performed good and faithful service in that capacity.

No alien shall be employed in any capacity on board a British ship, registered in the United Kingdom, at a rate of pay less than the standard rate of pay for the time being current on British ships for her rating.

Restriction on Employment of Young Persons and Children.

There are restrictions on the employment of children and young persons on board ship. Consult generally the Employment of Women, Young Persons and Children Act 1920 which, where it relates to employment in a ship, shall have effect as if it formed part of the Merchant Shipping Acts, 1894–1920.

By this Act, the expression 'child' meant a person under the age of 14 years, but this expression and definition of child has been repealed by the Education Act 1944. The definition of a child is now . . . 'any person who is not for the purposes of the Education Act 1944, over compulsory School age.'

The expression 'young person' means a person who has ceased to be a child and who is under the age of 18 years.

Certificates of Competency

Certificates of competency to be held by officers of ships.

92 (1) Every British foreign-going ship and every British home trade passenger ship, when going to sea from any place in the United Kingdom, and every foreign steamship carrying passengers between places in the United Kingdom, shall be provided with officers duly certificated under this Act according to the following scale:—

(*a*) In any case with a duly certificated master:

(*b*) If the ship is of one hundred tons burden or upwards, with at least one officer besides the master holding a certificate not lower than that of only mate in the case of a foreign-going ship, or of mate in the case of a home trade passenger ship:

(*c*) If the ship is a foreign-going ship, and carries more than one mate, with at least the first and second mate duly certificated:

(*d*) If the ship is a foreign-going steamship of one hundred nominal horse-power or upwards, with at least two engineers, one of whom shall be a first-class and the other a first-class or second-class engineer duly certificated:

(*e*) If the ship is a foreign-going steamship of less than one hundred nominal horse-power, or a sea-going home trade passenger steamship, with at least one engineer who is a first-class or second-class engineer duly certificated.

(2) If any person:—

(*a*) having been engaged as one of the above-mentioned officers goes to sea as such officer without being duly certificated; or

(*b*) employs a person as an officer, in contravention of this section, without ascertaining that the person so serving is duly certificated,

that person shall be liable for each offence to a fine not exceeding fifty pounds:

(3) An officer shall not be deemed duly certificated, within the meaning of this section, unless he is the holder for the time being of a valid certificate of competency under this Act of a grade appropriate to his station in the ship, or of a higher grade.

COMMENTS:

The provisions relating to the requirement of officers to hold a certificate of competency and to the production of those certificates are not applicable to officers of ships belonging to the general lighthouse authorities or to pleasure-yachts.

Consult section 413 for the requirements on board fishing-boats.

The words underlined above, that is sub-section 1(*b*), have been repealed as a result of section 85 of the Merchant Shipping Act 1906, which substitutes for the underlined words, section 56 of the Merchant Shipping Act 1906, viz.:

'If the ship is of one hundred tons burden, or upwards, with at least one officer besides the master holding a certificate not lower than that of:

(i) mate, in the case of a home trade passenger ship;

(ii) second mate, in the case of a foreign-going sailing-ship of not more than 200 tons burden, and;

(iii) only mate, in the case of any other foreign-going ship.'

Certificates.

For grades of certificates of competency, *see* section 93.

Naval Officers.

For certificates of service for naval officers, *see* section 99.

Steamship.

The provisions relating to steamships apply to ships propelled by electricity and other mechanical power, *see* section 743.

Tons Burden.

It was held in *The Brunel*, 1900, that tons burden in section 3 of the principal Act, meant net registered tonnage. It is submitted that this definition does not necessarily have the same meaning in other parts of the Act.

Passenger.

The word 'passenger' is defined for the purpose of Part (iii) of the principal Act, in the Merchant Shipping (Safety and Loadline Conventions) Act 1932, and in this Act the expression 'passenger' means any person carried in a ship except:

(*a*) a person employed or engaged in any capacity on board the ship on the business of the ship;

(*b*) a person on board the ship, either in pursuance of the obligation laid upon the master to carry shipwrecked, distressed or other persons, or by reason of any circumstance that neither the master nor the owner nor the charter (if any) could have prevented or forestalled, and

(*c*) a child under one year of age.

Passenger Ship.

In accord with the Merchant Shipping (Safety Convention) Act 1949, section 26, the expression 'passenger steamer' means a steamer carrying more than 12 passengers.

Steamships, Motor-ships, etc.

Section 743 of the principal Act provides that the provisions as to steamships apply also to ships propelled by electricity and other mechanical power.

⚓ ⚓ ⚓ ⚓

Grades of certificates of competency.

93 (1) Certificates of competency shall be granted in accordance with this Act, for each of the following grades (that is to say):

Master of a foreign-going ship:
First mate of a foreign-going ship:
Second mate of a foreign-going ship:
Only mate of a foreign-going ship:
Master of a home trade passenger-ship:
Mate of a home trade passenger ship:
First-class engineer:
Second-class engineer.

(2) A certificate of competency for a foreign-going ship shall be deemed to be of a higher grade than the corresponding certificate for a home trade passenger ship, and shall entitle the lawful holder thereof to go to sea in the corresponding grade in the last-mentioned ship; but a certificate for a home trade passenger ship shall not entitle the holder to go to sea as master or mate of a foreign-going ship.

COMMENTS.

Certificate of Competency.

Examinations for the certificate of competency for masters and mates are regulated by the Merchant Shipping (Certificates) Act 1914.

The grant of certificates	— Consult section 98.
The form of certificates	— Consult section 100.
Loss and forgery of certificates	— Consult M.S.A. 1906, 101, 104.
Cooks in foreign-going ships	— M.S.A. 1906, section 27, also M.S.A. 1948, section 6.

Certificate of Competency as AB.

See section 5 of the Merchant Shipping Acts 1948, The Merchant Shipping (Certificates of Competency as AB) Regulations 1959, S.I.

1959, No. 2148 as amended by the Merchant Shipping (Certificates of Competency as AB) (Amendment) Regulations 1962, S.I. 1962, No. 579.

Rules for Examinations: Masters and Mates.

These are not rules such as S.R. & O. (S.I.) but are regulations published by H.M. Stationer's Office, under the title 'Regulations relating to the Examination of Masters & Mates'.

⚓ ⚓ ⚓ ⚓

Examinations for certificates of competency.

94 (1) For the purpose of granting certificates of competency as masters, or mates, to persons desirous of obtaining the same, examinations shall be held by Local Marine Boards at their respective ports.

(2) The Board of Trade may make rules which shall be strictly adhered to by the examiners for:—

(*a*) the conduct of the examinations: and

(*b*) the qualification of the applicants:

and may depute any of their officers to attend and assist at any examination.

(3) The approval of the Board of Trade shall be necessary so far as regards the number and the remuneration of the examiners, and an examiner shall not be appointed, unless he holds a certificate of qualification to be from time to time granted or renewed by the Board of Trade.

(4) The Board of Trade may, if it appears to them that the examination for two or more ports can be held without inconvenience by the same examiners, provide that the examination be so held, and require the Local Marine Boards of those ports to act as one board for the purpose of the examination.

(5) Subject to the powers of the Board of Trade under this section the Local Marine Board may appoint, remove, and re-appoint examiners, and regulate the conduct of the examinations, and any member of the Local Marine Board may be present at and assist at the examinations held by that Board.

COMMENTS.

This section repealed by the Merchant Shipping (Certificates) Act 1914, section 1, sub-section 3 and replaced by section 1, sub-section 1 and 2 of that Act.

⚓ ⚓ ⚓ ⚓

Examinations by Board of Trade in certain cases.

95 Where the business of a mercantile marine office is conducted otherwise than under a Local Marine Board, the Board of Trade may exercise all such powers and make all such provisions for the holding of examinations as may be exercised and made by a Local Marine Board.

COMMENTS.

This section repealed by the Merchant Shipping (Certificates) Act 1914, section 1, sub-section 3 and replaced by section 1, sub-sections 1 and 2 of that Act.

Engineers certificates of competency.

96 (1) For the purpose of granting certificates of competency as engineers to persons desirous of obtaining the same, examinations shall be held at such places as the Board of Trade direct.

(2) The Board of Trade may appoint times for the examinations, and may appoint, remove, and re-appoint examiners to conduct the same, and determine the remuneration of those examiners, and may regulate the conduct of the examinations and the qualification of the applicants and may do all such acts and things as they think expedient for the purpose of the examinations.

COMMENTS.

Rules for the Examination of Engineers.

These are not such rules as S.R. & O. (S.I.) but are regulations published by H.M. Stationery Office, under the title 'Regulations relating to Examination of Engineers'.

See M.S. (Certificates) Act 1914.

Fees on examination.

97 An applicant for examination, whether as master, mate, or engineer, shall pay such fees, not exceeding those specified in the Fourth Schedule to this Act, as the Board of Trade direct, and the fees shall be paid to such persons as the Board appoint and carried to the Mercantile Marine Fund.

COMMENTS.

The words underlined in this section have been repealed by the Merchant Shipping (Safety Convention) Act 1949, section 37, sub-section 5 on Third Schedule.

Fees.

These are now paid to the Exchequer in accordance with Merchant Shipping (Mercantile Marine Fund) Act, section 1.

The fees now in force are contained in the Merchant Shipping (Fees) Regulations 1971, S.I. 1971, No. 643.

⚓ ⚓ ⚓ ⚓

98 (1) The Board of Trade shall, subject as herein-after mentioned, deliver to every applicant who is duly reported by the examiners to have passed the examination satisfactorily, and to have given satisfactory evidence of his sobriety, experience, ability, and general good conduct on board ship, such a certificate of competency as the case requires.

Grant of certificates on passing examination.

(2) The Board of Trade may in any case in which a report appears to them to have been unduly made, remit the case either to the examiners who made the report or to any other examiners, and may require a re-examination of the applicant, or a further inquiry into his testimonials and character, before granting him a certificate.

COMMENTS.

The Rules relating to examinations are contained in Merchant Shipping (Certificates) Act 1914.

The Regulations relating to the conduct of the examinations are published by H.M. Stationery Office, under the following titles:

(i) 'Regulations relating to the Examination of Masters and Mates.'

(ii) 'Regulations relating to the Examination of Engineers.'

⚓ ⚓ ⚓ ⚓

99 (1) A person who has attained the rank of lieutenant, sub-lieutenant, navigating lieutenant, or navigating sub-lieutenant in Her Majesty's Navy, or of lieutenant in Her Majesty's Indian Marine Service, shall be entitled to a certificate of service as master of a foreign-going ship without examination.

(2) A person who has attained the rank of engineer or assistant engineer in Her Majesty's Navy or Indian Marine Service shall be entitled without examination, if an engineer, to a certificate of service as first-class engineer, and if an assistant engineer to a certificate of service as second-class engineer.

(3) A certificate of service shall differ in form from a certificate of competency, and shall contain the name and rank of the person to whom it is delivered, and the Board of Trade shall deliver a certificate of service to any person who proves himself to be entitled thereto.

(4) The provisions of this Act (including the penal provisions) shall apply in the case of a certificate of service as they apply in the case of a certificate of competency, except that the provisions allowing a holder of a certificate of competency as master of a foreign-going ship to go to sea as master or mate of a home trade passenger ship shall not apply.

COMMENTS.

The words underlined, 'Marine Service', above have been replaced by the word 'Navy' in accord with the Government of India (Adaption of Acts of Parliament) Order 1937, S.R. & O. 1937, No. 230.

Fees.

The fees now in force are contained in the Merchant Shipping (Fees) Regulations 1971, S.I. 1971, No. 643.

Certificates of service must not be confused with certificates of competency, which can only be granted after examination.

Form and record of certificate.

100 (1) All certificates of competency shall be made in duplicate, one part to be delivered to the person entitled to the certificate, and one to be preserved.

(2) Such last-mentioned part of the certificate shall be preserved, and a record of certificates of competency and the suspending, cancelling, or altering of the certificates and any other matter affecting them shall be kept in such manner as the Board of Trade direct, by the Registrar-General of Shipping and Seamen or by such other person as the Board of Trade direct.

(3) Any such certificate and any record under this section shall be admissible in evidence in manner provided by this Act.

Loss of certificate.

101 If a master, mate, or engineer proves to the satisfaction of the Board of Trade that he has, without fault on his part, lost or been deprived of a certificate already granted to him, the Board of Trade shall, and in any other case may, upon payment of such fee (if any) as they direct, cause a copy of the certificate to which, by the record kept in pursuance of this Act, he appears to be entitled, to be certified by the Registrar-General of Shipping and Seamen, or other person directed to keep the record, and to be delivered to him; and a copy purporting to be so certified shall have all the effect of the original.

COMMENTS.

In the event of the certificate being a colonial certificate, then the operative authority is the authority granting the certificate.

102 Where the legislature of any British possession provides for the examination of, and grant of certificates of competency to, persons intending to act as masters, mates, or engineers on board ships, and the Board of Trade report to Her Majesty that they are satisfied that the examinations are so conducted as to be equally efficient with the examinations for the same purpose in the United Kingdom under this Act, and that the certificates are granted on such principles as to show the like qualifications and competency as those granted under this Act, and are liable to be forfeited for the like reasons and in the like manner, Her Majesty may by Order in Council:— Colonial certificates of competency.

(i) declare that the said certificates shall be of the same force as if they had been granted under this Act; and

(ii) declare that all or any of the provisions of this Act, which relate to certificates of competency granted under this Act, shall apply to the certificates referred to in the Order; and

(iii) impose such conditions and make such regulations with respect to the certificates, and to the use, issue, delivery, cancellation, and suspension thereof, as Her Majesty may think fit, and impose fines not exceeding fifty pounds for the breach of those conditions and regulations.

COMMENTS.

See various orders in Council relating to such certificates.

103 (1) The master of a foreign-going ship:— Production of certificates of competency to superintendent.

(*a*) on signing the agreement with the crew before a superintendent shall produce to him the certificates of competency which the master, mates, and engineers of the ship are by this Act required to hold; and

(*b*) in the case of a running agreement shall also, before the second and every subsequent voyage, produce to the superintendent the certificate of competency of any mate or engineer then first engaged by him who is required by this Act to hold a certificate.

(2) The master or owner of every home trade passenger ship of more than eighty tons burden shall produce to some superintendent within twenty-one days after the thirtieth of June and the thirty-first of December in every year the certificates of competency which the master, mates, and engineers of the ship are by this Act required to hold.

(3) Upon the production of the certificates of competency, the superintendent shall, if the certificates are such as the master, mates, and engineers of the ship ought to hold, give to the master a certificate to the effect that the proper certificates of competency have been so produced.

(4) The master shall, before proceeding to sea, produce the superintendent's certificate to the chief officer of customs, and the ship may be detained until the certificate is produced.

COMMENTS.

Certificates of competency, *see* section 92.

Tons burden—In *The Brunel* (*1900*), it was held that tons burden meant net registered tonnage. The court, however, intimated that these words in other parts of the Act may be interpreted differently.

Forgery, &c., of certificate of competency.

104 If any person:—

(*a*) forges or fraudulently alters, or assists in forging or fraudulently altering, or procures to be forged or fraudulently altered, any certificate of competency, or an official copy of any such certificate; or

(*b*) makes, assists in making, or procures to be made any false representation for the purpose of procuring either for himself or for any other person a certificate of competency; or

(*c*) fraudulently uses a certificate or copy of a certificate of competency which has been forged, altered, cancelled or suspended, or to which he is not entitled; or

(*d*) fraudulently lends his certificate of competency or allows it to be used by any other person, that person shall in respect of each offence be guilty of a misdemeanour.

COMMENTS.

These provisions also apply to certificates of competency as AB certificates of competency granted in Commonwealth countries, approved by regulations made under Merchant Shipping Act 1948, section 5, sub-section 4.

Punishment of Misdemeanours. *See* section 680.

⚓ ⚓ ⚓ ⚓

Merchant Shipping Act 1894

Part II

Sections 105–109

Repealed by Merchant Shipping Act 1970 (Commencement No. 1) Order 1972, Operative from 1st January, 1973

⚓ ⚓ ⚓ ⚓

Licences to Supply Seamen

110 The Board of Trade may grant to such persons as the Board think fit licences to engage or supply seamen or apprentices for merchant ships in the United Kingdom, and any such licence shall continue for such period, and may be granted and revoked on such terms and conditions as the Board think proper.

Licence for supply of seamen.

COMMENTS.

See section 742 for definition of seaman.

⚓ ⚓ ⚓ ⚓

111 (1) A person shall not engage or supply a seaman or apprentice to be entered on board any ship in the United Kingdom, unless that person either holds a licence from the Board of Trade for the purpose, or is the owner or master or mate of the ship, or is bona fide the servant and in the constant employment of the owner, or is a superintendent.

Penalty for engaging seamen without licence.

(2) A person shall not employ for the purpose of engaging or supplying a seaman or apprentice to be entered on board any ship in the United Kingdom any person, unless that person either holds a licence from the Board of Trade for

the purpose, or is the owner or master or mate of the ship, or is bona fide the servant and in the constant employment of the owner, or is a superintendent.

(3) A person shall not receive or accept to be entered on board any ship any seaman or apprentice, if that person knows that the seaman or apprentice has been engaged or supplied in contravention of this section.

(4) If a person acts in contravention of this section, he shall for each seaman or apprentice in respect of whom an offence is committed, be liable to a fine not exceeding twenty pounds, and, if a licensed person, shall forfeit his licence.

COMMENTS.

In R. *v* Stewart 1899, it was held that the words 'any ship' include a foreign ship. Also, the fine that may be imposed is a punishment for an offence and not a court debt.

⚓ ⚓ ⚓ ⚓

Penalty for receiving remuneration from seamen for engagement.

112 (1) A person shall not demand or receive directly or indirectly from a seaman or apprentice to the sea service, or from a person seeking employment as a seaman or apprentice to the sea service, or from a person on his behalf, any remuneration whatever for providing him with employment other than any fees authorised by this Act.

(2) If a person acts in contravention of this section, he shall for each offence be liable to a fine not exceeding five pounds.

⚓ ⚓ ⚓ ⚓

Merchant Shipping Act 1894

Part II

Sections 113–125

Repealed by Merchant Shipping Act 1970 (Commencement No. 1) Order 1972, Operative from 1st January, 1973

⚓ ⚓ ⚓ ⚓

Rating of Seamen

Rating of seamen.

126 (1) A seaman shall not be entitled to the rating of AB, that is to say, of an able-bodied seaman, unless he has served at sea for four years before the mast, but the employment of fishermen in decked fishing-vessels registered under the first part of this Act shall only count as sea service up to the period of three years of that employment; and the rating of AB shall only be granted after at least one year's sea service in a trading vessel in addition to three or more years' sea service on board of decked fishing-vessels so registered.

(2) The service may be proved by certificates of discharge, by a certificate of service from the Registrar-General of Shipping and Seamen (granted by the Registrar on payment of a fee not exceeding sixpence), specifying in each case whether the service was rendered in whole or in part in steamship or in sailing-ship, or by other satisfactory proof.

COMMENTS.

The words underlined in this section were substituted by: 'Three years before the mast . . .' *See* the Merchant Shipping Act 1906, section 58, sub-section 1.

Although the actual provisions relating to the certification of AB are contained in Merchant Shipping (Certificates of Competency as AB) Regulations 1959, No. 2148, as amended by Merchant Shipping (Certificates of Competency as AB) (Amendment) Regulations 1962, No. 579. *See* Merchant Shipping Act 1948, section 5, sub-section 6.

The officer, before whom the seaman is engaged, must refuse to enter him as an AB unless the proof required under the regulations is shewn.

Seaman.

Definition of. *See* section 742.

Merchant Shipping Act 1894

Part II

Sections 127–156

Repealed by Merchant Shipping Act 1970 (Commencement No. 1) Order 1972, Operative from 1st January, 1973

157 (1) The right to wages shall not depend on the earning of freight; and every seaman and apprentice who would be entitled to demand and recover any wages, if the

Wages not to depend on freight.

ship in which he has served had earned freight, shall, subject to all other rules of law and conditions applicable to the case, be entitled to demand and recover the same, notwithstanding that freight has not been earned; but in all cases of wreck or loss of the ship, proof that the seaman has not exerted himself to the utmost to save the ship, cargo, and stores, shall bar his claim to wages.

(2) Where a seaman or apprentice who would, but for death, be entitled by virtue of this section to demand and recover any wages, dies before the wages are paid, they shall be paid and applied in manner provided by this Act with respect to the wages of a seaman who dies during a voyage.

COMMENTS.

Sub-section 1 of this section is of interest, because the old rule of maritime law—freight is the mother of wages—ceased to be the law of this country. Merchant Shipping Act 1864, section 183, now repealed.

⚓ ⚓ ⚓ ⚓

Wages on termination of service by wreck or illness.

158 Where the service of a seaman terminates before the date contemplated in the agreement, by reason of the wreck or loss of the ship, or of his being left on shore at any place abroad under a certificate granted as provided by this Act of his unfitness or inability to proceed on the voyage, he shall be entitled to wages up to the time of such termination, but not for any longer period.

COMMENTS.

The Merchant Shipping (International Labour Conventions) Act 1925, materially modifies the effect of this section by providing that a seaman shall be entitled to wages for each day up to two months during which he remains unemployed by reason of the wreck or loss of his ship, unless the owner shows that the unemployment was not due to the wreck or loss of the ship, or that the seaman was able to obtain suitable employment elsewhere; and this is so even though the seaman's engagement would have terminated before the expiration of the two months had there been no wreck or loss of the ship.

Date of Termination.

The Terneuzen, 1938, invoking *The Olympic*, 1913. The vessel was wrecked on the 27th January. However, she was not declared a total loss on this date and salvage operations were commenced in order to try to save the vessel. These were not successful and three and a half months later the vessel was declared a total loss. The chief officer claimed for two months wages under Merchant Shipping Act 1925, section 1, from the date that the vessel was declared a total loss. The shipowners claimed that the chief officer had been employed over two months from the actual casualty. It was held, however, that the period of two months is calculated from the time of the cessation of the employment and not from the date of the initial occurrence.

See also Barras *v.* Aberdeen Fishing Company 1933, where the plaintiff claimed for wages whilst the vessel was in dry-dock as a result of collision. Also, Ellerman Lines Ltd. *v.* Murray 1931, and White Star Line *v.* Cometford 1931, where it was held that the shipowners were liable for wages for the period of two months after the date of the loss, irrespective of the expected date of the termination of the agreement. This decision is qualified insofar that if the shipowner can show that the seaman was able to take up suitable employment on any day, the shipowner has no need to pay wages in respect of that day.

See Merchant Shipping Act 1925, section 1.

Merchant Shipping Act 1894

Part II

Sections 159–199

Repealed by Merchant Shipping Act 1970 (Commencement No. 1) Order 1972, Operative from 1st January, 1973

200 (1) The Board of Trade shall issue scales of medicines and medical stores suitable for different classes of ships and voyages, and shall also prepare or sanction books containing instructions for dispensing the same. Regulations respecting medicines, anti-scorbutics, &c.

(2) The owner of every ship navigating between the United Kingdom and any place out of the same shall provide and cause to be kept on board a supply of medicine and medical stores according to the scale appropriate to the ship, and also the said books or one of them.

(3) The master or owner of every such ship, except in the case of:—

(*a*) ships bound to European ports or ports in the Mediterranean Sea; and

(*b*) such ships or classes of ships bound to ports on the eastern coast of America, north of the thirty-fifth degree of north latitude, and to any islands or places in the Atlantic Ocean north of the same limit as the Board of Trade may exempt;

shall provide and cause to be kept on board a sufficient quantity of anti-scorbutics in accordance with the regulations in the Fifth Schedule to this Act, and those regulations shall have effect as part of this section, and the master shall serve out the anti-scorbutics to the crew according to the said regulations, and if a seaman or apprentice refuses or neglects to take the anti-scorbutics when served out, that fact shall be entered in the official log-book, and the entry shall be signed by the master and by the mate or some other of the crew, and also by the medical practitioner on board, if any.

(4) If any requirement of this section with respect to the provision of medicines, medical stores, book of instruction, or anti-scorbutics is not complied with in the case of any ship, the owner or master of that ship shall, for each offence, be liable to a fine not exceeding twenty pounds, unless he can prove that the non-compliance was not caused through his inattention, neglect, or wilful default.

(5) If any requirement of this section with respect to the serving out of anti-scorbutics or making an entry in the official log-book is not complied with in the case of any ship to which the requirement applies, the master of the ship shall, for each offence, be liable to a fine not exceeding five pounds, unless he can prove that the non-compliance did not arise through any neglect, omission, or wilful default on his part.

(6) If it is proved that some person, other than the master or owner, is in default in any case under this section, that person shall, for each offence, be liable to a fine not exceeding twenty pounds.

(7) If any person manufactures, sells, or keeps, or offers for sale any medicines or medical stores for use on board ship which are of bad quality, he shall, for each offence, be liable to a fine not exceeding twenty pounds.

COMMENTS:

See sub-section 1.

These scales are contained in the Merchant Shipping Medical Scales Order 1953, No. 998, as amended S.I. 1953, No. 1446; S.I. 1955, No. 1157, S.I. 1961, No. 1045.

In respect of fishing-boats, the scales are found in the Merchant Shipping Medical Scales (Fishing-Boats) Order 1954, No. 1595, as amended S.I. 1961, No. 1046.

The Board of Trade, by order dated 30th October 1899, sanctioned the publication *Ship Captain's Medical Guide*, obtained from H.M. Stationery Office, or any bookseller.

Master's and Owner's Duty.

For the Master's and Owner's responsibilities in respect of the provision of a medical chest and providing treatment, *see* McRobbie *v.* George Robb & Sons Ltd. 1953.

Exemptions contained in section 3.

The general exemption under this act does not extend to vessels which may also be bound by the terms of their agreements to any place outside of these limits. Also, the exemption does not extend to the coast or islands of Greenland. This also applies to vessels passing through the Suez Canal.

Substitution.

Statutory Rule and Order 1927, No. 360, regulates the use of concentrated orange-juice in lieu of lime-juice in certain cases.

⚓ ⚓ ⚓ ⚓

Merchant Shipping Act 1894

Part II

Sections 201–206

Repealed by Merchant Shipping Act 1970 (Commencement No. 1)

Order 1972, Operative from 1st January 1973

⚓ ⚓ ⚓ ⚓

207

COMMENTS.

The section, which provided for the expenses of medical attendance in case of illness, was repealed by the Merchant Shipping Act 1906, which was then dealt with by section 34 of the 1906 Act. This has now been repealed by the Merchant Shipping Act 1970 (Commencement No. 1, Order 1972) operative from 1st January, 1973.

⚓ ⚓ ⚓ ⚓

208

COMMENTS.

This section, which provided for the recovery of expenses from the owner, was repealed by the Merchant Shipping Act 1906, which was then dealt with by section 35 of the 1906 Act. This has now been repealed by the Merchant Shipping Act 1970 (Commencement Order No. 1, 1972), operative from 1st January, 1973.

⚓ ⚓ ⚓ ⚓

Certain ships to carry medical practitioners.

209 (1) Every foreign-going ship, having one hundred persons or upwards on board, shall carry on board as part of her complement some duly qualified medical practitioner, and if she does not the owner shall for every voyage of the ship made without a duly qualified medical practitioner be liable to a fine not exceeding one hundred pounds.

(2) Nothing in this section shall apply to an emigrant ship within the meaning of the Third Part of this Act.

COMMENTS.

It would appear that a medical practitioner, carried under this section as part of a ship's complement, is a seaman, and accordingly, must sign the agreement.

⚓ ⚓ ⚓ ⚓

Accommodation for seamen.

210 (1) Every place in any British ship occupied by seamen or apprentices, and appropriated to their use, shall have for each of those seamen or apprentices a space of not less than seventy-two cubic feet, and of not less than twelve superficial feet measured on the deck or floor of that place, and shall be subject to the regulations in the Sixth Schedule to this Act, and those regulations shall have effect as part of this section, and if any of the foregoing requirements of this section is not complied with in the case of any ship, the owner of the ship shall for each offence be liable to a fine not exceeding twenty pounds.

(2) Every place so occupied and appropriated shall be kept free from goods and stores of any kind not being the personal property of the crew in use during the voyage, and if any such place is not so kept free, the master shall forfeit and pay to each seaman or apprentice lodged in that place the sum of one shilling for each day during which, after complaint has been made to him by any two or more of the seamen so lodged, it is not so kept free.

(3) Such fees as the Board of Trade fix shall be paid in respect of an inspection for the purposes of this section, not exceeding the fees specified in the Sixth Schedule to this Act.

COMMENTS.

By the Merchant Shipping Act 1948, section 1, regulations relating to crew accommodation in certain types of vessels came into operation on 1st January, 1954, S.I. 1953, No. 1036 refers.

The regulations referred to, the Merchant Shipping (Crew Accommodation) Regulations 1953, No. 1036, have been now amended by S.I. 1954, No. 1660; S.I. 1961, No. 393.

The words underlined in section 1 above, have been now amended by the Merchant Shipping Act 1906, section 64.

Surveys as a result of complaint of deficiency of accommodation, *see* section 463, nb the words 'or apprentice', wherever they occur in section 463, have been repealed by the Merchant Shipping Act 1970 (Commencement No. 1) Order 1972, as from 1st January, 1973.

The words 'Not exceeding the fees specified in the Sixth Schedule to this Act' were repealed by the Merchant Shipping (Safety Convention) Act 1949, section 37, sub-section 5 and Schedule III.

Merchant Shipping Act 1894

Part II

Sections 211 to 255

Repealed by Merchant Shipping Act 1970 (Commencement No. 1) Order 1972, Operative from 1st January, 1973

256 (1) All superintendents and all officers of customs shall take charge of all documents which are delivered or transmitted to or retained by them in pursuance of this Act, and shall keep them for such time (if any) as may be necessary for the purpose of settling any business arising at the place where the documents come into their hands, or for any other proper purpose, and shall, if required, produce them for any of those purposes, and shall then transmit them to the Registrar-General of Shipping and Seamen, and he shall record and perserve them, and they shall be admissible in evidence in manner provided by this Act, and they shall, on payment of a moderate fee fixed by the Board of Trade, or without payment if the Board so direct, be open to the inspection of any person.

Transmission of documents to registrar by superintendents and other officers.

(2) The documents aforesaid shall be public records and documents within the meaning of the Public Record Offices

Acts, 1838 and 1877, and those Acts shall, where applicable, apply to those documents in all respects, as if specifically referred to therein.

COMMENTS.

Sub-section 2 of this section has been repealed by the Public Records Act 1958, section 13, sub-section 2.

Merchant Shipping Act 1894

Part II

Sections 257–266

Repealed by Merchant Shipping Act 1970 (Commencement No. 1) Order 1972, Operative from 1st January, 1973

M.S.A. 1894

PART III

PASSENGER AND EMIGRANT SHIPS

PART III

PASSENGER AND EMIGRANT SHIPS

1. DEFINITIONS

Definition of Passenger Steamer and Passenger

267 For the purposes of this Part of this Act— Definition of 'passenger' and 'passenger steamer'.

The expression 'passenger' shall include any person carried in a ship other than the master and crew, and the owner, his family and servants; and

The expression 'passenger steamer' shall mean every British steamship carrying passengers to, from, or between any places in the United Kingdom, except steam ferry-boats working in chains (commonly called steam bridges) and every foreign steamship carrying passengers between places in the United Kingdom.

COMMENTS.

An addition to this section by the Merchant Shipping (Safety and Load Line Conventions) Act 1932, was repealed by the Merchant Shipping (Safety Convention) Act 1949, section 37 and the Third Schedule.

The words from 'the expression' to 'and' contained in the first paragraph have also been repealed by the 1949 Act referred to above.

The definition of passenger for the purposes of Part III of this Act is now as stated in section 26 of the 1949 Act, where the expression passenger is defined as any person carried in a ship, except:

(*a*) A person employed or engaged in any capacity on board the ship on the business of the ship;

(*b*) A person on board the ship either in pursuance of the obligation laid upon the Master to carry shipwrecked, distressed or other persons, or by reason of any circumstance that neither the Master nor the Owner, nor the Charterer (if any) could have prevented or forestalled; and

(*c*) A child under one year of age.

Obligation to carry distressed seamen on ships. *See* section 48 of the Merchant Shipping Act 1906.

Passenger Steamer.

The definition in this section is amended and widened by section 13 of the Merchant Shipping Act 1906. The words underlined . . . and . . . United Kingdom, have been repealed by section 85, Schedule II of the 1906 Act. This is the definition of 'Passenger Steamer' as it applies to this part of the Act. For the purposes of the Merchant Shipping (Safety and Load Line Conventions) Act 1949, the term 'Passenger Steamer' is defined by section 26, sub-section 2 of the 1949 Act, as a steamer carrying more than 12 passengers. Whereas in accord with this section, viz. 267 of Merchant Shipping Act 1894, a number less than 12 is sufficient to bring the steamer within the definition.

'Home-trade passenger ship' for the purpose of the Act generally is defined in section 742 of the 1894 Act.

Under the provisions of the Pilotage Act 1913, section II, it is evident that only one passenger is sufficient to attract compulsory pilotage, but this does not itself make the ship a passenger steamer. The question of whether the ship is a passenger steamer or not is in each case a question of fact; the mere presence of 'another person' being on board is not in itself sufficient to constitute the ship a passenger steamer. The term does not include every ship which on occasion carries passengers. Young *v.* Doherty 1929. It must be a steamer habitually, or substantially, used for carrying passengers. Graham *v.* Duncan 1950. The term 'passenger steamer' includes a tender for landing or embarking passengers. *See* section 15 of the Merchant Shipping Act 1906.

Steamship.

For the application of the Act to ships propelled by other means, *see* section 743 of this Act.

⚓ ⚓ ⚓ ⚓

Sections 268, 269, 270

Repealed by the Merchant Shipping Act 1970

(Commencement No. 1) Order 1972

As from 1st January, 1973

⚓ ⚓ ⚓ ⚓

2. Passenger Steamers

Survey of Passenger Steamers

Annual survey of passenger steamers.

271 (1) Every passenger steamer which carries more than twelve passengers shall—

(*a*) be surveyed once at least in each year in the manner provided in this Part of this Act; and (*b*) shall not ply or proceed to sea or on any voyage or excursion with any passengers on board, unless the owner or master has the certificate from the Board of Trade as to survey under this Part of this Act, the same being in force, and applicable to the voyage or excursion on which the steamer is about to proceed.

(2) A passenger steamer attempting to ply or go to sea may be detained until such certificate as aforesaid is produced to the proper officer of customs.

Sub-section 3

Repealed by Merchant Shipping Act 1970
The Merchant Shipping Act 1970
(Commencement No. 1) Order 1972
As from 1st January 1973

COMMENTS.

Passenger Steamer.

See section 267 of this Act for definition.

Certificates—Safety.

The Merchant Shipping (Safety Convention) Act 1949 gives details relating to 'Safety Certificates' in section 7 et. seq. As to the relationship of 'Safety Certificates' to 'Passenger Steamer Certificates', *see* section 13 of the same Act.

Proceeding to Sea Without the Required Certificate.

Held in Dudgeon *v.* Pembroke 1874, that in the case where the Master proceeds to sea without the requisite certificate, and carries passengers to sea without the knowledge of his Owner, he has exceeded his authority, and an insurance policy held by the innocent Owner is not vitiated.

In Cunard *v.* Hyde (No. 2) (1859), the reverse is true if the Owner is not innocent, but party to the illegal act.

⚓ ⚓ ⚓ ⚓

272 (1) The owner of every passenger steamer shall cause the same to be surveyed by a shipwright surveyor of ships and an engineer surveyor of ships, the shipwright surveyor being, in the case of an iron steamer, a person properly qualified in the opinion of the Board of Trade to survey an iron steamer.

A.D. 1894

Mode of survey and declaration of survey.

(2) The surveyors, if satisfied on the survey that they can with propriety do so, shall deliver to the owner declarations of survey in a form approved by the Board of Trade.

Repeal.

Sub-sections 3 to 5 of this section cease to have effect by sub-section 1 of section 13 of the Merchant Shipping (Safety Convention) Act 1949, and have been repealed by such section 5 of section 37 and the Third Schedule of the 1949 Act.

Amendment.

After 'an engineer surveyor of ships' the following words were added by sub-section 1 of section 9 of the Merchant Shipping (Safety and Load Line Conventions) Act 1932, as amended by sub-section 5 of section 35 of the Merchant Shipping (Safety Convention) Act 1949, viz. 'and, in the case of a sea-going passenger steamer required to be provided with a radio installation by a wireless telegraphy surveyor'.

COMMENTS.

In accord with section 8 of the 1932 Act, a person appointed a surveyor of ships under section 724 of the 1894 Act, may be appointed a wireless telegraphy surveyor. By the Merchant Shipping (Safety Convention) Act 1949, section 4, this person, i.e. a wireless telegraphy surveyor, is known as a 'radio surveyor'.

Passenger Steamer.

This term in this section means a steamer carrying more than 12 passengers.

Transmission of declaration.

273 (1) The owner of a steamer surveyed shall within fourteen days after the receipt by him of a declaration of survey transmit it to the Board of Trade.

(2) If an owner fails without reasonable cause so to transmit a declaration of survey, he shall forfeit a sum not exceeding ten shillings for every day during which the transmission is delayed, and any sum so forfeited shall be payable on the granting of a certificate in addition to the fee, and shall be applied in the same manner as the fee.

COMMENTS.

See sub-section 2 of section 13 of the Merchant Shipping (Safety Convention) Act 1949, for the application of the provisions of this section.

274 On the receipt of the declarations of survey, the Board of Trade shall, if satisfied that this Part of this Act has been complied with, issue in duplicate a passenger steamer's certificate, that is to say, a certificate stating such compliance and stating, according to the declarations— Issue of passenger steamer's certificate.

(*a*) the limits (if any) beyond which the steamer is not fit to ply; and

(*b*) the number of passengers which the steamer is fit to carry, distinguishing, if necessary, the number to be carried in each part of the steamer, and any conditions and variations to which the number is subject.

COMMENTS.

Consult section 7 of the Merchant Shipping (Safety Convention) Act 1949 for the issue of certificates referred to.

See section 720 of the 1894 Act as to the form of certificate.

Cancellation of the Survey Certificate.

Consult section 279 of the 1894 Act.

⚓ ⚓ ⚓ ⚓

275 (1) If the owner of a steamer feels aggrieved by the declaration of survey of a shipwright or engineer surveyor, or by the refusal of such a surveyor to give such a declaration, he may appeal to the court of survey for the port or district where the steamer for the time being is, in manner directed by the rules of that court. Appeal to court of survey.

(2) On any such appeal the judge of the court of survey shall report to the Board of Trade on the question raised by the appeal and the Board, when satisfied that the requirements of the report and of the foregoing provisions of this Part of this Act have been complied with, may grant a passenger steamer's certificate.

(3) Subject to any order made by the judge of the court of survey the costs of and incidental to the appeal shall follow the event.

(4) A shipwright or engineer surveyor in making a survey of a steamer for the purpose of a declaration of survey shall, if the owner of the steamer so requires, be accompanied on the survey by some person appointed by the owner, and in that case, if the surveyor and the person so appointed agree, there shall be no appeal under this section to the court of survey.

Amendment.

After 'engineer surveyor' in sub-section 1 above and 'engineer surveyor' in sub-section 4 above, the words 'or wireless telegraphy surveyor' were introduced. Merchant Shipping (Safety and Load Line Conventions) Act 1932. These are now known as'radio surveyors'—Merchant Shipping (Safety Convention) Act 1949, section 4.

COMMENTS.

For the issue of safety certificates consult section 13, sub-section 2 of of the Merchant Shipping (Safety Convention) Act 1949.

Transmission of certificate.

276 (1) The Board of Trade shall transmit the passenger steamer's certificate in duplicate to a superintendent or some other public officer at the port mentioned by the owner of the steamer for the purpose, or at the port where the owner or his agent resides, or where the steamer has been surveyed or is for the time lying.

(2) The Board of Trade shall cause notice of the transmission to be given to the master or owner or his agent, and the officer to whom the certificate has been transmitted shall, on the owner, master, or agent applying and paying the proper fee and other sums (if any) mentioned in this Act as payable in that behalf, deliver to him both copies of the certificate.

(3) In proving the issue of a passenger steamer's certificate it shall be sufficient to show that the certificate was duly received by the said officer, and that due notice of the transmission was given to the owner, master, or agent.

COMMENTS.

For the application of this section *see* section 13, sub-section 8 of the Merchant Shipping (Safety Convention) Act 1949.

Fees for certificate.

277 The grantee of a passenger steamer's certificate shall pay such fees, not exceeding those specified in Part One of the Ninth Schedule to this Act, as the Board of Trade fix.

Repeal.

The words underlined were repealed by section 37, sub-section 5 and the Third Schedule of the Merchant Shipping (Safety Convention) Act 1949.

COMMENTS.

By section 33 of the Merchant Shipping (Safety Convention) Act 1949, power is given to make regulations prescribing the fees payable under this section of the 1894 Act.

The fees at present in force are contained in Statutory Instrument No. 643 1971, The Merchant Shipping (Fees) Regulations 1971.

⚓ ⚓ ⚓ ⚓

278 (1) A passenger steamer's certificate shall not be in force for more than one year from the date of its issue, or any shorter time specified in the certificate, nor after notice is given by the Board of Trade to the owner, agent, or master of the steamer, that the Board have cancelled it. Duration of certificates.

(2) If a passenger steamer is absent from the United Kingdom at the time when her certificate expires, a fine shall not be incurred for want of a certificate until she first begins to ply with passengers after her next return to the United Kingdom.

COMMENTS.

For powers of cancellation *see* next section, viz. section 279.

⚓ ⚓ ⚓ ⚓

279 (1) The Board of Trade may cancel a passenger steamer's certificate where they have reason to believe— Cancellation of certificate.

(*a*) that any declaration of survey on which the certificate was founded has been in any particular made fraudulently or erroneously; or,

(*b*) that the certificate has been issued upon false or erroneous information; or,

(*c*) that since the making of the declaration, the hull, equipments, or machinery have sustained any injury, or are otherwise insufficient.

(2) In every such case the Board of Trade may require the owner to have the hull equipment or machinery of the steamer again surveyed, and to transmit further declarations of survey before they re-issue the certificate or grant a fresh one in lieu thereof.

COMMENTS.

For application *see* section 13, sub-section 8 of the Merchant Shipping (Safety Convention) Act 1949.

Consult also section II, sub-section 4, where alterations and/or damage are involved.

Delivery up of certificate.

280 (1) The Board of Trade may require a passenger steamer's certificate, which has expired or been cancelled, to be delivered up as they direct.

(2) If any owner or master fails without reasonable cause to comply with such requirements, he shall for each offence be liable to a fine not exceeding ten pounds.

COMMENTS.

For application *see* section 13, sub-section 8 of the Merchant Shipping (Safety Convention) Act 1949.

Posting up of certificate.

281 (1) The owner or master of every passenger steamer required to have a passenger steamer's certificate shall forthwith on the receipt of the certificate by him or his agent cause one of the duplicates to be put up in some conspicuous place on board the steamer, so as to be legible to all persons on board, and to be kept so put up and legible while the certificate remains in force, and the steamer is in use.

(2) If the owner or master fails without reasonable cause to comply with this section, he shall for each offence be liable to a fine not exceeding ten pounds.

(3) If a passenger steamer plies or goes to sea with passengers on board, and this section is not complied with, then for each offence the owner thereof shall be liable to a fine not exceeding one hundred pounds, and the master shall also be liable to a further fine not exceeding twenty pounds.

Amendment.

By Merchant Shipping (Load Line) Act 1967, the fine in sub-section 2 above of not exceeding £10 is replaced by a new penalty, 'on summary conviction, a fine not exceeding £20.'

By the Merchant Shipping (Load Line) Act 1967, the old penalty in sub-section 3 above is replaced by a new penalty, 'on summary conviction, in the case of the owner, a fine not exceeding £200, and in the case of the master, a fine not exceeding £50.

COMMENTS.

Consult Merchant Shipping (Safety Convention) Act 1949, sub-section 8 of section 13 regarding the certificates issued under the 1949 Act.

Passenger.

For meaning, consult section 271; also section 26 of the Merchant Shipping (Safety Convention) Act, 1949.

Passenger Steamer.

For meaning consult section 271; also section 26 of the Merchant Shipping (Safety Convention) Act 1949.

Consequence of Not Having a Certificate.

Consult section 271; it would not appear that section 21 of the 1906 Act is applicable.

⚓ ⚓ ⚓ ⚓

282 If any person—

Penalty for forgery of certificate or declaration.

(*a*) knowingly and wilfully makes, or assists in making, or procures to be made, a false or fraudulent declaration of survey or passenger steamer's certificate; or

(*b*) forges, assists in forging, procures to be forged, fraudulently alters, assists in fraudulently altering, or procures to be fraudulently altered, any such declaration or certificate, or anything contained in, or any signature to any such declaration or certificate;

that person shall in respect of each offence be guilty of a misdemeanour.

COMMENTS.

Consult the Merchant Shipping (Safety Convention) Act 1949, section 13, sub-section 8 for the application of this section to any certificate issued under the 1949 Act.

Misdemeanours.

For punishment consult section 680 of the Principal Act.

⚓ ⚓ ⚓ ⚓

283 The owner or master of any passenger steamer shall not receive on board thereof, or on or in any port thereof, any number of passengers which, having regard to the time, occasion, and circumstances of the case, is greater than the number allowed by the passenger steamer's certificate, and if he does so, he shall for each offence be liable to a fine not exceeding twenty pounds, and also to an additional fine not exceeding five shillings for every passenger above the number so allowed, or if the fare of any passenger on board exceeds five shillings, not exceeding double the amount of

Penalty for carrying passengers in excess.

the fares of all the passengers above the number so allowed, reckoned at the highest rate of fare payable by any passenger on board.

Amendment.

By the Merchant Shipping (Load Lines) Act of 1967, the fine contained in the above section from the words a fine not exceeding £20 to the end of the section is replaced by a new penalty, as follows:

'Irrespective of the number of passengers, on summary conviction, a fine not exceeding £400; and, on conviction on indictment, a fine.

COMMENTS.

Consult section 22 of the Merchant Shipping Act 1906 where it is an offence not only to have on board more passengers, but also to receive on board more passengers than permitted by the passenger certificate.

Consult section 27 of the Merchant Shipping (Safety Convention) Act 1949; where more persons are carried on board, as a result of a threat to their lives, no offence under such circumstances is committed.

⚓ ⚓ ⚓ ⚓

Colonial certificates for passenger steamers.

284 Where the legislature of any British possession provides for the survey of, and grant of certificates for, passenger steamers, and the Board of Trade report to Her Majesty the Queen that they are satisfied that the certificates are to the like effect, and are granted after a like survey, and in such manner as to be equally efficient with the certificates granted for the same purpose in the United Kingdom under this Act, Her Majesty in Council may—

(1) declare that the certificates granted in the said British possession shall be of the same force as if granted under this Act; and

(2) declare that all or any of the provisions of this Part of this Act which relate to passenger steamer's certificates shall, either without modification or with such modifications as to Her Majesty may seem necessary, apply to the certificates granted in the said British possession; and

(3) impose such conditions and make such regulations with respect to the certificates, and to the use, delivery, and cancellation thereof, as to Her Majesty may seem fit, and impose fines not exceeding fifty pounds for the breach of those conditions and regulations.

COMMENTS.

It would appear that this section is repealed by section 21, sub-section 3 of the Merchant Shipping (Safety and Load Line Conventions) Act 1932. The repeal remains effective by section 38, sub-section 2 of the Interpretation Act 1889, even though that the relevant section of the 1932 Act was itself repealed by the Merchant Shipping (Safety Convention) Act 1949, section 37. *See* also Schedule III of this Act.

There are various Orders in Council which remain in force by section 745 of the Principal Act:

Australia: 1924 (S.R. & O., No. 523);

Hong Kong: 1928 (S.R. & O., No. 250);

India: 1931 (S.R. & O., No. 848);

Mauritius: 1905 (S.R. & O., No. 137);

New Zealand: 1886 (S.R. & O., S.I. Rev., XIV P.209).

⚓ ⚓ ⚓ ⚓

General Equipment of Passenger Steamers

285 (1) A sea-going passenger steamer shall have her compasses properly adjusted from time to time, to the satisfaction of the shipwright surveyor and according to such regulations as may be issued by the Board of Trade. **Equipment of passenger steamers with compasses, hose, deck shelters, and safety appliances.**

(2) A sea-going passenger steamer shall be provided with a hose capable of being connected with the engines of the steamer, and adapted for extinguishing fire in any part of the steamer.

(3) A home trade passenger steamer shall be provided with such shelter for the protection of deck passengers (if any) as the Board of Trade, having regard to the nature of the passage, the number of deck passengers to be carried, the season of the year, the safety of the ship, and the circumstances of the case, require.

(4) A passenger steamer shall be provided with a safety-valve on each boiler, so constructed as to be out of the control of the engineer when the steam is up, and, if the safety-valve is in addition to the ordinary valve, so constructed as to have an area not less, and a pressure not greater, than the area of and pressure on the ordinary valve.

(5) If a passenger steamer plies or goes to sea from a port in the United Kingdom without being equipped as required by this section, then, for each matter in which default is made,

the owner (if in fault) shall be liable to a fine not exceeding one hundred pounds, and the master (if in fault) shall be liable to a fine not exceeding fifty pounds.

COMMENTS.

As to what vessels included in the term 'Ship', *see* section 742.

Meaning of sea-going, *see* The Salt Union *v*. Wood (1893), where it was held that a 'sea-going' ship is a ship that actually goes to sea, and not merely having the capacity to go to sea.

Section 2—A sea-going passenger steamer, etc., repealed by the Merchant Shipping (Safety and Load Line Conventions) Act 1932. The question of fire-extinguishing hoses is now dealt with by the rule making powers contained in section 427 and by the Merchant Shipping (Fire Appliances) Rules 1952.

See sections 286 and 433 regarding limit of weight upon safety-valves.

⚓ ⚓ ⚓ ⚓

Prohibition of increasing weight on safety valve.

286 A person shall not increase the weight on the safety-valve of a passenger steamer beyond the limits fixed by the surveyor, and, if he does so, he shall, in addition to any other liability he may incur by so doing, be liable for each offence to a fine not exceeding one hundred pounds.

COMMENTS.

See also section 433.

⚓ ⚓ ⚓ ⚓

Keeping Order in Passenger Steamers

Offences in connection with passenger steamers.

287 (1) If any of the following offences is committed in the case of a passenger steamer for which there is a passenger steamer's certificate in force (that is to say):

(*a*) If any person being drunk or disorderly has been on that account refused admission thereto by the owner or any person in his employment, and, after having the amount of his fare (if he has paid it) returned or tendered to him, nevertheless persists in attempting to enter the steamer;

(*b*) If any person being drunk or disorderly on board the steamer is requested by the owner or any person in his employ to leave the steamer at any place in the United Kingdom, at which he can conveniently do so, and, after having the amount of his fare (if he has paid it) returned or tendered to him, does not comply with the request;

(*c*) If any person on board the steamer, after warning by the master or other officer thereof, molests or continues to molest any passenger;

(*d*) If any person, after having been refused admission to the steamer by the owner or any person in his employ on account of the steamer being full, and having had the amount of his fare (if he has paid it) returned or tendered to him, nevertheless persists in attempting to enter the steamer;

(*e*) If any person having gone on board the steamer at any place, and being requested, on account of the steamer being full, by the owner or any person in his employ to leave the steamer, before it has quitted that place, and having had the amount of his fare (if he has paid it) returned or tendered to him, does not comply with that request;

(*f*) If any person travels or attempts to travel in the steamer without first paying his fare, and with intent to avoid payment thereof:

(*g*) If any person, having paid his fare for a certain distance, knowingly and wilfully proceeds in the steamer beyond that distance without first paying the additional fare for the additional distance, and with intent to avoid payment thereof:

(*h*) If any person on arriving in the steamer at a point to which he has paid his fare knowingly and wilfully refuses or neglects to quit the steamer; and

(*i*) If any person on board the steamer fails, when requested by the master or other officer thereof, either to pay his fare or exhibit such ticket or other receipt, if any, showing the payment of his fare, as is usually given to persons travelling by and paying their fare for the steamer:

the person so offending shall for each offence be liable to a fine not exceeding forty shillings, but that liability shall not prejudice the recovery of any fare payable by him.

(2) If any person on board any such steamer wilfully does or causes to be done anything in such a manner as to obstruct or injure any part of the machinery or tackle of the steamer, or to obstruct, impede, or molest the crew, or any of them, in the navigation or management of the steamer, or

otherwise in the execution of their duty on or about the steamer, he shall for each offence be liable to a fine not exceeding twenty pounds.

(3) The master or other officer of any such steamer, and all persons called by him to his assistance, may, without any warrant, detain any person who commits any offence against this section and whose name and address are unknown to the master or officer, and convey the offender with all convenient despatch before some justice of the peace to be dealt with according to law, and that justice shall with all convenient despatch try the case in a summary manner.

(4) If any person commits an offence against this section and on the application of the master of the steamer, or any other person in the employ of the owner thereof, refuses to give his name and address, or gives a false name or address, that person shall be liable to a fine not exceeding twenty pounds, and the fine shall be paid to the owner of the steamer.

COMMENTS.

See section 288 for powers in regard to drunken passengers on home-trade passenger vessels.

Issue of passenger steamer's certificate, *see* section 274.

The penalties for Drunkenness Act 1962, section 1, provides for an increase in the fines in respect of the offences under sub-section 1, paragraphs (*a*) and (*b*) to be increased to £5·00

The words underlined were repealed as from 1st April 1953 by the Justices of the Peace Act 1949, section 46 and Schedule VII.

⚓ ⚓ ⚓ ⚓

Power to exclude drunken passengers on home trade passenger steamers.

288 The master of any home trade passenger steamer may refuse to receive on board thereof any person who by reason of drunkenness or otherwise is in such a state, or misconducts himself in such a manner, as to cause annoyance or injury to passengers on board, and if any such person is on board, may put him on shore at any convenient place; and a person so refused admittance or put on shore shall not be entitled to the return of any fare he has paid.

COMMENTS.

See section 742 as to definition of 'home trade passenger steamer'.

⚓ ⚓ ⚓ ⚓

Sections 289 to 355

Repealed by Merchant Shipping Act 1970
(Commencement No. 1) Order 1972
As from 1st January, 1973

⚓ ⚓ ⚓ ⚓

Legal Proceedings

356 All fines and forfeitures under the provisions of this Part of this Act (other than the provisions relating to passenger steamers only) shall be sued for by the following officers; (that is to say), Recovery of fines.

(*a*) Any emigration officer;
(*b*) Any chief officer of customs; and also
(*c*) In the British Islands any person authorised by the Board of Trade and any officer of customs authorised by the Commissioners of Customs; and
(*d*) In a British possession any person authorised by the governor of that possession, or any officer of customs authorised by the Government department regulating the customs in that possession.

Paragraph (*a*) above
Repealed by Merchant Shipping Act 1970
The Merchant Shipping Act 1970
(Commencement No. 1) Order 1972
As from 1st January 1973

COMMENTS.

Definitions of the terms 'British Islands' and 'British Possessions' are contained in the Interpretation Act 1889, section 18, sub-sections 1 and 2. The term 'Commissioners of Customs', is now, by the Customs and Excise Act 1952, section 318, sub-section 1, Commissioners of Customs and Excise.

⚓ ⚓ ⚓ ⚓

Sections 357 and 358

Repealed by Merchant Shipping Act 1970
(Commencement No. 1) Order 1972
As from 1st January 1973

⚓ ⚓ ⚓ ⚓

Supplemental

Owner responsible for default in absence of agreement.

359 (1) In the absence of any agreement to the contrary, the owner of a ship shall be the person ultimately responsible as between himself and the other persons by this Part of this Act made liable in respect of any default in complying with any requirement thereof.

Sub-section 2 above
Repealed Merchant Shipping Act 1970
The Merchant Shipping Act 1970
(Commencement No. 1) Order 1972

COMMENTS.

The owner responsible depends upon the circumstances of the case.

See Meckhlereid *v.* West 1876, where it was held that the registered owner, who had let the ship under a Charter Party, giving the possession of the ship and all control over her and the crew, was not responsible for default.

See also Scheibier *v.* Furness 1893, and compare Steele *v.* Lester & Lilee 1877, where the registered managing owner was held liable for the negligence of the master.

Forms and fees.

360 (3) If any person employed under this Part of this Act demands or receives, directly or indirectly, otherwise than by the direction of the Board of Trade, any fee, remuneration, or gratuity whatever in respect of any duty performed by him under this Part of this Act, he shall for each offence be liable to a fine not exceeding fifty pounds.

Sections 1 and 2
Repealed by Merchant Shipping Act 1970
The Merchant Shipping Act 1970
(Commencement No. 1) Order 1972
As from 1st January 1973

Sections 361 and 362
Repealed by Merchant Shipping Act 1970
(Commencement No. 1) Order 1972
As from 1st January, 1973

363 Where a foreign ship is a passenger steamer or emigrant ship within the meaning of this Part of this Act, and the Board of Trade are satisfied, by the production of a foreign certificate of survey attested by a British consular officer at a port out of Her Majesty's dominions, that the ship has been officially surveyed at that port, and are satisfied that any requirements of this Act are proved by that survey to have been substantially complied with, the Board may, if they think fit, dispense with any further survey of the ship in respect of any requirement so complied with, and grant or direct one of their officers to grant a certificate, which shall have the same effect as if given upon survey under this Part of this Act:

Exemption from survey of foreign passenger steamer or emigrant ship in certain cases.

Provided that Her Majesty in Council may order that this section shall not apply in the case of an official survey at any port at which it appears to Her Majesty that corresponding advantages are not extended to British ships.

The words underlined, 'or emigrant ship'
Repealed by Merchant Shipping Act 1970
The Merchant Shipping Act 1970
(Commencement No. 1) Order 1972
As from 1st January 1973

⚓ ⚓ ⚓ ⚓

Sections 364 and 365
Repealed by Merchant Shipping Act 1970
(Commencement No. 1) Order 1972
As from 1st January 1973

⚓ ⚓ ⚓ ⚓

366 (1) The governor of a British possession may by proclamation—

Modification of provisions of Part III in their application to British posessions.

(*a*) determine what shall be deemed, for the purposes of this Part of this Act, to be the length of the voyage of any ship carrying steerage passengers from any port in that British possession to any other port; and

(*b*) fix dietary scales for steerage passengers during the voyage; and

(*c*) declare what medical stores shall be deemed necessary for the medical treatment of the steerage passengers during the voyage.

(2) Every such proclamation shall take effect from the issue thereof, and shall have effect without as well as within the possession, as if enacted in this Part of this Act.

(3) The governor of a British possession may authorise such persons as he thinks fit to make a like survey of emigrant ships sailing from that possession as is by this Act required to be made by two or more competent surveyors in the case of emigrant ships sailing from the British Islands.

(4) The governor of a British possession may authorise any competent person to act as medical practitioner on board an emigrant ship proceeding on a colonial voyage.

COMMENTS.

Definition of 'British Possession', *see* Interpretation Act 1889, section 18, sub-sections 1 and 2.

Power of governors of colonies as to numbers of passengers. steerage

367 (1) The governor of each of the Australasian colonies, that is to say, New South Wales, Victoria, South Australia, Western Australia, Queensland, Tasmania, New Zealand, and any colony hereafter established in Australia, may by proclamation make such rules as he thinks proper for determining the number of steerage passenges to be carried in any emigrant ship proceeding from one of such colonies to any other of those colonies, and for determining on what deck or decks, and subject to what reservations or conditions, steerage passengers may be carried in such ship.

(2) The governor of any British possession may, if he thinks fit, declare by proclamation that ships intended to pass within the Tropics from any port in such possession may convey steerage passengers, being natives of Asia or Africa, after the rate of one for every twelve superficial feet of the passenger deck instead of after the rate specified in the Tenth Schedule to this Act.

(3) Every such proclamation shall take effect from the issue thereof, or such other day as may be named therein, and shall have effect without as well as within the possession, as if it were enacted in this Part of this Act in substitution as respects the said ships for the Tenth Schedule to this Act.

(4) The provisions of the Tenth Schedule to this Act with respect to the number of superficial feet to be allowed to each steerage passenger shall not apply to any ship proceeding from any port in the island of Ceylon to any port in British

India in the Gulf of Manar or Palk's Straits, and the legislature of Ceylon may regulate by law the number of steerage passengers who may be carried on board such ships.

COMMENTS.

From the date of the establishment of the Dominions of Australia and New Zealand, sub-section 1 can be considered as having no effect.

The Tenth Schedule referred to has been repealed. *See* the Merchant Shipping Act 1906, section 17, sub-section 2; section 85, and Schedule II.

The reference to 'British India' should now be interpreted by the Indian Independence Act 1947, section 18, and the India (Consequential Provisions) Act 1949, section 1.

In reference to Ceylon, *see* Ceylon Independence Act 1947, section 1, Schedule 1.

⚓ ⚓ ⚓ ⚓

368 (1) The provisions of this Part of this Act (other than the provisions relating to passenger steamers only) shall not apply to British India, except as in this section provided.

Power for legislature of India to apply Part III.

(2) The Governor-General of India in Council may, by any Act passed for the purpose, declare that all or any provisions of this Part of this Act shall apply to the carriage of steerage passengers upon any voyage from any specified port in British India to any other specified port whatsoever; and may for the purposes of this Part of this Act—

(*a*) fix dietary scales for the voyage, and authorise the substitution of those scales for the scale enacted by this Act;

(*b*) determine what shall be deemed to be the length of any such voyage;

(*c*) determine the persons or officers who in British India shall take the place of emigration officers and officers of customs in the British Islands;

(*d*) declare the space necessary for steerage passengers, and the age at which two children shall be treated as one statute adult, in ships clearing out from any port in British India; and

(*e*) authorise the employment on board any ship of a medical practitioner duly qualified according to Indian law; and

(*f*) provide for the recovery and application in British India of fines and sums of money under this Part of the Act, and the provisions of any such Act while in force shall have effect without as well as within British India as if enacted by this Act.

(3) Provided that any such Act shall be of no effect under this section, unless it be reserved for the signification of Her Majesty's pleasure thereon, or contain a suspending clause providing that the Act shall not come into operation until Her Majesty's pleasure thereon has been publicly signified in British India.

COMMENTS.

The words underlined in sub-section 2 have been replaced by 'Legislature of India by S.R. & O. 1937, No. 230' as a result of the Government of India Act 1935. A new section brought into being by the same order was in turn repealed by the Burma Independence Act 1947.

This order continues in force in respect to all Acts insofar as they operate otherwise than as part of the law of British India, or India or Pakistan. Consult Indian Independence Act 1947, and India (Consequential Provisions) Act 1949.

Passenger Steamers.

See sections 271, sub-section 3 repealed, 272 to 288.

M.S.A. 1894

PART IV

FISHING-BOATS

PART IV

FISHING-BOATS

N.B.—For the General application of Part IV of the Principal Act to Scotland, *see* Merchant Shipping (Scottish Fishing-Boats) Act 1920.

FISHING-BOATS
Application of Part IV., &c.

369 (1) This Part of this Act relates partly— Application of Part IV.

(*a*) to all fishing-boats and to the whole fishing service; and partly

(*b*) to all fishing-boats of twenty-five tons tonnage and upwards; and partly

(*c*) to fishing-boats being trawlers of twenty-five tons tonnage and upwards, and where so expressly provided, to fishing-boats being trawlers of whatever tonnage.

(2) The Board of Trade may, by order published in the London Gazette—

(*a*) exempt from the date in the order mentioned, any class of such trawler or trawlers belonging to any port from the whole or any portion of this Part of this Act, and

(*b*) extend all or any of the provisions of this Part of this Act to any fishing-boats referred to in the order, and may revoke or alter any such order by an order published in like manner, but such order shall not extend to any of the provisions relating to the fishing-boat register, or to the boats and life-buoys to be carried on fishing-boats.

(3) The Board of Trade may, before making any order under this section, institute such inquiry as in their opinion may be required for enabling them to make the order, by such person as the Board may appoint, and the person so appointed shall for the purpose of the inquiry have all the powers of a Board of Trade inspector under this Act.

(4) The provisions of this Act with respect to fishing-boats being trawlers shall, save as otherwise expressly provided, apply to vessels employed as tenders or carriers to fishing-boats or for the purpose of collecting and conveying to the land the catch of fishing-boats.

COMMENTS.

Tonnage.

This is ascertained in accordance with section 371. *See* also Merchant Shipping (Fishing-boats Registry) Order 1927 (S.R. & O., No. 642).

Fishing-Boat.

Meaning of, *see* section 370.

Fishing-Boat Register.

The provisions of this Act relating to the fishing-boat register, *see* sections 373, 374.

For powers of the D.T.I. to make regulations restricting conveyance of fish from trawlers to collecting and carrying vessels, *see* section 417.

Applications of certain sections of Principal Act of Scotland, *see* Merchant Shipping Act 1906, section 81, sub-section 2.

Orders under this section.

B.O.T., 2nd November 1899, S.R. & O. 1899, No. 805 Merchant Shipping.

(Fishing-Boats) Order 1923, S. R. & O. 1923, No. 949, Merchant Shipping.

(Fishing-Boats) Order 1948, S.I. 1948, No. 366 Merchant Shipping.

(Fishing-Boats Agreements) Order 1948, S.I. 1948, No. 1853.

⚓ ⚓ ⚓ ⚓

Definitions. **370** In this Part of this Act, unless the context otherwise requires—

'Fishing-boat.' The expression 'fishing-boat' means a vessel of whatever size, and in whatever way propelled, which is for the time being employed in sea fishing or in the sea-fishing service, but save as otherwise expressly provided, that expression shall not include a vessel used for catching fish otherwise than for profit.

'Second hand.' The expression 'second hand' means, with respect to a fishing-boat, the mate or person next to the skipper in authority or command on board the boat.

The expression 'voyage' shall mean a fishing-trip commencing with a departure from a port for the purpose of fishing, and ending with the first return to a port thereafter upon the conclusion of the trip, but a return due to distress only shall not be deemed to be a return, if it is followed by a resumption of the trip. 'Voyage.'

The words underlined
Repealed by the Merchant Shipping Act 1970
The Merchant Shipping Act 1970
(Commencement No. 1) Order 1972
As from 1st January, 1973

COMMENTS.

Sea-Fishing.

This term is not defined in this Act, consult section 5, The Sea Fisheries Act 1868.

Fishing-Boat.

Certain fishing-boats are deemed to be foreign-going ships for the purpose of this Act, *see* section 744.

Port.

See section 742.

⚓ ⚓ ⚓ ⚓

371 (1) The tonnage of a fishing-boat for the purpose of this Part of this Act shall be taken to be in the case of a steam trawler her gross tonnage, but in any other case her register tonnage. Ascertainment of tonnage of fishing-boat.

The words underlined in sub-section 1
Repealed Merchant Shipping Act 1965, Schedule 2
Also sub-sections 2 and 3

COMMENTS.

For measurement and tonnage of ships, *see* sections 77–86. Also, the Merchant Shipping (Fishing-Boats Registry) Order, 1927, S.R. & O., No. 642.

⚓ ⚓ ⚓ ⚓

372 This Part of this Act shall not, except where otherwise expressly provided, apply to Scotland, or to any British possession. Extent of Part IV.

(1) PROVISIONS APPLYING TO ALL FISHING-BOATS AND TO THE WHOLE FISHING SERVICE

The following sections shall apply to all fishing-boats and the whole fishing service—

COMMENTS.

The words underlined were repealed by the Merchant Shipping (Scottish Fishing-Boats) Act 1920, section 1, sub-section 3, and Schedule.

For vessels engaged in the Whale, Seal, or Walrus fisheries, *see* section 744, also Merchant Shipping Act 1906, section 83.

Fishing-Boats Registry

Registry of British fishing-boat.

373 (1) This section shall apply to the British Islands, and to all British fishing-boats, including those used otherwise than for profit, and the expression 'fishing-boat' in this section shall be construed accordingly.

(2) Subject to any exemptions made by the regulations under this section, every fishing-boat shall be lettered and numbered and have official papers, and shall for that purpose be entered in the fishing-boat register.

(3) If a fishing-boat required to be so entered is not so entered, she shall not be entitled to any of the privileges or advantages of a British fishing-boat, but all obligations, liabilities, and penalties with reference to that boat, and the punishment of offences committed on board her, or by any persons belonging to her, and the jurisdiction of officers and courts, shall be the same as if the boat were actually so entered.

(4) If a fishing-boat required to be entered in the fishing-boat register is not so entered, and is used as a fishing-boat, the owner and skipper of such boat shall each be liable, for each offence, to a fine not exceeding twenty pounds, and the boat may be detained.

(5) Her Majesty, by Order in Council, may make regulations for carrying into effect and enforcing the entry of fishing-boats in the fishing-boat register, and any convention with a foreign country relative to the registry, lettering, and numbering of fishing-boats, which is for the time being in force by virtue of any statute, and may by such regulations—

(*a*) adopt any existing system of registry or lettering and numbering of boats, and provide for bringing any such system into conformity with the requirements of this Act and of any such convention, and the regulations; and

(*b*) define the boats or classes of boats to which the regulations or any of them are to apply, and provide for the exemption of any boats or classes of boats from the provisions of this section, and from the regulations or any of them; and

(*c*) apply to the entry of fishing-boats in the fishing-boat register, and to all matters incidental thereto, such (if any) of the enactments contained in this or any other Act relating to the registry of British ships, and with such modifications and alterations as may be found desirable; and

(*d*) impose fines not exceeding twenty pounds for the breach of any such regulations which cannot be punished by the application of any of those enactments.

(6) Section twenty-six of the Sea Fisheries Act, 1868, and sections eleven to fourteen of the Sea Fisheries Act, 1883, shall apply in like manner as if those sections referred to in this section and an Order in Council made thereunder, in substitution for sections twenty-two to twenty-four of the Sea Fisheries Act 1868, and any Order in Council made under those sections.

(7) Section one hundred and seventy-six of the Customs Consolidation Act 1876, shall not apply to any fishing-boat entered in the fishing-boat register in pursuance of this Act. *See* below.

COMMENTS.

British Islands.

This term includes the United Kingdom, the Channel Islands, and the Isle of Man. *See* Interpretation Act 1889, section 18.

Detention.

See section 692.

Repeal.

Sub-section 6 above. The words underlined repealed by S.L. Rev. Act 1908, sub-section 7 above; repealed by the Customs and Excise Act 1952, section 320, Schedule XII, Part 1, as from 1st January 1953.

See also section 68, sub-section 5 of the Customs and Excise Act 1952.

Consult the Sea Fisheries Act 1868, section 26 as to the compulsory carrying of certificates of registry or official papers by sea-fishing-boats.

Also, the Sea Fisheries Act, 1952, sections 11 to 14 for the enforcement of that Act by sea-fishery officers.

Important S.R. & O.

The Merchant Shipping (Fishing-Boats Registry) Order 1927 (S.R. & O. No. 642) revoked all earlier regulations as to the registry of fishing-boats; new regulations were brought into being, giving detailed provisions as to ports and places of registry, measurement of tonnage, etc.

Effect of registry of fishing-boat.

31 & 32 Vict. c. 45.
46 & 47 Vict. c. 22.

374 In all legal proceedings against the owner or skipper of, or any person belonging to, any boat entered in the fishing-boat register, either for an offence against the fishery regulations or regulations as to lights in the Sea Fisheries Act 1868, or for an offence against the Sea Fisheries Act 1883, or for the recovery of damages for injury done by such boat, the register shall be conclusive evidence that the persons entered therein at any date as owners of the boat were at that date owners thereof, and that the boat is a British sea-fishing boat: Provided that—

(*a*) this enactment shall not prevent any proceedings being instituted against any person not so entered who is beneficially interested in the boat; and

(*b*) this enactment shall not affect the rights of the owners among themselves, or the rights of any owner entered in the register against any person not so entered who is beneficially interested in the boat; and

(*c*) save as aforesaid, entry in the fishing-boat register shall not confer, take away, or affect any title to or interest in any fishing-boat.

COMMENTS.

Beneficial Interest.

See definition for the purposes of Part 1 of this Act, in section 57.

Merchant Shipping Act 1894

Part IV

Section 375

Repealed by Merchant Shipping Act 1937, section 2

Merchant Shipping Act 1894

Part IV

Sections 376–384

Repealed by Merchant Shipping Act 1970
(Commencement No. 1) Order 1972
As from 1st January, 1973

Provisions as to Deaths, Injuries, Ill-treatment Punishments, and Casualties in Fishing-Boats

Record and report of death, injury, ill-treatment, punishment, casualties, &c.

385 (1) The skipper of a fishing-boat shall keep a record of the following occurrences; namely—

(i) Of every death, injury, ill-treatment, or punishment of any member of his boat's crew while at sea or of any person on board his boat, and

(ii) Of every casualty to his fishing-boat or any boat belonging to her.

(2) The skipper shall produce the record so kept to any superintendent when required by him, and shall also send the same to the superintendent at the port to which the boat belongs at such periods as the Board of Trade require by any directions endorsed on the forms approved by them.

(3) If any such occurrence has happened in the case of a fishing-boat, the skipper of the boat shall make to the superintendent at the port where his boat's voyage ends, within twenty-four hours of the boat's arrival at that port, a report of the occurrence.

(4) The record and report under this section shall be in such form and contain such particulars as the Board of Trade require.

(5) If a skipper fails without reasonable cause to comply with any requirement of this section, he shall for each offence be liable to a fine not exceeding twenty pounds.

COMMENTS.

Inquiry.

In the event of such occurrence happening as is referred to in this section, an enquiry must be held by a Superintendent. *See* section 386.

Fishing-Boat.

Meaning of, *see* section 370.

Port.

Meaning of, *see* section 742.

Forms.

See section 720.

⚓ ⚓ ⚓ ⚓

Inquiry as to death, injury, ill-treatment, punishment, &c.

386 (1) Where any such occurrence as in the last preceding section mentioned happens or is supposed to have happened, the superintendent at or nearest to the port at which the fishing-boat arrives after the occurrence, or to which the boat belongs, may inquire into the cause and particulars of the occurrence, and, if a report as to the occurrence is made to him in pursuance of the said section, may make on the report an endorsement either that in his opinion the particulars in the report are true, or otherwise to such effect as in his opinion his information warrants.

(2) For the purpose of the inquiry, a superintendent shall have all the powers of a Board of Trade inspector under this Act.

(3) If in the course of the inquiry it appears to the superintendent that any such occurrence as aforesaid has been caused or was accompanied by violence or the use of any improper means, he shall report the matter to the Board of Trade, and shall also, if the emergency of the case in his opinion so requires, take immediate steps for bringing the offender to justice, and may for that purpose, if in his discretion he thinks it necessary, cause him to be arrested, and thereafter dealt with in due course of law.

COMMENTS.

Death.

If loss of life occurs through any casualty happening to, or on board any boat belonging to a fishery vessel, the D.T.I. may order an inquiry to be made or a formal investigation to be held. *See* section 468.

Powers of Inspectors.

See section 729.

⚓ ⚓ ⚓ ⚓

Merchant Shipping Act 1894

Part IV

Sections 387, 388

Repealed by Merchant Shipping Act 1970

(Commencement No. 1) Order 1972

As from 1st January 1973

Merchant Shipping Act 1894

Section 389

Repealed by

Merchant Shipping (Scottish Fishing-Boats) Act 1920

Section 1, sub-section 3, and Schedule

Merchant Shipping Act 1894

Part IV

Sections 391–412

Repealed by Merchant Shipping Act 1970

(Commencement No. 1) Order 1972

As from 1st January 1973

Certificates of Skippers and Second Hands

413 (1) A fishing-boat, being a trawler of twenty-five tons tonnage or upwards, shall not go to sea from any port of England or Ireland unless provided with a duly certificated skipper and a duly certificated second hand.

Skippers and second hands to hold certificate of competency.

(2) If a boat goes to sea contrary to this section, the owner thereof shall for each offence be liable to a fine not exceeding twenty pounds.

(3) If any person, except in case of necessity—

(*a*) having been engaged to serve as skipper or second hand of a fishing-boat, being a trawler of twenty-five tons tonnage and upwards, serves as skipper or second hand of that boat without being duly certificated; or

(*b*) employs any person as skipper or second hand of such a boat without ascertaining that he is duly certificated;

that person shall for each offence be liable to a fine not exceeding twenty pounds.

(4) A skipper or second hand shall not be deemed duly certificated for the purpose of this section unless he holds a certificate under this Part of this Act appropriate to his station in the boat or to a higher station.

(5) Where the skipper of such a boat is absent from his boat a superintendent may, on the request of the owner of the boat, and on being satisfied that the absence is due to an unavoidable cause, authorise the second hand of the boat to act, for a period not exceeding one month, as the skipper of the boat during the skipper's absence, and the second hand when acting under that authority shall for the purposes of this section be deemed to be a duly certificated skipper.

COMMENTS.

The words underlined were repealed by the Merchant Shipping Act 1906, section 85 and Second Schedule.

Extentions and Exemptions.

Sections 413–416 have been extended so as to apply to all fishing-boats engaged in seine net-fishing of 50 tons gross tonnage and upwards, propelled by steam or other mechanical power; but sub-section 4 of this section and the penal provisions in these sections are not to apply to the skipper or second hand of such boats if he is properly in possession of an authority issued by the Ministry of Transport authorising him to act in such capacity on fishing-boats, being liners or drifters of 50 tons or more, mechanically propelled, *see* the Merchant Shipping (Fishing-Boats) Order 1923, S.R. & O. 1923, No. 949.

See also the Merchant Shipping (Fishing-Boats) Order 1948, S.I. 1948, No. 366.

Fishing-Boat.

See section 370 for meaning.

Second Hand.

See section 370 for meaning.

414 (1) Certificates of competency as skipper or as second hand of fishing-boats, or any particular class of fishing-boats, may be granted by the Board of Trade in the same manner as certificates of competency as master or mate under the Second Part of this Act, and all the provisions of this Act with respect to or connected with the examination of applicants for certificates and the granting thereof, and the suspension and cancellation thereof, and inquiries and investigations into the conduct of the holders thereof, and all other provisions of this Act relating to or connected with certificates of masters or mates, shall apply to the certificates as skipper or second hand of fishing-boats, and the holders thereof, as if the certificates had been granted under Part II of this Act, and the holders thereof shall be entitled to such privileges, and subject to such liabilities as they would be if such certificates had been so granted. Granting of certificate of competency.

(2) A certificate of competency as skipper of a fishing-boat shall not be granted to any person unless he has previously held a certificate as second hand for at least twelve months.

COMMENTS.

This section applies to trawlers of 25 tons and upwards going to sea from any port in the United Kingdom. *See* section 81 of the Merchant Shipping Act 1906. Second Hand; Fishing-Boat, meaning of, *see* section 370.

Certificate of Service.

This Act applies to certificates of service granted under section 415 and to the holders thereof in a like manner as it applies to certificates of competency and to the holders thereof.

Inquiries.

See Part VI of this Act and repealing Acts.

Extensions.

See comments to section 413.

415 (1) If any person before the first day of September one thousand eight hundred and eighty-three served as a skipper or before the first day of July one thousand eight hundred and eighty-eight served as a second hand in fishing-boats, being trawlers of twenty-five tons tonnage and upwards or such other fishing-boats as the Board of Trade consider will have afforded that person sufficient experience, for a period amounting in all to not less than twelve months, that Certificate of service.

person shall be entitled to a certificate of service as skipper or second hand, as the case may be, of a fishing-boat, limited, if he has been exclusively employed in a particular class of such fishing-boats, to that particular class.

(2) If a person proves to the Board of Trade that he has served as required by this section and has been generally well conducted on board the boats in which he has served, the Board of Trade shall deliver a certificate of service to him.

(3) The certificate of service shall differ in form from a certificate of competency, and shall contain particulars of the name, place, and date of birth of the holder, and of the length and nature of his previous service.

(4) This Act shall apply to a certificate of service so granted and to the holder thereof in like manner as it applies to a certificate of competency granted under this Part of this Act and to the holder thereof.

COMMENTS.

This section applies to trawlers of 25 tons and upwards going to sea from any port in the United Kingdom. *See* Merchant Shipping Act 1906, section 81.

Extensions.

See comments to section 413.

Fishing-Boat; Second Hand, meaning of, *see* section 370.

⚓ ⚓ ⚓ ⚓

Registers of certificated skippers and second hands.

416 (1) The Board of Trade may cause a register of certificated skippers and second hands to be kept in such form and by such person, and containing such particulars, as the Board direct.

(2) Such register shall be admissible in evidence in manner provided by this Act, and the absence of an entry in the register of any person or matter shall be evidence of the non-registration of such person or matter, and if the question is whether the person has been certificated as a skipper or second hand, of his not being so certificated.

COMMENTS.

Extensions.

See comments regarding section 413.

Second Hand.

Meaning of, *see* section 370.

Certificated.

Those granted under section 414 and certificate of service under section 415.

Admissible in Evidence.

As to the admissibility of documents in evidence, *see* section 695, 719.

Conveyance of Fish from Trawlers

417 (1) The Board of Trade, on the application of any owners of a fleet of fishing-boats, or of any association of owners of fishing-boats, or of any persons having the charge or command of a fleet of fishing-boats, or without such application if the person or association entitled to make the application fails after request by the Board of Trade to do so, may make such regulations respecting the conveyance of fish from fishing-boats catching fish as trawlers to vessels engaged in collecting and carrying fish to port, as may appear to the Board expedient for preventing loss of life, or danger to life or limb. Board of Trade regulations as to conveyance of fish from trawlers.

(2) All regulations so made shall be laid for thirty days before both Houses of Parliament while in session, and shall not come into force till the expiration of those thirty days; and if either House within those thirty days resolves that the whole or any part of the regulations laid before them ought not to be in force, the same shall not have any force, without prejudice, nevertheless, to the making of any other regulation in its place.

(3) All regulations made under this section shall, whilst in force, have effect as if enacted in this Act.

(4) If any person to whom such a regulation applies fails without reasonable cause to comply therewith, he shall for each offence be liable to a fine not exceeding ten pounds.

(5) This section shall apply to fishing-boats of whatever tonnage.

COMMENTS.

Regulations laid before Parliament.

Regulations made under this section are now subject to the Statutory Instruments Act 1946.

There is an extension to the period of 30 days to one of 40 days.

Certificates

These granted under section 414 and certificate of [illegible] under section 415.

Admissible in Evidence

As to the admissibility of documents in evidence, see section 695 (1).

Compensation of [illegible] from Trinity [illegible]

[illegible] (1) The Board of Trade on the application of any owners of a fleet of [illegible] or of any association of owners or masters of [illegible] or of any persons having the charge or [illegible] of [illegible] under [illegible] without such application if the person or association [illegible] to make the application [illegible] by the Board or [illegible] may [illegible] such [illegible] the [illegible] and [illegible] from [illegible] as [illegible] [illegible] that [illegible] to the [illegible] of [illegible] to the [illegible].

(2) [illegible] shall be laid for thirty days before [illegible] and [illegible] and shall be [illegible] for the [illegible] [illegible] the [illegible] [illegible] days [illegible] that [illegible] of [illegible] [illegible] be [illegible] [illegible] to any [illegible] [illegible] in force.

(3) All Regulations [illegible] under [illegible] while in force have effect as if [illegible] in this Act.

(4) The [illegible] may [illegible] such [illegible] and [illegible] without [illegible] to [illegible] the [illegible] or [illegible] to [illegible] year.

(5) This section shall apply to [illegible] [illegible] [illegible].

COMMENT

Regulations to be laid before Parliament

Regulations made under this section are now subject to the Statutory Instruments Act 1946.

There is an extension of the period of 30 days to one of 40 days.

M.S.A. 1894

PART V

SAFETY

PART V

SAFETY

Prevention of Collisions

418 (1) Her Majesty may, on the joint recommendation of the Admiralty and the Board of Trade, by Order in Council, make regulations for the prevention of collisions at sea, and may thereby regulate the lights to be carried and exhibited, the fog-signals to be carried and used, and the steering and sailing rules to be observed, by ships, and those regulations (in this Act referred to as the collision regulations), shall have effect as if enacted in this Act. Collision regulations.

(2) The collision regulations, together with the provisions of this Part of this Act relating thereto, or otherwise relating to collisions, shall be observed by all foreign ships within British jurisdiction, and in any case arising in a British court concerning matters arising within British jurisdiction foreign ships shall, so far as respects the collision regulations and the said provisions of this Act, be treated as if they were British ships.

COMMENTS.

Regulations for preventing collisions at sea.

Present Rules.

NOTE—When carrying out investigations into the various decisions arising as a result of the Collision Regulations, it must be registered that these regulations have altered over the years, and that great care must be taken to understand the actual regulations which were in force at the material time, as well as the judgement obtaining.

At an International Conference on Safety of Life at Sea held in 1960, in London, new Collision Regulations were agreed, and the present Regulations, operative from September 1, 1965, are contained in S.I. 1965, No. 1525. Regulations for Preventing Collisions at Sea 1960, set out in Schedule 1 to the Collision Regulations (Ships and Seaplanes on the Water) and Signals of Distress (Ships) Order 1965.

Additional regulations for the prevention of collisions at sea which form part of the Collision Regulations for the purposes of the Merchant Shipping Act 1894, are contained in an Order in Council, S.I. 1972, No. 809. The Collision Regulations (Traffic Separation Schemes) Order 1972, operative from September 1, 1972. *See* 418 (*a*) 1.

The regulations set out in the Schedule to the Order make provision for regulating navigation in traffic-separation schemes, based on recommendations adopted by the Inter-Governmental Maritime Consultative Organisation (I.M.C.O.) together with the Collision Regulations (Traffic Separation Schemes) (Amendment) Order 1972, S.I. 1972, No. 1267. (Corrected reprint.)

Application of Regulations to Seaplanes.

The power to make regulations under this section includes power (with modifications) to make regulations for the prevention of collision at sea between seaplanes on the surface of the water, and between ships and seaplanes in the water. *See* section 52, sub-section 1, of the Civil Aviation Act 1949.

Hovercraft.

These are not classed as seaplanes. Their position in law is not absolutely clear although an Admiralty Notice to Mariners of August 25. 1962, No. 1849, has stated that they will comply as far as practicable with the Collision Regulations. Their permit to operate is issued under the air navigation legislation although, for the purposes of the Rules, they are to be considered as though they are power-driven vessels.

Hydrofoil Craft.

It would appear that for the purposes of the Rules these craft are to be considered as power-driven vessels.

Lights and Fog-Signals.

See section 420.

Foreign Ships.

See section 424, for the application of the collision regulations to foreign ships.

British Jurisdiction.

Consult Territorial Jurisdiction Act, 1878.

British jurisdiction extends over the open seas adjacent to the Coasts of the United Kingdom *and* of all other parts of H.M. Dominions to such a distance as is necessary for their defence and security. The expression United Kingdom normally means Great Britain and Northern Ireland. The expression Great Britain is given to the two Kingdoms of England and Scotland, as from May 1, 1907. The expression England includes Wales and Berwick on Tweed and the Isle of Wight (Wales and Berwick Act, 1746).

Accordingly, therefore, the Channel Islands and the Isle of Man are not contained in the term 'United Kingdom' in a statute, unless the term 'United Kingdom' is expressly or implicitly extended by the enactment in which it occurs.

For the inclusion of the Republic of Eire, *see* Irish Free State (Consequential Adaptation of Enactments) Order 1923.

⚓ ⚓ ⚓ ⚓

419 (1) All owners and masters of ships shall obey the collision regulations, and shall not carry or exhibit any other lights, or use any other fog-signals, than such as are required by those regulations. **Observance of collision regulations.**

(2) If an infringment of the collision regulations is caused by the wilful default of the master or owner of the ship, that master or owner shall, in respect of each offence, be guilty of a misdemeanor.

(3) If any damage to person or property arises from the non-observance by any ship of any of the collision regulations, the damage shall be deemed to have been occasioned by the wilful default of the person in charge of the deck of the ship at the time, unless it is shown to the satisfaction of the court that the circumstances of the case made a departure from the regulation necessary.

(4) Where in a case of collision it is proved to the court before whom the case is tried, that any of the collision regulations have been infringed, the ship by which the regulation has been infringed shall be deemed to be in fault, unless it is shown to the satisfaction of the court that the circumstances of the case made departure from the regulation necessary. Repealed. *See* below.

(5) The Board of Trade shall furnish a copy of the collision regulations to any master or owner of a ship who applies for it.

COMMENTS.

Repeal.

Sub-section 4 as well as sub-section 2 of section 422 repealed by the Maritime Conventions Act 1911, sub-section 4, sub-section 1 and 2. In addition, all actions of damage by collisions in which proceedings had been commenced since December 16, 1911, even though the collision, out of which the action arose, had taken place before that date. The *Enterprise* 1912.

Collision Regulations.

See comments under Her Majesty's Ships, below.

Where an uncompleted aircraft-carrier belonging to the Crown, but not yet commissioned, was involved in collision, it was held that although the collision Regulations of 1910 nor the Queen's Regulations and

Admiralty Instructions applied, the Collision Regulations nevertheless contained a standard of care to which those in charge of her should have conformed. The *Albion* 1953.

Regulations for Preventing Collisions at Sea; *see* comments to section 418.

Her Majesty's Ships.

Section 741 states: 'This Act shall not, except where specially provided, apply to ships belonging to Her Majesty.' Accordingly the Collision Regulations do not apply to ships belonging to Her Majesty, whether they are ships of war or ships employed in the service of any Government department. Young *v.* s.s. *Scotia* 1903. However, all H.M. ships are subject to exactly similar regulations for Navigation (the Queen's Regulations and Admiralty Instructions) so that the broad exemption contained in section 74, 1, is of little if any practical importance.

Damages.

For Rules as to division of loss, damages for personal injuries and provisions as to collisions generally, consult the Maritime Conventions Act 1911. Fundamentally, this means that the division of loss is in proportion to the degree in which each vessel was in fault, the rule of equal moieties being only applicable where it is not possible to establish different degrees of fault. This is also followed in relation to the cargo interests for, where formerly the owners of the cargo of the vessel could only recover half of their loss from the other vessel, the provisions of the Maritime Conventions Act 1911 allow that where damages have been assessed in proportion to the degree of fault, then the cargo owner of the vessel can recover the proportion of damage equal to the degree of fault of the other vessel.

Master, definition of, section 742.

⚓ ⚓ ⚓ ⚓

Inspection as to lights and fog-signals.

420 (1) A surveyor of ships may inspect any ship, British or foreign, for the purpose of seeing that the ship is properly provided with lights and the means of making fog-signals, in conformity with the collision regulations, and if the surveyor finds that the ship is not so provided, he shall give to the master or owner notice in writing, pointing out the deficiency, and also what is, in his opinion, requisite in order to remedy the same.

(2) Every notice so given shall be communicated in the manner directed by the Board of Trade to the chief officer of customs at any port at which the ship may seek to obtain a clearance or transire; and the ship shall be detained, until a certificate under the hand of a surveyor of ships is produced

to the effect that the ship is properly provided with lights and with the means of making fog-signals, in conformity with the collision regulations.

(3) For the purpose of an inspection under this section a surveyor shall have all the powers of a Board of Trade inspector under this Act.

(4) When the certificate as to lights and fog-signals is refused, an owner may appeal to the court of survey for the port or district where the ship for the time being is in manner directed by the rules of that court.

(5) On any such appeal the judge of the court of survey shall report to the Board of Trade on the question raised by the appeal, and the Board of Trade, when satisfied that the requirements of the report and of this Act as to lights and fog-signals have been complied with, may grant, or direct a surveyor of ships or other person appointed by them to grant, the certificate.

(6) Subject to any order made by the judge of court of survey the costs of and incidental to the appeal shall follow the event.

(7) A surveyor in making an inspection under this section shall, if the owner of the ship so require, be accompanied on the inspection by some person appointed by the owner and, if in that case the surveyor and the person so appointed agree, there shall be no appeal under this section to the court of survey.

(8) Such fees as the Board of Trade may determine shall be paid in respect of an inspection of lights and fog-signals under this section not exceeding those specified in the Sixteenth Schedule to this Act.

Repeal.

The words underlined above repealed Merchant Shipping (Safety Convention) Act 1949, section 37, sub-section 5 and Schedule III.

COMMENTS.

Exemption of Certain Ships.

Consult the Merchant Shipping (Safety Convention) Act 1949.

Surveyor of Ships.

See section 724. For powers of inspection, *see* section 729.

Collision Regulations.

See comments under sections 418, 419.

Enforcement of Detention.

See section 692.

Court of Survey.

For rules, etc., of this court, *see* section 487, 489. In respect of rights of appeal to other courts *see* Denny *v.* Board of Trade 1880.

Saving for local rules of navigation in harbours, &c.

421 (1) Any rules made before or after the passing of this Act under the authority of any local Act, concerning lights and signals to be carried, or the steps for avoiding collision to be taken, by vessels navigating the waters of any harbour, river, or other inland navigation, shall, notwithstanding anything in this Act, have full effect.

(2) Where any such rules are not and cannot be made, Her Majesty in Council on the application of any person having authority over such waters, or, if there is no such person, any person interested in the navigation thereof, may make such rules, and those rules shall, as regards vessels navigating the said waters, be of the same force as if they were part of the collision regulations.

COMMENTS.

It would appear that the distinction between rules arising out of sub-section 1 above and those arising out of sub-section 2 (Orders in Council) is of no practical importance since the abolition of the statutory presumption of fault. *See* sub-sections 419 and 422.

Duty of vessel to assist the other in case of collision.

422 (1) In every case of collision between two vessels, it shall be the duty of the master or person in charge of each vessel, if and so far as he can do so without danger to his own vessel, crew and passengers (if any),

(*a*) to render to the other vessel, her master, crew and passengers (if any) such assistance as may be practicable, and may be necessary to save them from any danger caused by the collision, and to stay by the other vessel until he has ascertained that she has no need of further assistance, and also

(*b*) to give to the master or person in charge of the other vessel the name of his own vessel and of the port to which she belongs, and also the names of the ports from which she comes and to which she is bound.

(2) If the master or person in charge of a vessel fails to comply with this section, and no reasonable cause for such failure is shown, the collision shall, in the absence of proof to the contrary, be deemed to have been caused by his wrongful act, neglect or default. Repealed.

(3) If the master or person in charge fails without reasonable cause to comply with this section, he shall be guilty of a misdemeanor, and, if he is a certificated officer, an inquiry into his conduct may be held, and his certificate cancelled or suspended.

Repeal.

Sub-section 2.

Repealed Maritime Convention Act 1911, section 4, sub-section 2.

COMMENTS.

The general duty to assist persons in danger at sea is contained in the Maritime Conventions Act 1911, section 6.

Question of Assistance/Salvage.

The duty to assist does not prevent a vessel rendering assistance to claim salvage. It would appear that the general rule is that where the vessel standing by is not to blame, then if her services are of the nature of salvage, then she may rank as a salvor. *See* the *Hannibal v. The Queen* 1867. *Melanie* (Owners) *v. San Onofre* (Owners) 1925.

Where she has been wholly or in part to blame, she is not entitled to claim salvage. *Beaverford v.* the *Kafiristan* 1938.

Tug and Tow.

It would appear that it is the duty of a tug to stand by and assist a vessel which has collided with the tug's tow. The *Hannibal v. The Queen* 1867.

This does not affect such tug's entitlement (if any) to remuneration (salvage/tonnage) for services rendered to the injured vessel.

Master or Person in Charge.

It would appear that a compulsory pilot is not a 'person in charge' and his presence on board does not relieve the master or mate or other person in charge from responsibility of rendering assistance. *The Queen* 1869.

Danger to Own Vessel.

Apprehension of capture. The *Thuringia* 1872.

Vessel Damaged While Assisting Another After Collision.

The *San Onofre* 1922.

Failure to Send Boat to Assist.

The *Adriatic* 1875.

Failure to Reply to Distress Signals.

The *Emmy Haase* 1884.

Duty to Go to Assistance of a Vessel in Distress.

See Merchant Shipping (Safety Convention) Act 1949, section 22.

NOTE—Sub-sections 6 and 7 repealed by the Merchant Shipping Act 1970. The Merchant Shipping Act 1970 (Commencement No. 1), Order 1972, as from January 1, 1973.

⚓ ⚓ ⚓ ⚓

Section 423

Repealed by Merchant Shipping Act 1970 (Commencement No. 1) Order 1972, as from 1st January, 1973

⚓ ⚓ ⚓ ⚓

Application of collision regulations to foreign ships.

424 Whenever it is made to appear to Her Majesty in Council that the Government of any foreign country is willing that the collision regulations, or the provisions of this Part of this Act relating thereto or otherwise relating to collisions, or any of those regulations or provisions should apply to the ships of that country when beyond the limits of British jurisdiction, Her Majesty may, by Order in Council, direct that those regulations and provisions shall, subject to any limitation of time, conditions and qualifications contained in the Order, apply to the ships of the said foreign country, whether within British jurisdiction or not, and that such ships shall for the purpose of such regulations and provisions be treated as if they were British ships.

COMMENTS.

Foreign Ships.

When within British jurisdiction all foreign ships are subject to the Collision Regulations. Consult section 418, sub-section 2.

British Jurisdiction.

See comments to section 418.

Collision Regulations.

See comments to section 418.

Countries which have accepted the collision regulations are:

Belgium, Burma, Cameroon, Denmark, Finland, France, Greece, Iceland,

Israel, Kuwait, Japan, Liberia, Madagascar, Morocco, Netherlands (Surinam and Netherlands Antilles), Norway, Paraguay, Peru, Philippines, Poland, Portugal, Roumania, Spain, Sweden, U.S.S.R., United Arab Republic, U.S.A., Vietnam, and Yugoslavia.

Sections 425–426

Repealed by Merchant Shipping Act 1970

The Merchant Shipping Act 1970

(Commencement No. 1), Order 1972

As from 1st January 1973

Life-saving Appliances

427 (1) The Board of Trade may make rules (in this Act called rules for life-saving appliances) with respect to all or any of the following matters; namely— Rules as to life-saving appliances.

(*a*) The arranging of British ships into classes, having regard to the services in which they are employed, to the nature and duration of the voyage and to the number of persons carried;

(*b*) The number and description of the boats, lifeboats, life-rafts, life-jackets, and life-buoys to be carried by British ships, according to the class in which they are arranged, and the mode of their construction, also the equipments to be carried by the boats and rafts, and the methods to be provided to get the boats and other life-saving appliances into the water, which methods may include oil for use in stormy weather; and

(*c*) The quantity, quality, and description of buoyant apparatus to be carried on board British ships carrying passengers, either in addition to or in substitution for boats, lifeboats, life-rafts, life-jackets, and life-buoys.

(2) All such rules shall be laid before Parliament so soon as may be after they are made, and shall not come into operation until they have lain for forty days before both Houses of Parliament during the session of Parliament; and on coming into operation shall have effect as if enacted in this Act.

(3) Rules under this section shall not apply to any fishing-boat for the time being entered in the fishing-boat register under Part IV of this Act.

N.B.—A new section has been substituted, *see* below.

Comments and Text of New Section.

By the Merchant Shipping (Safety Convention) Act 1949. The Merchant Shipping (Safety Convention) Act 1949 (Commencement Order) 1952, S.I. 1952, No. 1418, substituted section is:

Section 427.

(1) The Minister of Transport may, in relation to any ships to which this section applies, make rules (in this Act, called 'rules for life-saving appliances') with respect to all or any of the following matters, namely:

(*a*) The arranging of ships into classes, having regard to the services in which they are employed, to the nature and duration of the voyage and to the number of persons carried.

(*b*) The number, description, and mode of construction of the boats, life-rafts, line-throwing appliances, life-jackets, and life-buoys to be carried by ships according to the classes in which the ships are arranged.

(*c*) The equipment to be carried by any such boats and rafts and the methods to be provided to get the boats and other life-saving appliances into the water, including oil for use in stormy weather.

(*d*) The provision in ships of a proper supply of lights inextinguishable in water, and fitted for attachment to life-buoys.

(*e*) The quantity, quality and description of buoyant apparatus to be carried on board ships carrying passengers either in addition to or in substitution for boats, life-rafts, life-jackets, and life-buoys.

(*f*) The position and means of securing the boats, life-rafts, life-jackets, life-buoys, and buoyant apparatus.

(*g*) The marking of the boats, life-rafts, and buoyant apparatus so as to show their dimensions and the number of persons authorised to be carried on them.

(*h*) The manning of the lifeboats and the qualifications and certificates of lifeboatmen.

(*j*) The provision to be made for mustering the persons on board, and for embarking them in the boats (including provision for the lighting of, and the means of ingress to and egress from different parts of the ship).

(*k*) The provision of suitable means situated outside the engine-room whereby any discharge of water into the boats can be prevented.

(*l*) the assignment of specific duties to each member of the crew in the event of emergency.

(*m*) The methods to be adopted and the appliances to be carried in ships for the prevention, detection and extinction of fire.

(*n*) The practice in ships of boat-drills and fire-drills.

(*o*) The provision in ships of means of making effective distress-signals by day and by night.

(*p*) The provision in ships engaged on voyages in which pilots are likely to be embarked, of suitable pilot-ladders and of ropes, lights and other appliances designed to make the use of such ladders safe, and

(*q*) the examination at intervals to be prescribed by the rules of any appliance or equipment required by the rules to be carried.

(2) (*a*) British ships, except ships registered in a Dominion within the meaning of the Statute of Westminster 1931 or in India, Pakistan, Ceylon, Ghana, the Federation of Malaya, the Republic of Cyprus, Nigeria, Sierra Leone, Tanganyika, Jamaica, Trinidad and Tobago, or Uganda or in any territory administered by Her Majesty's Government in any such Dominion.

(*b*) Other ships while they are within any port in the United Kingdom: provided that this section shall not apply to a ship by reason of being within a port in the United Kingdom if she would not have been in any such port but for the stress of weather or any other circumstance that neither the master nor the owner, nor the charterer (if any) of the ship could have prevented or forestalled.

Exemption.

Safety Convention Ships (including passenger steamers) not registered in the United Kingdom are exempt from the rules for life-saving appliances, where accepted Safety Convention Certificates, applicable to such ships, are produced. Merchant Shipping (Safety Convention) Act 1949, section 16, sub-sections 1 and 2.

The rules at present in force are: The Merchant Shipping (Life-Saving Appliances) Rules 1965, S.I. 1965, No. 1105 as amended.

The Merchant Shipping (Life-Saving Appliances) (Amendment) Rules 1966, S.I. 1966, No. 744.

The Merchant Shipping (Life-Saving Appliances) (Second Amendment) Rules 1969, S.I. 1969, No. 409.

The Merchant Shipping (Fire Appliances) Rules 1965, S.I. 1965, No. 1106.

The Merchant Shipping (Musters) Rules 1965, S.I. 1965, No. 1113.

The Merchant Shipping (Signals of Distress) Rules 1965, S.I. 1965, No. 1550. Revoking: Signals of Distress Rules, S.I. 1954, No. 105.

The Merchant Shipping (Pilots Ladders) Rules 1965, S.I. 1965, No. 1046.

The Merchant Shipping (Pilots Ladders) (Amendment) Rules 1971, S.I. 1971, No. 724. Revoked by: The Merchant Shipping (Pilots Ladders) (Amendment No. 2) Rules 1972, S.I. 1972, No. 531.

N.B.—The Merchant Shipping (Life-Saving Appliances) Rules 1965.

COMMENTS.

In connection with the changeover in 1965 from the Merchant Shipping (Life-Saving Appliances) Rules 1958, to the 1965 Rules, the Secretary of State for Trade and Industry has now made the following general exemption for certain specified ships of Class VIII (*a*) from certain requirements of the 1965 Rules:

1. Any launch, lighter, dredger, barge, and hopper of Class VII (*a*), as defined in the Merchant Shipping (Life-Saving Appliances) Rules 1965 (hereinafter referred to as 'the 1965 Rules') being a ship, the keel of which was laid before the 26th May 1965, is hereby exempted from the requirements of Rule 14 of the 1965 Rules, subject to the following condition:

The ship shall comply with all the requirements of the Merchant Shipping (Life-Saving Appliances) Rules 1958, which would have been applicable to the ship, as a ship of Class IX under those Rules, if those Rules had not been revoked subject as follows:

(*a*) If the ship exceeds 100 feet in length and is engaged on a voyage which takes it substantial distances to sea, that is to say in excess of 10 miles from an adequate port of refuge, it shall carry life-rafts of sufficient aggregate capacity to accommodate at least twice the number of persons on board; and (*b*) Lifeboats and life-rafts carried by the ship shall be stowed as to be readily transferable to the water, but need not be stowed so as to be so transferable on either side of the ship.

2. This exemption shall come into operation on the 27th May 1973, and shall have effect in relation to any ship to which it respectively applies, until revoked either generally or in relation to that ship.

⚓ ⚓ ⚓ ⚓

428 It shall be the duty of the owner and master of every British ship to see that his ship is provided, in accordance with the rules for life-saving appliances, with such of those appliances as, having regard to the nature of the service on which the ship is employed, and the avoidance of undue encumbrance of the ship's deck, are best adapted for securing the safety of her crew and passengers.

Duties of owners and masters as to carrying life-saving appliances.

COMMENTS.

Application.

See comments to section 427.

Rules for Life-Saving Appliances.

Under section 427, rules may be made by the Minister of Transport. Consult also comment under that section.

⚓ ⚓ ⚓ ⚓

429 (1) For the purpose of preparing and advising on the rules for life-saving appliances, the Board of Trade may appoint a committee, the members of which shall be nominated by the Board in accordance with the Seventeenth Schedule to this Act.

Appointment of consultative committee for framing rules.

(2) A member of the committee shall hold office for two years from the date of his appointment, but shall be eligible for re-appointment.

(3) There shall be paid to the members of the committee, out of the Mercantile Marine Fund, such travelling and other allowances as the Board of Trade may fix.

(4) Her Majesty may, by Order in Council, alter the Seventeenth Schedule to this Act.

COMMENTS.

Rules for Life-Saving Appliances.

Consult comments to section 427.

Mercantile Marine Fund.

Consult Merchant Shipping (Mercantile Marine Fund) Act 1898, section 1, sub-section 1 (*b*) from which it will be seen that such payment is now out of moneys provided by Parliament.

Orders under sub-section 4.

To date, no orders have been made.

⚓ ⚓ ⚓ ⚓

Penalty for breach of rules.

430 (1) In the case of any ship—

(*a*) if the ship is required by the rules for life-saving appliances to be provided with such appliances and proceeds on any voyage or excursion without being so provided in accordance with the rules applicable to the ship; or

(*b*) if any of the appliances with which the ship is so provided are lost or rendered unfit for service in the course of the voyage or excursion through the wilful fault or negligence of the owner or master; or

(*c*) if the master wilfully neglects to replace or repair on the first opportunity any such appliances lost or injured in the course of the voyage or excursion; or

(*d*) if such appliances are not kept so as to be at all times fit and ready for use;

then the owner of the ship (if in fault) shall for each offence be liable to a fine not exceeding one hundred pounds, and the master of the ship (if in fault) shall for each offence be liable to a fine not exceeding fifty pounds.

(2) Nothing in the foregoing enactments with respect to life-saving appliances shall prevent any person from being liable under any other provision of this Act, or otherwise, to any other or higher fine or punishment than is provided by those enactments, provided that a person shall not be punished twice for the same offence.

(3) If the court before whom a person is charged with an offence punishable under those enactments thinks that proceedings ought to be taken against him for the offence under any other provision of this Act, or otherwise, the court may adjourn the case to enable such proceedings to be taken.

COMMENTS.

Amendment.

Merchant Shipping (Safety and Load Line Conventions) Act 1932, section 5, sub-section 2:

'Sub-section (1) of section 430 of the Principal Act (which imposes penalties for failure to comply with the rules for life-saving appliances) shall be amended by inserting after paragraph (*d*) thereof, the following paragraph:

(*e*) if any provision of the rules for life-saving appliances applicable to the ship is contravened, or not complied with.

Proceeds on Any Voyage.

A vessel which proceeded from the River Ouse at Kings Lynn to Lynn Roads, to lighten a vessel was held to be 'proceeding on a voyage or excursion' within the limits of this section. Genochio *v*. Steward 1907.

Life-Saving Rules.

Consult comments to section 427.

431 (1) A surveyor of ships may inspect any ship for the purpose of seeing that she is properly provided with life-saving appliances in conformity with this Act, and for the purpose of that inspection shall have all the powers of a Board of Trade inspector under this Act. Survey of ship with respect to life-saving appliances.

(2) If the said surveyor finds that the ship is not so provided, he shall give to the master or owner notice in writing, pointing out the deficiency, and also pointing out what in his opinion is requisite to remedy the same.

(3) Every notice so given shall be communicated in the manner directed by the Board of Trade to the chief officer of customs of any port at which the ship may seek to obtain a clearance or transire, and the ship shall be detained until a certificate under the hand of any such surveyor is produced to the effect that the ship is properly provided with life-saving appliances in conformity with this Act.

Substitution.

A new section, as a result of section 5, sub-section 3 of the Merchant Shipping (Safety and Load Line Conventions) Act 1932, is substituted, viz.:

431 (1) A surveyor of ships may inspect any ship for the purpose of seeing that the rules for life-saving appliances have been complied with in her case, and for the purpose of any such inspection shall have all the powers of a Ministry of Transport inspector under this Act.

(2) If the surveyor finds that the rules for life-saving appliances have not been complied with, he shall give written

notice to the owner or master, stating in what respect the said rules have not been complied with, and what, in his opinion, is required to rectify the matter.

COMMENTS.

Substitution.

A new section, as a result of section 5, sub-section 3 of the Merchant Shipping (Safety and Load Lines Conventions) Act 1932, is substituted, viz.:

431 (1) A Surveyor of Ships may inspect any ship for the purpose of seeing that the rules for the life-saving appliances have been complied with, in her case, and for the purpose of any such inspection shall have all the powers of a Ministry of Transport Inspector under this Act.

(2) If the Surveyor finds that the rules for life-saving appliances have not been complied with, he shall give written notice to the owner or master, stating in what respect the said rules have not been complied with, and what in his opinion, is required to rectify the matter.

(3) Every notice so given shall be communicated in manner directed by the Minister of Transport to the Chief Officer of Customs of any port at which the ship may seek to obtain a clearance or transire, and a clearance or transire shall not be granted to the ship, and the ship shall be detained until a certificate under the hand of a Surveyor of Ships is produced to the effect that the matter *has been* rectified.

The marginal note remains the same.

COMMENTS.

Detention of Ships.
See section 692.

Chief Officer of Customs.
See section 742 for definition.

Rules for Life-Saving Appliances.
Consult comments to section 427.

Powers of Inspection.
See sections 729, 730.

General Equipment

Adjustment of compasses and provision of hose.

432 (1) Every British sea-going steamship if employed to carry passengers, shall have her compasses properly adjusted from time to time; and every British sea-going steamship not used wholly as a tug shall be provided with a hose capable of being connected with the engines of the ship, and adapted for extinguishing fire in any part of the ship.

(2) If any such British sea-going steamship plies or goes to sea from any port in the United Kingdom and any requirement of this section is not complied with, then for each matter in which default is made, the owner (if in fault) shall be liable to a fine not exceeding one hundred pounds, and the master (if in fault) shall be liable to a fine not exceeding fifty pounds.

COMMENTS.

Sea-going Steamship.

See Salt Union *v.* Wood 1893, for meaning.

Equipment of Passenger Steamers.

See section 285.

It would appear that vessels not carrying passengers are not required to have their compasses adjusted, at least by statute.

433 A person shall not place an undue weight on the safety-valve of any steamship, and if he does so he shall, in addition to any other liability he may incur by so doing, be liable for each offence to a fine not exceeding one hundred pounds.

Placing undue weight on safety-valve.

COMMENTS.

Safety-valves of Passenger Steamers.

See section 272, sub-section (*d*).

Merchant Shipping Act 1894

Part V

Section 434

Signals of Distress.

This section was repealed, and re-enacted with modifications and extensions by the Merchant Shipping (Safety and Load Line Conventions) Act 1932, section 25, which in turn was repealed by the Merchant Shipping (Safety Convention) Act 1949, and re-enacted (with modifications) by section 21 of the same Act, i.e. Merchant Shipping (Safety Convention) Act 1949.

Merchant Shipping Act 1894

Part V

Section 435

Provisions of Signals of Distress.

This section repealed by Merchant Shipping (Safety Convention) Act 1949. The present details are contained in section 427 and by the rules made under that section q.v.

⚓ ⚓ ⚓ ⚓

Draught of Water and Load-Line

Ship's draught of water to be recorded.

436 (1) The Board of Trade may, in any case or class of cases in which they think it expedient to do so, direct any person appointed by them for the purpose, to record, in such manner and with such particulars as they direct, the draught of water of any sea-going ship, as shown on the scale of feet on her stem and stern-post, and the extent of her clear side in feet and inches, upon her leaving any dock, wharf, port, or harbour for the purpose of proceeding to sea, and the person so appointed shall thereupon keep that record, and shall forward a copy thereof to the Board of Trade.

(2) That record or copy, if produced out of the custody of the Board of Trade, shall be admissible in evidence in manner provided by this Act.

(3) The master of every British sea-going ship shall, upon her leaving any dock, wharf, port, or harbour for the purpose of proceeding to sea, record her draught of water and the extent of her clear side in the official log-book (if any) and shall produce the record to any chief officer of customs whenever required by him, and if he fails without reasonable cause to produce the record shall for each offence be liable to a fine not exceeding twenty pounds.

(4) The master of a sea-going ship shall, upon the request of any person appointed to record the ship's draught of water, permit that person to enter the ship and make such inspections and take such measurements as may be requisite for the purpose of the record; and if any master fails to do so, or impedes, or suffers anyone under his control to impede, any person so appointed in the execution of his duty, he shall for each offence be liable to a fine not exceeding five pounds.

(5) In this section the expression 'clear side' means the height from the water to the upper side of the plank of the deck from which the depth of hold as stated in the register is measured, and the measurement of the clear side is to be taken at the lowest part of the side.

Sub-section 3 above

Repealed by Merchant Shipping Act 1970

The Merchant Shipping Act 1970 (Commencement No. 1)

Order 1972 as from 1st January 1973

Sub-section 5 above was substituted by section 62 of the Merchant Shipping (Safety and Load Line Conventions) Act 1932, and now reads:

COMMENTS.

The words 'clear side' in sub-section 1 of this section was substituted by the word 'freeboard', Merchant Shipping (Safety and Load Line Conventions) Act 1932, section 62, sub-section 1.

Sub-section 5.

In this section the expression 'freeboard' means, in the case of any ship which is marked with a deck-line, the height from the water to the upper edge of the deck-line. And, in the case of any other ship the height amidships from the water to the upper edge of the deck from which the depth of hold as stated in the register is measured.

Sea-going Ship.

See Salt Union *v.* Wood 1893.

Ship.

See section 742.

Admissibility of Documents.

See section 695.

Declaration of Draught.

On request of pilot. *See* Pilotage Act 1913, section 31.

⚓ ⚓ ⚓ ⚓

Merchant Shipping Act 1894

Sections 437 to 445

Load Line Provisions.

Repealed by the Merchant Shipping (Safety and Load Line Conventions) Act 1932, section 67, sub-section 2 and Fourth Schedule, Part II.

Consult now Part II of the Merchant Shipping (Safety and Load Line Conventions) Act 1932.

The Orders in Council under the sections 444 and 445, now repealed, *see* section 67, sub-section 2 of the Merchant Shipping (Safety and Load Line Conventions) Act 1932 (Preservation of Order with Limited Effect).

⚓ ⚓ ⚓ ⚓

Dangerous Goods

Restrictions on carriage of dangerous goods.

446 (1) A person shall not send or attempt to send by any vessel, British or foreign, and a person not being the master or owner of the vessel, shall not carry or attempt to carry in any such vessel, any dangerous goods, without distinctly marking their nature on the outside of the package containing the same, and giving notice of the nature of those goods and of the name and address of the sender or carrier thereof to the master or owner of the vessel at or before the time of sending the same to be shipped or taking the same on board the vessel.

(2) If any person fails without reasonable cause to comply with this section he shall for each offence be liable to a fine not exceeding one hundred pounds, of if he shows that he was merely an agent in the shipment of any such goods as aforesaid, and was not aware and did not suspect and had no reason to suspect that the goods shipped by him were of a dangerous nature, then not exceeding ten pounds.

(3) For the purpose of this Part of this Act the expression 'dangerous goods' means aquafortis, vitriol, naphtha, benzine, gunpowder, lucifer matches, nitro-glycerine, petroleum, any explosives within the meaning of the Explosives Act 1875, and any other goods which are of a dangerous nature.

COMMENTS.

Dangerous Goods.

See sections 446–450, operation dealing with dangerous goods not affected by the Carriage of Goods by Sea Act 1971, q.v., also consult the Merchant Shipping (Safety Conventions) Act 1949, sections 23, 37.

Definition of, *see* sub-section 3 of this section. Consult also the Merchant Shipping (Safety Convention) Act 1949, section 23, sub-section 4 and the Merchant Shipping (Dangerous Goods) Rules 1952, No. 1977.

Petroleum.

For provisions as to loading and carrying of petroleum spirit, in harbours, *see* the Petroleum (Consolidation) Act 1928, Petroleum Spirit in Harbours Order 1939, S.R. & O. 1939, No. 927.

In L.N.W. Railway *v.* Farey 1920, it was held that a motor-car's tank containing petrol was a package containing dangerous goods, in sub-section 1 above.

Explosives.

Consult the Explosives Act 1875, section 34, also section 3. Also, Government Explosives in Harbours Order 1939, S.R. & O. 1939, No. 1181.

The Oil in Navigable Waters Act 1955 et seq.

Contains provisions regarding the discharge or escape of oil into navigable waters.

⚓ ⚓ ⚓ ⚓

447 A person shall not knowingly send or attempt to send by, or carry or attempt to carry in, any vessel, British or foreign, any dangerous goods under a false description, and shall not falsely describe the sender or carrier thereof, and if he acts in contravention of this section he shall for each offence be liable to a fine not exceeding five hundred pounds.

Penalty for misdescription of dangerous goods.

COMMENTS.

Dangerous Goods.

See section 446, sub-section 3, above.

⚓ ⚓ ⚓ ⚓

448 (1) The master or owner of any vessel, British or foreign, may refuse to take on board any package or parcel which he suspects to contain any dangerous goods, and may require it to be opened to ascertain the fact.

Power to deal with goods suspected of being dangerous.

(2) Where any dangerous goods, or any goods, which, in the judgement of the master or owner of the vessel, are dangerous goods, have been sent or brought aboard any vessel, British or foreign, without being marked as aforesaid, or without such notice having been given as aforesaid, the master or owner of the vessel may cause those goods to be thrown overboard, together with any package or receptacle

in which they are contained, and neither the master nor the owner of the vessel shall be subject to any liability, civil or criminal, in any court for so throwing the goods overboard.

COMMENTS.

See notes to section 446.

Rights and Immunities, Carriage of Dangerous Goods.

When goods are carried under contracts which come under the Provisions of the Carriage of Goods by Sea Act 1971, the Master has additional powers conferred on him by Part IV, Rule 6, in the Schedule to the Act, as follows:

'Goods of an inflammable, explosive, or dangerous nature to the shipment whereof the carrier, master or agent of the carrier has not consented with knowledge of their nature or character, may at any time before discharge be landed at any place, or destroyed or rendered innocuous by the carrier, without compensation, and the shipper of such goods shall be liable for all damages and expenses directly or indirectly arising out of, or resulting from, such shipment.

If any goods shipped with such knowledge and consent shall become a danger to the ship or cargo, they may be in like manner, landed at any place, or destroyed, or rendered innocuous by the carrier without liability, on the part of the carrier, except to general average, if any.

Forfeiture of dangerous goods improperly sent or carried.

449 (1) Where any dangerous goods have been sent or carried, or attempted to be sent or carried, on board any vessel, British or foreign, without being marked as aforesaid, or without such notice having been given as aforesaid, or under a false description, or with a false description of the sender or carrier thereof, any court having Admiralty jurisdiction may declare those goods and any package or receptacle in which they are contained, to be, and they shall thereupon be, forfeited, and when forfeited shall be disposed of as the court direct.

(2) The court shall have, and may exercise, the aforesaid powers of forfeiture and disposal notwithstanding that the owner of the goods has not committed any offence under the provisions of this Act relating to dangerous goods, and is not before the court, and has not notice of the proceedings, and notwithstanding that there is no evidence to show to whom the goods belong; nevertheless the court may, in their discretion, require such notice as they may direct to be given to the owner or shipper of the goods before they are forfeited.

COMMENTS.

Court Having Admiralty Jurisdiction.

For the jurisdiction of the High Court, *see* Administration of Justice Act 1956, section 1, sub-section 1. It is doubtful whether a claim for forfeiture under this section can be brought in a county court. *See* County Courts Act 1959, section 56.

Dangerous Goods.

Meaning of section 446, sub-section 3.

Marked as Aforesaid.

See section 446, section 1.

Notice as Aforesaid.

See section 446, section 1.

⚓ ⚓ ⚓ ⚓

Saving for other enactments relating to dangerous goods.

450 The provisions of this Part of this Act relating to the carriage of dangerous goods shall be deemed to be in addition to and not in substitution for, or in restraint of, any other enactment for the like object, so nevertheless that nothing in the said provisions shall be deemed to authorise any person to be sued or prosecuted twice in the same matter.

COMMENTS.

Consult generally section 446 and notes thereto regarding other enactments respecting dangerous goods.

⚓ ⚓ ⚓ ⚓

Section 451 repealed. *See* below

Loading of Deck Cargo.

Section 451, containing provisions regarding the loading of timber, was repealed by the Merchant Shipping Act 1906, section 85, Schedule II, when the subject-matter of the repealed section 451 was dealt with by the Merchant Shipping Act 1906, section 10. This was then in turn repealed by the Merchant Shipping (Safety and Load Line Conventions) Act 1932, Schedule IV, Part II, which has since been repealed as a result of the Merchant Shipping (Load-Lines) Act 1967, which now, by section 24, provides Regulations prescribing the requirements to be complied with in respect of cargo carried in uncovered space on the deck of a ship.

The regulations referred to are: The Merchant Shipping (Load Lines) (Deck Cargo) Regulations 1968, S.I. 1968, No. 1089, operative from the 29th July 1968.

⚓ ⚓ ⚓ ⚓

Merchant Shipping Acts

Sections 452, 453, 454, 455 and 456

These sections, which dealt with the carriage of grain, were repealed by Merchant Shipping (Safety Convention) Act 1949, their provisions being re-enacted (with modifications) by section 24 of that Act.

The rules at present in force under this section are the Merchant Shipping (Grain) Rules 1965, operative from 26th May 1965.

⚓ ⚓ ⚓ ⚓

Unseaworthy Ships

Sending unseaworthy ship to sea a misdemeanor.

457 (1) If any person sends or attempts to send, or is party to sending or attempting to send, a British ship to sea in such an unseaworthy state that the life of any person is likely to be thereby endangered, he shall in respect of each offence be guilty of a misdemeanor, unless he proves either that he used all reasonable means to insure her being sent to sea in a seaworthy state, or that her going to sea in such an unseaworthy state was, under the circumstances, reasonable and justifiable, and for the purpose of giving that proof he may give evidence in the same manner as any other witness.

(2) If the master of a British ship knowingly takes the same to sea in such an unseaworthy state that the life of any person is likely to be thereby endangered, he shall in respect of each offence be guilty of a misdemeanor, unless he proves that her going to sea in such an unseaworthy state was, under the circumstances, reasonable and justifiable, and for the purpose of giving such proof he may give evidence in the same manner as any other witness.

(3) A prosecution under this section shall not, except in Scotland, be instituted otherwise than by, or with the consent of, the Board of Trade, or of the governor of the British possession in which the prosecution takes place.

(4) A misdemeanor under this section shall not be punishable upon summary conviction.

(5) This section shall not apply to any ship employed exclusively in trading or going from place to place in any river or inland water of which the whole or part is in any British possession.

COMMENTS.

Unseaworthy.

Under the Marine Insurance Act 1906, a ship is deemed to be seaworthy when she is reasonably fit in all respects to encounter the ordinary perils of the seas of the adventure insured.

Warranty of Seaworthiness.

See the *Stranna* 1938.

Compare the Merchant Shipping Act 1921, section 2, as to unsafe lighters, barges, and like vessels.

Misdemeanour.

As to summary procedure, *see* section 680.

Evidences.

For competency of witnesses in criminal cases, *see and compare* Criminal Evidence Act 1898.

⚓ ⚓ ⚓ ⚓

458 (1) In every contract of service, express or implied, between the owner of a ship and the master or any seaman thereof, and in every instrument of apprenticeship whereby any person is bound to serve as an apprentice on board any ship, there shall be implied, notwithstanding any agreement to the contrary, an obligation on the owner of the ship, that the owner of the ship, and the master, and every agent charged with the loading of the ship, or the preparing of the ship for sea, or the sending of the ship to sea, shall use all reasonable means to insure the seaworthiness of the ship for the voyage at the time when the voyage commences, and to keep her in a seaworthy condition for the voyage during the voyage.

Obligation of shipowner to crew with respect to use of reasonable efforts to secure seaworthiness.

(2) Nothing in this section—

(*a*) shall subject the owner of a ship to any liability by reason of the ship being sent to sea in an unseaworthy state where, owing to special circumstances, the sending of the ship to sea in such a state was reasonable and justifiable; or

(*b*) shall apply to any ship employed exclusively in trading or going from place to place in any river or inland water of which the whole or part is in any British possession.

The words underlined on previous page are repealed by Merchant Shipping Act 1970.

The Merchant Shipping Act 1970 (Commencement No. 1) Order 1972 as from 1st January 1973

COMMENTS.

Contract of Services.

Consult the Merchant Shipping Act 1970, sections 1 to 11 and generally.

Seaman's Right to Refuse to Proceed to Sea.

See section 463.

Liability.

The decision arising in Waddle *v.* Wallsend Shipping Co. Ltd. 1952 appears to throw doubt upon the validity of this section, it being held, *inter alia*, that this section 'could now be treated as obsolete', invoking the Law Reform (Personal Injuries) Act 1948, per Devlin, J.

It is, however, considered by many that this section still provides an effective statutory provision, which has the effect of stating: (*a*), the extent of the owner's obligation as to seaworthiness and (*b*), preventing the owner from contracting out of that obligation.

In Cunningham *v.* Frontier S.S. Co. 1906, it was held that neglect to stow a grain cargo so as to prevent it from shifting, constituted a breach of the obligation created by this section.

⚓ ⚓ ⚓ ⚓

Power to detain unsafe ships, and procedure for detention.

459 (1) Where a British ship, being in any port in the United Kingdom, is an unsafe ship, that is to say, is by reason of the defective condition of her hull, equipments, or machinery, or by reason of overloading or improper loading, unfit to proceed to sea without serious danger to human life, having regard to the nature of the service for which she is intended, such ship may be provisionally detained for the purpose of being surveyed, and either finally detained or released as follows:—

(*a*) The Board of Trade, if they have reason to believe, on complaint or otherwise, that a British ship is unsafe, may order the ship to be provisionally detained as an unsafe ship for the purpose of being surveyed.

(*b*) When a ship has been provisionally detained there shall be forthwith served on the master of the ship a written statement of the grounds of her detention, and the Board of Trade may, if they think fit, appoint some competent person or persons to survey the ship and report thereon to the Board.

(*c*) The Board of Trade on receiving the report may either order the ship to be released or, if in their opinion the ship is unsafe, may order her to be finally detained, either absolutely, or until the performance of such conditions with respect to the execution of repairs or alterations, or the unloading or re-loading of cargo, as the Board think necessary for the protection of human life, and the Board may vary or add to any such order.

(*d*) Before the order for final detention is made a copy of the report shall be served upon the master of the ship, and within seven days after that service the owner or master of the ship may appeal to the court of survey for the port or district where the ship is detained in manner directed by the rules of that court.

(*e*) Where a ship has been provisionally detained, the owner or master of the ship, at any time before the person appointed under this section to survey the ship makes that survey, may require that he shall be accompanied by such person as the owner or master may select out of the list of assessors for the court of survey, and in that case if the surveyor and assessor agree, the Board of Trade shall cause the ship to be detained or released accordingly, but if they differ, the Board of Trade may act as if the requisition had not been made, and the owner and master shall have the like appeal touching the report of the surveyor as is before provided by this section.

(*f*) Where a ship has been provisionally detained, the Board of Trade may at any time, if they think it expedient, refer the matter to the court of survey for the port or district where the whip is detained.

(*g*) The Board of Trade may at any time, if satisfied that a ship detained under this section is not unsafe, order her to be released either upon or without any conditions.

(2) Any person appointed by the Board of Trade for the purpose (in this Act referred to as a detaining officer) shall have the same power as the Board have under this section of ordering the provisional detention of a ship for the purpose

of being surveyed, and of appointing a person or persons to survey her; and if he thinks that a ship so detained by him is not unsafe may order her to be released.

(3) A detaining officer shall forthwith report to the Board of Trade any order made by him for the detention or release of a ship.

(4) An order for the detention of a ship, provisional or final, and an order varying the same, shall be served as soon as may be on the master of the ship.

(5) A ship detained under this section shall not be released by reason of her British register being subsequently closed.

(6) The Board of Trade may with the consent of the Treasury appoint fit persons to act as detaining officers under this section, and may remove any such officer; and a detaining officer shall be paid such salary or remuneration (if any) out of money provided by Parliament as the Treasury direct, and shall for the purpose of his duties have all the powers of a Board of Trade Inspector under this Act.

(7) A detaining officer and a person authorised to survey a ship under this section shall for that purpose have the same power as a person appointed by a court of survey to survey a ship, and the provisions of this Act with respect to the person so appointed shall apply accordingly.

Amendment.

The following words were added by the Merchant Shipping Act 1897, section 1, sub-section 1: 'Section four hundred and fifty-nine of the Merchant Shipping Act 1894 (which gives power to detain unsafe ships) shall apply in the case of undermanning, and accordingly that section shall be construed as if the words 'or by reason of undermanning' were inserted therein after the word 'machinery' and as if the words 'or for ascertaining the sufficiency of her crew' were inserted after the word 'surveyed' and as if the words 'or the manning of the ship' were inserted therein after the words 'reloading of cargo' and the words 'exercisable under or for the purposes of that section shall include power to muster the crew.'

COMMENTS.

Safety Convention Passenger Steamer.

Miscellaneous Privileges.

See section 16 of the Merchant Shipping (Safety Convention) Act 1949 for the present provisions relating to miscellaneous privileges of ships holding Convention Certificates.

General.

Section 43 of the Merchant Shipping (Safety and Load Line Conventions) Act 1932, lays down that a British Load Line ship registered in the U.K., which does not comply with the 'conditions of assignment' of the Load Line Rules, shall be deemed to be unsafe in regard to section 459. The conditions of assignment are contained in the Merchant Shipping (Load Line) Rules 1968, operative from 21st July 1968.

Consult section 53, sub-section 5 of the Merchant Shipping (Safety and Load Line Conventions) Act 1932 as to British ships not registered in the United Kingdom, which have been materially altered so as to invalidate a Load Line Convention Certificate.

Consult section 56 of the Merchant Shipping (Safety and Load Line Conventions) Act 1932 as to a Load Line Convention Ship, not registered in the United Kingdom, or a foreign ship which does not comply with the conditions of assignment, for which *see* the Merchant Shipping (Load Line) Rules 1968.

See also, the Merchant Shipping (Safety Convention) Act 1949, section 23, sub-section 3; section 24, sub-sections 1 and 2, in regard to circumstances in which certain ships are deemed to be unsafe for the purposes of Part V (Safety) of the Merchant Shipping Act 1894, dealing with dangerous goods, and precautions in connection with the carriage of grain.

The Rules relating to the carriage of Grain are now contained in S.I. 1965, No. 1062, The Merchant Shipping (Grain) Rules 1965, which have superseded the Merchant Shipping (Grain) Rules 1952.

Amendment of Section.

The powers exercisable under, or for the purposes of, this section include a power to muster the crew.

Detention of Ship.

Application to foreign ships of provisions as to detention, *see* section 462.

Security for Costs.

See section 461.

⚓ ⚓ ⚓ ⚓

460 (1) If it appears that there was not reasonable and probable cause, by reason of the condition of the ship or the Act or default of the owner, for the provisional detention of a ship under this Part of this Act as an unsafe ship, the Board of Trade shall be liable to pay to the owner of the ship his costs of and incidental to the detention and survey of the ship, and also compensation for any loss or damage sustained by him by reason of the detention or survey. Liability for costs and damages.

(2) If a ship is finally detained under this Act, or if it appears that a ship provisionally detained was, at the time of that detention, an unsafe ship within the meaning of this Part of this Act, the owner of the ship shall be liable to pay to the Board of Trade their costs of and incidental to the detention and survey of the ship, and those costs shall, without prejudice to any other remedy.

(3) For the purpose of this section the costs of and incidental to any proceeding before a court of survey, and a reasonable amount in respect of the remuneration of the surveyor or officer of the Board of Trade, shall be part of the costs of the detention and survey of the ship, and any dispute as to the amount of those costs may be referred to one of the officers following, namely, in England or Ireland, to one of the masters or registrars of the High Court, and in Scotland to the Auditor of the Court of Session, and the officer shall, on request by the Board of Trade, ascertain and certifiy the proper amount of those costs.

(4) An action for any costs or compensation payable by the Board of Trade under this section may be brought against the Secretary of that Board by his official title as if he were a corporation sole, and if the cause of action arises in Ireland, and the action is brought in the High Court, that Court may order that the summons or writ may be served on the Crown and Treasury Solicitor for Ireland in such manner and on such terms respecting extension of time and otherwise as the Court thinks fit, and that that service shall be sufficient service of the summons or writ upon the Secretary of the Board of Trade.

Repeal.

Sub-section 4 above repealed by the Crown Proceedings Act 1947, section 39, sub-section 1 and Second Schedule.

COMMENTS.

Reasonable and Probable Cause.

For cases relating to the reasonable cause for detention, *see* Lewis *v.* Gray 1876; Thomas *v.* Farrer 1882.

Unreasonable Detention.

For the right of the Crown to change the place of the trial in an action for unreasonable detention, *see* Dixon *v.* Farrer 1886.

Compensation for Loss or Damage.

General damages in respect of injury to a shipowner's reputation, by reason of the detention of their ship, are not recoverable under this head. Dixon *v.* Calcraft 1802.

Cost of Detaining Ships.

See Merchant Shipping (Safety and Load Line Conventions) Act 1932; also Merchant Shipping (Safety Convention) Act 1949, section 35, sub-section 2.

Salvage.

It is presumed that sub-section 2 above referred to procedure only, in which regard consult section 547, and does not confer the maritime lien which a proper salvor would obtain.

Jurisdiction (High Court).

The jurisdiction in England under this Act was assigned by Rule 1 of the Rules of the Supreme Court (Merchant Shipping) 1894, to the Probate, Divorce, and Admiralty Division.

⚓ ⚓ ⚓ ⚓

Power to require from complainant security for costs.

461 (1) Where a complaint is made to the Board of Trade or a detaining officer that a British ship is unsafe, the Board or officer may, if they or he think fit, require the complainant to give security to the satisfaction of the Board for the costs and compensation which he may become liable to pay as hereinafter mentioned.

(2) Provided that such security shall not be required where the complaint is made by one-fourth, being not less than three, of the seamen belonging to the ship, and is not in the opinion of the Board or officer frivolous or vexatious, and the Board or officer shall, if the complaint is made in sufficient time before the sailing of the ship, take proper steps for ascertaining whether the ship ought to be detained.

(3) Where a ship is detained in consequence of any complaint, and the circumstances are such that the Board of Trade are liable under this Act to pay to the owner of the ship any costs or compensation, the complainant shall be liable to pay to the Board of Trade all such costs and compensation as the Board incur or are liable to pay in respect of the detention and survey of the ship.

COMMENTS.

Complaint by Seamen.

For survey of ships alleged by seamen to be unseaworthy, *see* section 463.

Power to Detain.

For power to detain unsafe ships and procedure for detention, *see* section 459.

⚓ ⚓ ⚓ ⚓

Application to foreign ships of provisions as to detention.

462 Where a foreign ship has taken on board all or any part of her cargo at a port in the United Kingdom, and is whilst at that port unsafe by reason of overloading or improper loading, the provisions of this Part of this Act with respect to the detention of ships shall apply to that foreign ship as if she were a British ship, with the following modifications:—

(i) A copy of the order for the provisional detention of the ship shall be forthwith served on the consular officer for the country to which the ship belongs at or nearest to the said port;

(ii) Where a ship has been provisionally detained, the consular officer, on the request of the owner or master of the ship, may require that the person appointed by the Board of Trade to survey the ship shall be accompanied by such person as the consular officer may select, and in that case, if the surveyor and that person agree, the Board of Trade shall cause the ship to be detained or released accordingly, but if they differ, the Board of Trade may act as if the requisition had not been made, and the owner and master shall have the like appeal to a court of survey touching the report of the surveyor as is hereinbefore provided in the case of a British ship; and

(iii) Where the owner or master of the ship appeals to the court of survey, the consular officer, on his request may appoint a competent person to be assessor in the case in lieu of the assessor who, if the ship were a British ship, would be appointed otherwise than by the Board of Trade.

Repeal.

The words underlined in this section were repealed by the Merchant Shipping Act 1906, section 85, Second Schedule.

Amendment.

After the word 'unsafe', the following group of words was added, by the Merchant Shipping Act 1906, section 2, sub-section 1: 'by reason of the defective condition of her hull, equipments, or machinery, or'.

After the words 'or improper loading' by the Merchant Shipping Act 1897, section 1, sub-section 2, 'or by reason of undermanning'.

COMMENTS.

Applications of Section.

This section applies with respect to any foreign ships being at any port in the United Kingdom, whether they take on board any cargo or not. Merchant Shipping Act 1906, section 2, sub-section 2.

See also Merchant Shipping Act 1906, section 6, where it is enacted that this provision as to foreign ships does not apply to ships not bound to a port in the U.K., putting in under stress of weather.

Provisions Respecting the Detention of Ships.

Consult section 459 and comments thereto.

Enforcement of Detention, etc.

The provisions for the enforcement of detention are contained in section 692. Where a foreign ship was detained and the copy of the Order in Council, under section 734, only referred to section 459, having been sent by registered post to the Consul, it was held that the notice was sufficient, and also that the Consul had been properly served within the meaning of this section. Larsen *v.* Hart 1900.

463 (1) Whenever in any proceeding against any seaman or apprentice belonging to any ship for the offence of desertion, or absence without leave or for otherwise being absent from his ship without leave, it is alleged by one-fourth, or if their number exceeds twenty by not less than five, of the seamen belonging to the ship, that the ship is by reason of unseaworthiness, overloading, improper loading, defective equipment, or for any other reason, not in a fit condition to proceed to sea, or that the accommodation in the ship is insufficient, the court having cognizance of the case shall take such means as may be in their power to satisfy themselves concerning the truth or untruth of the allegation, and shall for that purpose receive the evidence of the persons making the same, and may summon any other witnesses whose evidence they may think it desirable to hear, and shall, if satisfied that the allegation is groundless, adjudicate in the case, but if not so satisfied shall before adjudication cause the ship to be surveyed.

Survey of ships alleged by seamen to be unseaworthy.

(2) A seaman or apprentice charged with desertion, or with quitting his ship without leave, shall not have any right to apply for a survey under this section unless he has before quitting his ship complained to the master of the circumstances so alleged in justification.

(3) For the purposes of this section the court shall require any surveyor of ships appointed under this Act, or any person appointed for the purpose by the Board of Trade, or, if such a surveyor or person cannot be obtained without unreasonable

expense or delay, or is not, in the opinion of the court, competent to deal with the special circumstances of the case, then any other impartial surveyor appointed by the court, and having no interest in the ship, her freight, or cargo, to survey the ship, and to answer any question concerning her which the court think fit to put.

(4) Such surveyor or other person shall survey the ship, and make his written report to the court, including an answer to every question put to him by the court, and the court shall cause the report to be communicated to the parties, and, unless the opinions expressed in the report are proved to the satisfaction of the court to be erroneous, shall determine the questions before them in accordance with those opinions.

(5) Any person making a survey under this section shall for the purposes thereof have all the powers of a Board of Trade inspector under this Act.

(6) The costs (if any) of the survey shall be determined by the Board of Trade according to a scale of fees to be fixed by them, and shall be paid in the first instance out of the Mercantile Marine Fund.

(7) If it is proved that the ship is in a fit condition to proceed to sea, or that the accommodation is sufficient, as the case may be, the costs of the survey shall be paid by the person upon whose demand or in consequence of whose allegation the survey was made, and may be deducted by the master or owner out of the wages due or to become due to that person, and shall be paid over to the Board of Trade.

(8) If it is proved that the ship is not in a fit condition to proceed to sea, or that the accommodation is insufficient, as the case may be, the master or owner of the ship shall pay the costs of the survey to the Board of Trade, and shall be liable to pay to the seaman or apprentice, who has been detained in consequence of the said proceeding before the court under this section, such compensation for his detention as the court may award.

The words 'or apprentice', wherever they occur repealed by Merchant Shipping Act 1970. Merchant Shipping Act (Commencement No. 1) Order 1972. As from 1st January 1973.

COMMENTS.

Powers of Naval Courts.

See section 483, sub-section 1 (*j*) for equivalent powers of naval courts, where a survey is ordered of any ship which is the subject of investigation.

Accommodation.

See section 210 as to the accommodation to be provided for seamen in British ships. Consult also Merchant Shipping Act 1948, and in respect of fishing-boats, the Merchant Shipping Act 1950.

Mercantile Marine Fund.

The cost referred to are now payable out of moneys provided by Parliament as per Merchant Shipping (Mercantile Marine Fund) Act 1898, section 1, sub-section 1(*b*) q.v.

M.S.A. 1894

PART VI

SPECIAL SHIPPING ENQUIRIES AND COURTS

PART VI

SPECIAL SHIPPING ENQUIRIES AND COURTS

Inquiries and Investigations as to Shipping Casualties

464 For the purpose of inquiries and investigations under this Part of this Act a shipping casualty shall be deemed to occur— Shipping casualties.

(1) When or on near the coasts of the United Kingdom any ship is lost, abandoned, or materially damaged;

(2) When on or near the coasts of the United Kingdom any ship has been stranded or damaged, and any witness is found in the United Kingdom;

(3) When on or near the coasts of the United Kingdom any ship causes loss or material damage to any other ship;

(4) When any loss of life ensues by reason of any casualty happening to or on board any ship on or near the coasts of the United Kingdom;

(5) When in any place any such loss, abandonment, material damage, or casualty as above mentioned occurs, and any witness is found in the United Kingdom;

(6) When in any place any British ship is stranded or damaged, and any witness is found in the United Kingdom;

(7) When any British ship is lost or is supposed to have been lost, and any evidence is obtainable in the United Kingdom as to the circumstances under which she proceeded to sea or was last heard of.

COMMENTS.

On or Near the Coasts of the United Kingdom.

It would appear that this means within the territorial limit. *See* the *Fulham* 1898.

Ship.

For definition *see* section 742.

For ships to which the provisions as to naval courts apply, *see* section 486.

For enquiry in case of loss of life from a fishing-vessel's boat, *see* section 468.

⚓ ⚓ ⚓ ⚓

Preliminary inquiry into shipping casualties.

465 (1) Where a shipping casualty has occurred a preliminary inquiry may be held respecting the casualty by the following persons; namely—

(*a*) Where the shipping casualty occurs on or near the coasts of the United Kingdom, by the inspecting officer of the coastguard or chief officer of customs residing at or near the place at which the casualty occurs; or

(*b*) Where the shipping casualty occurs elsewhere, by the inspecting officer of the coastguard or chief officer of customs residing at or near any place at which the witnesses with respect to the casualty arrive or are found or can be conveniently examined; or

(*c*) In any case by any person appointed for the purpose by the Board of Trade.

(2) For the purpose of any such inquiry the person holding the same shall have the powers of a Board of Trade inspector under this Act.

COMMENTS.

Shipping Casualty.

Explanation of, consult section 464.

On or Near the Coasts of the United Kingdom.

See comments to section 464.

Chief Officer of Customs.

For definition, *see* section 742.

Enquiry.

The result of this enquiry is usually referred to as 'the deposition' of the person examined. Under the Merchant Shipping Act 1854, section 448 a deposition made by a master was held inadmissable as evidence on behalf of his owners, in an action brought against the ship for damages as a result of collision. The master had died before the trial. The *Henry Coxon* 1878.

It is submitted, however, that under the Evidence Act 1938, such evidence, subject to certain conditions, would now be admisable.

⚓ ⚓ ⚓ ⚓

Formal investigation of shipping casualties.

466 (1) A person authorised as aforesaid to make a preliminary inquiry shall in any case where it appears to him requisite or expedient (whether upon a preliminary inquiry or without holding such an inquiry) that a formal investigation should be held, and in any case where the Board of Trade so directs, apply to a court of summary jurisdiction to hold a formal investigation, and that court shall thereupon hold the formal investigation.

(2) A wreck commissioner appointed under this Act shall at the request of the Board of Trade hold any formal investigation into a shipping casualty under this section, and any reference to the court holding an investigation under this section includes a wreck commissioner holding such an investigation.

(3) The court holding any such formal investigation shall hold the same with the assistance of one or more assessors of nautical, engineering, or other special skill or knowledge, to be appointed out of a list of persons for the time being approved for the purpose by a Secretary of State in such manner and according to such regulations as may be prescribed by rules made under this Part of this Act with regard thereto.

(4) Where a formal investigation involves or appears likely to involve any question as to the cancelling or suspension of the certificate of a master, mate, or engineer, the court shall hold the investigation with the assistance of not less than two assessors having experience in the merchant service.

(5) It shall be the duty of the person who has applied to a court to hold a formal investigation to superintend the management of the case, and to render such assistance to the court as is in his power.

(6) The court, after hearing the case, shall make a report to the Board of Trade containing a full statement of the case and of the opinion of the court thereon, accompanied by such report of, or extracts from, the evidence, and such observations as the court think fit.

(7) Each assessor shall either sign the report or state in writing to the Board of Trade his dissent therefrom and the reasons for that dissent.

(8) The court may make such order as the court think fit respecting the costs of the investigation, or any part thereof, and such order shall be enforced by the court as an order for costs under the Summary Jurisdiction Acts.

(9) The Board of Trade may, if in any case they think fit so to do, pay the costs of any such formal investigation.

(10) For the purposes of this section the court holding a formal investigation shall have all the powers of a court of summary jurisdiction when acting as a court in exercise of their ordinary jurisdiction.

(11) Every formal investigation into a shipping casualty shall be conducted in such manner that if a charge is made against any person, that person shall have an opportunity of making a defence.

(12) Formal investigations into shipping casualties under this section shall be held in some town hall, assize or county court, or public building, or in some other suitable place to be determined according to rules made under this Part of this Act with regard thereto and, unless no other suitable place is in the opinion of the Board of Trade available, shall not be held in a court ordinarily used as a police court, and all enactments relating to the court shall for the purposes of the investigation have effect as if the place at which the court is held were a place appointed for the exercise of the ordinary jurisdiction of the court.

(13) Where an investigation is to be held in Scotland, the Board of Trade may remit the same to the Lord Advocate to be prosecuted in such manner as he may direct.

COMMENTS.

Person Authorised to Make Preliminary Enquiry.

See section 465.

Shipping Casualty.

For cases of, consult section 464.

Court of Summary Jurisdiction.

Now the Magistrates Courts Act 1952, in respect to England and Wales. The Court may proceed with an enquiry into the conduct of a master/officer, although the Minister makes no charge against him. *Ex Parte* Minto 1877.

Assessors.

List of, *see* section 467.

Certificate of Master, etc.

For power to cancel or suspend certificates, *see* section 470.

Rules Under This Part of This Act.

See Shipping Casualties Rules 1923, S.R. & O. 1923, No. 752, made under section 479.

Application of Sub-section II.

Consult the *Chelston* 1920; Nelson Steam Navigation Co. Ltd. *v.* Board of Trade 1931; and the *Princess Victoria* 1953. In this case it was held that the requirements of this sub-section were sufficiently complied with, if the person concerned, although not a party to the proceedings, and not named in any question put to the court, knew that his conduct was in issue and was aware of his rights.

The *Seistan* 1959. In this case an assessor, in a rider added to the findings of the court, criticised the conduct of an engineer, although no charge had been made against him, and he had not given evidence.

467 (1) The list of persons approved as assessors for the purpose of formal investigations into shipping casualties shall be in force for three years only, but persons whose names are on any such list may be approved for any subsequent list. List of assessors.

(2) The Secretary of State may at any time add or withdraw the name of any person to or from the list.

(3) The list of assessors in force at the passing of this Act shall, subject as aforesaid, continue in force till the end of the year one thousand eight hundred and ninety-five.

COMMENTS.

Consult section 466, sub-section 3, as to presence of assessors on a court holding a formal investigation. Also, Shipping Casualties Rules 1923.

468 When any loss of life arises by reason of any casualty happening to or on board any boat belonging to a fishing-vessel, the Board of Trade may, if they think fit, cause an inquiry to be made or a formal investigation to be held as in the case of a shipping casualty, and the provisions of this Act relating thereto shall apply accordingly. Inquiry in case of loss of life from fishing vessel's boat.

COMMENTS.

As to loss of life in fishing-boat casualties, *see* sections 385, 386.

Power as to Certificates of Officers, &c.

469 The Board of Trade may suspend or cancel the certificate of any master, mate, or engineer if it is shown that he has been convicted of any offence. Power of Board of Trade as to certificate.

COMMENTS.

Board of Trade *v.* Leith Local Marine Board 1896. In this case it was held that the words 'any offence' meant any 'criminal' offence and did not include an offence of, say, drunkenness, or even incompetency, for which a certificate could be cancelled by the court or tribunal conducting an enquiry into such a case. Also, it was held that the Board of Trade had no power to deal with a certificate except when the holder of the certificate had been convicted of a criminal offence.

For officers who must hold certificates of competency, *see* sections 92–96.

For delivery of certificates cancelled or suspended, *see* section 473.

For power to restore certificate *see* section 474.

⚓ ⚓ ⚓ ⚓

Power of court of investigation or inquiry as to certificates.

470 (1) The certificate of a master, mate, or engineer may be cancelled or suspended—

(*a*) by a court holding a formal investigation into a shipping casualty under this Part of this Act, or by a naval court constituted under this Act, if the court find that the loss or abandonment of, or serious damage to, any ship, or loss of life, has been caused by his wrongful act or default, provided that, if the court holding a formal investigation is a court of summary jurisdiction, that court shall not cancel or suspend a certificate unless one at least of the assessors concurs in the finding of the court:

(*b*) by a court holding an inquiry under this Part of this Act into the conduct of a master, mate, or engineer, if they find that he is incompetent, or has been guilty of any gross act of misconduct, drunkenness, or tyranny, or that in a case of collision he has failed to render such assistance or give such information as is required under the Fifth Part of this Act:

(*c*) by any naval or other court where under the powers given by this Part of this Act the holder of the certificate is superseded or removed by that court.

(2) Where any case before any such court as aforesaid involves a question as to the cancelling or suspending of a certificate, that court shall, at the conclusion of the case or as soon afterwards as possible, state in open court the decision to which they have come with respect to the cancelling or suspending thereof.

(3) The court shall in all cases send a full report on the case with the evidence to the Board of Trade, and shall also, if they determine to cancel or suspend any certificate, send the certificate cancelled or suspended to the Board of Trade with their report.

(4) A certificate shall not be cancelled or suspended by a court under this section, unless a copy of the report, or a statement of the case on which the investigation or inquiry has been ordered, has been furnished before the commencement of the investigation or inquiry to the holder of the certificate.

COMMENTS.

Cancelling or Suspending Certificate.

In the *Kestrel* 1881, it was held that it was not necessary for the court, in stating its decision, to give the reasons, although it is usual so to do. Consequently, it may in its report state reasons not given at the time of the decision.

In the *Corchester* 1957, it was held that the court has not the power to *recommend* that a certificate be cancelled or suspended, and that there is no machinery for any authority to act on any recommendation.

In the *Princess Victoria* 1953, the court criticised the designated manager, even though he was not a party, it being held that his conduct had contributed to the casualty.

The rights of appeal are contained in the Merchant Shipping Act 1906, section 66.

See the *Golden Sea* 1882, where a master's certificate was suspended where the loss was due to his taking improper ballast.

Wrongful Act or Default.

For necessity of proof of 'wrongful act or default', *see* the *Arizona* 1880, in which the master's certificate was restored on appeal because there was no evidence to connect the casualty with his alleged default.

Also consult the *Corchester* 1957, where it was held that there must be specific findings (i) that the officer was guilty of a specific wrongful act or default, and also that the casualty was caused or contributed to thereby.

In *Ex Parte* Story 1878 it was held that there was no power to suspend the master's certificate in the event of mere stranding, without material damage to the ship or loss of life.

In the *Princess Victoria* 1953, the words 'wrongful act or default' were considered, and were interpreted as 'a breach of legal duty of any degree which causes or contributes to the casualty'.

An error of judgement at a moment of difficulty or danger is excluded.

See the *Famenotl* 1882; Watson *v.* Board of Trade 1884. But in Brown *v.* Board of Trade 1890 it was held that these words: 'wrongful act or default' included such conduct arising from a surrender of the judgement to the influence of unreasonable panic.

Burden of Proof Required.

There does not appear to be any decision giving any clear indication of what 'burden of proof' is required. *See* the *Arizona* 1880 (master's certificate restored on appeal) and compare the judgement in the *Corchester* 1957, where it was held that proper action on the part of the officer concerned would *in all probability* have prevented the mistake of another officer.

Re-hearing of an Inquiry.

See section 475 and comments thereto.

⚓ ⚓ ⚓ ⚓

Inquiry into conduct of certificated officer.

471 (1) If the Board of Trade, either on the report of a local marine board or otherwise, have reason to believe that any master, mate, or certificated engineer is from incompetency or misconduct unfit to discharge his duties, or that in a case of collision he has failed to render such assistance or give such information as is required under the Fifth Part of this Act, the Board may cause an inquiry to be held.

(2) The Board may either themselves appoint a person to hold the inquiry or direct the local marine board at or nearest the place at which it is convenient for the parties or witnesses to attend to hold the same, or where there is no local marine board before which the parties and witnesses can conveniently attend, or the local marine board is unwilling to hold the inquiry, may direct the inquiry to be held before a court of summary jurisdiction.

(3) Where the inquiry is held by a local marine board, or by a person appointed by the Board of Trade, that board or person—

(*a*) shall hold the inquiry, with the assistance of a local stipendiary magistrate, or, if there is no such magistrate available, of a competent legal assistant appointed by the Board of Trade; and

(*b*) shall have all the powers of a Board of Trade inspector under this Act; and

(*c*) shall give any master, mate, or engineer against whom a charge is made an opportunity of making his defence either in person or otherwise, and may summon him to appear; and

(*d*) may make such order with regard to the costs of the inquiry as they think just; and

(*e*) shall send a report upon the case to the Board of Trade.

(4) Where the inquiry is held by a court of summary jurisdiction, the inquiry shall be conducted and the results reported in the same manner, and the court shall have the like powers, as in the case of a formal investigation into a shipping casualty under this Part of this Act, provided that, if the Board of Trade so direct, it shall be the duty of the person who has brought the charge against the master, mate, or engineer, to the notice of the Board of Trade to conduct the case, and that person shall in that case, for the purpose of this Act, be deemed to be the party having the conduct of the case.

COMMENTS.

Incompetency or Misconduct.

A condition of unfitness from incompetency implies a certain element of duration and, although conduct on a particular occasion may lead to the conclusion of incompetency, the circumstances must be quite exceptional to justify such a finding against a master with unimpeachable record. The *Empire Antelope*, the *Radchurch* 1943.

Duty of vessel to stand-by in cases of collision *see* section 422.

Court of Summary Jurisdiction.

See comments to section 466.

Inspector.

See section 729 for powers of inspectors. These powers include a discretionary power to grant summonses for witnesses for the defence.

The expense of such witnesses is to be borne by the public, and it is the proper course for the court, before granting summonses, to enquire as to the status of the witnesses, what they are expected to prove, and to prevent a witness being vexatiously summoned. *See* R. *v.* Collinbridge 1864.

False swearing at such an inquiry is indictable as perjury. R. *v.* Tomlinson 1866.

⚓ ⚓ ⚓ ⚓

472 (1) Any of the following courts, namely— Removal of master by Admiralty Court.

In England and Ireland the High Court,

In Scotland the Court of Session,

Elsewhere in Her Majesty's dominions any colonial court of Admiralty or Vice-Admiralty Court,

may remove the master of any ship within the jurisdiction of that court, if that removal is shown to the satisfaction of the court by evidence on oath to be necessary.

(2) The removal may be made upon the application of any owner of the ship or his agent, or of the consignee of the ship, or of any certificated mate, or of one-third or more of the crew of the ship.

(3) The court may appoint a new master instead of the one removed; but, where the owner, agent, or consignee of the ship is within the jurisdiction of the court, such an appointment shall not be made without the consent of that owner, agent, or consignee.

(4) The court may also make such order and require such security in respect of the costs of the matter as the court thinks fit.

COMMENTS.

Removal of Master.

For definition of 'Master', *see* section 742.

Section 483 is concerned with the power of naval court to remove master.

Power of Court to Cancel or Suspend Certificate.

See section 470.

Endorsement of Change of Master.

On certificate of registry, *see* section 19.

High Court in England.

The jurisdiction of the High Court under this Act was assigned to the Probate, Divorce, and Admiralty Division by the Rules of the Supreme Court (Merchant Shipping) 1894. S.R. & O., Rev. 1904.

High Court in Ireland.

The reference to the High Court in Ireland is construed as a reference to the High Court of Northern Ireland.

Delivery of certificate cancelled or suspended.

473 (1) A master, mate, or engineer whose certificate is cancelled or suspended by any court or by the Board of Trade shall deliver his certificate—

(*a*) if cancelled or suspended by a court to that court on demand:

(*b*) if not so demanded, or if it is cancelled or suspended by the Board of Trade, to that Board, or as that Board direct.

(2) If a master, mate, or engineer fail to comply with this section, he shall, for each offence, be liable to a fine not exceeding fifty pounds.

COMMENTS.

Certificates Cancelled or Suspended.

For powers of Minister to cancel or suspend, *see* section 469.

For powers of court to cancel or suspend, *see* section 470.

A record is kept by the Registrar-General of Shipping and Seamen of cancellations and suspensions. *See* section 100, sub-section 2.

⚓ ⚓ ⚓ ⚓

474 The Board of Trade may, if they think that the justice of the case requires it, re-issue and return the certificate of a master, mate, or engineer which has been cancelled or suspended, whether in the United Kingdom or in a British possession, or shorten the time for which it is suspended, or grant in place thereof a certificate of the same or any lower grade. **Power of Board of Trade to restore certificate.**

⚓ ⚓ ⚓ ⚓

Re-hearing of Investigations and Inquiries

475 (1) The Board of Trade may, in any case where under this Part of this Act a formal investigation as aforesaid into a shipping casualty, or an inquiry into the conduct of a master, mate, or engineer has been held, order the case to be re-heard either generally or as to any part thereof, and shall do so— **Re-hearing of inquiries and investigations.**

(*a*) if new and important evidence which could not be produced at the investigation or inquiry has been discovered; or

(*b*) if for any other reason there has in their opinion been ground for suspecting that a miscarriage of justice has occurred.

(2) The Board of Trade may order the case to be re-heard, either by the court or authority by whom the case was heard in the first instance, or by the wreck commissioner, or in England or Ireland by the High Court, or in Scotland by the Senior Lord Ordinary, or any other judge in the Court of

Session whom the Lord President of that court may appoint for the purpose, and the case shall be so re-heard accordingly.

(3) Where on any such investigation or inquiry, a decision has been given with respect to the cancelling or suspension of the certificate of a master, mate, or engineer, and an application for a re-hearing under this section has not been made or has been refused, an appeal shall lie from the decision to the following courts, namely—

(*a*) If the decision is given in England or by a naval court, to the High Court:

(*b*) If the decision is given in Scotland, to either division of the Court of Session:

(*c*) If the decision is given in Ireland, to the High Court in Ireland.

(4) Any re-hearing or appeal under this section shall be subject to and conducted in accordance with such conditions and regulations as may be prescribed by rules made in relation thereto under the powers contained in this Part of this Act.

COMMENTS.

The words 'and shall', in sub-section 1, impose a duty to grant a re-hearing when new and important evidence, which could not be produced at the time of the investigation, is discovered. The Board of Trade might be compelled by mandamus to grant it. The *Ida* 1866.

High Court in England.

An appeal or re-hearing under this section is to a Divisional Court of the Probate, Divorce, and Admiralty Division. *See* the *Seistan* 1959.

An appeal is not a re-hearing. The *Princess Victoria* 1953.

Appeal.

As to appeals by owners or any other persons affected by the decision of the court, having an interest in the investigation or inquiry, *see* section 66, Merchant Shipping Act 1906.

An appeal lies to the Court of Appeal from the Divisional Court if leave to appeal is obtained.

The Court will not permit witnesses to be called on questions of nautical knowledge or skill; it is the duty of the nautical assessors to advise the court on such matters. The *Kestrel* 1881.

Supplemental Provisions as to Investigations and Inquiries

Investigations before stipendiary magistrate.

476 (1) Where a stipendiary magistrate is in any place a member of the local marine board, a formal investigation at that place into a shipping casualty shall, whenever he happens to be present, be held before that stipendiary magistrate.

(2) There shall be paid out of the Mercantile Marine Fund to the stipendiary magistrates, if he is not remunerated out of money provided by Parliament under this Act, such remuneration by way of an annual increase of salary, or otherwise, as a Secretary of State, with the consent of the Board of Trade, may direct.

COMMENTS.

Formal Investigation into Shipping Casualty.

See section 466.

Mercantile Marine Fund.

Payments are now made out of moneys provided by Parliament. *See* Merchant Shipping (Mercantile Marine Fund) Act 1898, section 1, sub-section 1 (*b*).

⚓ ⚓ ⚓ ⚓

Merchant Shipping Act 1894

Section 477

Repealed Merchant Shipping Act 1970

Merchant Shipping Act 1970 (Commencement No. 1) Order 1972

⚓ ⚓ ⚓ ⚓

A.D. 1894

Authority for colonial court to make inquiries into shipping casualties and conduct of officers.

478 (1) The legislature of any British possession may authorise any court of tribunal to make inquiries as to shipwrecks, or other casualties affecting ships, or as to charges of incompetency, or misconduct on the part of masters, mates, or engineers of ships, in the following cases, namely—

(*a*) Where a shipwreck or casualty occurs to a British ship on or near the coasts of the British possession or to a British ship in the course of a voyage to a port within the British possession:

(*b*) Where a shipwreck or casualty occurs in any part of the world to a British ship registered in the British possession:

(*c*) Where some of the crew of a British ship which has been wrecked or to which a casualty has occurred, and who are competent witnesses to the facts, are found in the British possession:

(*d*) Where the incompetency or misconduct has occurred on board a British ship on or near the coasts of the British possession, or on board a British ship in the course of a voyage to a port within the British possession:

(*e*) Where the incompetency or misconduct has occurred on board a British ship registered in the British possession:

(*f*) When the master, mate, or engineer of a British ship who is charged with incompetency or misconduct on board that British ship is found in the British possession.

(2) A court or tribunal so authorised shall have the same jurisdiction over the matter in question as if it had occurred within their ordinary jurisdiction, but subject to all provisions, restrictions, and conditions which would have been applicable if it had so occurred.

(3) An inquiry shall not be held under this section into any matter which has once been the subject of an investigation or inquiry and has been reported on by a competent court or tribunal in any part of Her Majesty's dominions, or in respect of which the certificate of a master, mate, or engineer has been cancelled or suspended by a naval court.

(4) Where an investigation or inquiry has been commenced in the United Kingdom with reference to any matter, an inquiry with reference to the same matter shall not be held, under this section, in a British possession.

(5) The court or tribunal holding an inquiry under this section shall have the same powers of cancelling and suspending certificates, and shall exercise those powers in the same manner as a court holding a similar investigation or inquiry in the United Kingdom.

(6) The Board of Trade may order the re-hearing of any inquiry under this section in like manner as they may order the re-hearing of a similar investigation or inquiry in the United Kingdom, but if an application for re-hearing either is not made or is refused, an appeal shall lie from any order or finding of the court or tribunal holding the inquiry to the High Court in England: Provided that an appeal shall not lie—

(*a*) from any order or finding on an inquiry into a casualty affecting a ship registered in a British possession, or

(*b*) from a decision affecting the certificate of a master, mate, or engineer, if that certificate has not been granted either in the United Kingdom or in a British possession, under the authority of this Act.

(7) The appeal shall be conducted in accordance with such conditions and regulations as may from time to time be prescribed by rules made in relation thereto under the powers contained in this Part of this Act.

COMMENTS.

British Possession.

This is defined by the Interpretation Act 1889, section 18, as 'any part of Her Majesty's dominions, exclusive of the United Kingdom'.

Appeal.

An appeal lies to a Divisional Court of the Probate, Divorce and Admiralty Division.

It was probable that a master who was censured by a Colonial Court of Inquiry, but had not had his certificate suspended or cancelled, had a right of appeal under this section. There is certainly a right under the Merchant Shipping Act 1906, section 66. The *Royal Star* 1928.

Re-hearing of Inquiry.

See section 475.

Certificates of Officers.

See section 470.

⚓ ⚓ ⚓ ⚓

479 (1) The Lord Chancellor may (with the consent of the Treasury so far as relates to fees) make general rules for carrying into effect the enactments relating to formal investigations, and to the re-hearing of, or an appeal from, any investigation or inquiry held under this Part of this Act, and in particular with respect to the appointment and summoning of assessors, the procedure, the parties, the persons allowed to appear, the notice to those parties or persons or to persons affected, the amount and application of fees, and the place in which formal investigations are to be held. Rules as to investigations and inquiries.

(2) Any rule made under this section while in force shall have effect as if it were enacted in this Act.

(3) Any rule made under this section with regard to the re-hearing of, or appeals from, any investigation or inquiries, as to the appointment of assessors, and as to the place in which formal investigations are to be held, shall be laid before both Houses of Parliament as soon as may be after it is made.

COMMENTS.

Rules Under This Section.

Shipping Casualties and Appeals and Re-hearings Rules 1923, S.R. & O. 1923, No. 752.

The making of rules under this section is now subject to the Statutory Instruments Act 1946.

⚓ ⚓ ⚓ ⚓

Naval Courts on the High Seas and Abroad

Cases in which naval courts may be summoned.

480 A court (in this Act called a naval court) may be summoned by any officer in command of any of Her Majesty's ships on any foreign station, or, in the absence of such an officer, by any consular officer, in the following cases (that is to say)—

(i) Whenever a complaint which appears to that officer to require immediate investigation is made to him by the master of any British ship, or by a certificated mate, or by any one or more of the seamen belonging to any such ship;

(ii) Whenever the interest of the owner of any British ship or of the cargo thereof appears to that officer to require it; and

(iii) Whenever any British ship is wrecked, abandoned, or otherwise lost at or near the place where that officer may be, or whenever the crew or part of the crew of any British ship which has been wrecked, abandoned, or lost abroad arrive at that place.

COMMENTS.

Application of Provisions.

For ships to which provisions as to naval courts apply, *see* section 486.

⚓ ⚓ ⚓ ⚓

Constitution of naval courts.

481 (1) A naval court shall consist of not more than five and not less than three members, of whom, if possible, one shall be an officer in the naval service of Her Majesty not below the rank of lieutenant, one a consular officer, and one a master of a British merchant ship, and the rest shall be either officers in the naval service of Her Majesty, masters of British merchant ships, or British merchants, and the court may include the officer summoning the same, but shall not include the master or consignee of the ship to which the parties complaining or complained against belong.

(2) The naval or consular officer in the court, if there is only one such officer, or, if there is more than one, the naval or consular officer who, according to any regulations for settling their respective ranks for the time being in force, is of the highest rank, shall be the president of the court.

COMMENTS.

Naval Court.

See section 480.

482 (1) A naval court shall hear the complaint or other matter brought before them under this Act, or investigate the cause of the wreck, abandonment, or loss, and shall do so in such manner as to give every person against whom any complaint or charge is made an opportunity of making a defence. Functions of naval courts.

(2) A naval court may, for the purpose of the hearing and investigation, administer an oath, summon parties and witnesses, and compel their attendance and the production of documents.

COMMENTS.

Naval Court.

See section 480.

483 (1) Every naval court may, after hearing and investigating the case, exercise the following powers (that is to say)— Powers of naval courts.

(*a*) The court may, if unanimous that the safety of the ship or crew or the interest of the owner absolutely requires it, remove the master, and appoint another person to act in his stead; but no such appointment shall be made without the consent of the consignee of the ship if at the place where the case is heard:

(*b*) The court may, in cases in which they are authorised by this Act and subject to the provisions of this Act, cancel or suspend the certificate of any master, mate, or engineer:

(*c*) The court may discharge a seaman from his ship:

(*d*) The court may order the wages of a seaman so discharged or any part of those wages to be forfeited, and may direct the same either to be retained by way of compensation to the owner, or to be paid into the Exchequer, in the same manner as fines under this Act:

(*e*) The court may decide any questions as to wages or fines or forfeitures arising between any of the parties to the proceedings:

(*f*) The court may direct that all or any of the costs incurred by the master or owner of any ship in procuring the imprisonment of any seaman or apprentice in a foreign port, or in his maintenance whilst so imprisoned, shall be paid out of and deducted from the wages of that seaman or apprentice, whether then or subsequently earned:

(*g*) The court may exercise the same powers with regard to persons charged before them with the commission of offences at sea or abroad as British consular officers can under the Thirteenth Part of this Act:

(*h*) The court may punish any master of a ship or any of the crew of a ship respecting whose conduct a complaint is brought before them for any offence against this Act, which, when committed by the said master or member of the crew, is punishable on summary conviction, and shall for that purpose have the same powers as a court of summary jurisdiction would have if the case were tried in the United Kingdom: Provided that—

(i) where an offender is sentenced to imprisonment, the senior naval or consular officer present at the place where the court is held shall in writing confirm the sentence and approve the place of imprisonment, whether on land or on board ship, as a proper place for the purpose; and

(ii) copies of all sentences passed by any naval court summoned to hear any such complaint as aforesaid, shall be sent to the commander-in-chief or senior naval officer of the station:

(*j*) The court may, if it appears expedient, order a survey of any ship which is the subject of investigation to be made, and such survey shall accordingly be made, in the same way, and the surveyor who makes the same shall have the same powers as if such survey had been directed by a competent court in pursuance of the Fifth Part of this Act, in the course of proceedings against a seaman or apprentice for the offence of desertion.

(*k*) The court may order the costs of the proceedings before them, or any part of those costs, to be paid by any of the parties thereto, and may order any person making a frivolous or vexatious complaint to pay compensation for any loss or delay caused thereby; and any costs or compensation so ordered to be paid shall be paid by that person accordingly, and may be recovered in the same manner in which the wages of seamen are recoverable, or may, if the case admits, be deducted from the wages due to that person.

(2) All orders duly made by a naval court under the powers hereby given to it, shall in any subsequent legal proceedings be conclusive as to the rights of the parties.

(3) All orders made by any naval court shall, whenever practicable, be entered in the official log-book of the ship to which the parties to the proceedings before the court belong, and signed by the president of the court.

COMMENTS.

Certain punishments, imposed by naval courts, are now subject to review. *See* the Merchant Shipping Act 1950, section 3, also, the reviewing officer may revoke any direction by a naval court in exercise of their power.

For power of naval court to send person sentenced home to undergo sentence, *see* the Merchant Shipping Act 1906, section 67.

Appeal from Naval Courts.

See section 68, Merchant Shipping Act 1906, which was enacted to meet the position arising in Hutton *v.* Ras S.S. Co. 1907, where a naval court had discharged and forfeited the wages of a crew who had lawfully refused to continue a voyage in a ship carrying contraband; an action by the crew for their wages was dismissed on the ground that the findings of the naval court was conclusive.

Power of Court as to Certificates.

See section 470, sub-section 1 (*a*). *N.B.*—No provision is made for assessors to assist a naval court, and the requirement in respect of concurrence contained in section 470, sub-section 1 (*a*) is, therefore, not applicable under this section.

The words underlined in sub-section 1 (*h*), (i), on previous page, ceased to have effect, Merchant Shipping Act 1950, section 3, sub-section 8.

Report of proceedings of naval courts.

484 (1) Every naval court shall make a report to the Board of Trade containing the following particulars (that is to say)—

(*a*) A statement of the proceedings of the court, together with the order made by the court, and a report of the evidence;

(*b*) An account of the wages of any seaman or apprentice who is discharged from his ship by the court;

(*c*) If summoned to inquire into a case of wreck or abandonment, a statement of the opinion of the court as to the cause of that wreck or abandonment with such remarks on the conduct of the master and crew as the circumstances require.

(2) Every such report shall be signed by the president of the court, and shall be admissible in evidence in manner provided by this Act.

COMMENTS.

Admissible in Evidence.

See section 695.

⚓ ⚓ ⚓ ⚓

Penalty for preventing complaint or obstructing investigation.

485 If any person wilfully and without due cause prevents or obstructs the making of any complaint to an officer empowered to summon a naval court, or the conduct of any hearing or investigation by any naval court, he shall for each offence be liable to a fine not exceeding fifty pounds, or be liable to imprisonment, with or without hard labour, for any period not exceeding twelve weeks.

COMMENTS.

Hard Labour.

By the Criminal Justice Act 1948, section 1, sub-section 2, hard labour is abolished and enactments conferring power to sentence to imprisonment with hard labour are to be construed as conferring power to sentence of imprisonment.

⚓ ⚓ ⚓ ⚓

Application of provisions as to naval courts.

486 (1) The provisions of this Part of this Act with regard to naval courts on the high seas and abroad shall apply to all sea-going ships registered in the United Kingdom (with the exception, in their application elsewhere than in Scotland, of fishing-boats exclusively employed in fishing on the coasts of the United Kingdom) and to all ships registered in a British possession, when those ships are out of the jurisdiction of their respective governments, and where they apply to a ship, shall apply to the owners, master, and crew of that ship.

(2) For the purpose of the said provisions an unregistered British ship shall be deemed to have been registered in the United Kingdom.

Repeal.

The words underlined are repealed by Merchant Shipping (Scottish Fishing-Boats) Act 1920, section 1, sub-section 3 and schedule.

COMMENTS.

On the Coasts.

It would appear that this means within the territorial limit. *See* the *Fullam* 1898.

United Kingdom.

Where this phrase secondly occurs, it includes the Republic of Ireland.

Courts of Survey

487 (1) A court of survey for a port or district shall consist of a judge sitting with two assessors. Constitution of court of

(2) The judge shall be such person as may be summoned for the case in accordance with the rules made under this Act with respect to that court, out of a list approved for the port or district by a Secretary of State, of wreck commissioners appointed under this Act, stipendiary or metropolitan police magistrates, judges of county courts, and other fit persons; but in any special case in which the Board of Trade think it expedient to appoint a wreck commissioner, the judge shall be such wreck commissioner.

(3) The assessors shall be persons of nautical, engineering, or other special skill and experience; subject to the provisions of the Fifth Part of this Act as regards foreign ships, one of them shall be appointed by the Board of Trade, either generally or in each case, and the other shall be summoned, in accordance with the rules made as aforesaid, by the registrar of the court, out of a list of persons periodically nominated for the purpose by the local marine board of the port, or, if there is no such board, by a body of local shipowners or merchants

approved for the purpose by a Secretary of State, or, if there is no such list, shall be appointed by the judge: If a Secretary of State thinks fit at any time, on the recommendation of the government of any British possession or any foreign country, to add any persons to any such list, those persons shall, until otherwise directed by the Secretary of State, be added to the list, and if there is no such list shall form the list.

(4) The county court registrar or such other fit person as a Secretary of State may from time to time appoint shall be the registrar of the court, and shall, on receiving notice of an appeal or a reference from the Board of Trade, immediately summon the court to meet forthwith in manner directed by the rules.

(5) The name of the registrar and his office, together with the rules made as aforesaid, relating to the court of survey, shall be published in the manner directed by the rules.

(6) In the application of this section to Scotland the expression 'judge of a county court' means a sheriff, and the expression 'county court registrar' means sheriff clerk.

(7) In the application of this section to Ireland the expression 'stipendiary magistrate' includes any of the justices of the peace in Dublin metropolis and any resident magistrate.

(8) In the application of this section to the Isle of Man the expression 'judge of a county court' means the water bailiff, the expression 'stipendiary magistrate' means the high bailiff, the expression 'registrar of a county court' means a clerk to a deemster or a clerk to justices of the peace.

Repeal.

The words underlined on previous page, in sub-section 3, repealed by the Merchant Shipping Act 1970. Merchant Shipping Act 1970 (Commencement No. 1) Order 1972.

COMMENTS.

The words secondly underlined referred to Dublin, and may be omitted by S.L.R. Act 1927, section 3.

Court of Survey.

Rules for procedure. *See* section 489.

Provisions as Regard Foreign Ships.

For the appointment of assessors in the case of foreign ships, *see* section 462 (iii).

Ireland.

I.e. Northern Ireland only. Application to Northern Ireland and the Republic of Ireland, *see* the Irish Free State (Consequential Adaption of Enactments) Order 1923, S.R. & O. 1923, No. 405.

488 (1) The court of survey shall hear every case in open court.

Power and procedure of court of survey.

(2) The judge and each assessor of the court may survey the ship, and shall have for the purposes of this Act all the powers of a Board of Trade inspector under this Act.

(3) The judge of the court may appoint any competent person or persons to survey the ship and report thereon to the court.

(4) The judge of the court, any assessor of the court, and any person appointed by the judge of the court to survey a ship, may go on board the ship and inspect the same and every part thereof, and the machinery, equipments, and cargo, and may require the unloading or removal of any cargo, ballast, or tackle, and any person who wilfully impedes such judge, assessor, or person in the execution of the survey, or fails to comply with any requisition made by him, shall for each offence be liable to a fine not exceeding ten pounds.

(5) The judge of the court shall have the same power as the Board of Trade have to order the ship to be released or finally detained, but, unless one of the assessors concurs in an order for the detention of the ship, the ship shall be released.

(6) The owner and master of the ship and any person appointed by the owner or master, and also any person appointed by the Board of Trade, may attend at any inspection or survey made in pursuance of this section.

(7) The judge of the court shall send to the Board of Trade such report as may be directed by the rules, and each assessor shall either sign the report or report to the Board of Trade the reasons for his dissent.

COMMENTS.

Inspection Under this Act.

For powers of inspection, *see* sections 729, 730.

Power to Order Ship to be Released or Detained.

See sections 459 and 462.

Rules.

For rules of procedure, *see* section 489.

Rules for procedure of court of survey, &c.

489 The Lord Chancellor may (with the consent of the Treasury so far as relates to fees) make general rules to carry into effect the provisions of this Act with respect to a court of survey, and in particular with respect to the summoning of, and procedure before, the court, the requiring on an appeal security for costs and damages, the amount and application of fees, and the publication of the rules, and those rules shall have effect as if enacted in this Act.

Scientific Referees

Reference in difficult cases to scientific persons.

490 (1) If the Board of Trade are of opinion that an appeal to a court of survey involves a question of construction or design or of scientific difficulty or important principle, they may refer the matter to such one or more out of a list of scientific referees from time to time approved by a Secretary of State, as may appear to possess the special qualifications necessary for the particular case, and may be selected by agreement between the Board of Trade and the appellant, or in default of any such agreement by a Secretary of State, and thereupon the appeal shall be determined by the referee or referees, instead of by the court of survey.

(2) The Board of Trade, if the appellant in any appeal so requires and gives security to the satisfaction of the Board to pay the costs of and incidental to the reference, shall refer that appeal to a referee or referees so elected as aforesaid.

(3) The referee or referees shall have the same powers as a judge of the court of survey.

Merchant Shipping Act 1894

Section 491

Repealed by Merchant Shipping Act 1970

Merchant Shipping Act (Commencement No. 1) Order 1972

PART VII

DELIVERY OF GOODS AND LIEN FOR FREIGHT

PART VII

DELIVERY OF GOODS

Delivery of Goods and Lien for Freight

492 In this Part of this Act, unless the context otherwise requires— Definitions under Part VII.

The expression 'goods' includes every description of wares and merchandise:

The expression 'wharf' includes all wharves, quays, docks, and premises in or upon which any goods, when landed from ships, may be lawfully placed:

The expression 'warehouse' includes all warehouses, buildings, and premises in which goods, when landed from ships, may be lawfully placed:

The expression 'report' means the report required by the customs laws to be made by the master of an importing ship:

The expression 'entry' means the entry required by the customs laws to be made for the landing or discharge of goods from an importing ship:

The expression 'shipowner' includes the master of the ship and every other person authorised to act as agent for the owner or entitled to receive the freight, demurrage, or other charges payable in respect of the ship:

The expression 'owner' used in relation to goods means every person who is for the time entitled, either as owner or agent for the owner, to the possession of the goods, subject in the case of a lien (if any), to that lien:

The expression 'wharfinger' means the occupier of a wharf as herein-before defined:

The expression 'warehouseman' means the occupier of a warehouse as herein-before defined.

493 (1) Where the owner of any goods imported in any ship from foreign parts into the United Kingdom fails to make entry thereof, or, having made entry thereof, to land the same or take delivery thereof, and to proceed therewith Power of shipowner to enter and land goods on default by owner of goods.

with all convenient speed, by the times severally hereinafter mentioned, the shipowner may make entry of and land or unship the goods at the following times:—

(*a*) If a time for the delivery of the goods is expressed in the charter party, bill of lading, or agreement, then at any time after the time so expressed:

(*b*) If no time for the delivery of the goods is expressed in the charter party, bill of lading, or agreement, then at any time after the expiration of seventy-two hours, exclusive of a Sunday or holiday, from the time of the report of the ship.

(2) Where a shipowner lands goods in pursuance of this section he shall place them, or cause them to be placed—

(*a*) if any wharf or warehouse is named in the charter party, bill of lading, or agreement, as the wharf or warehouse where the goods are to be placed, and if they can be conveniently there received, on that wharf or in that warehouse; and

(*b*) in any other case on some wharf or in some warehouse on or in which goods of a like nature are usually placed; the wharf or warehouse being, if the goods are dutiable, a wharf or warehouse duly approved by the Commissioners of Customs for the landing of dutiable goods.

(3) If at any time before the goods are landed or unshipped the owner of the goods is ready and offers to land or take delivery of the same, he shall be allowed to do so, and his entry shall in that case be preferred to any entry which may have been made by the shipowner.

(4) If any goods are, for the purpose of convenience in assorting the same, landed at the wharf where the ship is discharged, and the owner of the goods at the time of that landing has made entry and is ready and offers to take delivery thereof, and to convey the same to some other wharf or warehouse, the goods shall be assorted at landing, and shall, if demanded, be delivered to the owner thereof within twenty-four hours after assortment; and the expense of and consequent on that landing and assortment shall be borne by the shipowner.

(5) If at any time before the goods are landed or unshipped the owner thereof has made entry for the landing and warehousing thereof at any particular wharf or warehouse other than that at which the ship is discharging, and has offered

and been ready to take delivery thereof, and the shipowner has failed to make that delivery, and has also failed at the time of that offer to give the owner of the goods correct information of the time at which the goods can be delivered, then the shipowner shall, before landing or unshipping the goods, in pursuance of this section, give to the owner of the goods or of such wharf or warehouse as last aforesaid twenty-four hours notice in writing of his readiness to deliver the goods, and shall, if he lands or unships the same without that notice, do so at his own risk and expense.

COMMENTS.

Definitions.

For the meaning of entry, goods, etc., *see* section 492.

Wharf—Approved.

Certain wharves and warehouses are approved by the Commissioners of Custom, now Commissioners of Customs and Excise, by the Customs and Excise Act 1952, for the landing and storing of dutiable goods.

Mode of Delivery.

This section does not vary the mode of delivery of the goods under (i) contract and (ii) the custom of the port. Margetti *v*. Smith & Co. 1883.

Shipowner may . . .

The shipowner is under no obligation to land goods and assert his lien. Hick *v*. Rodocanachi 1891.

Warehouseman.

. . . is entitled to rent, and expenses and has a distinct and separate lien for the same. *See* section 499.

494 If at the time when any goods are landed from any ship, and placed in the custody of any person as a wharfinger or warehouseman, the shipowner gives to the wharfinger or warehouseman notice in writing that the goods are to remain subject to a lien for freight or other charges payable to the shipowner to an amount mentioned in the notice, the goods so landed shall, in the hands of the wharfinger or warehouseman, continue subject to the same lien, if any, for such charges as they were subject to before the landing thereof; and the wharfinger or warehouseman receiving those goods shall retain them until the lien is discharged as herein-after mentioned, and shall, if he fails so to do, make good to the shipowner any loss thereby occasioned to him.

Lien for freight on landing goods.

COMMENTS.

General.

This section, as well as sections 495 and 496, apply when the goods are landed from any ship into the care of a wharfinger or warehouseman, accompanied by a notice in writing that they are to remain subject to a lien for freight, to an amount stated in the notice. It is not quite clear whether these sections 494–496, only apply to goods deposited under section 493. *See* Dennis *v.* Cork S.S. Co. 1913. The lien may be discharged in accordance with sub-sections 495 and 496. If it is not discharged the warehouseman may, and if so required by the shipowner, must, sell the goods by public auction after 90 days from the date the goods were deposited, or sooner if they are perishable. *See* section 497. Whether the notice should be contemporaneous with the landing has not been actually decided. *See* Lawther *v.* Belfast Harbour Commissioners 1864, where it is discussed. However, the precursor of this section was contained in the Bonded Warehouse Act 1945, section 51 which, whilst providing remedy for goods landed into a bonded warehouse, provided no limit as to the time within which notice must be given, and it would appear that the notice could be given at any time while the goods remained in the bonded store.

Notice.

A form of notice, which is submitted will satisfy the criteria of the statute is:

To: **Wharfinger or Warehouseman**

Take Notice that the goods mentioned in the schedule hereto which are being and/or have been landed from the motor vessel 'ARRIVED LATE' and placed in your custody as wharfinger and/or Warehouseman are to remain subject to a lien for freight and/or other charges payable to Shipowner to the amount ________________ mentioned in the said schedule.

This Notice is given pursuant to section 494 of the Merchant Shipping Act 1894, under which you are to retain the said goods until the said lien is discharged in accordance with the provisions of the Act and, on failure to do so, will be liable to make good to Shipowner any loss thereby occasioned to him.

Date Signature

Schedule

Quantity	Description of goods	Marks
Freight	Charges	Total

Amout mentioned in Notice: The amount must be due at the time when the goods are landed; it must not be excessive, and if the owner of the goods pays off one of the sums claimed, it is the duty of the Master to reduce the amount by that sum. *See* Miedbrodt *v.* Fitzsimon, *the Energie* 1875.

NOTE: If a Master wilfully inserts an amount which he is aware is in excess of the amount for which the lien exists, the delivery to the warehouseman is virtually a wrongful detention of the goods, and is therefore an actionable breach of duty. It would appear however, that where a Master inserted a bona fide claim for more than was due, particularly if it were not excessive, then no liability would be incurred.

Wharfinger . . . shall retain them: The wharfinger or warehouseman, the lien being discharged, 'is under an obligation cast upon him by the statute to deliver the goods to the same person to whom the shipowner was by his contract bound to deliver them'. Glyn, Mills & Co. *v.* East and West India Dock Co. 1882.

⚓ ⚓ ⚓ ⚓

495 The said lien for freight and other charges shall be discharged— Discharge of lien.

(1) upon the production to the wharfinger or warehouseman of a receipt for the amount claimed as due, and delivery to the wharfinger or warehouseman of a copy thereof or of a release of freight from the shipowner, and

(2) upon the deposit by the owner of the goods with the wharfinger or warehouseman of a sum of money equal in amount to the sum claimed as aforesaid by the shipowner;

but in the latter case the lien shall be discharged without prejudice to any other remedy which the shipowner may have for the recovery of the freight.

COMMENTS.

Said Lien.

This is the lien which the shipowner has under section 494.

Sum Claimed.

If the shipowner attempts to exercise his lien in regard to charges which he is not entitled to recover from the consignee, then he can be ordered to pay the consignee interest upon the additional sum. Red 'R' S.S. Co. *v*. Allatime 1908.

Sale of Goods.

See section 497.

⚓ ⚓ ⚓ ⚓

Provisions as to deposits by owners of goods.

496 (1) When a deposit as aforesaid is made with the wharfinger or warehouseman, the person making the same may, within fifteen days after making it, give to the wharfinger or warehouseman notice in writing to retain it, stating in the notice the sums, if any, which he admits to be payable to the shipowner, or, as the case may be, that he does not admit any sum to be so payable, but if no such notice is given, the wharfinger or warehouseman may, at the expiration of the fifteen days, pay the sum deposited over to the shipowner.

(2) If a notice is given as aforesaid the wharfinger or warehouseman shall immediately apprize the shipowner of it, and shall pay or tender to him out of the sum deposited the sum, if any, admitted by the notice to be payable, and shall retain the balance, or, if no sum is admitted to be payable, the whole of the sum deposited, for thirty days from the date of the notice.

(3) At the expiration of those thirty days unless legal proceedings have in the meantime been instituted by the shipowner against the owner of the goods to recover the said balance or sum, or otherwise for the settlement of any disputes which may have arisen between them concerning the freight or other charges as aforesaid, and notice in writing of those proceedings has been served on the wharfinger or warehouseman, the wharfinger or warehouseman shall pay the balance or sum to the owner of the goods.

(4) A wharfinger or warehouseman shall by any payment under this section be discharged from all liability in respect thereof.

COMMENTS.

Amount Mentioned in Notice.

See comments under this heading to section 494.

Legal Proceedings.

In the event of the freight being deposited by persons against whom the shipowner has no right of action for freight, then it is for the shipowner to apply for a declaration from his consignee that he, the shipowner, is entitled to be paid the freight deposited with the warehouseman. White & Co. *v*. Furness Withy & Co. 1895.

It is also proper for shippers of the cargo to be added as defendants for the purposes of counterclaim by them in respect of short delivery and damages to cargo. Montgomery *v*. Foy Morgan & Co. 1895.

The term legal proceedings in this section includes arbitration, *see* section 29, sub-section 1, Arbitration Act 1950.

Owner of the Goods.

In this section this means the owner of the goods at the time the deposit is made.

⚓ ⚓ ⚓ ⚓

497 (1) If the lien is not discharged, and no deposit is made as aforesaid, the wharfinger or warehouseman may, and, if required by the shipowner, shall, at the expiration of ninety days from the time when the goods were placed in his custody, or, if the goods are of a perishable nature, at such earlier period as in his discretion he thinks fit, sell by public auction, either for home use or for exportation, the goods or so much thereof as may be necessary to satisfy the charges herein-after mentioned.

Sale of goods by warehousemen.

(2) Before making the sale the wharfinger or warehouseman shall give notice thereof by advertisement in two local newspapers circulating in the neighbourhood, or in one daily newspaper published in London, and in one local newspaper, and also, if the address of the owner of the goods has been stated on the manifest of the cargo, or on any of the documents which have come into the possession of the wharfinger or warehouseman, or is otherwise known to him, send notice of the sale to the owner of the goods by post.

(3) The title of a bona fide purchaser of the goods shall not be invalidated by reason of the omission to send the notice required by this section, nor shall any such purchaser be bound to inquire whether the notice has been sent.

COMMENTS.

Sale.

See section 498 as to how the proceeds of the sale are applied.

The Lien.

This is the lien which the shipowner has under section 494.

⚓ ⚓ ⚓ ⚓

Application of proceeds of sale.

498 The proceeds of sale shall be applied by the wharfinger or warehouseman as follows, and in the following order—

(i) First, if the goods are sold for home use, in payment of any customs or excise duties owing in respect thereof; then

(ii) In payment of the expenses of the sale; then

(iii) In payment of the charges of the wharfinger or warehouseman and the shipowner according to such priority as may be determined by the terms of the agreement (if any) in that behalf between them; or, if there is no such agreement—

(*a*) in payment of the rent, rates, and other charges due to the wharfinger or warehouseman in respect of the said goods; and then

(*b*) in payment of the amount claimed by the shipowner as due for freight or other charges in respect of the said goods;

and the surplus, if any, shall be paid to the owner of the goods.

COMMENTS.

Warehouseman's Right to Rent and Expenses.

See section 499.

⚓ ⚓ ⚓ ⚓

Warehousemen's rent and expenses.

499 Whenever any goods are placed in the custody of a wharfinger or warehouseman, under the authority of this Part of this Act, the wharfinger or warehouseman shall be entitled to rent in respect of the same, and shall also have power, at the expense of the owner of the goods, to do all such reasonable acts as in the judgment of the wharfinger or warehouseman are necessary for the proper custody and preservation of the goods, and shall have a lien on the goods for the rent and expenses.

COMMENTS.

This Part of this Act.

This means sections 492 to 501 inclusive.

Lien.

The lien referred to herewith is distinct from the shipowner's lien for freight and other charges. The *Energie* 1875.

⚓ ⚓ ⚓ ⚓

500 Nothing in this Part of this Act shall compel any wharfinger or warehouseman to take charge of any goods which he would not have been liable to take charge of if this Act had not been passed; nor shall he be bound to see to the validity of any lien claimed by any shipowner under this Part of this Act.

Warehousemen's protection.

COMMENTS.

This part of this Act.

See comments to section 499.

501 Nothing in this Part of this Act shall take away or abridge any powers given by any local Act to any harbour authority, body corporate, or persons, whereby they are enabled to expedite the discharge of ships or the landing or delivery of goods; nor shall anything in this Part of this Act take away or diminish any rights or remedies given to any shipowner or wharfinger or warehouseman by any local Act.

Saving for powers under local Acts.

COMMENTS.

This Part of this Act.

See comments to section 499.

LIMITATION OF LIABILITY

M.S.A. 1894

PART VIII

PART VIII

LIABILITY OF SHIPOWNERS

STATUTORY PROVISIONS:

THE provisions relating to 'Limitation of Liability' have been taken out of their chronological order, and for the sake of clarity and good order, are grouped together under this general heading.

They include and comprise of:—

(i) M.S.A. 1894, Part VIII
which contains the main statutory provisions as to Limitation of Liability;

(ii) M.S. (Liability of Shipowners and Others) Act, 1900.
This extended the protection enjoyed by shipowners under Part VIII of the Principal Act to owners of docks and canals, harbour authorities, conservancy authorities, in respect of loss or damage caused to any vessel or goods on board any vessel;

(iii) M.S.A. 1906, Section 69.
This section altered the method of calculating the tonnage of steamships for assessment of tonnage in respect of limitation of liability;

(iv) M.S.A. 1921.
This Act extended the protection enjoyed by shipowners under Part VIII of the Principal Act (except in respect of loss of life, or personal injury to persons on board) to owners of lighters and barges, used in navigation in Great Britain, however propelled. It also provides for the registration and measurement of such vessels under Part I of the Principal Act, or under approved local registration;

(v) M.S. (Liability of Shipowners and Others) Act 1958.
This Act extended the protection of limitation in a most substantial manner as well as the limits set to liability.

SUMMARY: (To be read in conjunction with the Act itself.)

The provisions of this Act came into force on the 1st of August 1958. It follows that any claims arising out of incidents which occurred before the 1st of August 1958 are to be governed by the 'limitation' law, which was in being up to that date.

The main object of the 1958 Act is to give effect to the International Convention relating to the Limitation of the Liability of Owners of Seagoing Ships, held in Brussels, 1957.

The limits, set out in the 1894 Act and the 1900 Act, are increased from £15 to an amount equivalent to 3,100 gold francs and from £8 to 1,000 gold francs.

The sterling equivalents of these amounts, Statutory Instrument 1958, No. 1289 specified the initial equivalents, namely, £73 8s. $10\frac{5}{32}$d. in respect of the 3,100 gold francs, and £23 13s. $9\frac{27}{32}$d. in respect of the 1,100 gold francs.

This order was superseded by Statutory Instrument 1967, No. 1725, when the sterling equivalents were £85 13s. $7\frac{13}{16}$d. in respect of 3,100 gold francs, and £27 12s. $9\frac{1}{2}$d. in respect of the 1,100 gold francs.

This order in turn has been superseded by Statutory Instrument 1972, No. 734, The Merchant Shipping (Limitation of Liability) (Sterling Equivalents) Order, 1972, operational as from the 12th June, 1972. The sterling equivalents specified by the Secretary of State in this order, are:

3,100 gold francs — £85·6826
1,000 gold francs — £27·6396

This in turn has been superseded by the Merchant Shipping (Limitation of Liability) (Sterling Equivalents) Order 1973, S.I. No. 1190/1973, which in turn has been revoked and superseded by the Merchant Shipping (Limitation of Liability) (Sterling Equivalents) Order 1974, operative from the 12th April 1974.

Arising from this, for the purposes of Section 1 of the Merchant Shipping (Liability of Shipowners and Others) Act 1958, £108·1677 and £34·8928 are specified as the amounts which shall be taken as equivalent to 3,100 and 1,000 gold francs respectively.

Where there is a claim against the larger fund, and the tonnage of the ship concerned is less than 300 tons, then the amount must be multiplied by 300 to arrive at the amount of the limitation fund. *See* section 1 of the 1958 Act.

The right to limit in respect of loss of life or personal injury has been extended to claims of persons not on board the limiting ship. The right to limit liability for loss or damage to property or rights has been extended in respect of claims relating to any property or rights wherever situated. *See* section 2, subsection 1 of the 1958 Act.

It is sufficient to lay claim to limitation if the occurrence was caused through the act or omission of any person (whether on board the ship or not) in the navigation or management of the ship, or in loading, discharging, or embarkation and disembarkation of passengers, or through any other act or omission of any person on board the ship. *See* section 2, subsection 1 and 2 of the 1958 Act.

The class of claims for which liability may be limited now includes any liability arising in respect of any damage caused to harbour works, basins, or navigable waterways.

Limitation of liability has been extended to any charterer and to any person interested in or in possession of the ship and to any manager or operator of the ship, and to any employer of a person who by section 3, subsection 2, is entitled to limit his personal liability.

In addition, the master and members of the crew have been given the right to limit their personal liability. This is irrespective of their actual fault or privity, except in the case of the loss or of damage to undeclared valuables in circumstances of dishonesty. *See* section 3, sub-section 2 of the 1958 Act.

In respect of limitation, the definition of 'ship' has been extended to include any structure, whether completed or in the course of construction, launched and intended for use in navigation as a ship or part of a ship, and, further, the provisions of limitation apply to a British ship whether or not it has been registered. *See* section 4, sub-sections 1 and 2.

There are restrictions on enforcement of judgements after adequate security has been given, *see* section 6.

The 1958 Act, *see* section 7, allows for greater discretion than formerly in the distribution of the limitation fund. It now being enacted that liens no longer affect the proportions in which distribution is made.

The following extensions should be noted:—

Pilotage Authorities (Limitation of Liability) Act 1936, which gave pilotage authorities a right to limit in respect of a wide catalogue of loss or damage.

In accordance with section 35 of the Pilotage Act 1913, a licensed pilot is able to limit his liability q.v.

The Crown Proceedings Act 1947 allows amongst other things, the benefit of the provisions relating to limitation of liability in respect of H.M. Ships and in respect of Crown Docks and Harbours. This Act only applies in respect of liabilities and rights of H.M. Government in the United Kingdom. It does not apply in regard to proceedings against or by the Crown in regard to liabilities or rights of a Dominion Government.

M.S.A. 1894

PART VIII

LIABILITY OF SHIPOWNERS

502 The owner of a British sea-going ship, or any share therein, shall not be liable to make good to any extent whatever any loss or damage happening without his actual fault or privity in the following cases; namely—

Limitation of shipowner's liability in certain cases of loss of, or damage to, goods.

(i) Where any goods, merchandise, or other things whatsoever taken in or put on board his ship are lost or damaged by reason of fire on board the ship; or

(ii) Where any gold, silver, diamonds, watches, jewels, or precious stones taken in or put on board his ship, the true nature and value of which have not at the time of shipment been declared by the owner or shipper thereof to the owner or master of the ship in the bills of lading or otherwise in writing, are lost or damaged by reason of any robbery, embezzlement, making away with, or secreting thereof.

COMMENTS.

FIRE.

Damage by smoke and water in putting out a fire is damage 'by reason of fire' within the meaning of this section. *The Diamond* 1906.

Loss or Damage.

In an action by shipowners against cargo owners for contribution towards a general average expenditure, it was held that although relieved from liabilities for loss or damage, the plaintiffs were entitled to general average contribution. Louis Dreyfus & Co. *v.* Tempus Shipping Co. 1931.

There is no implication that the ship shall be seaworthy. Virginia Carolina Chemical Co. *v.* Norfolk & North American Steam Shipping Co. 1912, but the protection given by the Act may be excluded by the effect of a clause in the Bill of Lading, and this precludes a shipowner from setting up this section. *See* also, and compare: Ingram & Royle Ltd. *v.* Services Maritimes du Treport 1914.

However:—

If the unseaworthiness itself was the fault or privity of the owner, and if fire was brought about by the unseaworthiness, the shipowner is not relieved by section 502 . . . 'the *causa causans* of the loss was the unseaworthiness which occasioned the fire, which destroyed the goods. Lennards Carrying Co. *v.* Asiatic Petroleum Co. 1914, the onus being upon the shipowners to prove that loss happened without their actual fault or privity.

Declaration of Value.

In Williams *v.* African S.S. Co. 1856, it was held that the declaration . . . 'one box containing about 248 ounches of gold-dust'. . . was not sufficient.

Owner.

By the M.S. (Liability of Shipowners and Others) Act 1958, Section 3, sub-section 1, and Section 8, sub-section 4, it is now provided that . . . 'That the persons whose liability in connection with a ship is excluded or limited by Part VIII of the Merchant Shipping Act 1894, shall include any charterer and any person interested in, or in possession of, the ship, and, in particular any manager or operator of the ship' . . . *See* section 3 of the 1958 Limitation Act for extension of limitation or excursion to other persons of provisions applying to shipowners. Consult also section 8 of the same Act, sub-section 4.

Ship.

See M.S. (Liability of Shipowners and Others) Act 1958, section 4, sub-sections 1 and 2, for the extension and construction of the term 'ship'. Consult also section 8, sub-section 6 and Schedule. Also, amendment of section 5 of the Crown Proceedings Act 1947.

Valuables.

Belonging to a passenger and remaining under his control, *see* Smitten *v.* Orient Steam Navigation Co. Ltd. 1907

The word underlined, 'sea-going', is now to be omitted per M.S. (Liability of Shipowners and Others) Act 1958, section 8, sub-section 1.

⚓ ⚓ ⚓ ⚓

Limitation of owner's liability in certain cases of loss of life, injury, or damage.

503 (1) The owners of a ship, British or foreign, shall not, where all or any of the following occurrences take place without their actual fault or privity; (that is to say,)

(*a*) Where any loss of life or personal injury is caused to any person being carried in the ship;

(*b*) Where any damage or loss is caused to any goods, merchandise, or other things whatsoever on board the ship;

(*c*) Where any loss of life or personal injury is caused to any person carried in any other vessel by reason of the improper navigation of the ship;

(*d*) Where any loss or damage is caused to any other vessel, or to any goods, merchandise, or other things whatsoever on board any other vessel, by reason of the improper navigation of the ship;

be liable to damages beyond the following amounts; (that is to say,)

(i) In respect of loss of life or personal injury, either alone or together with loss of or damage to vessels, goods, merchandise, or other things, an aggregate amount not exceeding fifteen pounds for each ton of their ship's tonnage; and

(ii) In respect of loss of, or damage to, vessels, goods, merchandise, or other things, whether there be in addition loss of life or personal injury or not, an aggregate amount not exceeding eight pounds for each ton of their ship's tonnage.

(2) For the purposes of this section—

(*a*) The tonnage of a steam ship shall be her gross tonnage without deduction on account of engine room; and the tonnage of a sailing ship shall be her registered tonnage:

Provided that there shall not be included in such tonnage any space occupied by seamen or apprentices and appropriated to their use which is certified under the regulations scheduled to this Act with regard thereto.

(*b*) Where a foreign ship has been or can be measured according to British law, her tonnage, as ascertained by that measurement shall, for the purpose of this section, be deemed to be her tonnage.

(*c*) Where a foreign ship has not been and cannot be measured according to British law, the surveyor-general of ships in the United Kingdom, or the chief measuring officer of any British possession abroad, shall, on receiving from or by the direction of the court hearing the case, in which the tonnage of the ship is in question, such evidence concerning the dimensions of the ship as it may be practicable to furnish, give a certificate under his hand stating what would in his opinion have been the tonnage of the ship if she had been duly measured according to

British law, and the tonnage so stated in that certificate shall, for the purposes of this section, be deemed to be the tonnage of the ship.

(3) The owner of every sea-going ship or share therein shall be liable in respect of every such loss of life, personal injury, loss of or damage to vessels, goods, merchandise, or things as aforesaid arising on distinct occasions to the same extent as if no other loss, injury, or damage had arisen.

COMMENTS.

The words underlined in sub-section 1, (*c*) and (*d*), have been substituted by section 2, sub-section 1 of the M.S. (Liability of Shipowners and Others) Act 1958.

The words underlined in sub-section 1, paragraphs (i) and (ii) have been substituted by 'such loss, damage or infringement as is mentioned in paragraphs (*b*) and (*d*) of this sub-section'.

The words underlined in sub-section 1, paragraphs (i) and (ii), that is, fifteen and eight pounds respectively, have been substituted by: an amount equivalent to three thousand one hundred gold francs and one thousand gold francs. *See* Statutory Instrument 1972, No. 734, The Merchant Shipping (Limitation of Liability) (Sterling Equivalents) Order 1972. Consult now The Merchant Shipping (Limitation of Liability) (Sterling Equivalents) Order 1974, operative from 12th April 1974.

The words underlined in sub-section 2 (*a*) have ceased to have effect as a result of section 4, sub-section 3 of the Merchant Shipping Act 1948.

The words in sub-section 3, underlined above, have been substituted by section 8, sub-section 2 of the M.S. (Liability of Shipowners and Others) Act 1958.

It can be seen that this section of the Act has been considerably amended. The reader's attention is drawn to these amendments above, but in order to facilitate the reading and understanding of the section, it is fully written out as it now stands, viz:

Section 503.

(1) The owners of a ship, British or foreign, shall not, where all or any of the following occurrences take place without their actual fault or privity; (that is to say,)

(*a*) Where any loss of life or personal injury is caused to any person being carried in the ship;

(*b*) Where any damage or loss is caused to any goods, merchandise, or other things whatsoever on board the ship;

(*c*) Where any loss of life or personal injury is caused to any person not carried in the ship through the act or omission of any person (whether carried on board the ship or not) in the navigation or management of the ship or in the loading, carriage, or disembarkation of its passengers, or through any other act or omission of any person on board the ship;

(*d*) Where any loss or damage is caused to any property (other than any property mentioned in paragraph (*b*) of this sub-section) or any rights are infringed through the act or omission of any person (whether on board the ship or not) in the navigation or management of the ship or in the loading, carriage or discharge of its cargo, or in the embarkation, carriage, or disembarkation of its passengers, or through any other act or omission of any person on board the ship; be liable to damages beyond the following amounts; (that is to say,)

(i) in respect of loss of life or personal injury, either alone or together with such loss, damage or infringement as is mentioned in paragraphs (*b*) and (*d*) of this sub-section, an aggregate amount not exceeding an amount equivalent to three thousand one hundred gold francs for each ton of their ships' tonnage; and

(ii) in respect of such loss, damage or infringement as is mentioned in paragraphs (*b*) and (*d*) of this sub-section, whether there be in addition loss of life or personal injury or not, an aggregate amount not exceeding an amount equivalent to one thousand gold francs for each ton of their ship's tonnage.

(2) For the purposes of this section—

(*a*) The tonnage of a steam ship shall be net registered tonnage, with the addition of any engine room space deducted for the purposes of ascertaining that tonnage; and the tonnage of a sailing ship shall be her registered tonnage;

(*b*) Where a foreign ship has not been and cannot be measured according to British Law, the surveyor general of ships in the United Kingdom or the chief measuring officer of any British possession abroad, shall, on receiving from or by the direction of the court hearing the case, in which the tonnage of the ship is in question, such evidence concerning the dimensions of the ship as it may be practicable to furnish, give a certificate under his hand stating what would in his opinion, have been the tonnage of the ship if she had been duly measured according to British Law, and the tonnage so stated in that certificate shall, for the purposes of this section be deemed to be the tonnage of the ship.

(3) The limits set by this section to the liabilities mentioned therein, shall apply to the aggregate of such liabilities which are incurred on any distinct occasion without regard to any liability incurred on another occasion.

COMMENTS.

This section has been extended by:—

(*a*) M.S. (Liability of Shipowners and Others) Act 1900, section 2 q.v.

(*b*) M.S. Act 1921, section 1, q.v.

(*c*) Crown Proceedings Act 1947, section 5.

(*d*) M.S. (Liability of Shipowners and Others) Act 1958, section 2, sub-section 2 (*b*).

Section 3, sub-section 1.

Section 8, sub-section 4.

Section 3, sub-section 2.

Section 4, sub-section 1.

Section 4, sub-section 2.

Repeals.

The M.S. (Liability of Shipowners and Others) Act 1958, section 8, sub-section 6 and schedule, have repealed the following:—

(*a*) M.S. (Liability of Shipowners) Act 1898

(*b*) M.S. (Liability of Shipowners and Others) Act 1900, section 1.

(*c*) Merchant Shipping Act 1906, section 70 and 71.

(*d*) Merchant Shipping Act 1921, section 1, sub-section 2.

Restrictive Enactments.

(*a*) Merchant Shipping Act 1921, section 3.

(*b*) M.S. (Liability of Shipowners and Others) Act 1958, section 2 sub-section 4.

General Notes.

The operation of this section is not affected in its operation by the Carriage of Goods by Sea Act 1971 or the Maritime Conventions Act 1911.

Owner.

See The Spirit of the Ocean 1865, where it was held to include equitable owner. *See* also M.S. (Liability of Shipowners and Others) Act 1958, section 3, sub-section 1.

Liabilities of masters and members of the crew, *see* M.S. (Liability of Shipowners and Others) Act 1958, section 3, sub-section 2.

Liability of Her Majesty, managers, charterers and or sub-charterers by demise of H.M. ships, *see* Crown Proceedings Act 1947, section 5 as amended by the M.S. (Liability of Shipowners and Others) Act 1958, section 8, sub-section 5.

A shipowner may contract out of his right to limit liabilities, *The Satanita* 1897 (Clarke *v*. Dunraven).

Owners claiming to limit their liability in respect of damages as a result of collision are liable to pay interest on the amount for which they are liable under this section from the date of the collision, *The Northumbria* 1869, consult also Smith *v.* Kirby 1875 (interest on the amount for which owners liable in respect of loss of goods).

Ship.

It would appear that limitation can be claimed in respect of a ship which is defined in any one of the definitions contained in the following enactments:—

Merchant Shipping Act 1894, section 742.

Merchant Shipping Act 1921, section 1, sub-section 1.

M.S. (Liability of Shipowners and Others) Act 1958, section 4, sub-section 1.

NOTE:—It should be taken that section 3 of the Merchant Shipping Act 1921 appears to exclude the right of the owner of any lighter, barge or like vessel to limit their liability in respect of loss of life or personal injury caused to any person carried therein.

Fault or Privity.

Onus of Proof.

See generally Lennards Carrying Co. Ltd. *v.* Asiatic Petroleum Co. Ltd. 1915, where the principle was established that the onus is on the shipowners to prove that loss happened without their actual fault or privity.

In Paterson Steamships Ltd. *v.* Robin Hood Mills Ltd. 1937, it was held that the fault of privity of the owners must be the fault or privity in respect of that which caused the damage.

In *The Norman* 1960, it was laid down that where a shipowner is at fault, it is for him to prove that the fault did not contribute to the loss.

Circumstances which may or may not constitute fault or privity. Consult:—

The Warkworth 1884—Negligence of a person on shore in overlooking machinery.

The Fanny 1912—Appointment of incompetent master.

The Bristol City 1921—Sending an unfinished vessel to sea without proper tackle.

Standard Oil Co. Ltd. *v.* Clan Line Steamers 1924—Failure to acquaint the master of the unusual construction of ballast tanks.

The Thames 1940—Failure of the hirer of the barge to ascertain condition and where it was last surveyed.

The Hans Hoth 1952—Failure by the master to know local signals (the master was a part-owner).

The Truenlint 1952—Navigation lights on submarine misleading.

The Hildina 1957—Failure to provide a cut out on a trawling winch.

The Empire Jamaica 1957—The appointment of an uncertificated officer.

Radiant 1958—Inadequate tow-ropes and lack of deck lights.

The Norman 1960—Failure of owner to communicate to the vessel the latest navigational information.

The Anonity 1961—Inadequate notices regarding the prohibition of the use of a galley-stove whilst lying at an oil (petroleum) jetty.

The Lady Gwendolin 1964—Failure to give specific instructions to master regarding the use of radar.

Proof that owners have failed to observe a statutory duty or are in breach of an absolute common law duty, does not in itself give rise to being guilty of fault or privity. Beauchamp *v.* Turrel 1952—unsafe system of working, but *see* and *compare* Hook *v.* Consolidated Fisheries Ltd. 1953, where failure to provide a safe system of work would amount to actual fault or privity.

Difficulty arises where the owners are a corporate body. In Lennards Carrying Co. *v.* Asiatic Petroleum Co. 1915, Lord Holdane gave as his opinion, that the true construction required the fault or privity of somebody who is not merely a servant or agent for whom the company is liable upon the footing—respondeat superior—but somebody for whom the company is liable because his action is the very action of the company itself.

This precept was followed by the Privy Council in Paterson Steamships Ltd. *v.* Canadian Co-operative Wheat Producers Ltd. 1934, the same principle being accepted and applied in *The Truculent* 1952, where the court held amongst other things, that there was a fault in respect of the navigation lights shown by H.M.S. *Truculent*, and as the fault was one which the Third Sea Lord, a responsible member of the Board of Admiralty must have deemed to be aware, the claim of the Crown to limit their liability in accordance with the Act, failed.

The Phrase.

Any person being carried in the ship has been held to apply to a person who falls from the gangway whilst boarding a ship. Moore *v.* Metcalf Motor Coasters Ltd. 1958.

Improper Navigation.

The words 'improper navigation' are not restricted to the negligent navigation of a vessel by her master or crew, for the statute includes all damage wrongfully done by a ship to another whilst it is being navigated, where the wrongful action is due to the negligence of a person for whom the owner is responsible. *The Warkworth* 1884.

Improper navigation covers negligence of the master of a tug in transferring a tow rope, where such negligence is not a mere breach of contract. *The Vigilant* 1921.

Fire and explosion from escape of petrol through sea-valves was held not to be 'improper navigation' but improper management. *The Athelvictor* 1946.

Although the navigation of the ship must be by individuals, it is not the negligence of individuals for which relief is given under this section, but the improper navigation of the ship. *The Alde* 1926.

Other Things Whatsoever.

This phrase includes passengers' luggage, *The Stella* 1900. The decision in *The Bernina* 1886, is of interest; here, following a collision, the cargo of the vessel in fault was transhipped by the master into another vessel. These vessels were lost owing to the negligence of their masters and crews. The owners of the vessel in fault in the first instance obtained a decree limiting their liability as a result of the collision. An action was brought for the non-delivery of the cargo, and it was held that limitation of liability did not apply in respect of the loss of this cargo, because the loss did not occur on board the ship, that was able to limit her liability.

Tug and Tow.

In the event of the tug and tow being in the same ownership, and a collision occurs as a result of their negligence, the owners may limit on the combined tonnage of the tug and such of her tow as were in contact with the other vessel, or which by the weight contributed to the damage. *The Harlow* 1922.

The same principle is applicable if the tug and her tows are in the same ownership, even if the tug herself was not in collision, but was in control of the navigation of the tows. *The Freden* 1950.

Where, however, the tug and the tow are in different ownership, each owner is entitled to limit in respect of his own vessel. *The American* and *The Syria* 1874. *The Englishman* 1894. *The Morgengry* and *The Blackcock* 1900.

See also the decision of the Court of Appeal, *The Bramley Moore* 1964. Here, a collision occurred between the motorship *Egret* and the dumb barge *Millet* in tow of the tug *Bramley Moore*, with also the dumb barge *Buckwheat* in tow. The tug and her tows were in different ownership. The owners of the *Bramley Moore* sought to limit her liability in a sum of money based upon her tonnage alone. The defendants contended that the amount of this limitation fund should be based on the combined tonnage of the tug and one or both of the barges. It was held, invoking the M.S. (Liability of Shipowners and Others) Act 1958, that where damage was caused by a tow, due to the negligence of those on the tug, and not those on the tow, such damage was caused through an act or omission of a person on board the tug; and therefore, under the Merchant Shipping Act 1894, section 503, sub-section 1 (*d*), as amended by the 1958 Act, the owners of the tug could limit their liability according to the tonnage of the tug alone, and that, by the same reasoning, the flotilla could not be taken as a unit.

Loss, etc., Arising on Distinct Occasions.

Where a collision occurs with two vessels, one after the other, the collision occurring substantially at the same time, and because of one sole act of improper navigation, the owner of the vessel causing the two collisions is entitled to limit his liability to one payment for the both damages. *The Rajah* 1872. *The Creador* 1886.

In the event of damage being caused to two vessels by the improper helm action of the vessel in fault, it was held that as there was time to correct the improper helm action, the subsequent collision took place on a distinct occasion from the first. The test is whether both collisions are the result of the same act of improper seamanship. *The Schwan* 1882, or that there was sufficient time to remedy the improper seamanship.

Damages—Expenses of Wreck Raising.

With the enactment of the M.S. (Liability of Shipowners and Others) Act 1958, it was thought that by section 2, sub-section 2, paragraph 5, a statutory instrument would soon be brought into being, making the Act effective in respect of the provisions relating to removal of wreck. Some 16 years later no such statutory instrument has been brought into being, appointing the day when the parts of this section relating to removal of wreck becomes law.

It is worthy of note that if and when the order is made making paragraph (*a*) of sub-section 2 of section 2 law, the decisions described below in *The Millie* 1940, and *The Stonedale No. 4* 1956, will be reversed.

The shipowner has a common law liability for the removal of wreck as a result of negligence on the part of themselves or their servants. This common law liability has been extended by particular acts to ensure that the Dock, Harbour, or River Authority can still recover even if no negligence is involved.

In accord with the M.S. (Liability of Shipowners and Others) Act 1900, limitation was only possible as a result of negligence, and was not applicable in the event of the innocence of the shipowners' servants. This being, of course, prejudicial to the shipowner. This anomaly, amongst other things, was highlighted in the case of *The Millie* 1940. A collision occurred in the Manchester Ship Canal, as a result of which the steam barge *Millie* sank; it being held that she was solely to blame for the collision. She was able to limit her liability for the damage done to the innocent vessel, but she was not able to limit in respect of the removal expenses incurred by the canal authority, such expenses not being 'loss or damage to property or rights'.

The next 'limitation case' worthy of note was *The Stonedale No. 1* 1956. This followed the *Millie*, above, in material respects, went to the House of Lords, where it was also held that the liability for removal expenses was a liability as a debt under the canal authority's statutory powers, and not a liability by way of damage. And so we arrive at the case of *The Arabert* 1961.

Here, the vessels *Cyprian Coast* and the *Arabert* collided in December 1955. As a result of the collision, the *Cyprian Coast* was sunk, due to the negligence of the *Arabert*. In accord with the combined 'Limitation' Acts of 1894 and 1900, it was held that the sunken vessel was unable to limit her liability to the Tyne Improvement Commission in respect of the wreck-raising expenses for two reasons; firstly, because she was the innocent vessel, and secondly, because the liability was by way of a debt, and not as damages.

Of course, the innocent vessel, i.e. the *Cyprian Coast*, could include this in her claim against the *Arabert*, in addition to her other valid claims.

The full force of the apparent iniquity now becomes evident, for under the circumstances the *Arabert* could limit her liability in accordance with the 1894 and 1900 'Limitation Acts'.

It should be particularly noted that nothing in the M.S. (Liability of Shipowners and Others) Act 1958 applies in relation to any liability arising from an occurrence which took place before the commencement of this Act, 1st August 1958. *See* section 9 of the 1958 Act.

In *The Kirkness* 1957, it was held that a shipowner cannot limit his liability in respect of his liability to provide an indemnity under the United Kingdom Standard Towage Conditions for damage suffered by a tug, because such liability arises as a result of a contractual obligation and is not within the meaning of the word 'damages'. It should be noted, however, the liability for loss of life of persons on board the tug, being a right of action in fact, can be limited.

In Clarke *v.* Dunraven, *The Satanita* 1857, it was held that where under yacht racing rules, an infringement thereof imposed a liability on an owner of a yacht for all damages arising from improper navigation, it meant that the owner had contracted out of his right to limit his liability in respect of damage to a competing yacht.

So, owners are not prevented from contracting out of all liability for negligence, or from contracting to be liable for an amount exceeding the statutory liability. *The Satanita*—above, and *The Stella* 1900.

The exclusion by the contractual terms must be clear. *The Kirkness* 1957.

Tonnage.

As to measurement of Tonnage, *see* sections 77 et seq., Schedules 2 and 6—as extended by the Merchant Shipping Act 1954. *See* section 84 in respect of foreign ships.

The tonnage to be used as the basis in respect of limitation of liability of an owner is that which appears on the ship's register at the time of the collision and neither side is entitled to the benefit of any subsequent amendment. *The John Ormston* 1881. *The Dione* 1885.

The tonnage shown in the ship's register is not conclusive evidence, and evidence may be brought to show that the calculation was not made in accordance with the provisions of the Act. *The Franconia* 1878. *The Recepta* 1889.

The copy of the vessel's register shown to the court, must be a copy of the register at the time of the collision. *The Rosslyn* 1904.

Minimum Tonnage.

See the M.S. (Liability of Shipowners and Others) Act 1958, section 1, sub-section 1.

In the event that the limitation provisions are applied by the Crown Proceedings Act 1947, *see* section 5, sub-section 5 of such Act for the special provision made for the calculation of the tonnage where the ship is not registered under the Merchant Shipping Acts.

Where a British fishing vessel is registered under Part IV of the principal Act, but not Part 1, a deduction may be made for crew space which has been certified by Department of Trade and Industry's surveyor, for the purposes of registration under Part 1 of this Act, Couper *v.* McKenzie 1906.

Power of courts to consolidate claims against owners, &c.

504 Where any liability is alleged to have been incurred by the owner of a British or foreign ship in respect of loss of life, personal injury, or loss of or damage to vessels or goods, and several claims are made or apprehended in respect of that liability, then, the owner may apply in England and Ireland to the High Court, or in Scotland to the Court of Session, or in a British possession to any competent court, and that court may determine the amount of the owner's liability and may distribute that amount rateably among the several claimants, and may stay any proceedings pending in any other court in relation to the same matter, and may proceed in such manner and subject to such regulations as to making persons interested parties to the proceedings, and as to the exclusion of any claimants who do not come in within a certain time, and as to requiring security from the owner, and as to payment of any costs, as the court thinks just.

Amendment.

The words underlined above have been substituted by M.S. (Liability of Shipowners and Others) Act 1958, section 8, sub-section 3, viz. . . . "in respect of any occurrence in respect of which his liability is limited under section five hundred and three of this Act".

COMMENTS.

Extension of Section.

The Merchant Shipping Act 1911, section 1, extends the jurisdiction under this section to certain British courts in foreign countries. This was enacted because of the decision of the Privy Council in the s.s. *Maori King* 1909, when it was held that a British court in China had no jurisdiction to deal with a case of forfeiture. Obviously the importance of this has diminished with the passage of time, but the fact remains that it is still in the Statute Book.

See also section 2 of the M.S. (Liability of Shipowners and Others) Act 1900, for extension of jurisdiction to harbour or conservancy authority, etc., and also consult M.S. (Liability of Shipowners and Others) Act 1958, section 3, sub-section 1, for extension of 'Owner of a British or foreign ship'.

Practice.

In accordance with the Rules of the Supreme Court, the proceedings in respect of limitation takes the form of an Admiralty action. Consult also as to practice:—*British Shipping Laws* (Vol. 4)—'Collisions at Sea'—*Marsden on Collisions at Sea,* 11th Edition; Roscoe, *Admiralty Practice,* 5th Edition.

In such actions, the names and description of the owners seeking to limit liability should be stated in the writ, it is no longer sufficient to describe them simply as 'Owners of m.v. etc.'. *The Blanche* 1904. *The Inventor* 1905.

Rule 13 of the Rules of the Supreme Court preserves the right to reply on the provisions of section 503 by way of defence. Usually questions regarding limitation are raised by separate action, after the determination of liability, and it is in order in the Admiralty Division, as in the Queen's Bench Division (where the ascertainment of liability and damages is usually determined in the same proceedings) to raise a plea under section 503 by way of defence. *The Clutha* 1876. London Rangoon Trading Co. *v.* Ellerman Lines Ltd. 1923.

Where a claim merits a higher sum of damages than that resulting from limitation of liability, judgement will be given for the limit of liability. Wheeler *v.* London and Rochester Trading Co. 1957.

As to admission of liability before a decree can be obtained, *see* Hill *v.* Audus 1855.

It would appear from Commonwealth of Australia *v.* Asiatic Steam Navigation Co. Ltd. and Others 1955, that a qualified admission of partial blame will entitle a shipowner to a limitation decree, before final apportionment of blame has been made. Where liability is admitted, the court will stay actions brought for the purpose of establishing liability, Miller *v.* Powell 1875.

Before the plea is raised, in the Admiralty Division, it is not necessary that liability should be admitted. *The Amalia* 1863. *The Sisters* 1875. *See* also *The Karo* 1887.

However, before a decree can be obtained in the limitation proceedings it would appear that liability must be admitted or determined. Hill *v.* Audus 1855.

Costs.

There is a general rule that plaintiff in a limitation of liability suit must pay the costs. *The Teal* 1949. The practice is, however, not invariable. *The Rijnstroon* 1889.

May Distribute that Amount Rateably.

The practice now established is generally in accord with the International Convention dealing with the Limitation of Owners of Sea-going Ships, Brussels 1957, Article 3 referring.

The terms of this International Convention were generally enacted in this country by the M.S. Liability of Shipowners and Others) Act, 1958, with one notable omission. For the first time, a minimum tonnage was brought into being, namely 300 tons. However, Article 3 of this International Convention applied this minimum tonnage to all claims, whereas the Act specifically limits this minimum tonnage multiple to claims where loss of life or personal injury has occurred, either alone or together with loss of, or damage to, property.

Therefore, when a ship is less than 300 tons, it is submitted that where both types of claimants are present, that the calculation and distribution of the limitation fund would be as follows:—

Claims for loss of life or personal injury:—

Assuming a tonnage of 200 tons.

300 (minimum tonnage)	× 3,100 gold francs	= 930,000 gold francs
200 (actual tonnage)	× 1,000 gold francs	= 200,000 gold francs
Amount available for life or personal injury claimants:		= 730,000 gold francs

If this fund is not sufficient to satisfy the life or personal injury claimants, then they will rank *parri passu* with the 'property' claimants against the fund obtained by the actual tonnage of the ship, in this example:

$$200 \times 1{,}000 \text{ gold francs} = 200{,}000 \text{ gold francs}$$

As from 12th June 1972, *see* for the sterling equivalents of the gold francs above. The Merchant Shipping (Limitation of Liability) (Sterling Equivalents) Order 1972. Statutory Instrument 1972, No. 734.

The latest in the long line of Sterling Equivalent Orders is No. 536 of 1974, Merchant Shipping (The Merchant Shipping) (Limitation of Liability) (Sterling Equivalents) Order 1974, operative from 12th April

1974. Where the minimum tonnage of 300 tons is exceeded, but the amount which is calculated at the higher rate of 3,100 gold francs is insufficient to meet the combined claims of loss of life and personal injury, as well as for loss of goods, the procedure is as follows:—

The claimants in respect of loss of life and personal injury, rank first, and are entitled to be paid an amount equal to the difference between the higher and lower rate, i.e. 3,100 gold francs less 1,000 gold francs, making the difference 2,100 gold francs. Of course, the Sterling Equivalents as referred to earlier, S.I. 1974, No. 536, are applied in the final computation. If this amount satisfies the life claimants then no difficulty arises. If this amount does not satisfy the life claimants, then they are entitled to proceed and claim upon the fund calculated at 1,000 gold francs, ranking *parri passu* with the claimants in respect of damage to property. *See The Victoria* 1888.

Note, however, Canadian Pacific Railway Co. *v.* s.s. *Storstad* 1920, when the owners of the Storstad took no proceedings for limitation of their liability. The ship was sold, and the proceeds were paid into Court. Life and property claimant shared *pro rata*, it being held that in such a case, life claimants have no priority over the claimants for damage to property.

Distribution Among Several Life Claimants.

This has been most carefully enunciated and explained by Lord Romilly, M.R. in Glaholm *v.* Barker 1866—'Supposing the registered tonnage of the wrong-doing vessel was 100 tons, then the extent of the liability of the owners would be £1,500. (This is at the old rate of £15. Author's note.)

Supposing there were 100 persons drowned by the fault of the vessel, then the family of each person would only get £15, that amount being clearly less than the amount of damages sustained. But supposing two persons only were drowned, it does not therefore, follow that the £1,500 is to be divided between those two, but only the amount of damages which each family has sustained . . . In this case, the liability would be nearly £4,000 . . . In other words, in my opinion, the damages sufferers have sustained are to be ascertained in the same way as if the liability of the owners were unlimited, and then, the sum for which the owner is liable is to be applied in payment of the damages when so ascertained; if they are less than the amount of his liability, then there is to be paid to each family the damages sustained; but if the damages so ascertained exceed the amount of liability, then the whole amount for which the owner is liable must be distributed among the families rateably, according to the amount of damages sustained; if it is less, they are paid in full, and the balance paid over to the owner.

In the circumstances where rival claimants seek to recover from the limitation fund the same liability for payment of wreck-raising expenses, the procedure is in accord with *The Liverpool*, No. 2 1960.

The position where the owner has paid some claims out of court is contained in Rankine *v.* Raschen 1877, where it was held that he was entitled to have such payments taken into account in assessing the amount payable in respect of the remaining claims.

If payment is made under a judgement of a foreign court, the procedure is the same. *The Coaster* 1922.

Contingent Claims.

Formerly, an owner could not put forward such claims which may be made against him under the judgement of a foreign court. *The Kronprinz Olav* 1921. But *see* M.S. (Liability of Shipowners and Others) Act 1958, section 7, sub-section 1, which would appear to give a greater direction in this matter.

Where Vessel has been Sold.

If as a result of an action abroad the vessel has been sold the concerned in a limitation action in this country must credit such sums received out of the proceeds. *The Crathie* 1897.

Position where One Claimant has Possessionary Lien over the Ship.

See M.S. (Liability of Shipowners and Others) Act 1958, section 7, sub-section 2, which overrides the decision in Mersey Docks and Harbour Board *v.* Hay (*The Countess*) 1923, which allowed a claimant having a possessionary lien over the vessel, a superior right even to deprive other claimants of all right of recovery against the limitation fund.

Vessels Under Same Ownership, Position of Underwriters.

A vessel sank another under the same ownership, and the owner limited his liability. It was held that the underwriters, who had paid insurance out on the sunken vessel, were not entitled to claim upon the limitation fund, as they were only the assignees of the owner, who was not entitled to claim upon this fund. Simpson *v.* Thompson 1877.

Security.

Consult M.S. (Liability of Shipowners and Others) Act 1958, section 6.

Part owners to account in respect of damages.

505 All sums paid for or on account of any loss or damage in respect whereof the liability of owners is limited under the provisions of this Part of the Act, and all costs incurred in relation thereto, may be brought into account among part owners of the same ship in the same manner as money disbursed for the use thereof.

COMMENTS.

Liability of Owners.

Consult M.S. (Liability of Shipowners and Others) Act 1958, section 3; section 8, sub-section 4.

Part Owners.

Consult M.S. (Liability of Shipowners and Others) (Act 1958, section 8, sub-section 4.

⚓ ⚓ ⚓ ⚓

506 An insurance effected against the happening, without the owner's actual fault or privity, of any or all of the events in respect of which the liability of owners is limited under this Part of this Act shall not be invalid by reason of the nature of the risk.

Insurances of certain risks not invalid.

COMMENTS.

As to marine insurance generally, consult Marine Insurance Act 1906.

⚓ ⚓ ⚓ ⚓

Merchant Shipping Act 1894

PART VIII

Section 507

Repealed by Merchant Shipping Act 1970 (Commencement No. 1) Order 1972

⚓ ⚓ ⚓ ⚓

Merchant Shipping Act 1894

PART VIII

Section 508

Repealed by M.S. (Liability of Shipowners and Others) Act 1958 Section 8, Sub-section 6 and Schedule

Consult Now:

M.S. (Liability of Shipowners and Others) Act 1958
Section 3, Sub section 2; Section 4, Sub-sections 1 and 2

⚓ ⚓ ⚓ ⚓

509 This Part of this Act shall, unless the context otherwise requires, extend to the whole of Her Majesty's dominions.

COMMENTS.

Priority of Mortgages.

See section 33 and comments thereto.

Powers and Rights of Mortgages.

See sections 33-37 inclusive.

Entry of Discharge of Mortgage.

See section 32.

⚓ ⚓ ⚓ ⚓

MERCHANT SHIPPING
(Liability of Shipowners) Act 1898

This Act has been repealed by the Merchant Shipping (Liability of Shipowners and Others) Act 1958, section 8, sub-section 6, and Schedule.

The provisions now applicable are contained in section 3, sub-section 1; section 4, sub-sections 1 and 2 of the 1958 Act.

⚓ ⚓ ⚓ ⚓

MERCHANT SHIPPING
(Liability of Shipowners and Others) Act 1900

⚓ ⚓ ⚓ ⚓

MERCHANT SHIPPING
(Liability of Shipowners and Others) Act 1900
CHAPTER 32

An Act to amend the Merchant Shipping Act 1894, with respect to the Liability of Shipowners and others.

Merchant Shipping (Liability of Shipowners and Others) Act 1900, section 1.

Repealed by the Merchant Shipping (Liability of Shipowners and Others) Act 1958, section 8, sub-section 6 and Schedule.

Consult now:—

M.S. (Liability of Shipowners and Others) Act 1958, section 2.

⚓ ⚓ ⚓ ⚓

Limitation of liability of harbour conservancy authority.

2 (1) The owners of any dock or canal, or a harbour authority or a conservancy authority, as defined by the Merchant Shipping Act 1894, shall not, where without their actual fault or privity any loss or damage is caused to any vessel or vessels, or to any goods, merchandise, or other things whatsoever on board any vessel or vessels, be liable to damages beyond an aggregate amount not exceeding eight pounds for each ton of the tonnage of the largest registered British ship which, at the time of such loss or damage occurring, is, or within the period of five years previous thereto has been, within the area over which such dock or canal owner, harbour authority, or conservancy authority, performs any duty or exercises any power. A ship shall not be deemed to have been within the area over which a harbour authority or a conservancy authority performs any duty, or exercises any powers, by reason only that it has been built or fitted out within such area, or that it has taken shelter within or passed through such area on a voyage between two places both situate outside that area, or that it has loaded or unloaded mails or passengers within that area.

(2) For the purpose of this section the tonnage of ships shall be ascertained as provided by section five hundred and three, sub-section two, of the Merchant Shipping Act 1894, and the register of any ship shall be sufficient evidence that the gross tonnage and the deductions therefrom and the registered tonnage are as therein stated.

(3) Section five hundred and four of the Merchant Shipping Act 1894, shall apply to this section as if the words 'owner of a British or foreign ship' included a harbour authority, and the owner of a canal or of a dock.

(4) For the purpose of this section the term 'dock' shall include wet docks and basins, tidal docks and basins, locks, cuts, entrances, dry docks, graving docks, gridirons, slips, quays, wharves, piers, stages, landing-places, and jetties.

(5) For the purposes of this section the term 'owners of a dock or canal' shall include any person or authority having the control and management of any dock or canal, as the case may be.

(6) Nothing in this section shall impose any liability in respect of any such loss or damage on any such owners or authority in any case where no such liability would have existed if this Act had not passed.

COMMENTS.

Application to Crown.

Consult Crown Proceedings Act 1947.

Dock.

In Nicholson (J. & W.) & Co. Ltd. *v. Humorist* (Owners). The

Humorist 1946, it was held that a warehouse built on the bed of the river is a landing-place, and is therefore within this definition.

The Right to Limit Liability.

This right conferred by this section on dock owners, by whom damage is caused without their actual fault or privety, does not depend upon the quality of the act causing the damage, but upon the area within which the act was done.

The Ruapeha 1927. *See* also the subsequent proceedings in the *Ruapeha* (No. 2) 1929, relating to an action to limit liability, where the ship repairers who owned docks at two separate places, *A* and *B*, were not bound to take into account the size of vessel, at their place *B*, and were thus able to limit their liability on the tonnage of the largest vessel at place *A*.

Consult also the *City of Edinburgh* 1921, relating to an act done by dock owners in their capacity of ship repairers, it being held that they were not entitled to limit their liability in respect of damage whilst engaged in repairing a vessel in a dock not owned by them. The ownership of another dock being completely unconnected with their liability in respect of the repairs carried out in a dock not owned by them.

The Words 'not exceeding eight pounds'.

By the M.S. (Liability of Shipowners and Others) Act 1958, section 1, sub-section 1, the words 'not exceeding eight pounds', are substituted by 'equivalent to 1000 gold francs'. *See* Merchant Shipping, The Merchant Shipping (Limitation of Liability) (Sterling Equivalents) Order 1974, No. 536, where the specified equivalent is £34·8928.

Harbour Authority: Conservancy Authority.

For definitions consult the Merchant Shipping Act 1894, section 742.

Merchant Shipping Act 1894, section 503, sub-section 2, as referred to in section 2 of the 1900 Act, is amended by the Merchant Shipping Act 1906, section 69.

Limitation of liability where several claims arise on one occasion.

3. The limitation of liability under this Act shall relate to the whole of any losses and damages which may arise upon any one distinct occasion, although such losses and damages may be sustained by more than one person, and shall apply whether the liability arises at common law or under any general or private Act of Parliament, and notwithstanding anything contained in such Act.

COMMENTS.

It was formerly held, consult Mersey Docks and Harbour Board *v.* Hay, *The Countess*, 1923, that the lien conferred on a dock authority by its private Act is not affected by this Act beyond limiting the amount for which the lien could be exercised.

However, in this respect, the law has been changed; *see* the M.S. (Liability of Shipowners and Others) Act 1958, section 7, sub-section 2, viz.:

'No lien or other right in respect of any ship or property shall affect the proportions in which, under the said section five hundred and four, any amount is distributed amongst several claimants.'

4. This Act may be cited as the Merchant Shipping (Liability of Shipowners and Others) Act 1900. Short title.

5. This Act shall be construed as one with the Merchant Shipping Act 1894, and that Act and the Merchant Shipping Act 1897, the Merchant Shipping (Exemption from Pilotage) Act 1897, the Merchant Shipping (Liability of Shipowners) Act 1898, the Merchant Shipping (Mercantile Marine Fund) Act 1898, and this Act may be cited together as the Merchant Shipping Acts 1894 to 1900.

Construction. 57 and 58 Vict. *c.* 60. 60 and 61 Vict. *c.* 59. 60 and 61 Vict. *c.* 61. 61 and 62 Vict. *c.* 14. 61 and 62 Vict. *c.* 44.

COMMENTS.

Now the Merchant Shipping Acts 1894 to 1960.

MERCHANT SHIPPING ACT 1906

SECTION 69

For the purpose of the limitation under the Merchant Shipping Acts of the liability of owners of ships, docks, or canals, and of harbour authorities and conservancy authorities, the tonnage of a steamship shall be her registered tonnage, with the addition of an engine-room space deducted for the purpose of ascertaining that tonnage, and the words 'registered tonnage with the addition of any engine-room space deducted for the purpose of ascertaining that tonnage' shall accordingly be substituted in paragraph (*a*) of sub-section (2) of section five hundred and three of the principal Act for 'gross tonnage without deduction on account of engine-room'.

Calculation of tonnage of steamship for the purpose of limitation of liability.

COMMENTS.

This substituted the words in section 503, sub-section 2 (*a*) of the Principal Act.

For the provisions as to tonnage measurement, consult Merchant Shipping Act 1894, section 77 et seq, and Schedules 2 and 6 as extended by Merchant Shipping Act 1954.

MERCHANT SHIPPING ACT 1906

SECTION 70 AND SECTION 71

These two sections which amended the provisions of Part VIII of the Principal Act and also section 1 of the Liability Act of 1898, now repealed, have in turn been repealed by the M.S. (Liability of Shipowners and Others) Act 1958, section 8, sub-section 6, and schedule.

Consult now section 3, sub-section 1, and section 4 of the 1958 Liability Act.

PILOTAGE ACT 1913

SECTION 35

Limitation of Pilot's Liability where bond is given.

(1) A licensed pilot, who has given a bond in conformity with by-laws made for the purpose under this Act, shall not be liable for neglect or want of skill beyond the penalty of the bond and the amount payable to him on account of pilotage in respect of the voyage in which he was engaged when he became so liable.

(2) Any bond given by a pilot in conformity with by-laws made for the purpose under this Act, shall not be liable to stamp duty, and a pilot shall not be called upon to pay any expense in relation to the bond, other than the actual expense of preparing the same.

(3) Where any proceedings are taken against a pilot for any neglect or want of skill in respect of which his liability is limited as provided by this section and other claims are made or apprehended in respect of the same neglect or want of skill, the court in which the proceedings are taken may determine the amount of the pilot's liability, and, upon payment by the pilot of that amount into court, may distribute that amount rateably among the several claimants, and may stay any proceedings pending in any other court in relation to the same matter, and may proceed in such manner and subject to such regulations as to making persons interested parties to the proceedings and as to the exclusion of any claimants who do not come in within a certain time, and as to

requiring security from the pilot and as to payment of any costs as the court thinks just.

COMMENTS.

Beyond the Penalty of the Bond.

Section 17 of this 1913 Act allows a pilotage authority to make by-laws. Section 1, sub-section (i) states:—

. . . 'provide, if and so far as it appears to the authority to be generally desired by the pilots, for bonds (the penalty of which shall not in any case exceed one hundred pounds) being given by pilots for the purpose of the provisions of this Act limiting pilots' liability . . .'

Meaning of Pilot.

See section 742 of the Principal Act.

Pilotage Authorities (Limitation of Liability) Act 1936.

Consult this Act as to the limitation of liability of a Pilotage Authority.

THE MERCHANT SHIPPING ACT 1921

(1) The Merchant Shipping Act 1921.

Application of Parts I and VIII of the Merchant Shipping Act 1894, to lighters, etc.

(1) Notwithstanding anything in section seven hundred and forty-two of the Merchant Shipping Act 1894 (hereinafter referred to as 'the Principal Act'), the Principal Act shall have effect as though in the provisions of Parts I and VIII thereof (which relate respectively to the registry of ships and to the limitation of the liability of the owners of ships), as amended or extended by any subsequent enactment, the expression 'ship' included every description of lighter, barge, or like vessel used in navigation in Great Britain, however propelled:

Provided that a lighter, barge, or like vessel used exclusively in non-tidal waters, other than harbours, shall not, for the purposes of this Act, be deemed to be used in navigation.

(2) In the application of Part VIII of the principal Act to any such lighter, barge, or like vessel as aforesaid, the expression 'owner' shall include any hirer who has contracted to take over the sole charge and management thereof and is responsible for the navigation, manning and equipment thereof.

(3) Where the Board of Trade are satisfied that there are in force in any port under any Act or Order, regulations for the measurement or registration of lighters, barges, or like

vessels, which provide for the measurement of their tonnage in substantial agreement with the provisions of the Merchant Shipping Acts 1894 to 1920, and for an adequate system of identification of the vessels and their owners, the Board may by order declare that vessels measured or registered in accordance with such regulations shall, for the purposes of this Act, be deemed to be measured or registered under Part 1 of the Principal Act.

COMMENTS.

Repeal.

Sub-section 2, underlined above, has been repealed by the M.S. (Liability of Shipowners and Others) Act 1958, section 8, sub-section 6 and Schedule, and replaced by section 3, sub-section 1 of the 1958 Act.

Purposes of Limitation.

In respect of purposes of limitation, it is no longer material as to whether or not the ship has been registered. Consult the M.S. (Liability of Shipowners and Others) Act 1958, section 4, sub-section 2.

It would appear that limitation can be invoked in respect of a ship which falls within any one of these definitions contained in the following:—

(i) Section 742 of the Merchant Shipping Act 1894.

(ii) Section 1, sub-section 1 of the Merchant Shipping Act 1921.

(iii) Section 4, sub-section 1 of the M.S. (Liability of Shipowners and Others) Act 1958.

Attention is drawn to section 3 of this Act, that is, the Merchant Shipping Act 1921, which would appear to prevent the owners of any lighter, barge or like vessel from limiting their liability for loss of life or personal injury, caused to any person carried therein.

Hirer of Barge.

A Hirer does not cease to have sole charge and management because of an arrangement with the owner of the barge, who maintains responsibility for its upkeep, *The Thames* 1940.

⚓ ⚓ ⚓ ⚓

(2)

Use of unsafe lighters, etc.

(1) If any person uses or causes or permits to be used in navigation any lighter, barge, or like vessel when, through the defective condition of its hull or equipment or by reason of overloading or improper loading through undermanning, it is so unsafe that human life is likely to be thereby endangered, he shall be liable on summary conviction to a fine not exceeding one hundred pounds or to imprisonment for a term not exceeding six months.

(2) A prosecution under this section shall not, except in Scotland, be instituted otherwise than by, or with the consent of the Board of Trade.

COMMENTS.

Board of Trade.

For transfer of powers consult section 713 of the Principal Act.

Unsafe Lighters.

Consult and compare sections 457–463 of the Merchant Shipping Act 1894 as to unseaworthy ships.

⚓ ⚓ ⚓ ⚓

(3)

This Act shall not affect the liability of the owners of any lighter, barge, or like vessel in respect of loss of life or personal injury caused to any person carried therein. Saving for workmen.

COMMENTS.

Loss of Life.

Consult comments to section 1 of this Act.

⚓ ⚓ ⚓ ⚓

(4)

(1) This Act may be cited as the Merchant Shipping Act 1921, and shall be construed as one with the Merchant Shipping Acts 1894 to 1920, and those Acts and this Act may be cited together as the Merchant Shipping Acts 1894 to 1921. Short title, construction, and commencement.

(2) This Act shall come into operation on the first day of January, one thousand nine hundred and twenty-two.
(Sub-section (2) was repealed by the Shipping Liability Repeal Act 1950.)

COMMENTS.

Merchant Shipping Acts.

Now the Merchant Shipping Acts 1894 to 1970.

⚓ ⚓ ⚓ ⚓

THE PILOTAGE AUTHORITIES (LIMITATION OF LIABILITY) ACT 1936

General Comment

This Act makes provision with respect to the liability of pilotage authorities and others, and extends to

Pilotage Authorities (other than shipowners) privileges for limiting their liability similar to those granted to dock, canal, harbour, and conservancy authorities by section 2 of the M.S. (Liability of Shipowners and Others) Act 1900 as amended by the M.S. (Liability of Shipowners and Others) Act 1958.

Limitation of Liability of Pilotage Authorities. **(1)**

Limitation of liability of pilotage authorities.

(i) A pilotage authority (as defined in this Act) shall not where without their actual fault or privity any loss or damage is caused to any vessel or vessels, or to any goods, merchandise or other things whatsoever on board any vessel or vessels, or to any other property or rights of any kind, whether on land or on water, whether fixed or moveable, be liable to damages beyond the amount of one hundred pounds multiplied by the number of pilots holding licences from the pilotage authority under section sixteen of the Pilotage Act 1913, for the pilotage district of the pilotage authority at the date when the loss or damage occurs.

(ii) Nothing in this section shall impose any liability in respect of any such loss or damage as aforesaid on any pilotage authority in any case where no such liability would have existed if this Act had not been passed.

COMMENTS.

Pilotage Authority.

For definition, *see* section 8.

Pilotage District.

For definition, *see* the Pilotage Act 1913, section 8, as applied by section II, sub-section I of this, the 1936 Act.

Liability of Pilots.

If a pilot has given a bond in conformity with by-laws made under the Pilotage Act 1913, section 17, sub-section 1 (i), his liability for neglect or want of skill is limited to the penalty of the bond and the amount payable to him on account of pilotage in respect of the voyage in which he was engaged when he became liable.

Claims.

Where there are several claims on one occasion, consult section 2 of this Act and for the power of the court to consolidate claims, *see* section 3 of this Act.

(2) Limitation of Liability where Several Claims on One Occasion.

Limitation of liability where several claims on one occasion.

The limitation of liability under section one of this Act shall relate to the whole of any losses and damages which may arise upon any one distinct occasion, although such losses and damages may be sustained by more than one person, and shall apply whether the liability arises at common law or under any public general or local Act of Parliament and notwithstanding anything contained in such Act.

COMMENTS.

Claims.

Where the pilotage authority are the owners of a ship, *see* section 4.

Distinct Occasion.

See relevant comment to section 503 of the Principal Act.

(3) Power of Courts to Consolidate Claims.

Power of courts to consolidate claims.

Where any liability is alleged to have been incurred by a pilotage authority in respect of any loss or damage to which section one of this Act applies, and several claims are made or apprehended in respect of that liability, then the pilotage authority may apply in England to the High Court, or in Scotland to the Court of Session, or in Northern Ireland to the High Court of Justice in Northern Ireland, or in the Isle of Man to the High Court of Justice of the Isle of Man, and that court may determine the amount of liability of the pilotage authority, and may distribute that amount rateably among the several claimants, and may stay any proceedings pending in any other court in relation to the same matter, and may proceed in such manner and subject to such regulations as to making persons interested parties to the proceedings, and as to the exclusion of any claimants who do not come in within a certain time, and as to requiring security from the pilotage authority, and as to payment of any costs, as the court thinks just.

COMMENTS.

Consolidation of Claims.

Compare sections 504 of the 1894 Act, which applies to the consolidation of claims against owners, and section 35, sub-section 3 of the

Pilotage Act 1913, which applies to the consolidation of claims against pilots.

Various.

Consult generally section 504 of the Merchant Shipping Acts 1894.

⚓ ⚓ ⚓ ⚓

Act Not to Apply to Pilotage Authority as Owners of Ships. (4)

Act not to apply to pilotage authority as owners of Ships.

Where any pilotage authority are the owners of any ship, nothing in this Act shall affect any limitation of liability conferred on them or other rights to which they are entitled as such owners by or under Part VIII of the Merchant Shipping Act 1894 and the M.S. (Liability of Shipowners and Others) Act 1900, as respectively amended by subsequent Acts, and accordingly the foregoing provisions of this Act shall not apply to any loss or damage, the liability for which can be limited under the said enactments.

COMMENTS.

Pilotage Authority.

As to meaning, *see* section 8 of this Act.

Subsequent Act.

Consult the Limitation Acts 1900 et seq., and in particular the M.S. (Liability of Shipowners and Others) Act 1958.

⚓ ⚓ ⚓ ⚓

Saving for Funds for Benefit of Pilots, etc. (5)

Saving for funds for benefit of pilots, etc.

No pilots' benefit fund, pilotage annunity fund or other fund, formed or maintained by a pilotage authority for the benefit of pilots, their widows or children, shall be capable of being charged or attached or taken in execution or made available by any legal process or otherwise for meeting any liability of, or any claim against the pilotage authority.

COMMENTS.

Pilotage Authority.

As to meaning, *see* section 8.

Pilots' Benefit Fund.

Pilots' benefit funds may be formed under by-laws made by section 17, sub-section 1 (*j*) of the Pilotage Act 1913.

⚓ ⚓ ⚓ ⚓

As to Funds of Authorities Acting in Dual Capacity. **(6)**

If any body of persons, corporate or unincorporate, are the owners of any dock or canal (including any body of persons having the control or management of any dock or canal) or are a harbour authority or a conservancy authority and that body or a committee of that body are also a pilotage authority, then—

As to funds of authorities acting in dual capacity.

(i) No funds, revenues, moneys or other property whatsoever belonging to such a body in any capacity other than as pilotage authority shall be capable of being charged or attached or taken in execution or made available by any legal process or otherwise for meeting any liability of, or any claim against, such body or any committee of such body in their capacity as pilotage authority; and

(ii) No funds, revenues, moneys or other property whatsoever belonging to such body or a committee of such body in their capacity as pilotage authority shall be capable of being charged or attached or taken in execution or made available by any legal process, or otherwise for meeting any liability of, or any claim against, such body in any capacity other than as pilotage authority.

COMMENTS.

Harbour Authority, Conservancy Authority.

These terms are defined in section 742 of the Principal Act, and are applied in accord with section 9 of this Limitation Act of 1936.

Dock.

It is submitted that the definition of 'dock', as contained in section 2 of the Limitation Act of 1900, would apply.

Pilotage Authority.

See section 8.

Pilot Fund.

See section 21, sub-section 1 of the Pilotage Act 1913.

(7) As to Funds of Certain Trinity Houses.

(i) No funds, revenues, moneys, or other property whatsoever belonging to the Trinity House or the Trinity House of Newcastle-upon-Tyne, in any capacity other than as pilotage authority, shall be capable of being charged or attached or taken in execution or made available by any legal process or otherwise for meeting any liability of, or any claim against, either such body in their capacity as pilotage authority.

As to funds of certain Trinity Houses.

(ii) No funds, revenues, moneys, or other property whatsoever belonging to the Trinity House or any committee or sub-commissioners of the Trinity House or the Trinity House of Newcastle-upon-Tyne in their capacity as pilotage authority, shall be capable of being charged, or attached or taken in execution or made available by any legal process or otherwise for meeting any liability of, or any claim against, any such body in any capacity other than as pilotage authority.

COMMENTS.

The Trinity House.

I.e. the Trinity House of Deptford Strond. *See* section 742 of the Merchant Shipping Act 1894 as applied by section 9 of this, the 1936 Act.

The Trinity House of Newcastle-upon-Tyne.

See section 9 of this Act.

Pilotage Authority.

For definition, *see* section 8 of this Act.

Authorities Acting in Dual Capacity.

As to funds of these, consult section 6 of this Act.

Meaning of Pilotage Authority. **(8)**

Meaning of pilotage authority.

(i) In this Act, 'pilotage authority' means a body of persons or authority incorporated, constituted or established as a pilotage authority by a Pilotage Order made under the Pilotage Act 1913, and where any existing body of persons or authority constituted or established for any other purposes and with other duties or any committee of such existing body of persons or authority are constituted or established a pilotage authority by any such Order includes that body of persons, authority, or committee.

(ii) Where any body of persons or authority are incorporated, constituted or established by any such Order or Orders as the pilotage authority for more than one pilotage district, this Act shall have effect as though such body of persons or authority were a separate pilotage authority for each separate pilotage district.

COMMENTS.

The Pilotage Act of 1913, section 7, gives power to the Minister of Transport to make Pilotage Orders.

(9) Definitions.

In this Act, unless the context otherwise requires, words and expressions to which meanings are assigned by the Merchant Shipping Act 1894, as amended by subsequent Acts, shall have the same respective meanings; and the expression 'the Trinity House of Newcastle-upon-Tyne' means the Corporation of the Master Pilots and Seamen of he Trinity House of Newcastle-upon-Tyne. **Definitions.**

COMMENTS.

Merchant Shipping Act 1894.

Consult section 742 of that Act as to the meaning of various expressions.

Extent of Act. (10)

This Act extends to Great Britain, Northern Ireland and the Isle of Man. **Extent of Act.**

Short Title and Construction. (11)

(i) This Act may be cited as the Pilotage Authorities (Limitation of Liability) Act 1936, and shall be construed as one with the Pilotage Act 1913, and the Acts amending that Act. **Short title and construction.**

(ii) The Pilotage Act 1913, and this Act may be cited together as the Pilotage Acts 1913 and 1936.

COMMENTS.

Construed as One.

Every part of each of the Acts has to be construed . . . 'as if it had been contained in one Act, unless there is some manifest discrepancy, making it necessary to hold that the later Act has to some extent, modified something found in the earlier Act', per Earl of Selbourne L.C. in Canada Southern Railway Co. *v.* International Bridge Co. 1883.

This principle has been applied in Hart *v.* Hudson Bros., Ltd. 1928; Phillips *v.* Parnaby 1934.

MERCHANT SHIPPING

(Liability of Shipowners and Others) Act 1958

MERCHANT SHIPPING

(Liability of Shipowners and Others) Act 1958

An Act to amend Part VIII of the Merchant Shipping Act 1894, and section two of the Merchant Shipping (Liability of Shipowners and Others) Act 1900; and for purposes connected therewith.

[1st August 1958]

Be it enacted by the Queen's most Excellent Majesty, by and with the advice and consent of the Lords Spiritual and Temporal, and Commons, in this present Parliament assembled, and by the authority of the same, as follows:—

1. (1) In ascertaining the limits set to the liability of any persons by section five hundred and three of the Merchant Shipping Act 1894, or section two of the Merchant Shipping (Liability of Shipowners and Others) Act 1900, there shall be substituted—

Increase in liability of shipowners and others. 57 and 58 Vict. *c.* 60. 63 and 64 Vict. *c.* 32.

(*a*) for the amount of fifteen pounds mentioned in the said section five hundred and three, an amount equivalent to three thousand one hundred gold francs;

(*b*) for each of the amounts of eight pounds mentioned in the said sections, an amount equivalent to one thousand gold francs;

and the number by which the amount substituted by paragraph (*a*) of this sub-section is to be multiplied shall be three hundred in any case where the tonnage concerned is less than three hundred tons.

(2) For the purposes of this section a gold franc shall be taken to be a unit consisting of sixty-five and a half milligrams of gold of millesimal fineness nine hundred.

(3) The Minister of Transport and Civil Aviation may from time to time by order made by statutory instrument specify the amounts which for the purposes of this section are to be taken as equivalent to three thousand one hundred and one thousand gold francs respectively.

(4) Where money has been paid into court (or, in Scotland, consigned in court) in respect of any liability to which a limit

is set as aforesaid, the ascertainment of that limit shall not be affected by a subsequent variation of the amounts specified under sub-section (3) of this section unless the amount paid or consigned was less than that limit as ascertained in accordance with the order then in force under that sub-section.

COMMENTS.

Sterling Equivalents.

See the Merchant Shipping (Limitation of Liability) (Sterling Equivalents) Order 1974, operative from 12th April 1974, where the equivalents of 1000 gold francs is to be taken as £34·8929 and 3100 gold francs as £108·1673.

Consult Generally.

Section 503 of the Principal Act as amended.

⚓ ⚓ ⚓ ⚓

Amendments as to nature of liability limited by Merchant Shipping Act 1894, *s.* 503.

2. (1) In sub-section (1) of section five hundred and three of the Merchant Shipping Act 1894, the following paragraphs shall be substituted for paragraphs (*c*) and (*d*)—

'(*c*) where any loss of life or personal injury is caused to any person not carried in the ship through the act or omission of any person (whether on board the ship or not) in the navigation or management of the ship or in the loading, carriage or discharge of its cargo or in the embarkation, carriage or disembarkation of its passengers, or through any other act or omission of any person on board the ship;

(*d*) where any loss or damage is caused to any property (other than any property mentioned in paragraph (*b*) of this sub-section) or any rights are infringed through the act or omission of any person (whether on board the ship or not) in the navigation or management of the ship, or in the loading, carriage or discharge of its cargo or in the embarkation, carriage or disembarkation of its passengers, or through any other act or omission of any person on board the ship;'

and for the words 'loss of or damage to vessels, goods, merchandise or other things', both where they occur in paragraph (i) and where they occur in paragraph (ii), there shall be substituted the words 'such loss, damage or infringement as is mentioned in paragraphs (*b*) and (*d*) of this sub-section'.

(2) For the purposes of the said sub-section (1), where any obligation or liability arises—

(*a*) in connection with the raising, removal or destruction of any ship which is sunk, stranded or abandoned or of anything on board such a ship, or

(*b*) in respect of any damage (however caused) to harbour works, basins or navigable waterways,

the occurrence giving rise to the obligation or liability shall be treated as one of the occurrences mentioned in paragraphs (*b*) and (*d*) of that sub-section, and the obligation or liability as a liability to damages.

(3) The application of the said section five hundred and three to any liability shall not be excluded by reason only that the occurrence giving rise to the liability was not due to the negligence of any person.

(4) Nothing in the said section five hundred and three shall apply to any liability in respect of loss of life or personal injury caused to, or loss of or damage to any property or infringement of any right of, a person who is on board or employed in connection with the ship under a contract of service with all or any of the persons whose liabilities are limited by that section, if that contract is governed by the law of any country outside the United Kingdom and that law either does not set any limit to that liability or sets a limit exceeding that set to it by that section.

(5) Paragraph (*a*) of sub-section (2) of this section shall not come into force until such day as the Minister of Transport and Civil Aviation may by order made by statutory instrument appoint.

(6) The Minister of Transport and Civil Aviation may by order make provision for the setting up and management of a fund, to be used for the making to harbour or conservancy authorities of payments needed to compensate them for the reduction, in accordance with paragraph (*a*) of sub-section (2) of this section, of amounts recoverable by them in respect of the obligations and liabilities mentioned in that paragraph, and to be maintained by contributions from such authorities raised and collected by them in respect of vessels in like manner as other sums so raised by them; and any such order may contain such incidental and supplementary provisions as appear to the Minister to be necessary or expedient.

(7) The power to make an order under sub-section (6) of this section shall include power to vary or revoke any such order by a subsequent order and any such power shall be exercisable by statutory instrument, which shall be subject to

annulment in pursuance of a resolution of either House of Parliament.

COMMENTS.

Section 2, Sub-section (2) (a).

This provision is not effective until such day as may be appointed by statutory instrument.

Sub-section (3).

It would appear that the right to limit is not extended to liabilities other than 'damages', for example a contractual liability to indemnify irrespective of negligence or breach of contract, *The Kirkness* 1957.

Sub-section (4): The Term 'United Kingdom'.

The term in this section means Great Britain and Northern Ireland. Consult also section 11 of this Act.

Sub-section (5).

Where this sub-section becomes effective it will override the decision in *The Millie* 1940, and *The Stonedale*, No. 1 1956.

⚓ ⚓ ⚓ ⚓

Extension to other persons of provisions applying to shipowners.

(3) (1) The persons whose liability in connection with a ship is excluded or limited by Part VIII of the Merchant Shipping Act 1894, shall include any charterer and any person interested in or in possession of the ship, and, in particular, any manager or operator of the ship.

(2) In relation to a claim arising from the act or omission of any person in his capacity as master or member of the crew or (otherwise than in that capacity) in the course of his employment as a servant of the owners or of any such person as is mentioned in sub-section (1) of this section,—

(*a*) the persons whose liability is excluded or limited as aforesaid shall also include the master, member of the crew or servant, and, in a case where the master or member of the crew is the servant of a person whose liability would not be excluded or limited apart from this paragraph, the person whose servant he is; and

(*b*) the liability of the master, member of the crew or servant himself shall be excluded or limited as aforesaid notwithstanding his actual fault or privity in that capacity, except in the cases mentioned in paragraph (ii) of section five hundred and two of the said Act of 1894.

COMMENTS

The persons . . . excluded.

In this regard consult section 502 of the Principal Act, and comments, by which liability may be completely excluded.

Liability of Master.

The words of this Act, 'in that capacity', intend to prevent a master, owner from limiting his liability when the loss or damage occurs, as a result of fault or privity in respect of a matter for which owners are normally responsible.

⚓ ⚓ ⚓ ⚓

4. (1) Part VIII of the Merchant Shipping Act 1894, shall apply to any structure, whether completed or in course of completion, launched and intended for use in navigation as a ship or part of a ship, and the expression 'ship' in the said Part VIII and in this Act shall be construed accordingly. **Unregistered ships and ships in course of completion or construction.**

(2) The said Part VIII shall apply to any British ship notwithstanding that it has not yet been registered.

(3) The tonnage of any ship or structure to which the said Part VIII applies by virtue of this section shall, for the purposes of that Part, be ascertained as provided by sub-section (2) of section five hundred and three of the said Act of 1894 with regard to foreign ships.

COMMENTS.

The Expression 'ship'.

Consult section 742 of the Principal Act for the definition of 'ship'. Also, section 1 of the Merchant Shipping Act 1921, by which the application of Part VIII of the Principal Act is extended.

⚓ ⚓ ⚓ ⚓

5. (1) Where a ship or other property is arrested in connection with a claim which appears to the court to be founded on a liability to which a limit is set by section five hundred and three of the Merchant Shipping Act 1894, or security is given to prevent or obtain release from such an arrest, the court may, and in the circumstances mentioned in sub-section (3) of this section shall, order the release of the ship, property or security, if the conditions specified in sub-section (2) of this section are satisfied; but where the release is ordered the person on whose application it is ordered shall be deemed to have submitted to **Release of ship, etc.**

the jurisdiction of the court to adjudicate on the claim (or, in Scotland, to have prorogated that jurisdiction).

(2)The said conditions are—

(*a*) that security which in the opinion of the court is satisfactory (in this section referred to as 'guarantee') has previously been given, whether in the United Kingdom or elsewhere, in respect of the said liability or any other liability incurred on the same occasion and the court is satisfied that, if the claim is established, the amount for which the guarantee was given or such part thereof as corresponds to the claim will be actually available to the claimant; and

(*b*) that either the guarantee is for an amount not less than the said limit or further security is given which, together with the guarantee, is for an amount not less than that limit.

(3) The circumstances mentioned is sub-section (1) of this section are that the guarantee was given in a port which, in relation to the claim, is the relevant port (or, as the case may be, a relevant port and that that port is in a Convention country.

(4) For the purposes of this section—

(*a*) a guarantee given by the giving of security in more than one country shall be deemed to have been given in the country in which security was last given;

(*b*) any question whether the amount of any security is (either by itself or together with any other amount) not less than any limit set by section five hundred and three of the Merchant Shipping Act 1894, shall be decided as at the time at which the security is given;

(*c*) where part only of the amount for which a guarantee was given will be available to a claimant that part shall not be taken to correspond to his claim if any other part may be available to a claimant in respect of a liability to which no limit is set as mentioned in sub-section (1) of this section.

(5) In this section—

'Convention country' means any country in respect of which the Convention is in force (including any country to which the Convention extends by virtue of Article 14 thereof);

'relevant port'—

(*a*) in relation to any claim, means the port where the event giving rise to the claim occurred or, if that event did not occur in a port, the first port of call after the event occurred; and

(*b*) in relation to a claim for loss of life or personal injury or for damage to cargo, includes the port of disembarkation or discharge.

'the Convention' means the International Convention relating to the Limitation of the Liability of Owners of Seagoing Ships signed in Brussels on the tenth day of October, nineteen hundred and fifty-seven.

(6) If Her Majesty by Order in Council declares that any country specified in the Order is a Convention country within the meaning of this section, the Order shall, while in force, be conclusive evidence that the country is a Convention country; but any Order in Council under this section may be varied or revoked by a subsequent Order in Council.

(7) In the application of this section to Scotland, the references to arrest shall be construed as referring to arrestment on the dependence of an action or *in rem* and for the references to release from arrest or to the ordering of such a release there shall be substituted references to the recall of an arrestment.

COMMENTS.

Section 1, the Court.

For the Admiralty jurisdiction for actions *in rem*, consult sections 1 and 3 of the Administration of Justice Act 1956.

⚓ ⚓ ⚓ ⚓

6. (1) No judgment or decree for a claim founded on a liability to which a limit is set by section five hundred and three of the Merchant Shipping Act 1894, shall be enforced, except so far as it is for costs (or, in Scotland, expenses), if security for an amount not less than the said limit has been given, whether in the United Kingdom or elsewhere, in respect of the liability or any other liability incurred on the same occasion and the court is of opinion that the security is satisfactory and is satisfied that the amount for which it was given or such part thereof as corresponds to the claim will be actually available to the person in whose favour the judgment or decree was given or made.

Restriction on enforcement after giving of security.

(2) For the purposes of this section—

(*a*) any question whether the amount of any security is

not less than any limit set by section five hundred and three of the Merchant Shipping Act 1894, shall be decided as at the time at which the security is given;

(*b*) where part only of the amount for which security has been given will be available to the person in whose favour the judgment or decree was given or made that part shall not be taken to correspond to his claim if any other part may be available to a claimant in respect of a liability to which no limit is set as mentioned in sub-section (1) of this section.

⚓ ⚓ ⚓ ⚓

Distribution of limitation fund.

7. (1) In making any distribution in accordance with section five hundred and four of the Merchant Shipping Act 1894, the court may, if it thinks fit, postpone the distribution of such part of the amount to be distributed as it deems appropriate having regard to any claims that may later be established before a court of any country outside the United Kingdom.

(2) No lien or other right in respect of any ship or property shall affect the proportions in which under the said section five hundred and four any amount is distributed amongst several claimants.

COMMENTS.

Section 1, sub-section 1. Claims . . . outside the United Kingdom.

It would appear that this Act, and particularly this section, gives a wider discretion than formerly. Consult *The Kronprinz Olav* 1921, in which the Court of Appeal decided that if no payment has been made as a result of a foreign judgement, the owner could not put forward a contingent claim which may be awarded against him, but the court could delay the distribution, pending the complete ascertainment of the claims, as long as application was made in good time.

Sub-section 2.

This overrides the decision on Mersey Docks and Harbour Boards *v.* Hay (*The Countess*) 1923, where it was held by the House of Lords that a possessary lien over the ship has a superior right, even to the extent of depriving other claimants of all right of recovery against the limitation fund.

⚓ ⚓ ⚓ ⚓

8. (1) In section five hundred and two of the Merchant Shipping Act 1894, the word 'sea-going' shall be omitted.

Minor and consequential amendments and repeals.

(2) For sub-section (3) of section five hundred and three of the Merchant Shipping Act 1894, there shall be substituted the following sub-section—

'(3) The limits set by this section to the liabilities mentioned therein shall apply to the aggregate of such liabilities which are incurred on any distinct occasion, and shall so apply in respect of each distinct occasion without regard to any liability incurred on another occasion.'

(3) In section five hundred and four of the Merchant Shipping Act 1894, for the words 'in respect of loss of life, personal injury or loss of or damage to vessels or goods' there shall be substituted the words 'in respect of any occurrence in respect of which his liability is limited under section five hundred and three of this Act'.

(4) In Part VIII of the Merchant Shipping Act 1894, the expression 'owner' shall be construed as including, where it occurs in section five hundred and two, every person whose liability is excluded by section three of this Act, and elsewhere, except in the second place where it occurs in section five hundred and five, every person whose liability is limited by that section.

(5) In section five of the Crown Proceedings Act 1947, the following shall be substituted for paragraph (*a*) of sub-section (6)—

'(*a*) any structure to which Part VIII of that Act is applied by section four of the Merchant Shipping (Liability of Shipowners and Others) Act 1958; and'

and in sub-section (8) for the reference to the Merchant Shipping (Liability of Shipowners) Act 1898, there shall be substituted a reference to sections three and four of this Act.

(6) The enactments mentioned in the Schedule to this Act are hereby repealed to the extent specified in the third column of that Schedule.

⚓ ⚓ ⚓ ⚓

9. Nothing in this Act applies in relation to any liability arising from an occurrence which took place before the commencement of this Act.

Saving for occurrences taking place before commencement.

⚓ ⚓ ⚓ ⚓

10. (1) This Act extends to Northern Ireland.

(2) In the application of this Act to Northern Ireland the reference in section eight to the Crown Proceedings Act 1947, is a reference to that Act as it applies in Northern Ireland.

(3) For the purposes of section six of the Government of Ireland Act 1920 (which relates to the powers of the Parliament of Northern Ireland to make laws), this Act shall be deemed to have been passed before the day appointed for the purposes of that section.

⚓ ⚓ ⚓ ⚓

Application to British possessions, etc.

11. (1) Her Majesty may by Order in Council direct that the provisions of this Act, and (so far as they do not so extend apart from the Order) the existing limitation enactments, shall extend, with such exceptions, adaptations and modifications as may be specified in the Order, to—

(*a*) the Isle of Man;

(*b*) any of the Channel Islands;

(*c*) any colony, or any country or place outside Her Majesty's dominions in which for the time being Her Majesty has jurisdiction, or any territory consisting partly of one or more colonies and partly of one or more such countries or places.

(2) In this section 'the existing limitation enactments' means Part VIII of the Merchant Shipping Act 1894, sections two of the M.S. (Liability of Shipowners and Others) Act 1900, and any incidental or supplementary provisions of any enactment applying the said Part or section.

COMMENTS.

Isle of Man.

Consult the M.S. (Liability of Shipowners and Others) Act 1958 (Isle of Man) Order 1960, No. 1379, for extension to the Isle of Man.

⚓ ⚓ ⚓ ⚓

Construction, short title and citation.

12. (1) Any reference in this Act to any other enactment is a reference thereto as amended, and includes references thereto as applied, by or under any subsequent enactment, including, except where the context otherwise requires, this Act.

(2) This Act shall be construed as one with the Merchant Shipping Acts 1894 to 1954.

(3) This Act may be cited as the M.S. (Liability of Shipowners and Others) Act 1958, and this Act and the Merchant Shipping Acts 1894 to 1954 may be cited together as the Merchant Shipping Acts 1894 to 1958.

COMMENTS.

It is submitted that definitions in previous Acts may be taken into account in regard to the construction of the provisions of this, the 1958 Act.

SCHEDULE

ENACTMENTS REPEALED

Table of Statutes referred to in this Act

Session and Chapter	Short Title	Extent of Repeal
57 & 58 Vict. *c.* 60.	The Merchant Shipping Act 1894.	In section five hundred and two, the word 'sea-going'. Section five hundred and eight.
61 & 62 Vict. *c.* 14.	The Merchant Shipping (Liability of Shipowners) Act 1898.	The whole Act.
63 & 64 Vict. *c.* 32.	The Merchant Shipping (Liability of Shipowners and others) Act 1900.	Section one.
6 Edw. 7. *c.* 48.	The Merchant Shipping Act 1906.	Sections seventy and seventy-one.
11 & 12 Geo 5 *c.* 28.	The Merchant Shipping Act 1921.	Sub-section (2) of section one.

Short Title	Session and Chapter
Merchant Shipping Act 1894	57 & 58 Vict. *c.* 60.
Merchant Shipping (Liability of Shipowners) Act 1898	61 & 62 Vict. *c.* 14.
Merchant Shipping (Liability of Shipowners and Others) Act 1900	63 & 64 Vict. *c.* 32.
Government of Ireland Act 1920	10 & 11 Geo. 5. *c.* 67.
Crown Proceedings Act 1947	10 & 11 Geo. 6 *c.* 44.

The Crown Proceedings Act 1947, applied the provisions of the M.S. Acts in regard to limitation of liability of Her

Majesty, in respect of H.M. Ships, the liability of demise or sub-demise charterers of ships from Her Majesty, and to the liability of managers of Her Majesty's Ships.
The relevant sections are:—Numbers 5 and 7.

THE CROWN PROCEEDINGS ACT 1947

Section 5

Liability in respect of Crown ships, etc.

(1) The provisions of the Merchant Shipping Acts 1894 to 1940, which limit the amount of the liability of the owners of ships shall, with any necessary modifications, apply for the purpose of limiting the liability of His Majesty, in respect of His Majesty's Ships, and any provision of the said Acts which relates to or is ancillary to or consequential on the provisions so applied shall have effect accordingly.

(2) Without prejudice to the provisions of the preceding sub-section, where a ship is built at any port or place within His Majesty's dominions, and His Majesty is interested in her by reason of the fact that she is built by or on behalf of or to the order of His Majesty in right of his Government in the United Kingdom, the provisions of the Merchant Shipping Acts 1894 to 1940, which limit the amount of liability of the owners of ships, shall, with any necessary modifications, apply for the purposes of limiting liabilities in respect of that ship of His Majesty, her builders, her owners, and any other persons interested in her; and any provision of the said Acts which relates to or is ancillary to or consequential on the provisions so applied shall have effect accordingly.

This sub-section shall have effect only in respect of the period from and including the launching of the ship until the time of her completion, and shall not in any event have effect in respect of any period during which His Majesty is not interested in the ship as aforesaid. In relation to a ship built to the order of His Majesty in right of His Government in the United Kingdom, the time of her completion shall be taken for the purposes of this sub-section to be the time when His Majesty, acting in His said right, finally takes delivery of her under the building contract.

(3) Where any ship has been demised or sub-demised by His Majesty acting in right of His Government in the United Kingdom, then whether or not the ship is registered for the purposes of the Merchant Shipping Acts 1894 to 1940, the provisions of those Acts which limit the amount of the liability of the owners of ships, shall, in respect of the period

for which the demise or sub-demise continues, apply with any necessary modifications, for the purpose of limiting the liabilities in respect of the ship of any person entitled to her by demise or sub-demise and any provisions of the said Acts which relates to or is ancillary to or consequential on the provisions so applied shall have effect accordingly.

This sub-section shall be deemed to always have had effect.

(4) Where by virtue of any arrangement between His Majesty and some other person (not being a seservant of His Majesty) that other person (hereinafter referred to as 'the manager') is entrusted with the management of any of His Majesty's Ships, the provisions of the Merchant Shipping Acts 1894 to 1940, which limit the amount of the liability of the owners of ships, shall apply for the purpose of limiting the manager's liability in respect of the ship while so entrusted; and any provision of the said Acts which relates to or is ancillary to or consequential on the provisions so applied shall have effect accordingly.

This sub-section shall be deemed always to have had effect.

(5) Where for the purposes of any enactment as applied by this section it is necessary to ascertain the tonnage of any ship, and that ship is not registered for the purposes of the Merchant Shipping Acts 1894 to 1940, the tonnage of the ship shall be taken for the purposes of that enactment to be the tonnage arrived at by:—

(*a*) ascertaining her tonnage in accordance with section seventy-seven of the Merchant Shipping Act 1894, and the Rules contained in the Second Schedule to that Act, or those Rules as modified or altered from time to time under sub-section (7) of the said section seventy-seven and deducting from her tonnage as so ascertained ten percent thereof; *or*

(*b*) where it is impossible to ascertain her tonnage as provided by paragraph (*a*) of this sub-section, taking her estimated tonnage as certified for the purposes of this paragraph, and deducting from her estimated tonnage as so certified ten percent thereof.

Where it is necessary to ascertain the tonnage of a ship in the manner provided by paragraph (*b*) of this sub-section, the Chief Ships Surveyor of the Ministry of Transport or the Officer for the time being discharging the functions of the said surveyor, shall, upon the direction of the court concerned, and after considering such evidence of the dimensions of the ship as it may be practicable to obtain, estimate what her tonnage would have been found to be in she could have been duly measured for the purpose, and issue a certificate stating her tonnage as so estimated by him.

(6) For the purposes of this section the expression 'ship' has the meaning assigned to it by section seven hundred and forty-two of the Merchant Shipping Act 1894, but includes also:—

(*a*) (any structure to which Part VIII of that Act is applied by section four of the M.S. (Liability of Shipowners and Others) Act 1958; and

(*b*) every description of lighter, barge or like vessel used in navigation in Great Britain however propelled, so, however, that a vessel used exclusively in non-tidal waters, other than harbours, shall not for the purposes of this paragraph, be deemed to be used in navigation.

(7) Any reference in this section to the provisions of the Merchant Shipping Acts 1894 to 1940, which limit the amount of the liability of the owners of ships, shall be construed as including a reference to any provisions of those Acts which negatives the liability of the owner of a ship, and accordingly any reference in this section to limiting the liability of any person shall be construed as including a reference to negativing his liability.

(8) Relief shall not be available by virtue of (sections three and four of the M.S. (Liability of Shipowners and Others) Act 1958) in any case in which it is available by virtue of this section.

COMMENTS.

General.

The right to limit liability is not affected by the Maritime Conventions Act 1911, nor by the Carriage of Goods by Sea Act 1971.

H.M. Ships.

In *The Truculent* 1952, it was held that the expression 'His Majesty' is not used in any personal sense, but in a corporate sense. Accordingly, therefore, the Board of Admiralty were held to be in the position of owners of His Majesty's ship in question.

Section 6, sub-section (a) Section 8.

This paragraph, underlined and within brackets, has been substituted for a reference to the definition of 'ship' formerly contained in the

Liability Act of 1898, now repealed by the M.S. (Liability of Shipowners) Act 1958, section 8, sub-section 5.

THE CROWN PROCEEDINGS ACT 1947

SECTION 7

Liability in respect of Crown docks, harbours, etc.

(1) It is hereby declared that the provisions of the Merchant Shipping Acts 1894 to 1940, which limit the amount of the liability of the owners of docks and canals, and of harbour and conservancy authorities, apply for the purpose of limiting the liability of His Majesty in His capacity as the owner of any dock or canal, or in His capacity as a harbour or conservancy authority, and that all the relevant provisions of the said Acts have effect in relation to His Majesty accordingly.

(2) In this section the expressions 'dock', 'harbour', 'owner', 'harbour authority', and 'conservancy authority' have respectively the same meanings as they have for the purposes of section two of the M.S. (Liability of Shipowners and Others) Act 1900.

(3) In this section, references to His Majesty include references to any Government department and to any officer of the Crown in his capacity as such.

COMMENTS.

The Provisions of the Merchant Shipping Acts 1894 to 1940.

For these provisions, consult the M.S. (Liability of Shipowners and Others) Act 1900, section 2, as amended by section 1, sub-section 1 of the 1958 Liability Act.

M.S.A. 1894

PART IX

WRECK AND SALVAGE

PART IX

WRECK AND SALVAGE

Vessels in Distress

510 In this Part of this Act, unless the context otherwise requires— Definition of "wreck and salvage".

(1) The expression 'wreck' includes jetsam, flotsam, lagan, and derelict found in or on the shores of the sea or any tidal water:

(2) The expression 'salvage' includes all expenses properly incurred by the salvor in the performance of the salvage services.

COMMENTS.

Application to Aircraft.

For application of law of wreck and salvage to aircraft, consult the Civil Aviation Act 1949, section 51. Also, the Aircraft (Wreck and Salvage) Order 1938.

Wreck.

To constitute wreck, goods must have touched the ground, though they need not have been left dry. R. *v.* Forty-nine cases of Brandy 1836; also, R. *v.* Two Casks of Tallow 1837.

This term was held not to include a barge which had parted from her moorings in the Thames and was drifting. *The Zeta* 1875. Consult also Palmer *v.* Rouse 1858; Cargo ex Schiller 1877, where it was held that timber which had drifted from its moorings did not come under the term 'wreck'.

Jetsam, Flotsam, Lagan, and Derelict.

For the meaning of these terms, consult Constables' Case 1601; *The Pauline* 1845. The Gas-float *Whitton* 1896, as well as cases cited under 'wreck' above.

The term 'derelict' is applied to a ship abandoned or deserted at sea. Crossman *v.* West 1887, *see* also *The Aquila* 1798, *The Cosmopolitan* 1848, *The Genessee* 1848, *The Coromandel* 1857, *The Gertrude* 1861, and the *F. D. Lambert* 1917.

For the distinction between 'derelict' and 'wreck', *see* also *The Sophie* 1841.

Tidal Water.

For definition, *see* section 742, M.S.A. 1894.

⚓ ⚓ ⚓ ⚓

Duty of receiver where vessel in distress.

511 (1) Where a British or foreign vessel is wrecked, stranded, or in distress at any place on or near the coasts of the United Kingdom or any tidal water within the limits of the United Kingdom, the receiver of wreck for the district in which that place is situate shall, upon being made acquainted with the circumstance, forthwith proceed there, and upon his arrival shall take the command of all persons present, and shall assign such duties and give such directions to each person as he thinks fit for the preservation of the vessel and of the lives of the persons belonging to the vessel (in this Part of this Act referred to as shipwrecked persons) and of the cargo and apparel of the vessel.

(2) If any person wilfully disobeys the direction of the receiver, he shall for each offence be liable to a fine not exceeding fifty pounds; but the receiver shall not interfere between the master and the crew of the vessel in reference to the management thereof, unless he is requested to do so by the master.

COMMENTS.

Coasts of the United Kingdom.

It is submitted that this means territorial waters. *See* also *The Fulham* 1898.

Receiver of Wreck.

For appointment, *see* section 566 of this Act. For exercise of powers of receiver, in his absence, *see* section 516 below.

Definitions.

'Vessel', 'tidal water', 'master', *see* section 742 below.

⚓ ⚓ ⚓ ⚓

Powers of the receiver in case of vessels in distress.

512 (1) The receiver may, with a view to such preservation as aforesaid of shipwrecked persons or of the vessel, cargo, or apparel—

(*a*) require such persons as he thinks necessary to assist him:

(*b*) require the master, or other person having the charge, of any vessel near at hand to give such aid with his men, or vessel, as may be in his power:

(*c*) demand the use of any waggon, cart, or horses that may be near at hand.

(2) If any person refuses without reasonable cause to comply with any such requisition or demand, that person shall, for each refusal, be liable to a fine not exceeding one hundred pounds; but a person shall not be liable to pay any duty in respect of any such waggon, cart, or horses, by reason only of the use of the same under this section.

COMMENTS.

Repeal.

The words underlined from "but . . . to section," repealed by section 49, Schedule V of the Finance Act 1944 as from 1st January 1945.

It would appear that motor vehicles are exempt from the requirements of third party insurance at a time when they are being driven on a journey to or from any place, undertaken for salvage purposes pursuant to Part IX of the Principal Act, by section 202, sub-section 2 (*c*) Road Traffic Act 1960. *See* also section 251 of the same act, when there is power to vary speed limits for motor vehicles used for salvage purposes pursuant to Part IX of the Principal Act.

⚓ ⚓ ⚓ ⚓

513 (1) Whenever a vessel is wrecked, stranded, or in distress as aforesaid, all persons may, for the purpose of rendering assistance to the vessel, or of saving the lives of the shipwrecked persons, or of saving the cargo or apparel of the vessel, unless there is some public road equally convenient, pass and repass, either with or without carriages or horses, over any adjoining lands without being subject to interruption by the owner or occupier, so that they do as little damage as possible, and may also, on the like condition, deposit on those lands any cargo or other article recovered from the vessel.

Power to pass over adjoining lands.

(2) Any damage sustained by an owner or occupier in consequence of the exercise of the rights given by this section shall be a charge on the vessel, cargo, or articles in respect of or by which the damage is occasioned, and the amount payable in respect of the damage shall, in case of dispute, be determined and shall, in default of payment, be recoverable in the same manner as the amount of salvage is under this Part of this Act determined or recoverable.

(3) If the owner or occupier of any land—

(*a*) impedes or hinders any person in the exercise of the rights given by this section by locking his gates, or refusing, upon request, to open the same, or otherwise; or

(*b*) impedes or hinders the deposit of any cargo or other article recovered from the vessel as aforesaid on the land; or

(*c*) prevents or endeavours to prevent any such cargo or other article from remaining deposited on the land for a reasonable time until it can be removed to a safe place of public deposit;

he shall for each offence be liable to a fine not exceeding one hundred pounds.

COMMENTS.

Salvage Determined or Recoverable.

For procedure on salvage cases consult sections 547 et seq. For definitions of salvage *see* section 510.

Fine.

For summary prosecution for fines, *see* section 680, sub-section 1 (*b*).

⚓ ⚓ ⚓ ⚓

Power of receiver to suppress plunder and disorder by force.

514 (1) Whenever a vessel is wrecked, stranded or in distress as aforesaid, and any person plunders, creates disorder, or obstructs the preservation of the vessel or of the shipwrecked persons or of the cargo or apparel of the vessel, the receiver may cause that person to be apprehended.

(2) The receiver may use force for the suppression of any such plundering, disorder, or obstruction, and may command all Her Majesty's subjects to assist him in so using force.

(3) If any person is killed, maimed, or hurt by reason of his resisting the receiver or any person acting under the orders of the receiver in the execution of the duties by this Part of this Act committed to the receiver, neither the receiver nor the person acting under his orders shall be liable to any punishment, or to pay any damages by reason of the person being so killed, maimed, or hurt.

COMMENTS.

For Offences in Respect of Wreck.

Consult comments to section 536.

⚓ ⚓ ⚓ ⚓

515 Where a vessel is wrecked, stranded, or in distress as aforesaid, and the vessel or any part of the cargo and apparel thereof, is plundered, damaged, or destroyed by any persons riotously and tumultuously assembled together, whether on shore or afloat, compensation shall be made to the owner of the vessel, cargo, or apparel: *Liability for damage in case of a vessel plundered.*

In England in the same manner, by the same authority, and out of the same rate as if the plundering, damage, injury, or destruction were an injury, stealing, or destruction in respect of which compensation is payable under the provisions of the Riot (Damages) Act, 1886, and in the case of the vessel, cargo, or apparel not being in any police district, as if the plundering, damage, injury, or destruction took place in the nearest police district; *49 and 50 Vict. c. 38.*

In Scotland by the inhabitants of the county, city, or borough in or nearest to which such offence is committed, in manner provided by the Riot Act, with respect to prosecutions for repairing the damages of any churches and other buildings, or as near thereto as circumstances permit, and *1 Geo. 1. st. 2, c. 5.*

In Ireland in manner provided by the Act of the Session held in the sixteenth and seventeenth year of the reign of Her present Majesty, chapter thirty-eight, entitled 'An Act to extend the remedies for the compensation of malicious injuries to property in Ireland with respect to damage to any dwelling-house or other property therein mentioned.' *16 and 17 Vict. c. 38.*

COMMENTS.

The paragraph underlined, 'In Ireland to mentioned', has been altered by section 23, sub-section 1 of the Northern Ireland Act 1962, which reads: 'In Northern Ireland, in pursuance of an application in that behalf to the County Court.'

Compensation will not be made under this section in Northern Ireland unless the aggregate amount of the plunder, damage, or destruction exceeds twenty pounds.

516 (1) Where a receiver is not present, the following officers or persons in succession (each in the absence of the other, in the order in which they are named), namely, any chief officer of customs, principal officer of the coastguard, officer of inland revenue, sheriff, justice of the peace, commissioned officer on full pay in the naval service of Her *Exercise of powers of receiver in his absence.*

Majesty, or a commissioned officer on full pay in the military service of Her Majesty, may do anything by this Part of this Act authorised to be done by the receiver.

(2) An officer acting under this section for a receiver shall, with respect to any goods or articles belonging to a vessel the delivery of which to the receiver is required by this Act, be considered as the agent of the receiver, and shall place the same in the custody of the receiver; but he shall not be entitled to any fees payable to receivers, or be deprived by reason of his so acting of any right to salvage to which he would otherwise be entitled.

COMMENTS.

Receiver.

For duty of receiver where vessel is in distress, consult section 511.

Coastguard.

Remuneration for services, *see* section 568.

Chief Officer of Customs.

Definition of contained in section 742.

Delivery required by this Act.

See section 518 (*b*).

Right to Salvage.

Consult sections 544 et seq.

Examination in respect of ships in distress.

517 (1) Where any ship, British or foreign, is or has been in distress on the coasts of the United Kingdom, a receiver of wreck, or at the request of the Board of Trade a wreck commissioner or deputy approved by the Board, or, in the absence of the persons aforesaid, a justice of the peace, shall, as soon as conveniently may be, examine on oath (and they are hereby respectively empowered to administer the oath) any person belonging to the ship, or any other person who may be able to give any account thereof or of the cargo or stores thereof, as to the following matters; (that is to say,)

(*a*) The name and description of the ship;

(*b*) The name of the master and of the owners;

(*c*) The names of the owners of the cargo;

(*d*) The ports from and to which the ship was bound;

(*e*) The occasion of the distress of the ship;

(*f*) The services rendered; and

(*g*) Such other matters or circumstances relating to the ship, or to the cargo on board the same, as the person holding the examination thinks necessary.

(2) The person holding the examination shall take the same down in writing, and shall send one copy thereof to the Board of Trade, and another to the secretary of Lloyd's in London, and the secretary shall place it in some conspicuous situation for inspection.

(3) The person holding the examination shall, for the purposes thereof, have all the powers of a Board of Trade inspector under this Act.

COMMENTS.

Compare sections 464 et seq., for inquiries, and investigations as to shipping casualties.

Accordingly, this section does not apply to ships in distress near the coasts of the United Kingdom. Consult also *The Fulham* 1898 as to the meaning of the words 'on or near'.

Receiver of Wreck.

See sections 566 as to appointment.

Wreck Commissioner.

See section 477 as to appointment.

Inspector.

For powers of inspectors, *see* sections 728, 729, and 730. For Board of Trade, substitute Ministry of Transport.

Dealing with Wreck

518 Where any person finds or takes possession of any wreck within the limits of the United Kingdom he shall— **Provisions as to wreck found in the United Kingdom.**

(*a*) if he is the owner thereof, give notice to the receiver of the district stating that he has found or taken possession of the same, and describing the marks by which the same may be recognised;

(*b*) if he is not the owner thereof, as soon as possible deliver the same to the receiver of the district:

and if any person fails, without reasonable cause, to comply with this section, he shall, for each offence, be liable to a fine not exceeding one hundred pounds, and shall in addition, if he is not the owner, forfeit any claim to salvage, and shall be liable to pay to the owner of the wreck if it is claimed, or, if it is unclaimed to the person entitled to the same, double the value thereof, to be recovered in the same way as a fine of a like amount under this Act.

COMMENTS.

United Kingdom.

This section applies to wrecks found or taken possession of outside the limits of the United Kingdom and brought within those limits. M.S.A. 1906, section 72.

As to meaning of 'United Kingdom', *see* relevant comments to section 742.

Wreck and Salvage.

For definitions, *see* section 510.

Owner.

For claims of owners to wreck, *see* section 521.

Receiver.

For appointment of receivers of wreck, *see* section 566.

For notice of wreck to be given by receiver, *see* section 520.

In certain cases a receiver may sell wreck, *see* section 522.

General.

This section is meant to prevent a criminal and improper detention, this bringing into being a fraud upon the Crown or the owner. Persons who found a laden barge floating on the Thames and restored it to the owners were held not to have forfeited their right to salvage through not complying with the provisions of this section. *The Zeta* 1875.

Where a finder took possession believing property to be his own, he was not deprived of right to recover salvage. *The Liffey* 1887.

It does not apply to salvors who remain in possession for the safety of the vessel. *The Glynderon* 1905.

Penalty for taking wreck at time of casualty.

519 (1) Where a vessel is wrecked, stranded, or in distress at any place on or near the coasts of the United Kingdom or any tidal water within the limits of the United Kingdom, any cargo or other articles belonging to or separated from the vessel, which may be washed on shore or otherwise lost or taken from the vessel, shall be delivered to the receiver.

(2) If any person, whether the owner or not, secretes or keeps possession of any such cargo or article, or refuses to deliver the same to the receiver or any person authorised by him to demand the same, that person shall for each offence be liable to a fine not exceeding one hundred pounds.

(3) The receiver or any person authorised as aforesaid may take any such cargo or article by force from the person so refusing to deliver the same.

COMMENTS.

Coasts of the United Kingdom.

It is submitted this means 'within territorial waters'. *See The Fulham* 1898.

Tidal Water.

See section 742 for definition.

Receiver.

See section 566.

Notice of Wreck.

See section 520.

Fine.

For summary prosecution for fines, *see* section 680, sub-section 1 (*b*).

⚓ ⚓ ⚓ ⚓

520 Where a receiver takes possession of any wreck he shall within forty-eight hours— Notice of wreck to be given by receiver.

(*a*) cause to be posted in the custom house nearest to the place where the wreck was found or was seized by him a description thereof and of any marks by which it is distinguished; and

(*b*) if in his opinion the value of the wreck exceeds twenty pounds, also transmit a similar description to the secretary of Lloyd's in London, and the secretary shall post it in some conspicuous position for inspection.

COMMENTS.

Wreck.

Defined in section 510.

Receiver.

For appointment of, *see* section 566.

⚓ ⚓ ⚓ ⚓

521 (1) The owner of any wreck in the possession of the receiver, upon establishing his claim to the same to the satisfaction of the receiver within one year from the time at Claims of owners to wreck.

which the wreck came into the possession of the receiver, shall, upon paying the salvage, fees, and expenses due, be entitled to have the wreck or the proceeds thereof delivered up to him.

(2) Where any articles belonging to or forming part of a foreign ship, which has been wrecked on or near the coasts of the United Kingdom, or belonging to and forming part of the cargo, are found on or near those coasts, or are brought into any port in the United Kingdom, the consul-general of the country to which the ship or in the case of the cargo to which the owners of the cargo may have belonged, or any consular officer of that country authorised in that behalf by any treaty or arrangement with that country, shall, in the absence of the owner and of the master or other agent of the owner, be deemed to be the agent of the owner, so far as relates to the custody and disposal of the articles.

COMMENTS.

Disposal of Unclaimed Wreck.

See section 525.

Delivery of Wreck to the Receiver.

See section 518.

Coasts of the United Kingdom.

See relevant comment to section 519.

Consul General.

The powers of a consul-general or other consular officer and sub-section 2 extend to the custody and disposal of the wrecked ship itself, as well as to the custody and disposal of the articles referred to. Consult section 5, sub-section 2 of the Consular Conventions Act 1949.

Immediate sale of wreck by receiver in certain cases.

522 A receiver may at any time sell any wreck in his custody if in his opinion—

(*a*) it is under the value of five pounds, or

(*b*) it is so much damaged or of so perishable a nature that it cannot with advantage be kept, or

(*c*) it is not of sufficient value to pay for warehousing, and the proceeds of the sale shall, after defraying the expenses thereof, be held by the receiver for the same purposes and subject to the same claims, rights, and liabilities as if the wreck had remained unsold.

COMMENTS.

Proceeds.

In regard to sums paid in respect of claims to money on account of proceeds of wreck, *see* section 677, sub-section (*h*).

⚓ ⚓ ⚓ ⚓

Unclaimed Wreck

523 Her Majesty and Her Royal successors are entitled to all unclaimed wreck found in any part of Her Majesty's dominions, except in places where Her Majesty or any of Her Royal predecessors has granted to any other person the right to that wreck.

Right of Crown to unclaimed wreck.

COMMENTS.

Wreck.

For definition, *see* section 510.

Wreck found outside the limits of the United Kingdom, and brought within such limits, has to be delivered to the Receiver of Wreck, though the Crown may have no title to it.

See section 72 of the M.S.A. 1906.

⚓ ⚓ ⚓ ⚓

524 (1) Where any admiral, vice-admiral, lord of the manor, heritable proprietor duly infeft, or other person entitled for his own use to unclaimed wreck found on any place within the district of a receiver, he shall deliver to the receiver a statement containing the particulars of his title, and an address to which notices may be sent.

Notice of unclaimed wreck to be given to persons entitled.

(2) When a statement has been so delivered and the title proved to the satisfaction of the receiver, the receiver shall, on taking possession of any wreck found at a place to which the statement refers, within forty-eight hours send to the address delivered a description of the wreck and of any marks by which it is distinguished.

COMMENTS.

Wreck must be delivered to the receiver under section 518 (*b*).

⚓ ⚓ ⚓ ⚓

525 Where no owner establishes a claim to any wreck, found in the United Kingdom and in the possession of the receiver, within one year after it came into his possession, the wreck shall be dealt with as follows; (that is to say,)

Disposal of unclaimed wreck.

(1) If the wreck is claimed by any admiral, vice-admiral, lord of the manor, heritable proprietor, or other person who has delivered such a statement to the receiver as herein-before provided, and has proved to the satisfaction of the receiver his title to receive unclaimed wreck found at the place where that wreck was found, the wreck after payment of all expenses, costs, fees, and salvage due in respect thereof, shall be delivered to him;

(2) If the wreck is not claimed by any admiral, vice-admiral, lord of the manor, heritable proprietor, or other person as aforesaid, the receiver shall sell the same and shall pay the proceeds of the sale (after deducting therefrom the expenses of the sale, and any other expenses incurred by him, and his fees, and paying thereout to the salvors such amount of salvage as the Board of Trade may in each case, or by any general rule, determine for the benefit of the Crown, as follows; (that is to say,)

(*a*) If the wreck is claimed in right of Her Majesty's duchy of Lancaster, to the receiver-general of that duchy or his deputies as part of the revenues of that duchy;

(*b*) If the wreck is claimed in right of the duchy of Cornwall, to the receiver-general of that duchy or his deputies as part of the revenues of that duchy; and

(*c*) If the wreck is not so claimed, the receiver shall pay the proceeds of sale to the Mercantile Marine Fund during the life of Her present Majesty, and after the decease of Her present Majesty to her heirs and successors.

COMMENTS.

The words underlined above have been repealed by the Statute Law Revision Act 1908.

Wreck in Possession of Receiver.

For delivery of wreck to the receiver, *see* section 518.

Delivery of unclaimed wreck does not prejuduce title to the wreck. *see* section 527.

As to disputed title to unclaimed wreck, *see* section 526.

526 (1) Where any dispute arises between any such admiral, vice-admiral, lord of a manor, heritable proprietor, or other person as aforesaid and the receiver respecting title to wreck found at any place, or, where more persons than one claim title to that wreck and a dispute arises between them as to that title, that dispute may be referred and determined in the same manner as if it were a dispute as to salvage to be determined summarily under this Part of this Act. **Disputed title to unclaimed wreck.**

(2) If any party to the dispute is unwilling to have the same so referred and determined, or is dissatisfied with the decision on that determination, he may within three months after the expiration of a year from the time when the wreck has come into the receiver's hands, or from the date of the decision, as the case may be, take proceedings in any court having jurisdiction in the matter for establishing his title.

COMMENTS.

Title to Wreck.

See section 525, sub-section 1.

Dispute as to Salvage.

See section 548 for summary disposal of salvage disputes.

⚓ ⚓ ⚓ ⚓

527 Upon delivery of wreck or payment of the proceeds of sale of wreck by a receiver, in pursuance of the provisions of this Part of this Act, the receiver shall be discharged from all liability in respect thereof, but the delivery thereof shall not prejudice or affect any question which may be raised by third parties concerning the right or title to the wreck, or concerning the title to the soil of the place on which the wreck was found. **Delivery of unclaimed wreck by receivers not to prejudice title.**

COMMENTS.

Delivery of Wreck.

For disposal of unclaimed wreck, *see* section 525.

⚓ ⚓ ⚓ ⚓

528 (1) The Board of Trade may, with the consent of the Treasury, out of the revenue arising under this Part of this Act, purchase for and on behalf of Her Majesty any rights to wreck possessed by any person other than Her Majesty. **Power to Board of Trade to purchase rights to wreck.**

(2) For the purpose of a purchase under this section, the provisions of the Lands Clauses Acts relating to the purchase of lands by agreement shall be incorporated with this Part of this Act, and in the construction of those Acts for the purposes of this section this Part of this Act shall be deemed to be the special Act, and any such right to wreck as aforesaid shall be deemed to be an interest in land authorised to be taken by the special Act, and Her Majesty shall be deemed to be the promoter of the undertaking.

COMMENTS.

See section 523 for right of Crown, with certain exceptions, to unclaimed wreck.

Admiral not to interfere with wreck.

529 No admiral, vice-admiral, or other person, under whatever denomination, exercising Admiralty jurisdiction, shall, as such, by himself or his agents, receive, take, or interfere with any wreck except as authorised by this Act.

Removal of Wrecks

Removal of wreck by harbour or conservancy authority.

530 Where any vessel is sunk, stranded, or abandoned in any harbour or tidal water under the control of a harbour or conservancy authority, or in or near any approach thereto, in such manner as in the opinion of the authority to be, or be likely to become, an obstruction or danger to navigation or to lifeboats engaged in lifeboat service in that harbour or water or in any approach thereto, that authority may—

(*a*) take possession of, and raise, remove, or destroy the whole or any part of the vessel; and

(*b*) light or buoy any such vessel or part until the raising, removal, or destruction thereof; and

(*c*) sell, in such manner as they think fit, any vessel or part so raised or removed, and also any other property recovered in the exercise of their powers under this section, and out of the proceeds of the sale reimburse themselves for the expenses incurred by them in relation thereto under this section, and the authority shall hold the surplus, if any, of the proceeds in trust for the persons entitled thereto.

Provided as follows:—

(1) A sale shall not (except in the case of property which is of a perishable nature, or which would deteriorate in value by delay) be made under this section until at least seven clear days notice of the intended sale has been given by advertisement in some local newspaper circulating in or near the district over which the authority have control; and

(2) At any time before any property is sold under this section, the owner thereof shall be entitled to have the same delivered to him on payment to the authority of the fair market value thereof, to be ascertained by agreement between the authority and the owner, or failing agreement by some person to be named for the purpose by the Board of Trade, and the sum paid to the authority as the value of any property under this provision shall, for the purposes of this section, be deemed to be the proceeds of sale of that property.

COMMENTS.

General.

For power of harbourmaster to remove wreck or obstruction, *see* also the Harbours, Docks, and Piers Clauses Act 1847, and to various Acts referring specifically to particular ports. For a similar power in respect of dockyard ports, *see* the Dockyard Ports Regulation Act 1865, section 13. In some cases, the powers under such Acts are more advantageous to the Authority than those under this Act.

Vessel.

For definition, *see* section 742. For extention of meaning of 'vessel' for the purposes of these provisions—*see* section 532. The term 'vessel' here does not include H.M. ships. *See* Christie *v.* Trinity House Corporation 1919.

Light or Buoy.

Where control of the wreck has been legitimately transferred by the owners to a harbour authority, although owners were still in possession, then in the absence of negligence on the part of the owners, they are not liable for a collision which occurs through insufficient lighting, buoying, or other protection. *Utopia* (Owners) *v. Primula* (Owners), *The Utopia* 1893, *The Douglas* 1882, Brown *v.* Mallett 1848, White *v.* Crisp 1854.

However, where the owner employs a contractor on salvage operations, being still in possession, he is not relieved from his liabilities in regard to the protection of other vessels, and will be liable for damage caused by the negligent lighting of the wreck. *The Snark* 1900.

For liability for expenses of lighting, *see The Ella* 1915.

The authority may, instead of acting under this section, agree with a salvor to allow him to attempt salvage in undertaking to indemnify the authority in respect of any liabilities incurred by the authority. Trinity House *v* Maritime Salvors, Ltd. 1923.

See also Hoclock *v.* Isachen 1928 for power of the authority to compromise its claim under the indemnity.

An authority is liable for damages for not surveying. Dormont *v.* Furness Railway Co. 1883, Anchor Line (Henderson Bros.), Ltd. *v.* Dundee Harbour Trustees 1922.

Expenses Incurred.

A wreck-raising authority has no power under this Act to recover from the owner expenses incurred in raising wreck. A remedy may be given by special Act, or under the Harbours, Docks and Piers Clauses Act 1847 as incorporated. *See* Tyne Improvement Commissioners *v.* The Armement Anversois S/A, *The Brabo* 1949, where an action was not properly brought by a conservancy authority against shipowners out of the jurisdiction for expenses incurred in removing wreck.

Particular note should be taken of Sheppey and Chemical Works *v.* Conservators of River Medway 1926.

Under section 120 of the Medway Conservancy Act 1881, a personal remedy for the recovery of expenses of removing the wreck is given. It is, however, only against the owner at the time the expenses were incurred. Therefore, where the owners at the time of the casualty had abandoned before the expenses were incurred, the Authority could not recover against him under the Act.

Attention is once again directed to the Harbour, Docks, and Piers Clauses Act 1847, and in particular section 56, where the particular form of words used relieves the original owner of the vessel from liability for expenses incurred after abandonment.

See The Crystal (Arrow Shipping Co. *v.* Tyne Improvement Commissioners 1894); Barraclough *v.* Brown 1897; Boston Corporation *v.* Fennick 1923.

As to what are considered legitimate expenses, *see The Harrington* 1888, *The Ousel* 1957.

Power of lighthouse authority to remove wreck.

531 (1) Where any vessel is sunk, stranded, or abandoned in any fairway, or on the seashore or on or near any rock, shoal, or bank, in the British Islands, or any of the adjacent seas or islands, and there is not any harbour or conservancy authority having power to raise, remove, or destroy the vessel, the general lighthouse authority for the place in or near which the vessel is situate shall, if in their opinion the vessel is, or is likely to become, an obstruction or danger to navigation or to lifeboats engaged in the lifeboat service, have the same powers in relation thereto as are by this Part of this Act conferred upon a harbour or conservancy authority.

(2) All expenses incurred by the general lighthouse authority under this section, and not reimbursed in manner provided by this Part of this Act, shall be paid out of the Mercantile Marine Fund, but shall be subject to the like estimate, account, and sanction as the expenses of a general lighthouse authority, other than establishment expenses.

COMMENTS.

Vessel.

This does not include H.M. Ships.

British Islands.

This means the United Kingdom, the Channel Islands and the Isle of Man, *see* section 18, sub-section 1, of the Interpretation Act 1889.

General Lighthouse Authority.

For definition, *see* section 634. For the rights of servants of a general lighthouse authority to claim salvage in respect of services rendered by them outside their statutory duties, *see The Citos* 1925.

The opinion that a wreck is dangerous to navigation must be formed with a view to action within a reasonable time.

Christie *v.* Trinity House Corporation 1919. For observations on the powers of Trinity House in dealing with a wreck under the authority of this section, *see* Trinity House *v.* Maritime Salvors, Ltd. 1923.

Expenses.

As to the expenses of lighthouse authorities, *see* sections 660 et seq.

Mercantile Marine Fund.

Now the General Lighthouse Fund. *See* M.S. (Mercantile Marine Fund) Act. 1898, section 1, sub-section 1 (*b*) and (*c*).

532 The provisions of this Part of this Act relating to removal of wrecks shall apply to every article or thing or collection of things being or forming part of the tackle, equipments, cargo, stores, or ballast of a vessel in the same manner as if it were included in the term 'vessel', and for the purposes of these provisions any proceeds of sale arising from a vessel and from the cargo thereof, or any other property recovered therefrom, shall be regarded as a common fund.

Powers of removal to extend to tackle, cargo, &c.

COMMENTS.

Vessel.

Compare the definition in section 742.

Exercise of power, 530–532 of this Act. *See* Oil in Navigable Waters Act 1955, section 4, sub-section 6, for defence to any person who in exercise of any power as a result of section 530–532 allows oil or a mixture containing oil into prohibited sea areas outside United Kingdom waters, or into United Kingdom waters.

⚓ ⚓ ⚓ ⚓

Power for Board of Trade to determine certain questions between authorities.

533 If any question arises between a harbour or conservancy authority on the one hand and a general lighthouse authority on the other hand as to their respective powers under this Part of this Act for the removal of wrecks, in relation to any place being in or near an approach to a harbour or tidal water, that question shall, on the application of either authority, be referred to the decision of the Board of Trade, and the decision of that Board shall be final.

COMMENTS.

Wreck—Removal of.

See sections 530–531.

Harbour—Tidal Water.

For definitions, *see* section 742.

⚓ ⚓ ⚓ ⚓

Powers to be cumulative.

534 The powers conferred by this Part of this Act on a harbour, conservancy, or lighthouse authority, for the removal of wrecks shall be in addition to and not in derogation of any other powers for a like object.

COMMENTS.

See the general comment at the beginning of section 530. The Authority is able to act under the relevant statute most advantageous to it.

See The Elerick 1881. Compare the various acts which may be available regarding the removal of wrecks and their consequences.

OFFENCES IN RESPECT OF WRECK.

GENERAL COMMENTS.

Penal Servitude.

By section 1, sub-section 1 of the Criminal Justice Act 1948, penal servitude is abolished and enactments conferring power to sentence to penal servitude are to be construed as conferring power to sentence to imprisonment.

Persons in Possession of Shipwrecked Goods Not Giving a Satisfactory Account and Offering Shipwrecked Goods for Sale.

See the Larceny Act 1861, section 65.

Stealing Goods from a Wrecked Vessel.

See the Larceny Act 1916, section 15, sub-section 3.

Destroying Wrecked Ships or Articles Therein.

Compare the Malicious Damage Act 1861, section 49.

Assaults on Officers or Persons Preserving Wrecked Vessel or Goods.

See Offences Against the Person Act 1861, section 37.

Offences in respect of Wreck

535 If any person takes into any foreign port any vessel, stranded, derelict, or otherwise in distress, found on or near the coasts of the United Kingdom or any tidal water within the limits of the United Kingdom, or any part of the cargo or apparel thereof, or anything belonging thereto, or any wreck found within those limits, and there sells the same, that person shall be guilty of felony, and on conviction thereof shall be liable to be kept in penal servitude for a term not less than three years and not exceeding five years.

Taking wreck to foreign port.

COMMENTS.

Near the Coasts of the United Kingdom.

See The Fulham 1898.

Definitions.

Vessel: Tidal Water, *see* section 742.

Wreck, *see* section 530.

536 (1) A person shall not without the leave of the master board or endeavour to board any vessel which is wrecked, stranded, or in distress, unless that person is, or acts by command of, the receiver or a person lawfully acting as such, and if any person acts in contravention of this enactment, he shall for each offence be liable to a fine not exceeding fifty pounds, and the master of the vessel may repel him by force.

Interfering with wrecked vessel or wreck.

(2) A person shall not—

(*a*) impede or hinder, or endeavour in any way to impede or hinder, the saving of any vessel stranded or in danger of being stranded, or otherwise in distress on or near any coast or tidal water, or of any part of the cargo or apparel thereof, or of any wreck;

(*b*) secrete any wreck, or deface or obliterate any marks thereon; or

(*c*) wrongfully carry away or remove any part of a vessel stranded or in danger of being stranded, or otherwise in distress, on or near any coast or tidal water, or any part of the cargo or apparel thereof, or any wreck,

and if any person acts in contravention of this enactment, he shall be liable for each offence to a fine not exceeding fifty pounds, and that fine may be inflicted in addition to any punishment to which he may be liable by law under this Act or otherwise.

COMMENTS.

Definitions.

Master; vessel; tidal water, *see* section 742.

Wreck, *see* section 510.

Summary Prosecution.

See section 680, sub-section 1.

⚓ ⚓ ⚓ ⚓

Summary procedure for concealment of wreck.

537 (1) Where a receiver suspects or receives information that any wreck is secreted or in the possession of some person who is not the owner thereof, or that any wreck is otherwise improperly dealt with he may apply to any justice of the peace for a search warrant and that justice shall have power to grant such a warrant, and the receiver, by virtue thereof, may enter any house, or other place, wherever situate, and also any vessel, and search for, seize, and detain any such wreck there found.

(2) If any such seizure of wreck is made in consequence of information given by any person to the receiver, on a warrant being issued under this section, the informer shall be entitled, by way of salvage, to such sum not exceeding in any case five pounds as the receiver may allow.

COMMENTS.

Wreck: for definition, *see* section 510.

Merchant Shipping Act 1894

Wreck and Salvage

Marine Store Dealer, etc.

Sections 538 to 542

Repealed by Scrap Metal Dealers Act 1964

As from 1st April, 1965

Marking of Anchors

543 (1) Every manufacturer of anchors shall mark on every anchor manufactured by him in legible characters and both on the crown and also on the shank under the stock his name or initials, and shall in addition mark on the anchor a progressive number and the weight of the anchor. Marking of Anchors

(2) If a manufacturer of anchors fails without reasonable cause to comply with this section, he shall be liable for each offence to a fine not exceeding five pounds.

COMMENTS:

Marking of Anchors.

For anchors and cables generally, *see*:—

Anchors and Chain Cables Act 1967.

The Anchors and Chain Cables Rules 1970, in operation on 19th October 1970.

The Anchors and Chain Cables Act 1967 (Commencement) Order1970, in operation on 19th October 1970.

Salvage

544 (1) Where services are rendered wholly or in part within British waters in saving life from any British or foreign vessel, or elsewhere in saving life from any British vessel, there shall be payable to the salvor by the owner of the vessel, cargo, or apparel saved, a reasonable amount of salvage, to be determined in case of dispute in manner herein-after mentioned. Salvage payable for saving life.

(2) Salvage in respect of the preservation of life when payable by the owners of the vessel shall be payable in priority to all other claims for salvage.

(3) Where the vessel, cargo, and apparel are destroyed, or the value thereof is insufficient after payment of the actual expenses incurred, to pay the amount of salvage payable in respect of the preservation of life, the Board of Trade may, in their discretion, award to the salvor, out of the Mercantile Marine Fund, such sum as they think fit in whole or part satisfaction of any amount of salvage so left unpaid.

COMMENTS.

General—Saving of Life.

The right to salvage for saving life, where no property was saved, was not recognised by general maritime law, or by the Court of Admiralty, there being no property to which the claim could attach, and therefore no claim *in rem*. *See The Aid* 1822.

Consider also, the well-known dictum of Brett, M. R., in *The Rempor* 1883—'There is one element invariably required by Admiralty Law in order to found an action for salvage; there must be something saved more than life, which will form a fund from which salvage may be paid, in other words, for the saving of life alone, without the saving of ship, freight, or cargo, salvage is not recoverable in the Admiralty Court.'

The harshness of this doctrine has, however, been softened by section 544, sub-section 3, above, *q.v.*

Also, where property has been saved, the court of the salvors thereof have also saved life, would make a liberal estimate of the services, with a corresponding degree of award. Consult *The Johannes* 1860; Bligh *v.* Simpson, *The Fusilier* 1865; *The Willem III* 1871.

Note should be taken also of the Maritime Marine Act 1911, section 6, which lays down a general duty to render assistance to persons in danger at sea. *See* also section 22, the M.S. (Safety Conventions) Act 1949, which imposes a qualified duty on the master of a British ship registered in the U.K. when he receives a wireless distress call to proceed to the assistance of persons in distress.

The liability for salvage extends to persons having a beneficial interest in the property saved and subject to pecuniary loss if it were not saved. The Five Steel Barges 1890. *See* also Duncan *v.* Dundee Shipping Co. 1878; the Cargo ex *Port Victor* 1901.

Where Property has been Saved.

In this case, there is a fund out of which a reward for the saving of life may be made, and this is immaterial whether the property saved has been salved by one or several salvors, contemporaneously or subsequently, as the following cases will show; following generally the words of Bagally, L. J.:—

'The liability to pay a reasonable amount of salvage to life salvors is imposed upon owners of cargo as well as upon owners of the ship . . . said liability is not a general personal liability to be enforced in any circumstances, whether the ship and cargo are lost or not, but a liability limited to the value of the property saved from destruction . . . as regards the right of life salvors to claim a reasonable amount of salvage, it is immaterial whether the property has been saved by salvors as the expression is ordinarily understood, or by other means.'

The owners of cargo which has been saved are liable to contribute to life salvage even though the salvors have rendered no direct benefit to the cargo. *See The Fusilier* 1865; *see* also the Cargo ex *Schiller* 1877 and compare the Cargo ex *Sarpedon* 1877, where it was held that where the ship was lost but cargo and life were saved, the cargo owner was held liable for life salvage and could not recoup from the owners of the ship.

In the event of a harbour authority acting under its statutory powers, sold a raised wreck for less than it cost to raise the vessel, and subsequently, recovered the difference from the vessel's owners, it was held that there was nothing to which a life-salvage claim could attach.

Also, in the event that the owners of the wreck could recover from the owners of a vessel through whose fault she was sunk, then they are also not liable for life salvage. *The Annie* 1886.

Life salvage is not normally recoverable by insurance, but may be specifically insured against, Nourse *v.* Liverpool Sailing Ship Owners, etc., 1896.

Where the master of a stranded vessel arranges for onward transmission by another steamer, the original contractual obligations having been ended, he acts as agent for the passengers and no claim by the second ship for life salvage will attach. *The Mariposa* 1896. Compare also *The Medina* 1876.

Where a ship was wrecked, but passengers and crew were taken to the port of destination by the salving steamer, as a result of which the owner of the wrecked vessel earned the passage money, it was held that this money constituted a fund out of which the life salvors might be paid. Before the enactment of the Crown Proceedings Act 1947, salvage could not be claimed for services to the property of the Crown. *The Scotia* 1903.

British Waters.

It is a question of fact whether or not services were rendered in part within British waters. Regarding these words, consult: *The Willem III* 1871; *The Pacific* 1898; Jorgensen *v.* Neptune Steam Fishing Co. Ltd. 1902.

Salvage.

For definition, *see* section 510.

Salvage of life from foreign vessels.

545 When it is made to appear to Her Majesty that the government of any foreign country is willing that salvage should be awarded by British courts for services rendered in saving life from ships belonging to that country, when the ship is beyond the limits of British jurisdiction, Her Majesty may, by Order in Council, direct that the provisions of this Part of this Act with reference to salvage of life shall, subject to any conditions and qualifications contained in the Order, apply, and those provisions shall accordingly apply to those services as if they were rendered in saving life from ships within British jurisdiction.

COMMENTS.

Beyond Limits of British Jurisdiction.

See the Territorial Waters Jurisdiction Act 1878.

Salvage.

For definition, *see* section 510. *See* also Maritime Conventions Act 1911 regarding the appointment of salvage amongst owners, etc., of a foreign ship.

⚓ ⚓ ⚓ ⚓

Salvage of cargo or wreck.

546 Where any vessel is wrecked, stranded, or in distress at any place on or near the coasts of the United Kingdom or any tidal water within the limits of the United Kingdom, and services are rendered by any person in assisting that vessel or saving the cargo or apparel of that vessel or any part thereof, and where services are rendered by any person other than a receiver in saving any wreck, there shall be payable to the salvor by the owner of the vessel, cargo, apparel, or wreck, a reasonable amount of salvage to be determined in case of dispute in manner herein-after mentioned.

COMMENTS.

Near the Coasts.

It is submitted that this means within territorial waters. *The Fulham* 1898.

United Kingdom.

Here includes the Republic of Ireland.

Any Person: Definition of a Salvor.

In *The Neptune* 1824, Lord Stowell gave the following definition of a salvor, which has stood the test of time:—

'A person who, without any particular relation to the ship in distress, proffers useful service, and gives it as a volunteer adventurer, without any pre-existing covenant that connected him with the duty of employing himself in the preservation of that ship.'

Difficulty is sometimes created where there is already a contract of towage and or pilotage in being.

The test as to whether a pilot is entitled to a salvage award, as to where the particular circumstances of the case are such as to make his services more than pilotage. In other words, could the pilot be expected to perform such duties for ordinary pilotage fees, or even for an extraordinary pilotage award.

As stated by Sir S. Evans, P., in *The Bedeburn* 1914, 'It is not in the interests of the mercantile community to give any countenance to the idea that a pilot compulsorily in charge of a disabled vessel can easily convert himself into a salvor.'

Again, in Akerblom *v.* Price, Potter, Walker & Co. 1880 . . . 'to exercise such unusual skill or perform such an unusual kind of service, as to make it unjust that he should be paid otherwise than upon the terms of salvage award. Consult also: *The Frederick* 1838; *The Saratoga* 1861; *The Aglaia* 1886; *The Driade* 1959'.

The burden of proof is on the pilot. *The Aeolus* 1873.

Similar considerations apply to salvage services of a tug that has a pre-existing contract with the ship. The test is whether the additional services become necessary as a result of circumstances beyond her control, thus making the services wholly different from those contemplated by the parties when entering into the towage contract.

Consult generally: *The Saratoga* 1861; *The Minnehaha* 1861; *The White Star* 1866; *The Westbourne* 1889; *The Marechal Sachet* 1911; *The Glenmorven* 1913; *The Leon Blum* 1915.

For salvage by Her Majesty's Ships, *see* section 577 and comments thereto.

Miscellaneous Salvors.

(*a*) Passengers;

(*b*) The crew.

In regard to passengers, it is accepted that they cannot normally claim salvage as their acts are deemed to be in the nature of self-preservation. However, if any specialised act is performed by a passenger above and beyond what would normally be expected of him, e.g. swimming without a connecting line in heavy seas to a salving steamer, then doubtless such an act would rank for salvage award.

Likewise, the crew of a salved vessel will normally not rank for an award, *see The Albionic* 1942 and compare *The Lomonosoff* 1921, where it was held that there was no objection to a salvage claim in that a sailor in performing the salvage services, saved himself at the same time.

The servants of a general lighthouse authority engaged in performing their statutory duty of removing wrecks under section 531 may be entitled to salvage if the services they render are adjudged outside of their statutory duty. *The Citos* 1925.

Coastguards.

These are civil service personnel, and are paid in accordance with civil service scales. Within their official duties they are not entitled to salvage and will only be granted extra money if they do more than their office demands. Before they can claim they must receive the consent of the Admiralty.

Lifeboat Crews.

These exist to save life. If, however, they salvage property when life salvage is not required, then these services are adjudged to be beyond their duty, and therefore rank as salvors. *The Marguerite Molinas* 1903; *The Cayo Bonito* 1904.

Salvage Against the Crown and Foreign State-owned Vessels.

The Admiralty Court will not enforce claims *in rem* or *in personam* in relation to salvage services in assisting H.M. Ships or aircraft, or in saving life therefrom or any Government cargo or apparel. *See* the Crown Proceedings Act 1947, section 8; section 9, sub-section 6, section 29, sub-section (1) and (II), such claims *in rem* or *in personam* for salvage of ships or goods belonging to a foreign power, even though the ship is employed in ordinary commercial trade. *See The Parlement Belge* 1880.

Consult also, Compania Naviera Vascongada *v.* S.S. *Christina* 1938, where a writ *in rem* was issued claiming possession of the ship. The House of Lords held that the writ be set aside as the ship had been requisitioned by the Government, and as such, was immune from process. They did, however, cast some doubt on the correctness of the decision in the *Porto Alexandre* 1920. This case involved a vessel owned by the Portuguese Government, and used solely for trading purposes. It was held that she was immune from process. It would appear, however, that where the goods are carried at a private charterer's risk the Admiralty Law of salvage applies. *Port Victor* (Cargo ex) 1901, *The Jassy* 1906.

In accordance with Admiralty practice, the British Government normally, and foreign governments at times, do submit to the jurisdiction of the court, when claims are made, but it must always be borne in mind that no claim *in rem* or *in personam*, will be enforced by an Admiralty Court.

⚓ ⚓ ⚓ ⚓

Procedure in Salvage

Determination of salvage disputes.

547 (1) Disputes as to the amount of salvage whether of life or property, and whether rendered within or without the United Kingdom arising between the salvor and the owners of any vessel, cargo, apparel, or wreck, shall, if not settled by agreement, arbitration, or otherwise, be determined summarily in manner provided by this Act, in the following cases; namely,—

(*a*) In any case where the parties to the dispute consent:

(*b*) In any case where the value of the property saved does not exceed one thousand pounds:

(*c*) In any case where the amount claimed does not exceed in Great Britain three hundred pounds, and in Ireland two hundred pounds.

(2) Subject as aforesaid, disputes as to salvage shall be determined by the High Court in England or Ireland, or in Scotland the Court of Session, but if the claimant does not recover in any such court in Great Britain more than three hundred pounds, and in any such court in Ireland more than two hundred pounds, he shall not be entitled to recover any costs, charges, or expenses incurred by him in the prosecution of his claim, unless the court before which the case is tried certify that the case is a fit one to be tried otherwise than summarily in manner provided by this Act.

(3) Disputes relating to salvage may be determined on the application either of the salvor or of the owner of the property saved, or of their respective agents.

(4) Where a dispute as to salvage is to be determined summarily under this section it shall be referred and determined as follows:—

(*a*) In England it shall be referred to and determined by a county court having Admiralty jurisdiction by virtue of the County Courts Admiralty Jurisdiction Act 1868, of any Act amending the same:

(*b*) In Scotland it shall be referred to and determined by the sheriff's court:

(*c*) In Ireland it shall be referred to the arbitration of and determined by two justices of the peace, or a stipendiary magistrate, or the recorder of any borough having a recorder, or the chairman of quarter sessions in any county, and any such justices, stipendiary magistrate, recorder, or chairman are herein-after included in the expression 'arbitrators'.

(5) Nothing in this Act relating to the procedure in salvage cases shall affect the jurisdiction or procedure in salvage cases of a county court having Admiralty jurisdiction by virtue of the County Courts Admiralty Jurisdiction Act,

1868, or the Court of Admiralty (Ireland) Act 1867, or any Act amending either of those Acts.

COMMENTS.

High Court in England: Partial Repeal.

Sub-sections 2 and 3 of this section, so far as they relate to the High Court in England, are repealed by the Judicature (Consolidation) Act 1925, section 226, and the Sixth Schedule. The jurisdiction of the High Court is now governed by the Administration of Justice Act 1956, section 7, sub-section 2. The following is relevant: Administration of Justice Act 1956, section 1, sub-section 1. The Admiralty jurisdiction shall be as follows, that is to say, jurisdiction to hear and determine any of the following questions as claims: . . . sub-section 1, paragraph (*j*):

Any claim in the nature of salvage (including any claim arising by virtue of the application, by, or under section 51 of the Civil Aviation Act 1949, of the law relating to salvage to aircraft and their apparel and cargo); sub-section 3:

The reference in paragraph (*j*) of sub-section 1 of this section to claims in the nature of salvage includes a reference to such claims for services rendered in saving life from a ship or an aircraft, or in preserving cargo apparel, or wreck, as under sections 544 to 546 of the Merchant Shipping Act 1894, or any Order in Council made under section 51 of the Civil Aviation Act 1949 are authorised to be made in connection with a ship or aircraft.

(4) The preceding provisions of this section apply . . .

(*b*) in relation to all claims, wheresoever arising (including in the case of cargo or wreck salvage, claims in respect of cargo or wreck found on land); . . .

Jurisdiction of County Courts.

This section, as well as sections 548 and 549, were repealed in so far as they relate to the summary determination in a county court in England, of dispute as to salvage by the County Courts (Amendment) Act 1934, section 13, sub-section 8; section 34, sub-section 1; section 35, sub-sections 3 and 4, and Fifth Schedule, Part 1.

Now, *see* County Courts Act 1959, as to jurisdiction of County Courts in England and Wales.

Owners.

This term includes mortgagees and all interested in the property. *The Louisa* 1863.

Vessel, Cargo, Apparel, or Wreck.

Does not apply to all property saved from peril at sea, and a floating beacon not able to be navigated is not the subject of salvage, as was said with regard to such a structure in The Gas-float *Whitton*, (No. 2) 1897, per Lord Herschell:

'It is not constructed for the purpose of being navigated or of conveying passengers. It was, in truth, a lighted buoy or beacon. The suggestion that the gas stored in the float can be regarded as cargo carried by it, is more ingenious than sound.'

Value of the Property.

This is the value when first brought into safety. *The Stella* 1867.

In the Craig-an-Eran 1939, the Court of Session in Scotland held that it had no jurisdiction in regards to salvage action where the value had been determined as less than £1000.

The Amount Claimed.

This was held in *The William and John* 1863, preceding legal proceedings. *See* also, 'sum in dispute', section 549, sub-section 1, paragraph (*b*) which has been held to mean the sum claimed by the salvors, and not the amount awarded. *The Andrew Wilson* 1863; *The Mary Ann* 1865; *The Generous* 1868.

Appeals in Salvage Disputes.

See section 549.

Determination of Disputes as to Salvage Summarily.

See section 548.

⚓ ⚓ ⚓ ⚓

548 (1) Disputes as to salvage which are to be determined summarily in manner provided by this Act shall— Determination of disputes as to salvage summarily.

(*a*) where the dispute relates to the salvage of wreck be referred to a court or arbitrators having jurisdiction at or near the place where the wreck is found:

(*b*) where the dispute relates to salvage in the case of services rendered to any vessel or to the cargo or apparel thereof or in saving life therefrom be referred to a court or arbitrators having jurisdiction at or near the place where the vessel is lying, or at or near the port in the United Kingdom into which the vessel is first brought after the occurrence by reason whereof the claim of salvage arises.

(2) Any court or arbitrators to whom a dispute as to salvage is referred for summary determination may, for the purpose of determining any such dispute, call in to their assistance any person conversant with maritime affairs as assessor, and there shall be paid as part of the costs of the proceedings to every such assessor in respect of his services such sum not exceeding five pounds as the Board of Trade may direct.

COMMENTS.

Where the Wreck is Lying.

This means the place where the ship is brought immediately after the accident. Summers *v.* Bucham 1891.

Wreck.

For definition, *see* section 510.

Jurisdiction.

See comments to section 547.

Appeal in case of salvage disputes.

549 (1) Where a dispute relating to salvage has been determined summarily in manner provided by this Act, any party aggrieved by the decision may appeal therefrom—

(*a*) in Great Britain, in like manner as in the case of any other judgment in an Admiralty or maritime cause of the county court or sheriff's court, as the case may be; and

(*b*) In Ireland, to the High Court, but only if the sum in dispute exceeds fifty pounds, and the appellant within ten days after the date of the award gives notice to the arbitrators of his intention to appeal and, within twenty days after the date of the award, takes such proceedings as, according to the practice of the High Court, are necessary for the institution of an appeal.

(2) In the case of an appeal from arbitrators in Ireland the arbitrators shall transmit to the proper officer of the court of appeal a copy on unstamped paper certified under their hands to be a true copy of the proceedings had before them or their umpire (if any) and of the award so made by them or him, accompanied with their or his certificate in writing of the gross value of the article respecting which salvage is claimed; and such copy and certificate shall be admitted in the court of appeal as evidence in the case.

COMMENTS.

Jurisdiction.

See comments to section 547.

Amount of Award.

Normally, the Court will not alter the amount of award unless plainly inadequate or exhorbitant. Cases have arisen where attempts have been made to enforce a high price upon the vessel requiring assistance. There are several instances where these high figures have been reduced.

The Mark Lane 1890.

The Mark Lane, on passage from the Gulf towards Belfast, suffered engine and propeller trouble when in position about 350 miles from Halifax, Nova Scotia. The s.s. *Crete*, which came upon the disabled steamer, offered to tow her the 350-odd miles to Halifax for £5000 and refused to do it for less.

The Court held the amount agreed was exorbitant, and set aside the agreement, awarding only £3000 for the salvage services.

Again, in the *Sir Garnet Wolsely* 1891, it was stated:—

'I quite agree that the £1000 agreed upon is a great deal more than I myself should have thought of giving for the services rendered . . . but I am not prepared to say that this amount is so wholly exorbitant as to induce me to set the agreement aside. I think, however, the screw was put on to the Captain, in a way it should not have been, so shall make no order as to costs.'

See also *The Caba* 1860, *The Harriett* 1857, *The Clarissa* 1856. Again, per Buckley, L. J. in *The Port Hunter* 1910:

'The amount of the award is so much a matter for judicial discretion that unless the judge has gone wrong on a matter of principle, so far as any principle can be laid down in a salvage case, the court will decline to interfere.'

Compare the House of Lords decision in *The Glengyle* 1889. An instance where the court increased the salvage amount is contained in *The Westbourne* 1889.

The contract is generally one incorporating the utmost good faith; where, however, there is non-disclosure of material facts, the court may set aside the agreement and fix a reward as if no agreement had been made. *See The Crus V* 1862, *The Generous* 1868, *The Kingalock* 1854, *The Henry* 1851.

Sum in Dispute.

This means the sum claimed by the salvors and not the sum awarded by the justices and appealed against. *The Andrew Wilson* 1863, *The Mary Ann* 1865.

550 (1) The Lord Lieutenant in Ireland may appoint, out of the justices for any borough or county, a rota of justices, by whom jurisdiction in salvage cases under this Part of this Act shall be exercised.

As to arbitrators in Ireland.

(2) Where no such rota is appointed the salvors may, by writing addressed to the justices clerk, name one justice and the owner of the property saved may in like manner name

another justice to be arbitrators; and if either party fails to name a justice within a reasonable time the case may be tried by two or more justices at petty sessions.

(3) Where a dispute as to salvage is referred to justices under this Act, they may, if a difference of opinion arises between them, or without such difference, if they think fit, appoint some person conversant with maritime affairs as umpire to decide the point in dispute.

(4) The arbitrators, within forty-eight hours after any such dispute has been referred to them, and the umpire (if any) within forty-eight hours after his appointment, shall make an award as to the amount of salvage payable, with power nevertheless for such arbitrators or umpire, by writing, duly signed, to extend the time for so making the award.

(5) There shall be paid to every umpire appointed as aforesaid, in respect of his services, such sum not exceeding five pounds as the Board of Trade may direct.

(6) All the costs of such arbitration, including any such payment to an umpire as aforesaid, shall be paid by the parties to the dispute, in such manner, and in such shares and proportions, as the arbitrators or umpire may direct by the award.

(7) The arbitrators or umpire may call for the production of any documents in the possession or power of either party which they or he may think necessary for determining the question in dispute, and may examine the parties and their witnesses on oath, and administer the oaths necessary for that purpose.

(8) A Secretary of State may determine the scale of costs to be awarded in salvage cases determined by arbitrators under this Part of this Act.

COMMENTS.

Ireland.

Here means Northern Ireland only.

⚓ ⚓ ⚓ ⚓

Valuation of property by receiver.

551 (1) Where any dispute as to salvage arises, the receiver of the district where the property is in respect of which the salvage claim is made, may, on the application of either party, appoint a valuer to value that property, and shall give copies of the valuation to both parties.

(2) Any copy of the valuation purporting to be signed by the valuer, and to be certified as a true copy by the receiver, shall be admissible as evidence in any subsequent proceeding.

(3) There shall be paid in respect of the valuation by the person applying for the same such fee as the Board of Trade may direct.

COMMENTS.

Exclusion of Section.

This section as well as sections 552, 553 and 554 are excluded in relation to salvage claims against the Crown.

See Crown Proceedings Act 1947, section 8, sub-section 1.

⚓ ⚓ ⚓ ⚓

552 (1) Where salvage is due to any person under this Act, the receiver shall— **Detention of property liable for salvage by a receiver.**

(*a*) if the salvage is due in respect of services rendered in assisting any vessel, or in saving life therefrom, or in saving the cargo or apparel thereof, detain the vessel and cargo or apparel; and

(*b*) if the salvage is due in respect of the saving of any wreck, and the wreck is not sold as unclaimed under the Act, detain the wreck.

(2) Subject as herein-after mentioned, the receiver shall detain the vessel and the cargo and apparel, or the wreck (herein-after referred to as detained property) until payment is made for salvage, or process is issued for the arrest or detention thereof by some competent court.

(3) A receiver may release any detained property if security is given to his satisfaction or, if the claim for salvage exceeds two hundred pounds, and any question is raised as to the sufficiency of the security, to the satisfaction in England or Ireland of the High Court, and in Scotland of the Court of Session, including any division of that court, or the Lord Ordinary officiating on the bills during vacation.

(4) Any security given for salvage in pursuance of this section to an amount exceeding two hundred pounds may be enforced by such court as aforesaid in the same manner as if bail had been given in that court.

COMMENTS.

Exclusion of section.

See comments to section 551.

Salvage Due Under this Act.

The words 'due to any person under this Act' appear to cover any salvage which the Act contemplates being awarded by the courts mentioned in it, the jurisdiction is conferred or recognised by it. *The Fulham* 1898.

Salvage Due.

See sections 544, 546 for salvage payable for saving life, cargo, or wreck. The term 'salvage' is defined in section 510.

The Receiver shall.

It is submitted that the receiver has no discretion to refuse to detain if a claim for salvage is made. *The Fulham* 1899.

After Release.

After release by the receiver on security being given, salvors had no right to detain the property or arrest it by warrant of the Admiralty Court. *The Lady Katherine Barham* 1861.

⚓ ⚓ ⚓ ⚓

Sale of detained property by receiver.

553 (1) The receiver may sell any detained property if the persons liable to pay the salvage in respect of which the property is detained are aware of the detention, in the following cases; namely,—

(*a*) Where the amount is not disputed, and payment of the amount due is not made within twenty days after the amount is due, or,

(*b*) Where the amount is disputed, but no appeal lies from the first court to which the dispute is referred, and payment is not made within twenty days after the decision of the first court, or

(*c*) Where the amount is disputed and an appeal lies from the decision of the first court to some other court, and within twenty days of the decision of the first court neither payment of the sum due is made nor proceedings are commenced for the purpose of appeal.

(2) The proceeds of sale of detained property shall, after payment of the expenses of the sale, be applied by the receiver in payment of the expenses, fees, and salvage, and, so far as not required for that purpose, shall be paid to the owners of the property, or any other persons entitled to receive the same.

COMMENTS.

Exclusion of section.

See comments to section 511.

Salvage.

For definition, *see* section 510.

⚓ ⚓ ⚓ ⚓

554 (1) Where services for which salvage is claimed are rendered either by the commander or crew or part of the crew of any of Her Majesty's ships or of any other ship, and the salvor voluntarily agrees to abandon his lien upon the ship, cargo, and property alleged to be salved, then, upon the master entering into a written agreement attested by two witnesses to abide the decision of the High Court in England, or of a Vice-Admiralty Court or Colonial Court of Admiralty, and thereby giving security in that behalf to an amount agreed on by the parties to the agreement, that agreement shall bind the ship, and the cargo, and freight respectively, and the respective owners of the ship, cargo, and freight, and their respective heirs, executors, and administrators, for the salvage which may be adjudged to be payable in respect of the ship, cargo, and freight respectively to the extent of the security given. A.D. 1894. Agreement as to salvage.

(2) Any agreement made under this section may be adjudicated on and enforced in the same manner as a bond executed under the provisions of this Part of this Act relating to salvage by Her Majesty's ships, and on any such agreement being made the salvor and the master shall respectively make the statements required by this Part of this Act to be made in the case of the bond, but their statements need not be made on oath.

(3) The salvor shall transmit the statements made, as soon as practicable to the court in which the agreement is to be adjudicated upon.

COMMENTS.

Exclusion of Section.

See comments to section 551.

Salvage by H.M. Ships.

See also sections 557 et seq.

Bond.

For provisions as to bond executed under this part of the Act, *see* section 559.

Definitions.

For 'salvor' in the case of H.M. Ships, and 'master', *see* section 742.
For 'salvage', *see* section 510.

⚓ ⚓ ⚓ ⚓

Apportionment of salvage under 200*l*. by receiver.

555 (1) Where the aggregate amount of salvage payable in respect of salvage services rendered in the United Kingdom has been finally determined, either summarily in manner provided by this Act or by agreement, and does not exceed two hundred pounds, but a dispute arises as to the apportionment thereof among several claimants, the person liable to pay the amount may apply to the receiver for liberty to pay the same to him; and the receiver shall, if he thinks fit, receive the same accordingly, and shall grant to the person paying the amount a certificate of the amount paid and of the services in respect of which it is paid, and that certificate shall be a full discharge and indemnity to the person by whom the money is paid, and to his vessel, cargo, apparel, and effects against the claims of all persons whomsoever in respect of the services mentioned in the certificate.

(2) The receiver shall with all convenient speed distribute any amount received by him under this section among the persons entitled to the same on such evidence, and in such shares and proportions, as he thinks fit, and may retain any money which appears to him to be payable to any person who is absent.

(3) A distribution made by a receiver in pursuance of this section shall be final and conclusive as against all persons claiming to be entitled to any portion of the amount distributed.

COMMENTS.

Amendment.

Between the words "agreement . . . and does not" . . . insert 'or by a County Court in England'.

See County Courts Act 1959, section 56, sub-section 8, which replaced section 56, sub-section 8 of the County Courts Act 1934.

Amount of Salvage Determined.

See section 547 as to determination of salvage dispute.

⚓ ⚓ ⚓ ⚓

Apportionment of salvage by Admiralty Courts.

556 Whenever the aggregate amount of salvage payable in respect of salvage service rendered in the United Kingdom has been finally ascertained, and exceeds two hundred pounds, and whenever the aggregate amount of salvage payable in respect of salvage services rendered elsewhere has been finally ascertained, whatever that amount may be, then, if any delay or dispute arises as to the apportionment thereof, any court having Admiralty jurisdiction may cause the same to be apportioned amongst the persons entitled thereto in such manner as it thinks just, and may for that purpose, if it thinks fit, appoint any person to carry that apportionment into effect, and may compel any person in whose hands or under whose control the amount may be to distribute the same, or to bring the same into court to be there dealt with as the court may direct, and may for the purposes aforesaid issue such processes as it thinks fit.

⚓ ⚓ ⚓ ⚓

Salvage by Her Majesty's Ships

557 (1) Where salvage services are rendered by any ship belonging to Her Majesty or by the commander or crew thereof, no claim shall be allowed for any loss, damage, or risk caused to the ship or her stores, tackle, or furniture, or for the use of any stores or other articles belonging to Her Majesty, supplied in order to effect those services, or for any other expense or loss sustained by Her Majesty by reason of that service, and no claim for salvage services by the commander or crew, or part of the crew of any of Her Majesty's ships shall be finally adjudicated upon, unless the consent of the Admiralty to the prosecution of that claim is proved. Salvage by Her Majesty's ships.

(2) Any document purporting to give the consent of the Admiralty for the purpose of this section, and to be signed by the Secretary to the Admiralty or on his behalf, shall be evidence of that consent.

(3) If a claim is prosecuted and the consent is not proved, the claim shall stand dismissed with costs.

COMMENTS.

Repeal.

The words underlined above, from "where to service," were repealed by the Merchant Shipping (Salvage) Act 1940, section 4, sub-section 3, and Schedule.

General.

The Crown Proceedings Act 1947 reformed the whole system of actions by and against the Crown, and since 1948, not only can the Crown claim salvage, like any other shipowner, but also ordinary shipowners can claim salvage against the Crown for assistance rendered to H.M. Ships. No action *in rem* may, however, be brought.

See the Crown Proceedings Act 1947, sections 8 and 29.

The provisions of sub-section 1 above remained, apparently to prevent improper claims such as that which had been censured by the Court in *The Rapid* 1938.

See also per Lord Wright in Admiralty Commissioners *v. Valverda* 1938, where it was held that this sub-section 1 could not be excluded by agreement. In this same case it was held that this section as modified by the Merchant Shipping (Salvage) Act 1916 (Repealed) excluded all claims for salvage by the Admiralty.

H.M. Ships.

In cases on the meaning of H.M. Ships, *see The Cybele* 1878, where a harbour tug owned and employed by the Board of Trade as Trustees of Ramsgate Harbour, were held not to be ships belonging to Her Majesty.

Symons *v.* Baker 1905. Vessel on Navy List, exclusively employed in carrying coal for the Navy, was held to be a ship belonging to Her Majesty within the meaning of section 741 of this Act, although neither master nor crew were in the Navy.

Elliott Steam Tug Co. Ltd. *v.* Admiralty Commissioners 1921. Where vessel registered on terms amounting to demise to Admiralty, the tug was held to be a ship belonging to Her Majesty, and therefore, the Admiralty were held entitled to sue for salvage under M.S. (Salvage) Act 1916 (Repealed).

The Sarden 1916. Where tug requisitioned on terms which did not amount to a demise, was not debarred from claiming salvage, hence, was not held to be a ship belonging to Her Majesty. *See* also *The Nile* 1875, *The Bertie* 1886. Where an enemy ship seized as a prize and requisitioned by the Admiralty, it was held to be a ship belonging to Her Majesty, and under the legislation then prevailing, was held not entitled to salvage.

Commander or Crew.

Where services rendered by the officers and crew are of Her Majesty's ships were outside the scope of their duties they were held entitled to substantial award. *The Ulysses* (Cargo ex) 1888.

Prize Salvage.

See the Prize Salvage Act 1944, where the consent of the Admiralty must be obtained before enforcing a claim for prize salvage.

⚓ ⚓ ⚓ ⚓

Salvage by Her Majesty's ships abroad.

558 (1) Where services are rendered at any place out of the limits of the United Kingdom or the four seas adjoining thereto by the commander or any of the crew of Her Majesty's ships, in saving any vessel or cargo or property, belong to a vessel, the vessel, cargo, or property, alleged to be saved shall, if the salvor is justified by the circumstances of the case in detaining it, be taken to some port where there is a consular officer or a Colonial Court of Admiralty, or a Vice-Admiralty Court.

(2) The salvor and the master, or other person in charge of the vessel, cargo, or property salved, shall within twenty-four hours after arriving at the port each deliver to the consular officer or judge of the Colonial Court of Admiralty or Vice-Admiralty Court, as the case may be, a statement on oath, specifying so far as possible, and so far as those particulars are applicable, the particulars set out in the first part of the Nineteenth Schedule to this Act, and also in the case of the master or other person his willingness to execute a bond in the form, so far as circumstances will permit, set out in the second part of that schedule.

COMMENTS.

Commander or Crew of H.M. Ships.

It is submitted that this section, in concert with Schedule 19, does not give the officer commanding a H.M. Ship to enter into an agreement with the master of a merchantman as to the amount of salvage.

In any event, if ordered to assist a wrecked ship, he cannot impose terms and then refuse to assist unless the terms laid down are accepted. *The Wousung* (Cargo Ex) 1876.

United Kingdom.

Here includes the Republic of Ireland.

559 (1) The bond shall be in such sum as the consular officer or judge thinks sufficient to answer the demand for salvage service, but the sum fixed shall not exceed one half of the amount which, in the opinion of the consular officer or judge, is the value of the property in respect of which salvage has been rendered.

Provisions as to bond to be executed.

(2) Where the vessel, cargo, or property in respect of which salvage services are rendered is not owned by persons domiciled in Her Majesty's dominions, the master shall procure such security for the due performance of the bond as the consular officer or judge thinks sufficient to be lodged with that officer or judge, or with that officer or judge and such other persons jointly as the salvor may appoint.

(3) The consular officer or judge shall fix the amount of the bond within four days after the receipt of the statements required by this Part of this Act, but if either of those

statements is not delivered within the time required by this Part of this Act, he may proceed *ex parte*.

(4) A consular officer may for the purposes of this section take affidavits.

(5) Nothing in this section shall authorise the consular officer or judge to require the cargo of any ship to be unladen.

COMMENTS.

Bond.

See section 558, sub-section 2 for requirements as to bonds.

Definitions.

Consular officer, salvor, and master, *see* section 742.

Execution of bond.

560 (1) The consular officer or judge on fixing the sum to be inserted in the bond shall send notice thereof to the salvor and master, and on the execution of the bond by the master in the sum fixed in the presence of the consular officer or judge (who shall attest the same), and upon delivery thereof to the salvor, and in cases where security is to be lodged, on that security being duly lodged, the right of the salvor to detain the vessel, cargo, or property shall cease.

(2) The bond shall bind the respective owners of the vessel, cargo, and freight, and their heirs, executors, and administrators, for the salvage adjudged to be payable in respect of the vessel, cargo, and freight respectively.

COMMENTS.

See comments to section 559.

Enforcement of bond.

561 (1) The bond shall be adjudicated on and enforced in the High Court in England, unless the salvor and master agree at the time of the execution of the bond that the bond may be adjudicated on and enforced in any specified Colonial Court of Admiralty or Vice-Admiralty Court, but that court shall in that case have the same power and authorities for the purpose as the High Court in England.

(2) The High Court in England shall have power to enforce any bond given in pursuance of this Part of this Act in any Colonial Court of Admiralty or Vice-Admiralty Court in any part of Her Majesty's dominions, and any court exercising Admiralty jurisdiction in Scotland, Ireland,

the Isle of Man, or the Channel Islands shall assist that court in enforcing those bonds.

(3) Where security has been given for the performance of a bond, the persons with whom the security is lodged shall deal with the same as the court adjudicating upon the bond direct.

(4) The consular officer or judge shall at the earliest opportunity transmit the statements and documents delivered to him, and the notice of the sum fixed in the bond to the High Court in England or the Colonial Court of Admiralty or Vice-Admiralty Court in which the bond is to be enforced, as the case may be.

COMMENTS.

Bond.

See section 558, sub-section 2 for requirements as to bonds.

Definition.

For 'Master', 'Crew', and 'Salvor', *see* section 742.

⚓ ⚓ ⚓ ⚓

Saving for other salvage rights.

562 (1) Nothing contained in this Part of this Act shall prejudice the right of the salvor, where salvage services have been rendered by one of Her Majesty's ships, or by the commander of any of the crew thereof, to proceed for the enforcement of the salvage claim otherwise than in manner provided by this Act, but the salvor shall have no right to detain the vessel, cargo, or property saved, unless he elects to proceed under this Part of this Act.

(2) Nothing contained in this Part of this Act shall affect the right of the salvor, where salvage services have been rendered by one of Her Majesty's ships or by the commander or any of the crew thereof, in any case which is not provided for therein.

COMMENTS.

Definition.

'Salvor', *see* section 742.

Salvage by H.M. Ships.

See sections 557 and 558.

Enforcement of Claim.

See sections 547 and 548, and comments thereto.

⚓ ⚓ ⚓ ⚓

Exemption from stamp duty.

563 Any bond, statement, agreement, or other document made or executed in pursuance of the provisions of this Part of this Act relating to salvage by Her Majesty's ships shall, if made or executed out of the United Kingdom, be exempt from stamp duty.

COMMENTS.

Bond, etc., Relating to Salvage.

See sections 557 and 558.

⚓ ⚓ ⚓ ⚓

Punishment for forgery and false representations.

564 If any person in any proceeding under the provisions of this Part of this Act relating to salvage by Her Majesty's ships—

(*a*) forges, assists in forging, or procures to be forged, fraudulently alters, assists in fraudulently altering, or procures to be fraudulently altered, any document; *or*

(*b*) puts off or makes use of any forged or altered document, knowing the same to be so forged or altered; *or*

(*c*) gives or makes, or assists in giving or making, or procures to be given or made, any false evidence or representation, knowing the same to be false,

that person shall for each offence be liable to imprisonment, with or without hard labour, for any period not exceeding two years, or, on summary conviction, to imprisonment, with or without hard labour, for any period not exceeding six months.

COMMENTS.

Salvage by H.M. Ships.

See sections 557 and 558.

Hard Labour.

By section 1, sub-section 2 of the Criminal Justice Act 1948, hard labour is abolished, and enactments conferring power to sentence to imprisonment with hard labour are to be construed as conferring power to sentence to imprisonment.

⚓ ⚓ ⚓ ⚓

Jurisdiction of High Court in Salvage

Jurisdiction of High Court in salvage.

565 Subject to the provisions of this Act, the High Court, and in Scotland the Court of Session, shall have jurisdiction to decide upon all claims whatsoever relating to salvage, whether the services in respect of which salvage is claimed were performed on the high seas or within the body of any county, or partly on the high seas and partly within the body of any county, and whether the wreck in respect of which salvage is claimed is found on the sea or on the land, or partly on the sea and partly on the land.

COMMENTS.

High Court in England.

So far as it relates to the High Court in England, this section is repealed by the Supreme Court of Judicature (Consolidation) Act 1925, now re-enacted in section 1 of the Administration of Justice Act 1956.

Northern Ireland.

This section so far as it relates to Northern Ireland, has been repealed by the Administration of Justice Act 1956, section 55, sub-section 1, Schedule 1, Part III.

Appointment of Receivers of Wreck

566 The Board of Trade shall have the general superintendence throughout the United Kingdom of all matters relating to wreck, and may, with the consent of the Treasury, appoint any officer of customs or of the coastguard, or any officer of inland revenue, or, where it appears to such Board to be more convenient, any other person, to be a receiver of wreck (in this Part of this Act referred to as a receiver), in any district, and to perform the duties of receiver under this Part of this Act, and shall give due notice of the appointment. Appointment of receivers of wreck.

Fees of Receivers of Wreck

567 (1) There shall be paid to every receiver the expenses properly incurred by him in the performance of his duties, and also, in respect of the several matters specified in the Twentieth Schedule to this Act, such fees not exceeding the amounts therein mentioned as may be directed by the Board of Trade, but a receiver shall not be entitled to any remuneration other than those payments. Receivers' fees.

(2) The receiver shall, in addition to all other rights and remedies for the recovery of those expenses or fees, have the same rights and remedies in respect thereof as a salvor has in respect of salvage due to him.

(3) Whenever any dispute arises in any part of the United Kingdom as to the amount payable to any receiver in respect of expenses or fees, that dispute shall be determined by the Board of Trade, and the decision of that Board shall be final.

(4) All fees received by a receiver in respect of any services performed by him as receiver shall be carried to, and form part of, the Mercantile Marine Fund, but a separate account shall be kept of those fees, and the moneys arising from them shall be applied in defraying any expenses duly incurred in carrying into effect this Act in such manner as the Board of Trade direct.

COMMENTS.

The words underlined in this section were repealed as from 19th November 1952 by the M.S. (Safety Convention) Act 1949, section 37, sub-section 5, and Schedule.

Fees.

The fees of receivers of wreck are now contained in Part 20 of the Schedule to the M.S. (Fees) Regulations 1971 (S.I. 1971, No. 643) in operation as from 1st May 1971.

Expenses.

The expenses of burial of carcases washed ashore are recoverable by the receiver from the local authority, who can recover from the shipowner, *see* now Diseases of Animals Act 1950, section 75, as amended by the Administration of Justice Act 1956.

In Northern Ireland, regard should be paid to the Diseases of Animals Act 1925, which still substantially applies.

Salvors Rights and Remedies.

See section 552.

Mercantile Marine Fund.

Fees are now payable to the exchequer, *see* the Merchant Shipping (Mercantile Marine Fund) Act 1898, section 1, sub-section 1, paragraph (*a*).

⚓ ⚓ ⚓ ⚓

Remuneration for services by coastguard.

568 (1) Where services are rendered by any officers or men of the coastguard service in watching or protecting shipwrecked property, then, unless it can be shown that those services have been declined by the owner of the property or his agent at the time they were tendered, or that salvage has been claimed and awarded for those services, the owner of the property shall pay in respect of those services remuneration according to a scale to be fixed by the Board of Trade; and that remuneration shall be recoverable by the same means, and shall be paid to the same persons, and accounted for and applied in the same manner as fees received by receivers under the provisions of this Part of this Act.

(2) The scale fixed by the Board of Trade shall not exceed the scale by which remuneration to officers and men of the coastguard for extra duties in the ordinary service of the Commissioners of Customs is for the time being regulated.

COMMENTS.

Fees Received by Receivers.

See comments to section 567.

Shipwrecked Property.

For exercise of powers of receiver of wreck in their absence by coastguards, *see* section 516.

Commissioners of Customs and Excise.

See Customs and Excise Act 1952.

Duties on Wreck

Provisions as to duties, &c., on wrecked goods.

569 (1) All wreck, being foreign goods brought or coming into the United Kingdom or Isle of Man, shall be subject to the same duties as if the same was imported into the United Kingdom or Isle of Man respectively, and if any question arises as to the origin of the goods, they shall be deemed to be the produce of such country as the Commissioners of Customs may on investigation determine.

(2) The Commissioners of Customs and Inland Revenue shall permit all goods, wares, and merchandise saved from any ship stranded or wrecked on her homeward voyage to be forwarded to the port of her original destination, and all goods, wares, and merchandise saved from any ship stranded or wrecked on her outward voyage to be returned to the port at which the same were shipped; but those Commissioners shall take security for the due protection of the revenue in respect of those goods.

COMMENTS.

Repeal.

Sub-section (1), underlined above, was repealed by the Customs and Excise Act 1952, section 320, Schedule XII, Part 1, as from 1st January 1953.

It has been replaced by section 34, sub-section 3 of the Repealing Act, viz.:

'Any goods brought or coming into the United Kingdom by sea, otherwise than as cargo, stores or baggage carried in a ship, shall be chargeable with the like duty, if any, as would be applicable to those goods if they had been imported as merchandise; and if any question arises as to the origin of the goods, they shall be deemed to be the produce of such country as the Commissioners may, on investigation, determine' . . .

Wreck.

For definition, *see* section 510.

Commissioners of Customs.

The management of customs duties is now vested in the Commissioners of Customs and Excise.

⚓ ⚓ ⚓ ⚓

Supplemental

Powers of sheriff in Scotland.

570 Any matter or thing which may be done under this Part of this Act by or to a justice of the peace, or a court of summary jurisdiction, may in Scotland be done by or to the sheriff of the county.

⚓ ⚓ ⚓ ⚓

Saving for Cinque ports.

571 Nothing in this Part of this Act shall prejudice or affect any jurisdiction or powers of the Lord Warden or any officers of the Cinque ports or of any court of those ports or of any court having concurrent jurisdiction within the boundaries of these ports, and disputes as to salvage arising within those boundaries shall be determined in the manner in which they have been hitherto determined.

COMMENTS.

For jurisdiction as to salvage in the Cinque Ports, *see* the Cinque Ports Act 1821.

⚓ ⚓ ⚓ ⚓

M.S.A. 1894

PART XI

LIGHTHOUSES

PART XI

LIGHTHOUSES

General Management

634 (1) Subject to the provisions of this Part of this Act, and subject also to any powers or rights now lawfully enjoyed or exercised by any person or body of persons having by law or usage authority over local lighthouses, buoys, or beacons (in this Act referred to as 'local lighthouse authorities',) the superintendence and management of all lighthouses, buoys, and beacons shall within the following areas be vested in the following bodies; namely,— **Management of lighthouses, buoys, and beacons.**

(*a*) Throughout England and Wales, and the Channel Islands, and the adjacent seas and islands, and at Gibraltar, in the Trinity House;

(*b*) Throughout Scotland and the adjacent seas and islands, and the Isle of Man, in the Commissioners of Northern Lighthouses; and

(*c*) Throughout Ireland and the adjacent seas and islands, in the Commissioners of Irish Lights,

and those bodies are in this Act referred to as the general lighthouse authorities and those areas as lighthouse areas.

(2) Subject to the provisions of this Part of this Act, the general lighthouse authorities shall respectively continue to hold and maintain all property now vested in them in that behalf in the same manner and for the same purposes as they have hitherto held and maintained the same.

COMMENTS.

Commissioners of Irish Lights.

The functions of the Commissioners were, as regards the Republic of Ireland, transferred to the Provisional Government by the Provisional Government (Transfer of Functions) Order 1922, S.R. & O., No. 315, 1922.

The Commissioners of Irish Lights at Dublin still exercise jurisdiction over Northern Ireland Lights.

The Trinity House.

For meaning, *see* section 742.

Construction of Lighthouses.

See sections 638 to 642 for the powers and duties of general lighthouse authorities in respect of the construction of lighthouses.

Exhibition of False Lights.

It is an offence to injure a lighthouse or to exhibit false lights. *See* sections 666 and 667.

⚓ ⚓ ⚓ ⚓

Returns and information to Board of Trade.

635 The general lighthouse authorities, and their respective officers, shall at all times give to the Board of Trade all such returns, explanations, or information, in relation to the lighthouses, buoys, or beacons within their respective areas, and the management thereof, as the Board require.

COMMENTS.

Inspection.

On a complaint being made, the Ministry has power to inspect lighthouses, buoys, and beacons. For definition of such terms, *See* section 742.

⚓ ⚓ ⚓ ⚓

Power of Board of Trade to inspect on complaint made.

636 (1) The Board of Trade may, on complaint that any lighthouse, buoy, or beacon under the management of any of the general lighthouse authorities, or any work connected therewith, is inefficient or improperly managed or is unnecessary, authorise any persons appointed by them to inspect the same.

(2) A person so authorised may inspect the same accordingly, and make any inquiries in respect thereof, and of the management thereof, which he thinks fit; and all officers and others having the care of any such lighthouses, buoys, or beacons, or concerned in the management thereof, shall furnish any information and explanations in relation thereto which the person inspecting requires.

⚓ ⚓ ⚓ ⚓

Inspection by Trinity House.

637 The Trinity House, and any of their engineers, workmen, and servants, may at all times enter any lighthouse within any of the lighthouse areas for the purpose of viewing their condition or otherwise for the purposes of this Act.

COMMENTS.

The Trinity House.

For meanings, *see* section 742 as to the powers of the Trinity House in areas other than their own, *see* sections 640 and 641.

⚓ ⚓ ⚓ ⚓

Construction of Lighthouses, &c.

638 A general lighthouse authority shall, within their area but subject, in the case of the Commissioners of Northern Lighthouses and the Commissioners of Irish Lights, to the restrictions enacted in this Part of this Act, have the following powers (in this Act referred to as lighthouse powers); namely, powers— **General powers of lighthouse authorities.**

(*a*) to erect or place any lighthouse, with all requisite works, roads, and appurtenances:

(*b*) to add to, alter, or remove any lighthouse:

(*c*) to erect or place any buoy or beacon, or alter or remove any buoy or beacon:

(*d*) to vary the character of any lighthouse or the mode of exhibiting lights therein.

COMMENTS:

To Erect.

Development required for the purposes of the exercise of the functions of a general lighthouse authority under this Act is permitted by the Town and Country Planning (General Development) Order 1948, S.I. 1948, No. 958, Part 3 the First Schedule, Class XVIIIg.

The undertakers, as defined in the Harbour Docks and Piers Clauses Act 1847, may not erect any lighthouse or exhibit any light without the sanction of the appropriate general lighthouse authority.

⚓ ⚓ ⚓ ⚓

639 (1) A general lighthouse authority may take and purchase any land which may be necessary for the exercise of their lighthouse powers, or for the maintenance of their works or for the residence of the light keepers, and for that purpose the Lands Clauses Acts shall be incorporated with this Act and shall apply to all lighthouses to be constructed and all land to be purchased under the powers thereof. Powers as to land.

(2) A general lighthouse authority may sell any land belonging to them.

COMMENTS.

Lighthouse Powers.

For meaning, *see* section 638.

⚓ ⚓ ⚓ ⚓

Restrictions on exercise of lighthouse powers by Commissioners.

640 (1) When the Commissioners of Northern Lighthouses or the Commissioners of Irish Lights propose to exercise any of their lighthouse powers, they shall submit a scheme to the Trinity House specifying the mode in which they propose to exercise the power, and their reasons for wishing to exercise the same, and they shall not exercise any such power until they have so submitted a scheme to the Trinity House and obtained the sanction of the Board of Trade in manner provided by this Act.

(2) The Trinity House shall take into consideration any scheme so submitted to them, and shall make a report, stating their approval or rejection of the scheme with or without modification, and shall send a copy of the report to the Commissioners by whom the scheme is submitted.

(3) For the purpose of obtaining the sanction of the Board of Trade to any scheme so submitted to the Trinity House, the Trinity House shall send a copy of the scheme and of their report thereon, and of any communications which have passed with reference thereto between them and the Commissioners by whom the scheme is submitted, to the Board of Trade, and that Board may give any directions they think fit with reference to the scheme, and may grant or withhold their sanction either wholly or subject to any conditions or modifications they think fit.

(4) The Commissioners by whom a scheme is submitted may, before a decision on the scheme is given by the Board of Trade, forward either to that Board or to the Trinity House any suggestions or observations with respect to the scheme or the report of the Trinity House thereon, and the Board of Trade in giving any decision on the scheme shall consider those suggestions or observations.

(5) The decision of the Board of Trade with reference to any scheme shall be communicated by that Board to the Trinity House, and by the Trinity House to the Commissioners by whom the scheme is submitted, and those Commissioners shall act in conformity with the decision.

COMMENTS.

Lighthouse Powers.

For meaning, *see* section 638.

Definitions.

See sections 742.

⚓ ⚓ ⚓ ⚓

641 (1) The Trinity House may, with the sanction of the Board of Trade, direct the Commissioners of Northern Lighthouses or the Commissioners of Irish Lights— Power of Trinity House to direct lighthouse works to be done.

(*a*) to continue any lighthouse, buoy, or beacon:

(*b*) to erect or place any lighthouse, buoy, or beacon, or add to, alter, or remove any existing lighthouse, buoy, or beacon:

(*c*) to vary the character of any lighthouse or the mode of exhibiting lights therein:

and the Commissioners shall be bound within a reasonable time to obey any directions so given and sanctioned.

(2) For the purpose of obtaining the sanction of the Board of Trade to any direction under this section, the Trinity House shall make a written application to the Board of Trade showing fully the work which they propos e to direct and their reasons for directing the same, and shall give notice in writing of the application to the Commissioners to whom they propose to give the direction at their principal office in Edinburgh or Dublin, as the case may be.

(3) Before the Board of Trade decide on any such application an opportunity shall be given to the Commissioners to whom it is proposed to give the direction for making any representation which they may think fit to make with regard to the application to the Board of Trade or the Trinity House.

COMMENTS.

Definitions.

See section 742.

⚓ ⚓ ⚓ ⚓

642 Where any improved light, or any siren or any description of fog signal has been added to an existing Additions to lighthouses.

lighthouse, the light siren or signal may, for the purposes of this Part of this Act, be treated as if it were a separate lighthouse.

COMMENTS.

Lighthouse.

For meaning, *see* section 742.

Light Dues

Continuance of light dues.

643 Subject to any alterations to be made under the powers contained in this Part of this Act, a general lighthouse authority shall, in respect of any lighthouses, buoys, or beacons which at the commencement of this Act are under their management, continue to levy dues (in this Act called light dues), subject to the samel imitations as to the amount thereof as are in force at the commencement of this Act; and those light dues shall be payable in respect of all ships whatever, except ships belonging to Her Majesty, and ships exempted from payment thereof in pursuance of this Act.

COMMENTS.

Repeal.

The words underlined in this section were repealed by the M.S. (Mercantile Marine Fund) Act 1898, section 8, and Fourth Schedule.

Light Dues.

See now Merchant Shipping, The Merchant Shipping (Light Dues) Order 1972, S.I. 1972, No. 456, operative from 1st April 1972.

This consolidates, with amendments, the scale of payments, rules and exemptions relating to the levying of light dues set out in Schedule 2 to the M.S. (Mercantile Marine Fund) Act 1898, as previously amended.

Merchant Shipping Act 1894

Part XI

Sections 644–646

Repealed by the Merchant Shipping (Mercantile Marine Fund) Act 1898 Section 8 and Fourth Schedule

647 Tables of all light dues, and a copy of the regulations for the time being in force in respect thereof, shall be posted up at all custom houses in the United Kingdom, and for that purpose each of the general lighthouse authorities shall furnish copies of all such tables and regulations to the Commissioners of Customs in London, and to the chief officers of customs resident at all places where light dues are collected on account of that lighthouse authority; and those copies shall be posted up by the Commissioners of Customs at the Custom House in London, and by the chief officers of customs at the custom houses of the places at which they are respectively resident. Publication of light dues and regulations.

COMMENTS.

Light Dues.

These dues are payable by virtue of section 643.

For scale of payments, etc., *see* comments to this section.

⚓ ⚓ ⚓ ⚓

648 (1) All light dues coming into the hands of any general lighthouse authority under this Act shall be carried to the Mercantile Marine Fund. Application and collection of light dues.

(2) Every person appointed to collect light dues by any of the general lighthouse authorities shall collect all light dues payable at the port at which he is so appointed, whether they are collected on account of the authority by whom he was appointed or on account of one of the other general lighthouse authorities.

(3) Any person so appointed to collect light dues shall pay over to the general lighthouse authority by whom he was appointed, or as that authority directs, the whole amount of light dues received by him; and the authority receiving the dues shall keep accounts thereof, and shall cause the dues to be remitted to Her Majesty's Paymaster-General in such manner as the Board of Trade direct.

COMMENTS.

General Lighthouse Authority.

For meaning, *see* section 634.

Mercantile Marine Fund.

This fund has now been abolished and light dues are now payable into the General Lighthouse Fund. *See* section 676—section 1, paragraph (i) in Part XII of the Principal Act.

Receipts for Light Dues.

The person collecting light dues must give a receipt for them, and a ship may be detained until the receipt is produced to the proper officer of customs, *see* section 651.

Light Dues.

For ships liable to pay light dues, *see* section 634.

⚓ ⚓ ⚓ ⚓

Recovery of light dues.

649 (1) The following persons shall be liable to pay light dues for any ship in respect of which light dues are payable; namely,—

(*a*) The owner or master; or

(*b*) Such consignees or agents thereof as have paid, or made themselves liable to pay, any other charge on account of the ship in the port of her arrival or discharge;

and those dues may be recovered in the same manner as fines of a like amount under this Act.

(2) Any consignee or agent (not being the owner or master of the ship) who is hereby made liable for the payment of light dues in respect of any ship, may, out of any moneys received by him on account of that ship or belonging to the owner thereof, retain the amount of all light dues paid by him, together with any reasonable expenses he may have incurred by reason of the payment of the dues or his liability to pay the dues.

COMMENTS.

Light Dues.

These dues are payable by virtue of section 643. For collection of light dues, *see* section 648. Distress for non-payment, *see* section 650. A receipt for light dues must be obtained, and a ship may be detained until it is produced to the proper officer of Customs. *See* section 651.

See The Andalania, 1886, as to the competing claims of seamen for wages and that of a person who has paid light dues.

Where it is provided that the charterers shall pay 'Port Charges', this includes light dues which the ship may be required to pay before obtaining her clearance. Newman & Dale *v.* Lamport & Holt 1896.

Master; Port; Ship.

For definitions, *see* section 742.

⚓ ⚓ ⚓ ⚓

650 (1) If the owner or master of any ship fails, on demand of the authorised collector, to pay the light dues due in respect thereof, that collector may, in addition to any other remedy which he or the authority by whom he is appointed is entitled to use, enter upon the ship, and distrain the goods, guns, tackle, or any thing belonging to, or on board, the ship, and detain that distress until the light dues are paid.

Distress on ship for light dues.

(2) If payment of the light dues is not made within the period of three days next ensuing the distress, the collector may, at any time during the continuance of the non-payment, cause the distress to be appraised by two sufficient persons or sworn appraisers, and thereupon sell the same, and apply the proceeds in payment of the light dues due, together with all reasonable expenses incurred by him under this section, paying the surplus (if any), on demand, to the owner or master of the ship.

⚓ ⚓ ⚓ ⚓

651 A receipt for light dues shall be given by the person appointed to collect the same to every person paying the same, and a ship may be detained at any port where light dues are payable in respect of any ship, until the receipt for the light dues is produced to the proper officer of customs.

Receipt for light dues.

⚓ ⚓ ⚓ ⚓

Local Lighthouses

652 (1) It shall be the duty of each of the general lighthouse authorities, or of any persons authorised by that authority for the purpose, to inspect all lighthouses, buoys, and beacons situate within their area, but belonging to or under the management of any local lighthouse authority, and to make such inquiries in respect thereof and of the management thereof as they think fit.

Inspection of local lighthouses.

(2) All officers and others having the care of any such local lighthouses, buoys, or beacons, or concerned in the management thereof, shall furnish all such information and explanations concerning the same as the general lighthouse authority require.

(3) All local lighthouse authorities and their officers shall at all times give to the general lighthouse authority all such returns, explanations, or information concerning the lighthouses, buoys, and beacons under their management and the

management thereof, as the general lighthouse authority require.

(4) The general lighthouse authority shall communicate to each local lighthouse authority the results of the inspection of their lighthouses, buoys, and beacons, and shall also make general reports of the results of their inspection of local lighthouses, buoys, and beacons to the Board of Trade; and those reports shall be laid before Parliament.

COMMENTS.

Laid Before Parliament.

The procedure for laying documents before Parliament is now regulated by the Laying of Documents before Parliament (Interpretation) Act 1948.

Lighthouse Authority.

For the meaning of 'local' and 'general lighthouse authority', *see* section 634.

Local Lighthouse.

A general lighthouse authority may exercise control over local lighthouse authorities within their area and may accept the surrender or purchase of local lighthouses, *see* sections 653 and 654.

⚓ ⚓ ⚓ ⚓

Control of local lighthouse authorities by general lighthouse authorities.

653 (1) A general lighthouse authority may, within their area, with the sanction of the Board of Trade, and after giving due notice of their intention, direct a local lighthouse authority to lay down buoys, or to remove or discontinue any lighthouse, buoy, or beacon, or to make any variation in the character of any lighthouse, buoy, or beacon, or in the mode of exhibiting lights in any lighthouse, buoy, or beacon.

(2) A local lighthouse authority shall not erect or place any lighthouse, buoy, or beacon, or remove or discontinue any lighthouse, buoy, or beacon, or vary the character of any lighthouse, buoy or beacon, or the mode of exhibiting lights in any lighthouse, buoy, or beacon, without the sanction of the general lighthouse authority.

(3) If a local lighthouse authority having power to erect, place, or maintain any lighthouse, buoy, or beacon, at any place within a lighthouse area, fail to do so, or fail to comply with the direction of a general lighthouse authority under this section with respect to any lighthouse, buoy, or beacon, Her Majesty may, on the application of the general lighthouse authority by Order in Council, transfer any powers of the

local lighthouse authority with respect to that lighthouse, buoy, or beacon, including the power of levying dues, to the general lighthouse authority.

(4) On the making of any Order in Council under this section, the powers transferred shall be vested in the general lighthouse authority to whom they are transferred, and the lighthouse, buoy, or beacon in respect of which the Order is made, and the dues leviable in respect thereof, shall respectively be subject to the same provisions as those to which a lighthouse, buoy, or beacon provided by that general lighthouse authority under this Part of this Act, and the light dues leviable under this Part of this Act are subject.

(5) Nothing in this section shall apply to local buoys and beacons placed or erected for temporary purposes.

COMMENTS.

Lighthouse Authority.

General and/or local, *see* section 634 for definition, also lighthouse area.

Lighthouse; Buoy or Beacon.

Defined in section 742.

⚓ ⚓ ⚓ ⚓

654 (1) A local lighthouse authority may, if they think fit, surrender or sell any lighthouse, buoy, or beacon held by them to the general lighthouse authority within whose area it is situated, and that general lighthouse authority may, with the consent of the Board of Trade, accept or purchase the same. Surrender of local lighthouses.

(2) The purchase money for any lighthouse, buoy, or beacon so sold to a general lighthouse authority shall be paid out of the Mercantile Marine Fund.

(3) On the surrender or sale of a lighthouse, buoy, or beacon under this section to a general lighthouse authority,—

(*a*) the lighthouse, buoy, or beacon surrendered or sold shall, together with its appurtenances, become vested in the general lighthouse authority, and shall be subject to the same provisions as if it has been provided by that authority under this Part of this Act; and

(*b*) the general lighthouse authority shall be entitled to receive either the dues which were leviable in respect of the lighthouse, buoy, or beacon surrendered or sold at the time of the surrender or sale, or, if Her Majesty so directs by Order in Council, such dues as may be fixed by Order in Council, and those dues shall be subject to the same provisions and regulations as light dues for a lighthouse completed by a general lighthouse authority under this Act.

COMMENTS.

Lighthouse Authority.

Defined in section 634.

Lighthouse Buoy or Beacon.

See section 742 for definition.

Lighthouse Dues.

For the provisions relating to light dues for lighthouses completed by a general lighthouse authority, *see* sections 643–651, and for those relating to lighthouses completed by a local lighthouse authority, *see* sections 655 and 656.

Mercantile Marine Fund.

This fund has now been abolished, and the purchase money is now paid out of the General Lighthouse Fund, *see* the M.S. (Mercantile Marine Fund) Act 1898, section 1, sub-section 1.

Light dues for local lights.

655 (1) If any lighthouse, buoy, or beacon is erected or placed, or reconstructed, repaired, or replaced by a local lighthouse authority, Her Majesty may, on the application of that authority, by Order in Council, fix such dues to be paid to that authority in respect of every ship which enters the port or harbour under the control of that authority or the estuary in which the lighthouse, buoy, or beacon is situate, and which passes the lighthouse, buoy, or beacon and derives benefit therefrom as Her Majesty may think reasonable.

(2) Any dues fixed under this section (in this Act referred to as local light dues) shall be paid by the same persons and may be recovered in the same manner as light dues under this Part of this Act.

(3) Her Majesty may by Order in Council reduce, alter, or increase any local light dues, so that those dues, so far as possible, may be sufficient and not more than sufficient for the payment of the expenses incurred by the local lighthouse authority in respect of the lighthouses, buoys, or beacons for which the dues are levied.

COMMENTS.

Repeal.

In the above section, sub-section 1; sub-section 3; and the words in sub-section 2—'dues fixed under this section (In the Act referred to as'—have been repealed by the Harbours Act) 1964, section 63, sub-section 3, Schedule 6.

The part of the section remaining is thus:

'(2) Any local light dues shall be paid by the same persons and may be recovered in the same manner as light dues under this Part of this Act.' Consult also section 29 of the Harbours Act 1964.

Light Dues.

As to the recovery of light dues, *see* sections 649–651.

⚓ ⚓ ⚓ ⚓

656 (1) All local light dues shall be applied by the authority by whom they are levied for the purpose of the construction, placing, maintenance, and improvement of the lighthouses, buoys, and beacons in respect of which the dues are levied, and for no other purpose. Application of local light dues.

(2) The local lighthouse authority to whom any local light dues are paid shall keep a separate account of the receipt and expenditure of those dues, and shall, once in every year or at such other time as the Board of Trade may determine, send a copy of that account to the Board of Trade, and shall send the same in such form and shall give such particulars in relation thereto as the Board of Trade requires.

COMMENTS.

Local Light Dues.

Now exigible by section 29 of the Harbours Act 1964, q.v.

Lighthouse, Buoy and Beacon.

Defined in section 742.

⚓ ⚓ ⚓ ⚓

Merchant Shipping Act 1894

Section 657

Repealed by The Harbours Act 1964, section 29

⚓ ⚓ ⚓ ⚓

Expenses of General Lighthouse Authorities

Payment of lighthouse expenses out of Mercantile Marine Fund.

658 The expenses incurred by the general lighthouse authorities in the works and services of lighthouses, buoys, and beacons under this Part of this Act, or in the execution of any works necessary or expedient for the purpose of permanently reducing the expense of those works and services, shall be paid out of the Mercantile Marine Fund.

COMMENTS.

Mercantile Marine Fund.

This fund has now been abolished, and the expenses are now paid out of the General Lighthouse Fund, *see* the M.S. (Mercantile Marine Fund) Act 1898, section 1.

Lighthouse; Buoy; Beacon.

Defined in section 742.

Establishments of general lighthouse authorities.

659 (1) Her Majesty may by Order in Council fix the establishments to be maintained by each of the general lighthouse authorities on account of the services of lighthouses, buoys, and beacons, or the annual or other sums to be paid out of the Mercantile Marine Fund in respect of those establishments.

(2) If it appears that any part of the establishments of the general lighthouse authorities is maintained for other purposes as well as for the purposes of their duties as general lighthouse authorities, Her Majesty may by Order in Council fix the portion of the expense of those establishments to be paid out of the Mercantile Marine Fund.

(3) An increase of any establishment or part of an establishment fixed under this section shall not be made without the consent of the Board of Trade.

COMMENTS.

Mercantile Marine Fund.

This fund has been abolished, and the expenses are now paid out of the General Lighthouse Fund, *see* the M.S. (Mercantile Marine Fund) Act 1898.

Annual or Other Sums.

This section has been extended to fixing the annual or other sums to be paid to members of the general lighthouse authority for England and Wales. *See* the M.S. (Amendment) Act 1920.

General Lighthouse Authorities.

Defined in section 634.

Lighthouse; Buoy; and Beacon.

Defined in section 742.

⚓ ⚓ ⚓ ⚓

660 (1) An expense of a general lighthouse authority in respect of the services of lighthouses, buoys, and beacons shall not be paid out of the Mercantile Marine Fund, or allowed in account, unless either it has been allowed as part of the establishment expenses under this Act, or an estimate or account thereof has been approved by the Board of Trade.

Estimates or accounts of expenses sent to Board of Trade.

(2) For the purpose of approval by the Board of Trade, each of the general lighthouse authorities shall submit to that Board an estimate of all expenses to be incurred by them in respect of lighthouses, buoys, or beacons, other than expenses allowed under this Act on account of their establishments, or, in case it is necessary in providing for any sudden emergency to incur any such expense without waiting for the sanction of an estimate, shall as soon as possible submit to the Board of Trade a full account of the expense incurred.

(3) The Board of Trade shall consider any estimates and accounts so submitted to them, and may approve them either with or without modification.

COMMENTS.

Mercantile Marine Fund.

Such references to the Mercantile Marine Fund are to be construed as references to the General Lighthouse Fund. Consult the M.S. (Mercantile Marine Fund) Act 1898, section 1.

General Lighthouse Authority.

Defined in section 634.

Lighthouse; Buoy; or Beacons.

Defined in section 742.

Advances.

The Treasury and the Public Works Loan Commissioners may, for extraordinary purposes, make loans to general lighthouse authorities, *see* sections 661 and 663.

⚓ ⚓ ⚓ ⚓

Advances by Treasury for lighthouse expenses.

661 (1) For the purpose of the construction and repair of lighthouses, and of other extraordinary expenses connected with lighthouses, buoys, and beacons, the Treasury may, upon the application of the Board of Trade, advance out of the growing produce of the Consolidated Fund such sums, and upon such terms and at such rate of interest, as they think fit, and pay the same into the Mercantile Marine Fund, but the total amount due in respect of any such advances shall not at any one time exceed two hundred thousand pounds.

(2) Where the Treasury advance any sum under this section, that sum and the interest thereon shall be a charge upon the Mercantile Marine Fund, and upon any dues, rates, fees, or other payments payable thereto, and the Board of Trade shall make such provision for the repayment thereof out of that fund either by way of sinking fund or otherwise as the Treasury require.

(3) A charge under this section for the purpose of an advance by the Treasury shall not prevent the reduction of any dues, rates, fees, or other payments payable to the Mercantile Marine Fund, if the reduction is sanctioned by the Treasury.

COMMENTS.

Colonial Lights.

This section, sections 662 and 663, now apply in the case of Colonial lights by virtue of the M.S. (Mercantile Marine Fund) Act 1898, section 2.

Mercantile Marine Fund.

This fund has been abolished, and reference thereto are to be construed as reference to the General Lighthouse Fund. *See* the M.S. (Mercantile Marine Fund) Act 1898.

Lighthouse; Buoy; and Beacon.

Defined in section 742.

Advances.

See comments to section 660 and section 663.

Mortgage of Mercantile Marine Fund for lighthouse expenditure.

662 (1) The Board of Trade may mortgage the Mercantile Marine Fund and any dues, rates, fees, or other payments payable thereto, or any part thereof, for the purpose of the construction and repair of lighthouses or other extraordinary expenses connected with the services of lighthouses, buoys, and beacons.

(2) Any mortgage under this section shall be made in such form and executed in such manner as the Board of Trade may direct.

(3) A person lending money on a mortgage under this section shall not be bound to inquire as to the purpose for which the money is raised or the manner in which it is applied.

COMMENTS.

Colonial Lights.

This section and sections 661 and 663 are applied to Colonial lights by the M.S. (Mercantile Marine Fund) Act, 1898, section 2.

Mercantile Marine Fund.

This fund has been abolished, and references thereto are to be construed as references to the General Lighthouse Fund. *See* the M.S. (Mercantile Marine Fund) Act 1898, section 1.

Lighthouse; Buoy, and Beacon.

Defined in section 742.

Advances.

For the powers of the Treasury and the Public Works Loan Commissioners to make advances for extraordinary expenses, *see* sections 661 and 663.

⚓ ⚓ ⚓ ⚓

663 (1) The Public Works Loan Commissioners may, for the purpose of the construction and repair of lighthouses or other extraordinary expenses connected with the service of lighthouses, buoys, and beacons, advance money upon mortgage of the Mercantile Marine Fund, and the several dues, rates, fees, and payments to be carried thereto under this Act, or any of them, or any part thereof, without requiring any further security than that mortgage.

Advances by Public Works Loan Commissioners.

(2) Notwithstanding anything in this Act, every mortgage so made to the Public Works Loan Commissioners shall be made in accordance with the Acts regulating loans by the Public Works Loan Commissioners.

(3) An advance by the Public Works Loan Commissioners shall not prevent any lawful reduction of any dues, rates, fees, or other payments payable to the Mercantile Marine Fund if that reduction is assented to by the Public Works Loan Commissioners.

COMMENTS.

Colonial Lights.

This section, as well as sections 661 and 662, apply in the case of colonial lights. *See* the M.S. (Mercantile Marine Act) 1898, section 2.

Mercantile Marine Fund.

See comments to section 662.

Public Works Loan Commissioners.

The Commissioners were constituted under the Public Works Loan Act 1875. *See* now, in regard to loans on the Security of the General Lighthouse Fund, section 11 Public Works Loan Act 1897.

⚓ ⚓ ⚓ ⚓

Accounts of general lighthouse authorities.

664 Each of the general lighthouse authorities shall account to the Board of Trade for their receipts from light dues and for their expenditure in respect of expenses paid out of the Mercantile Marine Fund, in such form, and at such times, and with such details, explanations, and vouchers, as the Board of Trade require, and shall, when required by that Board, permit all books of accounts kept by or under their respective direction to be inspected and examined by such persons as that Board appoint for that purpose.

COMMENTS.

Mercantile Marine Fund.

See comments to section 662.

⚓ ⚓ ⚓ ⚓

Power to grant pensions.

665 (1) A general lighthouse authority may, with the sanction of the Board of Trade, grant superannuation allowances or compensation to persons whose salaries are paid out of the Mercantile Marine Fund on their discharge or retirement.

(2) No superannuation allowance or compensation granted under this section to a person shall exceed the proportion of his salary which may be granted to a person in the public civil service under the Acts relating to superannuation allowances or compensation for the time being in force.

COMMENTS.

Mercantile Marine Fund.

See comments to section 662.

Personal Representatives.

In regard to payment of superannuation benefits to legal personal representatives and dependants, *see* the Superannuation (Various Services) Act 1938, section 1.

Double Payments.

For the prevention of double payments under this section and the War Pensions (Mercantile Marine) Scheme 1949, Statutory Instrument No. 1852 of 1949, or the Naval Order as applied by the scheme, *see* Act 22 of the Scheme.

Acts Relating to Superannuation Allowances.

See Superannuation Acts 1834–1960.

⚓ ⚓ ⚓ ⚓

Offences in connection with Lighthouses, &c.

666 (1) A person shall not wilfully or negligently— **Injury to lighthouses, &c.**

(*a*) injure any lighthouse or the lights exhibited therein, or any buoy or beacon;

(*b*) remove, alter, or destroy any lightship, buoy, or beacon; or

(*c*) ride by, make fast to, or run foul of any lightship or buoy.

(2) If any person acts in contravention of this section, he shall, in addition to the expenses of making good any damage so occasioned, be liable for each offence to a fine not exceeding fifty pounds.

COMMENTS.

Fine.

Fines are received in accordance with section 680.

Offences in Connection with Lights, etc.

Consult also the Malicious Damage Act 1861, sections 47 and 48.

⚓ ⚓ ⚓ ⚓

667 (1) Whenever any fire or light is burnt or exhibited at such place or in such manner as to be liable to be mistaken for a light proceeding from a lighthouse, the general lighthouse authority within whose area the place is situate, may serve a notice upon the owner of the place where the fire or light is burnt or exhibited, or on the person having the charge of the fire or light, directing that owner or person, within a reasonable time to be specified in the notice, to take effectual means **Prevention of false lights.**

for extinguishing or effectually screening the fire or light, and for preventing for the future any similar fire or light.

(2) The notice may be served either personally or by delivery of the same at the place of abode of the person to be served, or by affixing the same in some conspicuous spot near to the fire or light to which the notice relates.

(3) If any owner or person on whom a notice is served under this section fails, without reasonable cause, to comply with the directions contained in the notice, he shall be guilty of a common nuisance, and, in addition to any other penalties or liabilities he may incur, shall for each offence be liable to a fine not exceeding one hundred pounds.

(4) If any owner or person on whom a notice under this section is served neglects for a period of seven days to extinguish or effectually screen the fire or light mentioned in the notice, the general lighthouse authority may, by their servants or workmen, enter upon the place where the fire or light is, and forthwith extinguish the same, doing no unnecessary damage; and may recover the expenses incurred by them in so doing from the owner or person on whom the notice has been served in the same manner as fines may be recovered under this Act.

COMMENTS.

False Lights.

It is an offence under the Malicous Damage Act 1861, sections 47 and 48, to exhibit false lights, or to remove or conceal buoys or other sea-marks. *See* section 733 regarding the use of registered private signals.

Lighthouse.

Defined in section 742.

General Lighthouse Authority.

For meaning, consult section 634.

Fine.

Fines are received in accordance with section 680.

⚓ ⚓ ⚓ ⚓

Commissioners of Northern Lighthouses

Incorporation of Commissioners of Northern Lights.

668 (1) The persons holding the following offices shall be a body corporate under the name of the Commissioners of Northern Lighthouses; (that is to say,)

(*a*) The Lord Advocate and the Solicitor-General for Scotland;

(*b*) The lords provosts of Edinburgh, Glasgow, and Aberdeen, and the provosts of Inverness and Campbeltown;

(*c*) The eldest bailies of Edinburgh and Glasgow;

(*d*) The sheriffs of the counties of the Lothians and Peebles, Lanark, Renfrew and Bute, Argyll, Inverness, Elgin and Nairn, Ross Cromarty and Sutherland, Caithness, Orkney and Shetland, Aberdeen, Kincardine and Banff, Ayr, Fife and Kinross, Dumfries and Galloway; and

(*e*) Any persons elected under this section.

(2) The Commissioners shall have a common seal; and any five of them shall constitute a quorum, and shall have power to do all such matters and things as might be done by the whole body.

(3) The Commissioners may elect the provost or chief magistrate of any royal or parliamentary burgh on or near any part of the coasts of Scotland and the sheriff of any county abutting on those coasts to be a member of their body.

Provision as to Channel Islands

669 (1) The powers of the Trinity House under this Part of this Act with respect to lighthouses, buoys, or beacons already erected or placed, or hereafter to be erected or placed, in the islands of Guernsey or Jersey (other than their powers with respect to the surrender or purchase of local lighthouses, buoys, and beacons, and the prevention of false lights) shall not be exercised without the consent of Her Majesty in Council. **Restriction on exercise of powers in Channel Islands.**

(2) Dues for any lighthouse, buoy, or beacon erected or placed in or near the islands of Guernsey, Jersey, Sark, or Alderney shall not be taken in the islands of Guernsey or Jersey without the consent of the States of those Islands respectively.

COMMENTS.

The Trinity House.

For meaning, *see* section 742.

Lighthouse, buoy, or beacon.

Defined in section 742.

False Lights.

For the powers of the Trinity House in respect of false lights, *see* section 667.

Dues.

As to light dues generally, *see* sections 643 to 651, and sections 655 to 657.

⚓ ⚓ ⚓ ⚓

Lighthouses, &c., in Colonies

Dues for colonial lighthouses, &c.

670 (1) Where any lighthouse, buoy, or beacon has, either before or after the passing of this Act, been erected or placed on or near the coasts of any British possession by or with the consent of the legislature of that possession, Her Majesty may by Order in Council, fix such dues (in this Act referred to as colonial light dues) to be paid in respect of that lighthouse, buoy, or beacon by the owner or master of every ship which passes the same and derives benefit therefrom, as Her Majesty may deem reasonable, and may be like order increase, diminish, or repeal such dues, and those dues shall from the time mentioned in the Order be leviable throughout Her Majesty's dominions.

(2) Colonial light dues shall not be levied in any British possession unless the legislature of that possession has by address to the Crown, or by Act or ordinance duly passed, signified its opinion that the dues ought to be levied.

COMMENTS.

Colonial Lights.

The lights referred to in this section and various others contained in Schedule 111 to the M.S. (Mercantile Marine Fund) Act 1898, are colonial lights, but *see* the M.S. (Ministry Lighthouse) Act 1960, section 1.

Consult also, generally, the Colonial Light Dues (Revocation) Order 1960 (S.I. No. 471).

⚓ ⚓ ⚓ ⚓

Collection and recovery of colonial light dues.

671 (1) Colonial light dues shall in the United Kingdom be collected and recovered so far as possible as light dues are collected and recovered under this Part of this Act.

(2) Colonial light dues shall in each British possession be collected by such persons as the governor of that possession may appoint for the purpose, and shall be collected by the

same means, in the same manner, and subject to the same conditions so far as circumstances permit, as light dues under this Part of this Act, or by such other means, in such other manner, and subject to such other conditions as the legislature of the possession direct.

COMMENTS.

Colonial Dues.

Generally, *see* comments to section 670.

Light Dues—Recovery.

See section 649.

672 Colonial light dues levied under this Act shall be paid over to Her Majesty's Paymaster-General at such times and in such manner as the Board of Trade direct, and shall be applied, paid, and dealt with by him for the purposes authorised by this Act, in such manner as that Board direct. **Payment of colonial light dues to Paymaster-General.**

COMMENTS.

Colonial Dues.

See comments to section 670.

Merchant Shipping Act 1894

Part XI

Section 673

Repealed by The Merchant Shipping (Mercantile Marine Fund) Act 1858, section 8, and Fourth Schedule

NB—The expenses of colonial lights are payable out of the General Lighthouse Fund

674 (1) The Board of Trade may raise such sums as they think fit for the purpose of constructing or repairing any lighthouse, buoy, or beacon in respect of which colonial light dues are levied or are to be levied on the security of those dues so levied or to be levied. **Advances for construction and repair of colonial lighthouses, &c.**

(2) Any sums so to be raised may be advanced by the Treasury out of moneys provided by Parliament, or by the Public Works Loan Commissioners or by any other persons, but any such advances shall be made and secured in the same manner and subject to the same provisions as similar advances for the purpose of lighthouses in the United Kingdom under this Part of this Act.

COMMENTS.

Lighthouse, Buoy, and Beacon.

Defined in section 742.

Colonial Lighthouse.

Defined in section 670.

Advances by Treasury.

See section 661.

Mortgage of Mercantile Marine Fund.

See section 662.

Advances by Public Works Loan Commissioners.

See section 663.

⚓ ⚓ ⚓ ⚓

Accounts of colonial light dues.

675 (1) Accounts shall be kept of all colonial light dues received under this Act and of all sums expended in the construction, repair, or maintenance of the lighthouse, buoy, or beacon in respect of which those dues are received.

(2) These accounts shall be kept in such manner as the Board of Trade direct, and shall be laid annually before Parliament and audited in such manner as may be directed by Order in Council.

COMMENTS.

Laid Before Parliament.

The procedure for laying documents before Parliament is now regulated by the Laying of Documents before Parliament (Interpretation) Act 1948.

Orders Under this Section.

See Order in Council dated 13 May 1875, S. R. & O. REV. 1904.

⚓ ⚓ ⚓ ⚓

M.S.A. 1894

PART XII

MERCANTILE MARINE FUND

PART XII

MERCANTILE MARINE FUND

676 (1) The common fund called the Mercantile Marine Fund shall continue to exist under that name, and subject to the provisions of this Act there shall be accounted for and paid to that fund— Sums payable to the Mercantile Marine Fund.

(*a*) all fees, charges, and expenses payable in respect of the survey or measurement of ships under this Act:

(*b*) all fees and other sums (other than fines and forfeitures) received by the Board of Trade under the Second and Fifth Parts of this Act, including all fees payable in respect of the medical inspection of seamen under the Second Part of this Act:

(*c*) the moneys arising from the unclaimed property of deceased seamen, except where the same are required to be paid as directed by the Accountant-General of Her Majesty's Navy:

(*d*) any sums recovered by the Board of Trade in respect of expenses incurred in relation to distressed seamen and apprentices under the Second Part of this Act:

(*e*) all fees and other sums payable in respect of any services performed by any person employed under the authority of the Third Part of this Act:

(*f*) all fees paid upon the engagement or discharge of members of the crews of fishing boats when effected before a superintendent:

(*g*) such proceeds of the sale of unclaimed wreck as are directed to be paid thereto during the life-time of Her present Majesty under the Ninth Part of this Act:

(*h*) any fees received by receivers of wreck under the Ninth Part of this Act:

(*i*) all light dues or other sums received by or accruing to any of the General Lighthouse Authorities under the Eleventh Part of this Act:

(*k*) all costs and expenses ordered by the court to be paid to the Board of Trade in pursuance of the Boiler Explosions Acts, 1882 and 1890:

(*l*) any sums which under this or any other Act are directed to be paid to the Mercantile Marine Fund.

(2) All fees mentioned in this section shall be paid at such time and in such manner as the Board of Trade direct.

COMMENTS.

Paragraph (*g*) been repealed as spent by the Statute Law Revision Act 1908.

Mercantile Marine Fund.

All sums accounted for and paid to this fund, except the sums mentioned in paragraph 1 (i), are now paid into the Exchequer.

Payments in respect of paragraph 1 (i) are to be made to the General Lighthouse Fund.

Measurement . . . under this Act.

See section 724 (4).

All fees . . . under the Second Part of this Act.

See sections 97, 420, and 463 as amended.

All fees . . . of the Third Part of this Act.

See section 277.

All fees . . . before a Superintendent.

See section 390.

Any fees . . . under the Ninth Part of this Act.

See section 567.

All light dues . . . under the Eleventh Part of this Act.

See section 648.

⚓ ⚓ ⚓ ⚓

Application of Mercantile Marine Fund.

677 Subject to the provisions of this Act and to any prior charges that may be subsisting on the Mercantile Marine Fund under any Act of Parliament or otherwise there shall be charged on and payable out of that fund the following expenses so far as they are not paid by any private person:—

(*a*) The salaries and other expenses connected with local marine boards and mercantile marine offices and with the examinations conducted under the Second and Fourth Parts of this Act:

(*b*) The salaries of all surveyors of ships and officers appointed under this Act and all expenses incurred in connexion with the survey and measurement of ships under this Act, and the remuneration of medical inspectors of seamen under the Second Part of this Act:

(*c*) The salaries and expenses of persons employed under the Third Part of this Act:

(*d*) The superannuation allowances, gratuities, pensions, and other allowances granted either before or after the passing of this Act to any of the said surveyors, officers, or persons:

(*e*) The allowances and expenses paid for the relief of distressed British seamen and apprentices, including the expenses declared under this Act to be payable as such expenses, and any contributions to seamen's refuges and hospitals:

(*f*) Any sums which the Board of Trade, in their discretion, think fit to pay in respect of claims to moneys carried to the Mercantile Marine Fund on account of the property of deceased seamen, or on account of the proceeds of wreck:

(*g*) All expenses of obtaining depositions, reports, and returns respecting wrecks and casualties:

(*h*) All expenses incurred in carrying into effect the provisions of this Act with regard to receivers of wrecks and the performance of their duties under this Act:

(*i*) All expenses incurred by the general lighthouse authorities in the works and services of lighthouses, buoys, and beacons, or in the execution of any works necessary or expedient for the purpose of permanently reducing the expense of those works and services:

(*k*) Any pensions or other sums payable in relation to the duties formerly performed by the Trinity House in respect of lastage and ballastage in the River Thames:

(*l*) Such expenses for establishing and maintaining on the coasts of the United Kingdom proper lifeboats with the necessary crews and equipments, and for affording assistance towards the preservation of life and property in cases of shipwreck and distress at sea, and for rewarding the preservation of life in such cases, as the Board of Trade direct:

(*m*) Such reasonable costs, as the Board of Trade may allow, of advertising or otherwise making known the establishment of, or alterations in, foreign lighthouses, buoys, and beacons to owners, and masters of, and other persons interested in, British ships:

(*n*) All costs and expenses incurred by the Board of Trade under the Boiler Explosions Act, 1882 and 1890 (so far as not otherwise provided for), including any remuneration paid in pursuance of section seven of the Boiler Explosions Act, 1882, and any costs and expenses ordered by the court in pursuance of those Acts to be paid by the Board of Trade:

(*o*) Any expenses which are charged on or payable out of the Mercantile Marine Fund under this or any other Act of Parliament.

COMMENTS.

Payable out of that fund.

See Merchant Shipping (Mercantile Marine Fund) Act 1898, section 1.

Examinations . . . Second and Fourth Parts of this Act.

See sections 96, 414, and section 1 of the Merchant Shipping (Certificates) Act 1914.

Paragraph 'g'.

See sections 464 and 517.

Paragraph 'k'.

Consult generally the Merchant Shipping Act 1970 in accordance with the Merchant Shipping Act 1970 (Commencement No. 1) Order 1972, as from 1st January 1973.

Merchant Shipping Act 1894

Section 678

Repealed by The Merchant Shipping (Mercantile Marine Fund) Act 1898 Section 8 and Fourth Schedule

Accounts and audit. 29 & 30 Vict. c. 39.

679 (1) The accounts of the Mercantile Marine Fund shall be deemed to be public accounts within the meaning of section thirty-three of the Exchequer and Audit Departments Act, 1866, and shall be examined and audited accordingly.

(2) The Board of Trade shall as soon as may be after the meeting of Parliament in every year cause the accounts of the Mercantile Marine Fund for the preceding year to be laid before both Houses of Parliament.

COMMENTS.

General.

This section applies to the sums and expenses referred to in sections 676 and 677.

Mercantile Marine Fund.

Now the General Lighthouse Fund.

Exchequer and Audit Departments Act 1866.

Repealed by the Exchequer and Audit Departments Act 1921 q.v.

M.S.A. 1894

PART XIII

LEGAL PROCEEDINGS

PART XIII

LEGAL PROCEEDINGS

Prosecution of Offences

680 (1) Subject to any special provisions of this Act and to the provisions hereinafter contained with respect to Scotland,— Prosecution of offences.

(*a*) an offence under this Act declared to be a misdemeanor, shall be punishable by fine or by imprisonment not exceeding two years, with or without hard labour, but may, instead of being prosecuted as a misdemeanor, be prosecuted summarily in manner provided by the Summary Jurisdiction Acts, and if so prosecuted shall be punishable only with imprisonment for a term not exceeding six months, with or without hard labour, or with a fine not exceeding one hundred pounds,

(*b*) an offence under this Act made punishable with imprisonment for any term not exceeding six months, with or without hard labour, or by a fine not exceeding one hundred pounds, shall be prosecuted summarily in manner provided by the Summary Jurisdiction Acts.

(2) Any offence committed or fine recoverable under a byelaw made in pursuance of this Act may be prosecuted or recovered in the same manner as an offence or fine under this Act.

COMMENTS.

Special provisions of this Act.

Consult section 457, sub-section 4, by which a misdemeanour under that section is not punishable upon summary conviction. But note section 72 of the M.S. (Safety and Load Line Conventions) Act 1932, which provides that notwithstanding anything in this section, any offence whatsoever under Part I or Part II of that Act may be prosecuted summarily.

Hard Labour.

Imprisonment with hard labour has now been abolished. Criminal Justice Act 1948, section 1. Enactments conferring power to sentence to imprisonment with hard labour are to be construed as conferring power to sentence to imprisonment.

Term not exceeding six months.

A person charged with an offence for which he is liable to imprisonment for a term exceeding three months, is entitled to be tried by a jury. Rex *v.* Goldberg 1904.

See section 25 of the Magistrates' Courts Act 1952.

⚓ ⚓ ⚓ ⚓

Application of Summary Jurisdiction Acts in certain cases.

681 (1) The Summary Jurisdiction Acts shall, so far as applicable, apply—

(*a*) to any proceeding under this Act before a court of summary jurisdiction, whether connected with an offence punishable on summary conviction or not; and

(*b*) to the trial of any case before one justice of the peace, where, under this Act, such a justice may try the case.

(2) Where under this Act any sum may be recovered as a fine under this Act, that sum, if recoverable before a court of summary jurisdiction, shall, in England, be recovered as a civil debt in manner provided by the Summary Jurisdiction Acts.

COMMENTS.

Sum recovered as a fine.

Consult, for example, section 649 in respect of light dues. Section 667 regarding expenses of extinguishing false lights, and also section 49 of the Pilotage Act 1913, in respect of pilotage dues.

Summary Jurisdiction Acts.

For meaning consult the Interpretation Act 1889 and, in particular, section 13. The Summary Jurisdiction Acts have been substantially repealed, and replaced by the Magistrates Courts Act 1952, in respect of England and Wales.

Summary procedure in Salvage.

Consult sections 648 *et seq.*

⚓ ⚓ ⚓ ⚓

Appeal on summary conviction.

682 Where a person is convicted summarily in England of an offence under this Act, and the fine inflicted or the sum ordered to be paid exceeds five pounds in amount, that person may appeal to quarter sessions against the conviction in manner provided by the Summary Jurisdiction Acts.

⚓ ⚓ ⚓ ⚓

683 (1) Subject to any special provisions of this Act neither a conviction for an offence nor an order for payment of money shall be made under this Act in any summary proceeding instituted in the United Kingdom unless that proceeding is commenced within six months after the commission of the offence or after the cause of complaint arises as the case may be; or, if both or either of the parties to the proceeding happen during that time to be out of the United Kingdom, unless the same is commenced, in the case of a summary conviction within two months, and in the case of a summary order within six months, after they both first happen to arrive, or to be at one time, within the United Kingdom. Limitation of time for summary proceedings.

(2) Subject to any special provisions of this Act neither a conviction for an offence nor an order for payment of money shall be made under this Act in any summary proceeding instituted in any British possession, unless that proceeding is commenced within six months after the commission of the offence or after the cause of complaint arises as the case may be; or if both or either of the parties to the proceeding happen during that time not to be within the jurisdiction of any court capable of dealing with the case, unless the same is commenced in the case of a summary conviction within two months, and in the case of a summary order within six months after they both first happen to arrive, or to be at one time, within that jurisdiction.

(3) No law for the time being in force under any Act, ordinance, or otherwise, which limits the time within which summary proceedings may be instituted shall affect any summary proceeding under this Act.

(4) Nothing in this section shall affect any proceeding to which the Public Authorities Protection Act, 1893, applies.

COMMENTS.

Parties to the proceedings.

In Austin *v*. Olsen 1868, it was held that this phrase meant the person committing the offence and the person against whom it was committed. The position arose where a seaman took proceedings against a person for attempting to persuade him to neglect to join a ship.

Public Authorities Protection Act 1893.

Now repealed by the Law Reform Act 1954.

Jurisdiction

Provision as to jurisdiction in case of offences.

684 For the purpose of giving jurisdiction under this Act, every offence shall be deemed to have been committed and every cause of complaint to have arisen either in the place in which the same actually was committed or arose, or in any place in which the offender of person complained against may be.

COMMENTS.

Application of section.

This section 684, and section 685 and 686, are applied to jurisdiction under the Aliens Order 1953 (S.I., No. 1671). Section 693 is applied to fines paid by a master of a ship under that order.

This section is applied by section 3, sub-section 5 of the Sea-Fish Industry Act 1933 (as amended) by section 2, sub-section 4 of the White Fish and Herring Industries Act 1948, and by section 7, sub-section 5 of the Sea-Fish Industry Act 1959.

Jurisdiction over ships lying off the coasts.

685 (1) Where any district within which any court, justice of the peace, or other magistrate, has jurisdiction either under this Act or under any other Act or at common law for any purpose whatever is situate on the coast of any sea, or abutting on or projecting into any bay, channel, lake, river, or other navigable water, every such court, justice, or magistrate, shall have jurisdiction over any vessel being on, or lying or passing off, that coast, or being in or near that bay, channel, lake, river, or navigable water, and over all persons on board that vessel or for the time being belonging thereto, in the same manner as if the vessel or persons were within the limits of the original jurisdiction of the court, justice, or magistrate.

(2) The jurisdiction under this section shall be in addition to and not in derogation of any jurisdiction or power of a court under the Summary Jurisdiction Acts.

COMMENTS.

Application of section.

See Comments to section 684.

686 (1) Where any person, being a British subject, is charged with having committed any offence on board any British ship on the high seas, or in any foreign port or harbour or on board any foreign ship to which he does not belong, or, not being a British subject, is charged with having committed any offence on board any British ship on the high seas, and that person is found within the jurisdiction of any court in Her Majesty's dominions, which would have had cognizance of the offence if it had been committed on board a British ship within the limits of its ordinary jurisdiction, that court shall have jurisdiction to try the offence as if it had been so committed. Jurisdiction in case of offences on board ship.

(2) Nothing in this section shall affect the Admiralty Offences (Colonial) Act, 1849.

COMMENTS.

Application of Section.

See comments to section 684.

British Subject.

See Comments to section 1.

Within British Territorial Waters.

Consult the Territorial Waters Jurisdiction Act 1878, as to offences on board a foreign ship within British Territorial waters.

Found within the jurisdiction.

It is not material as to the liability of a foreigner to punishment, or to the jurisdiction of the court to try him, that he was illegally and by force taken on board the English ship and there detained in custody at the time of the committal of the offence, the act alleged to be a crime not being committed for the purpose of releasing himself from the illegal duress; such person is 'found within the jurisdiction'. R. *v.* Lopez; R. *v.* Sattler 1858. An alien may be tried for secreting himself in a British Ship. Robey *v.* Vladinier 1935.

⚓ ⚓ ⚓ ⚓

687 All offences against property or person committed in or at any place either ashore or afloat out of Her Majesty's dominions by any master, seaman, or apprentice who at the time when the offence is committed is, or within three months previously has been, employed in any British ship shall be deemed to be offences of the same nature respectively, and be liable to the same punishments respectively, and be inquired of, heard, tried, determined, and adjudged in the same manner and by the same courts and in the same places as if those Offences committed by British seamen at foreign ports to be within Admiralty jurisdiction.

offences had been committed within the jurisdiction of the Admiralty of England; and the costs and expenses of the prosecution of any such offence may be directed to be paid as in the case of costs and expenses of prosecutions for offences committed within the jurisdiction of the Admiralty of England.

COMMENTS.

Jurisdiction of Admiralty.

The numerous statutes dealing with the trial of offences within the Admiralty jurisdiction, may be found set out in the yearly Index to the Statutes under 'SEA'.

Consult also Archbold's 'Criminal Pleading, etc.', paragraphs 82 to 87 of the 35th edition under 'offences in the Admiralty Jurisdiction'.

Merchant Shipping Act 1894

Section 688

Repealed by the Administration of Justice Act 1956 and replaced by Section 3, Sub-section 3, and Sub-section 4 of the same Act.

Provisions in Case of Offences Abroad

Conveyance of offenders and witnesses to United Kingdom or British possession.

689 (1) Whenever any complaint is made to any British consular officer—

(*a*) that any offence against property or person has been committed at any place, either ashore or afloat, out of Her Majesty's dominions by any master, seaman, or apprentice, who at the time when the offence was committed, or within three months before that time, was employed in any British ship; or

(*b*) that any offence on the high seas has been committed by any master, seaman, or apprentice belonging to any British ship,

that consular officer may inquire into the case upon oath, and may, if the case so requires, take any steps in his power for the purpose of placing the offender under the necessary restraint and of sending him as soon as practicable in safe custody to the United Kingdom, or to any British possession in which there is a court capable of taking cognizance of the offence, in any ship belonging to Her Majesty or to any of Her subjects, to be there proceeded against according to law.

(2) The consular officer may order the master of any ship belonging to any subject of Her Majesty bound to the United Kingdom or to such British possession as aforesaid to receive and afford a passage and subsistence during the voyage to any such offender as aforesaid, and to the witnesses, so that the master be not required to receive more than one offender for every one hundred tons of his ship's registered tonnage, or more than one witness for every fifty tons of that tonnage; and the consular officer shall endorse upon the agreement of the ship such particulars with respect to any offenders or witnesses sent in her as the Board of Trade require.

(3) Any master of a ship to whose charge an offender has been so committed shall, on his ship's arrival in the United Kingdom or in such British possession as aforesaid, give the offender into the custody of some police officer or constable, and that officer or constable shall take the offender before a justice of the peace or other magistrate by law empowered to deal with the matter, and the justice or magistrate shall deal with the matter as in cases of offences committed upon the high seas.

(4) If any master of a ship, when required by any British consular officer to receive and afford a passage and subsistence to any offender or witness, does not receive him and afford a passage and subsistence to him, or does not deliver any offender committed to his charge into the custody of some police officer or constable as herein-before directed, he shall for each offence be liable to a fine not exceeding fifty pounds.

(5) The expense of imprisoning any such offender and of conveying him and the witness to the United Kingdom or to such British possession as aforesaid in any manner other than in the ship to which they respectively belong, shall, where not paid as part of the costs of the prosecution, be paid out of moneys provided by Parliament.

COMMENTS.

Consult the Merchant Shipping Act 1906, section 67, for power of Naval courts to send a person sentenced to imprisonment home, to undergo sentence.

Witnesses.

A seaman sent home as witness was held not be be entitled to any wages after he left the ship. Melville *v.* DeWolf 1855.

Merchant Shipping Act 1894

Section 690

Repealed by Merchant Shipping Act 1970

(Commencement No. 1) Order 1972

⚓ ⚓ ⚓ ⚓

Depositions to be received in evidence when witness cannot be produced.

691 (1) Whenever in the course of any legal proceeding instituted in any part of Her Majesty's dominions before any judge or magistrate, or before any person authorised by law or by consent of parties to receive evidence, the testimony of any witness is required in relation to the subject matter of that proceeding, then upon due proof, if the proceeding is instituted in the United Kingdom that the witness cannot be found in that kingdom, or if in any British possession that he cannot be found in that possession, any deposition that the witness may have previously made on oath in relation to the same subject matter before any justice or magistrate in Her Majesty's dominions, or any British consular officer elsewhere, shall be admissible in evidence, provided that—

(*a*) if the deposition was made in the United Kingdom, it shall not be admissible in any proceeding instituted in the United Kingdom; and

(*b*) if the deposition was made in any British possession, it shall not be admissible in any proceeding instituted in that British possession; and

(*c*) if the proceeding is criminal it shall not be admissible, unless it was made in the presence of the person accused.

(2) A deposition so made shall be authenticated by the signature of the judge, magistrate, or consular officer before whom it is made; and the judge, magistrate, or consular officer shall certify, if the fact is so, that the accused was present at the taking thereof.

(3) It shall not be necessary in any case to prove the signature or official character of the person appearing to have signed any such deposition, and in any criminal proceeding a certificate under this section shall, unless the contrary is proved, be sufficient evidence of the accused having been present in manner thereby certified.

(4) Nothing herein contained shall affect any case in which depositions taken in any proceeding are rendered admissible in evidence by any Act of Parliament, or by any

Act or ordinance of the legislature of any colony so far as regards that colony, or interfere with the power of any colonial legislature to make those depositions admissible in evidence, or to interfere with the practice of any court in which depositions not authenticated as herein-before mentioned are admissible.

COMMENTS.

For foreign places where there is no British Consular officer, *see* section 737.

Detention of Ship and Distress on Ship

692 (1) Where under this Act a ship is to be or may be detained, any commissioned officer on full pay in the naval or military service of Her Majesty, or any officer of the Board of Trade, or any officer of customs, or any British consular officer may detain the ship, and if the ship after detention or after service on the master of any notice of or order for detention proceeds to sea before it is released by competent authority, the master of the ship, and also the owner, and any person who sends the ship to sea, if that owner or person is party or privy to the offence, shall be liable for each offence to a fine not exceeding one hundred pounds. **Enforcing detention of ship.**

(2) Where a ship so proceeding to sea takes to sea when on board thereof in the execution of his duty any officer authorised to detain the ship, or any surveyor or officer of the Board of Trade or any officer of customs, the owner and master of the ship shall each be liable to pay all expenses of and incidental to the officer or surveyor being so taken to sea, and also to a fine not exceeding one hundred pounds, or, if the offence is not prosecuted in a summary manner, not exceeding ten pounds for every day until the officer or surveyor returns, or until such time as would enable him after leaving the ship to return to the port from which he is taken, and the expenses ordered to be paid may be recovered in like manner as the fine.

(3) Where under this Act a ship is to be detained an officer of customs shall, and where under this Act a ship may be detained an officer of customs may, refuse to clear that ship outwards or to grant a transire to that ship.

(4) Where any provision of this Act provides that a ship may be detained until any document is produced to the proper officer of customs, the proper officer shall mean, unless the

context otherwise requires, the officer able to grant a clearance or transire to such ship.

COMMENTS.

This section is applied to the detention of ships under the following Acts:—

Seal Fisheries North Pacific Act 1912, section 3.

Diseases of Animals Act 1950, section 74, sub-section 3.

Detention of foreign ships when unseaworthy.

See section 462 and the Merchant Shipping Act 1906, section 2.

For further powers of Customs Officers to refuse or cancel clearance of ships, consult section 63 of the Customs and Excise Act 1952.

Sums ordered to be paid leviable by distress on ship.

693 Where any court, justice of the peace, or other magistrate, has power to make an order directing payment to be made of any seaman's wages, fines, or other sums of money, then, if the party so directed to pay the same is the master or owner of a ship, and the same is not paid at the time and in manner prescribed in the order, the court, justice of the peace, or magistrate who made the order may, in addition to any other powers they may have for the purpose of compelling payment, direct the amount remaining unpaid to be levied by distress or poinding and sale of the ship, her tackle, furniture, and apparel.

COMMENTS.

Seaman's Wages.

In *The Westmorland* 1845, it was held that distress was not leviable on vessel under arrest of Court of Admiralty, at the suit of seamen for wages.

Evidence, Service of Documents, and Declarations

Proof of attestation not required.

694 Where any document is required by this Act to be executed in the presence of or to be attested by any witness or witnesses, that document may be proved by the evidence of any person who is able to bear witness to the requisite facts without calling the attesting witness or the attesting witnesses or any of them.

COMMENTS.

Consult the Evidence Act 1845, section 1, by which certain documents purporting to be sealed and signed may be received in evidence without proof of the seal and signature.

Also, the Evidence Act 1938, section 3 (proof of instruments to validity of which attestation is necessary).

695 (1) Where a document is by this Act declared to be admissible in evidence, such document shall, on its production from the proper custody, be admissible in evidence in any court or before any person having by law or consent of parties authority to receive evidence, and, subject to all just exceptions, shall be evidence of the matters stated therein in pursuance of this Act or by any officer in pursuance of his duties as such officer.

Admissibility of documents in evidence.

(2) A copy of any such document or extract therefrom shall also be so admissible in evidence if proved to be an examined copy or extract, or if it purports to be signed and certified as a true copy or extract by the officer to whose custody the original document was entrusted, and that officer shall furnish such certified copy or extract to any person applying at a reasonable time for the same, upon payment of a reasonable sum for the same, not exceeding fourpence for every folio of ninety words, but a person shall be entitled to have—

(*a*) a certified copy of the particulars entered by the registrar in the register book on the registry of the ship, together with a certified statement showing the ownership of the ship at the time being; and

(*b*) a certified copy of any declaration, or document, a copy of which is made evidence by this Act, on payment of one shilling for each copy.

(3) If any such officer wilfully certifies any document as being a true copy or extract knowing the same not to be a true copy or extract, he shall for each offence be guilty of a misdemeanor, and be liable on conviction to imprisonment for any term not exceeding eighteen months.

(4) If any person forges the seal, stamp, or signature of any document to which this section applies, or tenders in evidence any such document with a false or counterfeit seal, stamp, or signature thereto, knowing the same to be false or counterfeit, he shall for each offence be guilty of felony, and be liable to penal servitude for a term not exceeding seven years, or to imprisonment for a term not exceeding two years, with or without hard labour, and whenever any such document has been admitted in evidence, the court or the person

who admitted the same may on request direct that the same shall be impounded, and be kept in the custody of some officer of the court or other proper person, for such period or subject to such conditions as the court or person thinks fit.

COMMENTS.

The words underlined with double lines ceased to have effect by reason of the M.S. (Safety Convention) Act 1949, section 37, sub-section 5, and Schedule III, which also repealed the words underlined by a single line.

Proper custody.

See, as to proper custody of an expired indenture of apprenticeship, Hall *v*. Hall 1841.

Copies of documents.

See the Evidence Act 1851, section 14, as to the admissibility of examined or certified copies of public documents.

Penal servitude.

This is now abolished, and the reference is to be construed as one to imprisonment. Criminal Justice Act 1948, section 1.

General.

It is submitted that this section does not exclude evidence in explanation of the document.

⚓ ⚓ ⚓ ⚓

Service of documents.

696 (1) Where for the purposes of this Act any document is to be served on any person, that document may be served—

(*a*) in any case by delivering a copy thereof personally to the person to be served, or by leaving the same at his last place of abode; and

(*b*) if the document is to be served on the master of a ship, where there is one, or on a person belonging to a ship, by leaving the same for him on board that ship with the person being or appearing to be in command or charge of the ship; and

(*c*) if the document is to be served on the master of a ship, where there is no master, and the ship is in the United Kingdom, on the managing owner of the ship, or, if there is no managing owner, on some agent of the owner residing in the United Kingdom, or where no such agent is known or can be found, by affixing a copy thereof to the mast of the ship.

(2) If any person obstructs the service on the master of a ship of any document under the provisions of this Act

relating to the detention of ships as unseaworthy, that person shall for each offence be liable to a fine not exceeding ten pounds, and, if the owner or master of the ship is party or privy to the obstruction, he shall in respect of each offence be guilty of a misdemeanor.

COMMENTS.

For application of this section to a demand (in writing) that a clearance be returned by a Customs officer for the purpose of detaining a ship, *see* Customs and Excise Act 1952, section 53.

Master.

Defined in section 742.

Managing Owner.

See section 59 as to registration of Managing Owner.

Detention of unsafe ship.

See section 459.

697 Any exception, exemption, proviso, excuse, or qualification, in relation to any offence under this Act, whether it does or does not accompany in the same section the description of the offence, may be proved by the defendant, but need not be specified or negatived in any information or complaint, and, if so specified or negatived, no proof in relation to the matter so specified or negatived shall be required on the part of the informant or complainant. Proof, &c. of exception.

698 Any declaration required by this Act to be taken before a justice of the peace or any particular officer may be taken before a commissioner for oaths. Declaration.

COMMENTS.

Commissioners for Oaths.

See section 742 for definition.

Application of Penalties and Costs of Prosecutions

699 (1) Where any court, justice of the peace, or other magistrate, imposes a fine under this Act for which no specific application is herein provided, that court, justice of the peace, or magistrate, may if they think fit, direct the whole Application of penalties.

or any part of the fine to be applied in compensating any person for any wrong or damage which he may have sustained by the act or default in respect of which the fine is imposed, or to be applied in or towards payment of the expenses of the proceedings.

(2) Subject to any directions under this section or to any specific application provided under this Act, all fines under this Act shall, notwithstanding anything in any other Act—

(*a*) if recovered in the United Kingdom, be paid into the Exchequer in such manner as the Treasury may direct, and be carried to and form part of the Consolidated Fund; and

(*b*) if recovered in any British possession, be paid over into the public treasury of that possession, and form part of the public revenue thereof.

COMMENTS.

The words underlined were repealed by the Justices of the Peace Act 1949, section 46, and Schedule VII as from 1st April 1953. *See* Statutory Instrument 1951, No. 1941.

United Kingdom.

The term 'Great Britain' was substituted for 'United Kingdom' by the Northern Ireland Act 1962, section 25, sub-section 1, paragraph (*a*) so that the proceeds of fines imposed upon the conviction of a person in Northern Ireland should not be paid thereafter into the Exchequer of the United Kingdom.

⚓ ⚓ ⚓ ⚓

Expenses of prosecution of misdemeanor.

700 Where an offence under this Act is prosecuted as a misdemeanor, the court before whom the offence is prosecuted may in England make the same allowances and order payment of the same costs and expenses as if the offence were a felony, and in any other part of Her Majesty's dominions may make such allowances and order payment of such costs and expenses as are payable or allowable upon the trial of any misdemeanor or under any law for the time being in force therein.

⚓ ⚓ ⚓ ⚓

Merchant Shipping Act 1894

Section 701
Repeal

COMMENTS.

This section was repealed by the Costs in Criminal Cases Act 1908, section 10 and schedule, being contained in section 4, sub-section 1 of that Act. This, in turn, has been repealed by the Costs in Criminal Cases Act 1952, section 1, and Schedule, the relevant matter of the repealed section now being contained in section 7 of the 1952 Act, viz: Costs in Criminal Cases Act 1952, section 7.

7 (1) Costs payable out of local funds under this Act shall be paid:—

(*a*) in the case of offences committed in an administrative county, out of the county fund.

(*b*) in the case of offences committed in a county borough, out of the general rate fund of the county borough.

(2) For the purposes of the preceding sub-section, offences committed within Admiralty jurisdiction shall be deemed to have been committed in the place where the accused is tried at, the Central Criminal Court, in the County of London.

(3) Costs paid out of the fund of any county or county borough under the last preceding sub-section shall be repayed out of moneys provided by Parliament.

(*b*) In this section, any reference to an offence shall be construed as including a reference to an alleged offence committed in any county or borough shall be construed as including a reference to an offence alleged to have been committed there.

Merchant Shipping Act 1894

Sections 702–710

apply to Scotland

Procedure in Scotland

702 In Scotland every offence which by this Act is described as a felony or misdemeanor may be prosecuted by indictment or criminal letters at the instance of Her Majesty's Advocate before the High Court of Justiciary, or by criminal libel at the instance of the procurator fiscal of the county before the sheriff, and shall be punishable with fine and with imprisonment with or without hard labour in default of payment, or with imprisonment with or without hard labour, or with both, as the court may think fit, or in the case of

Offences punishable as misdemeanors.

felony with penal servitude where the court is competent thereto; and such court may also, if it think fit, order payment by the offender of the costs and expenses of the prosecution.

COMMENTS.

Repeal.

The words underlined in this section were repealed by the Merchant Shipping Act 1906, section 82, sub-section 3, q.v.

Summary proceedings.

703 In Scotland, all prosecutions, complaints, actions, or proceedings under this Act, other than prosecutions for felonies or misdemeanors, may be brought in a summary form before the sheriff of the county, or before any two justices of the peace of the county or burgh where the cause of such prosecution or action arises, or where the offender or defender may be for the time, and when of a criminal nature or for fines or penalties, at the instance of the procurator fiscal of court, or at the instance of any party aggrieved, with concurrence of the procurator fiscal of court; and the court may, if it think fit, order payment by the offender or defender of the costs of the prosecution or action.

COMMENTS.

Repeal.

The words underlined in this section were repealed by the Merchant Shipping Act 1906, section 82, sub-section 4 q.v.

Form of complaint.

704 Where in any summary proceedings under this Act in Scotland any complaint or action is brought in whole or in part for the enforcement of a pecuniary debt or demand, the complaint may contain a prayer for warrant to arrest upon the dependence.

Warrants on summary proceedings.

705 On any summary proceedings in Scotland the deliverance of the sheriff clerk or clerk of the peace shall contain warrant to arrest upon the dependence in common form, where that warrant has been prayed for in the complaint or other proceeding: Provided always, that where the apprehension of any party, with or without a warrant, is authorised by this Act, such party may be detained in custody until he can be brought at the earliest opportunity before any two justices or the sheriff who may have jurisdiction in the place, to be dealt with as this Act directs, and no citation or induciae shall in such case be necessary.

706 When it becomes necessary to execute such arrestment on the dependence against goods or effects of the defender within Scotland, but not locally situated within the jurisdiction of the sheriff or justices of the peace by whom the warrant to arrest has been granted, it shall be competent to carry the warrant into execution on its being endorsed by the sheriff clerk, or clerk of the peace of the county or burgh respectively within which such warrant comes to be executed. Backing arrestments.

707 Where on any summary proceedings in Scotland there is a decree for payment of any sum of money against a defender, the decree shall contain warrant for arrestment, poinding, and imprisonment in default of payment. Form of decree for payment of money.

708 In all summary complaints and proceedings for recovery of any penalty or sum of money in Scotland if a defender who has been duly cited shall not appear at the time and place required by the citation, he shall be held as confessed, and sentence or decree shall be pronounced against him in terms of the complaint, with such costs and expenses as to the court shall seem fit: Provided that he shall be entitled to obtain himself reponed against any such decree at any time before the same be fully implemented, by lodging with the clerk of court a reponing note, and consigning in his hands the sum decerned for, and the costs which had been awarded by the court, and on the same day delivering or transmitting through the post to the pursuer or his agent a copy of such reponing note; and a certificate by the clerk of court of such note having been lodged shall operate as a sist of diligence till the cause shall have been reheard and finally disposed of, which shall be on the next sitting of the court, or on any day to which the court shall then adjourn it. Sentence and penalties in default of defender's appearance.

Orders not to be quashed for want of form and to be final.

709 No order, decree, or sentence pronounced by any sheriff or justice of the peace in Scotland under the authority of this Act shall be quashed or vacated for any misnomer, informality, or defect of form; and all orders, decrees, and sentences so pronounced shall be final and conclusive, and not subject to suspension, reduction, or to any form of review or stay of execution, except on the ground of corruption or malice on the part of the sheriff or justices, in which case the suspension, or reduction must be brought within fourteen days of the date of the order, decree, or sentence complained of: Provided that no stay of execution shall be competent to the effect of preventing immediate execution of such order, decree, or sentence.

General rules, so far as applicable, to extend to penalties and proceedings in Scotland.

710 Nothing in this Act shall be held in any way to annul or restrict the common law of Scotland with regard to the prosecution or punishment of offences at the instance or by the direction of the Lord Advocate, or the rights of owners or creditors in regard to enforcing a judicial sale of any ship and tackle, or to give to the High Court in England any jurisdiction in respect of salvage in Scotland which it has not heretofore had or exercised.

COMMENTS.

Admiralty Jurisdiction and Arrestment of Ships in Scotland.

See Administration of Justice Act 1956, sections 45 to 50.

Prosecution of Offences in Colonies

Prosecution of offences in British possession.

711 Any offence under this Act shall, in any British possession, be punishable by any court or magistrate by whom an offence of a like character is ordinarily punishable, or in such other manner as may be determined by any Act or ordinance having the force of law in that possession.

COMMENTS.

British possession.

See the Interpretation Act 1889, section 18, sub-section 2.

Application of Part XIII

Application of Part XIII.

712 This Part of this Act shall, except where otherwise provided, apply to the whole of Her Majesty's dominions.

COMMENTS.

Application.

By the Foreign Jurisdiction Act 1890, Her Majesty has power by Order in Council, to extend the provisions of the Merchant Shipping Acts to any foreign country in which for the time being Her Majesty has jurisdiction.

M.S.A. 1894

PART XIV

SUPPLEMENTAL

PART XIV

SUPPLEMENTAL

General Control of Board of Trade

713 The Board of Trade shall be the department to undertake the general superintendence of all matters relating to merchant shipping and seamen and are authorised to carry into execution the provisions of this Act and of all Acts relating to merchant shipping and seamen for the time being in force, except where otherwise provided by those Acts, or except so far as those Acts relate to the revenue. Superintendence of merchant shipping by Board of Trade.

COMMENTS.

Board of Trade.

See preface to this edition, where by Statutory Instrument No. 1537/1970, the B.O.T. was merged into a new department, called the Department of Trade and Industry.

⚓ ⚓ ⚓ ⚓

714 All consular officers and officers of customs abroad, and all local marine boards and superintendents, shall make and send to the Board of Trade such returns or reports on any matter relating to British merchant shipping or seamen as the Board may require. Returns as to merchant shipping to Board of Trade.

COMMENTS.

Repeal.

These underlined words 'local marine boards and' are repealed, The Merchant Shipping Act 1970 (Commencement No. 1) Order 1972.

⚓ ⚓ ⚓ ⚓

715 All superintendents shall, when required by the Board of Trade, produce to that Board or to its officers all official log-books and other documents which are delivered to them under this Act. Production of log-books, &c. by superintendents.

⚓ ⚓ ⚓ ⚓

A.D. 1894.

Application of fees, fines, &c.

716 (1) All fees and other sums (other than fines) received by the Board of Trade under the Second, Fourth, and Fifth Parts of this Act shall be carried to the account of the Mercantile Marine Fund.

(2) All fines coming into the hands of the Board of Trade under this Act shall be paid into the Exchequer as the Treasury may direct, and shall be carried to and form part of the Consolidated Fund.

COMMENTS.

Mercantile Marine Fund.

The sums referred to are now paid into the Exchequer. *See* the M.S. (Mercantile Marine Fund) Act 1898, section 1, sub-section 1 (*a*). Consult section 33, sub-section 4 of the M.S. (Safety Convention) Act 1949, where the provisions of sub-section 2 above apply. Also to fines under the 1949 Act as it applies under this Act.

Legal proceedings.

717 The Board of Trade may take any legal proceedings under this Act in the name of any of their officers.

COMMENTS.

Board of Trade.

See comments to section 713.

Expenses of Commissioners of Customs

Expenses incurred by Commissioners of Customs.

718 All expenses incurred by the Commissioners of Customs in the conduct of suits or prosecutions or otherwise in carrying into effect the provisions of this Act, shall be considered as expenses having reference to the Revenues of Customs, and shall be paid accordingly; but the Board of Trade may, with the consent of the Treasury, repay out of the Mercantile Marine Fund all or any part of such of the expenses so paid as are under this Act chargeable on that fund.

COMMENTS.

Mercantile Marine Fund.

Expenses are now paid out of moneys provided by Parliament, *see* M.S. (Mercantile Marine Fund) Act 1898, section 1, sub-section 1 (*b*).

Documents and Forms

719 All documents purporting to be made, issued, or written by or under the direction of the Board of Trade, and to be sealed with the seal of the Board, or to be signed by their secretary or one of their assistant secretaries, or, if a certificate, by one of the officers of the Marine Department, shall be admissible in evidence in manner provided by this Act. Proof of documents.

COMMENTS.

Consult *The Yarmouth*, 1909, where the court refused to admit as evidence a document purporting to issue from the Board of Trade, which was not sealed or signed as provided by this section.

720 (1) Subject to any special provisions of this Act the Board of Trade may prepare and sanction forms for any book, instrument, or paper required under this Act, other than those required under the First Part of this Act, and may make such alterations in these forms as they think fit. Power of Board of Trade to prescribe forms.

(2) The Board shall cause every such form to be sealed with their seal or marked with some other distinguishing mark, and before finally issuing any form or making any alteration in a form shall cause public notice thereof to be given in such manner as the Board think requisite in order to prevent inconvenience.

(3) The Board of Trade shall cause all such forms to be supplied at all custom houses and mercantile marine offices in the United Kingdom, free of charge, or at such moderate prices as the Board may fix, or the Board may license any persons to print and sell the forms.

(4) Every such book, instrument, or paper, required under this Act shall be made in the form (if any) approved by the Board of Trade, or as near thereto as circumstances permit, and unless so made shall not be admissible in evidence in any civil proceeding on the part of the owner or master of any ship.

(5) Every such book, instrument, or paper, if made in a form purporting to be the proper form, and to be sealed or marked in accordance with this section, shall be deemed to be in the form required by this Act unless the contrary is proved.

COMMENTS.

Board of Trade.

See preface to this edition, where by Statutory Instrument No. 1537/1970, the B.O.T., was merged into a new Department, called the Department of Trade and Industry.

Forms under the First Part of this Act.

Consult section 65 as to forms of documents and note that the form of salvage bond per section 558 is contained in the 19th Schedule of the Principal Act.

Admissible in Evidence.

Consult sections 695, 696 as to the admissibility of documents generally.

⚓ ⚓ ⚓ ⚓

Exemption from stamp duty.

721 The following instruments shall be exempt from stamp duty:—

(*a*) Any instruments used for carrying into effect the First Part of this Act; and

(*b*) Any instruments used by or under the direction of the Board of Trade in carrying into effect the Second, Fifth, Eleventh, and Twelfth Parts of this Act; and

(*c*) any instruments which are by those Parts of this Act required to be in a form approved by the Board of Trade, if made in that form.

COMMENTS.

First Part of this Act.

See section 65 and Schedule 1.

⚓ ⚓ ⚓ ⚓

Offences as to use of forms.

722 (1) If any person—

(*a*) forges, assists in forging, or procures to be forged, the seal or any other distinguishing mark of the Board of Trade on any form issued by the Board of Trade under this Act; or

(*b*) fraudulently alters, or assists in fraudulently altering, or procures to be fraudulently altered any such form,

that person shall in respect of each offence be guilty of a misdemeanor.

(2) If any person—

(*a*) when a form approved by the Board is, under the Second Part of this Act, required to be used, uses without reasonable cause a form not purporting to be a form so approved; or

(*b*) prints, sells, or uses any document purporting to be a form approved by the Board of Trade knowing the same not to be the form approved for the time being, or not to have been prepared or issued by the Board of Trade,

that person shall, for each offence, be liable to a fine not exceeding ten pounds.

COMMENTS.

Fines.

See section 680.

⚓ ⚓ ⚓ ⚓

Powers for Enforcing Compliance with Act

723 (1) Where any of the following officers; namely,— any officer of the Board of Trade, any commissioned officer of any of Her Majesty's ships on full pay, any British consular officer, the Registrar-General of Shipping and Seamen or his assistant, any chief officer of customs in any place in Her Majesty's dominions, or any superintendent, — Powers for seeing that Act is complied with.

has reason to suspect that the provisions of this Act, or any law for the time being in force relating to merchant seamen or navigation, is not complied with, that officer may—

(*a*) require the owner, master, or any of the crew of any British ship to produce any official log-books or other documents relating to the crew or any member thereof in their respective possession or control;

(*b*) require any such master to produce a list of all persons on board his ship, and take copies of the official log-books, or documents, or of any part thereof;

(*c*) muster the crew of any such ship; and

(*d*) summon the master to appear and give any explanation concerning the ship or her crew or the official log-books or documents produced or required to be produced.

(2) If any person, on being duly required by an officer authorised under this section, fails without reasonable cause to produce to that officer any such official log-book or

document as he is required to produce under this section, or refuses to allow the same to be inspected or copied, or impedes any muster of the crew required under this section or refuses or neglects to give any explanation which he is required under this section to give, or knowingly misleads or deceives any officer authorised under this section to demand any such explanation, that person shall for each offence be liable to a fine not exceeding twenty pounds.

COMMENTS.

Muster the crew of any such ships.

For provisions as to mustering of persons on board ship, *see* the M.S. (Musters) Rules 1952. S.I. 1951/1952.

Surveyors of Ships

Appointment of surveyors.

724 (1) The Board of Trade may, at such ports as they think fit, appoint either generally or for special purposes, and on special occasion, any person they think fit to be a surveyor of ships for the purposes of this Act, and a person so appointed (in this Act referred to as a surveyor of ships) may be appointed either as a shipwright surveyor or as an engineer surveyor or as both.

(2) The Board of Trade may also appoint a surveyor general of ships for the United Kingdom.

(3) The Board of Trade may remove any surveyors of ships and fix and alter their remuneration, and may make regulations as to the performance of their duties, and in particular as to the manner in which surveys of passenger steamers are to be made, as to the notice to be given by them when surveys are required, and as to the amount and payment of any travelling or other expenses incurred by them in the execution of their duties, and may by such regulations determine the persons by whom and the conditions under which the payment of those expenses is to be made.

(4) If a surveyor of ships demands or receives directly or indirectly any fee, remuneration, or gratuity whatever in respect of any duties performed by him under this Act otherwise than by the direction of the Board of Trade, he shall for each offence be liable to a fine not exceeding fifty pounds.

(5) The duties of a surveyor of ships shall be performed under the direction of the Board of Trade, and in accordance with the regulations made by that Board.

COMMENTS.

Shipwright.

This word, underlined above, has been replaced by 'ship'. *See* section 75 of the Merchant Shipping Act 1906.

Passenger Steamers.

These words underlined in sub-section 3 have been replaced by the term 'Ships'. *See* the M.S. (Safety Convention) Act 1949, section 35.

Regulations under this section.

These are contained in the 'Instructions' to surveyors, issued by the Department of Trade and Industry.

Surveyor-general of Ships.

Other principal officers in connection with the survey of ships and other matters pertaining thereto may be appointed. *See* the Merchant Shipping Act 1906, section 75, sub-section 4.

See section 503, sub-section 2 (*c*) in respect of measurement of a foreign ship.

Merchant Shipping Act 1894

Section 725

Repealed by Merchant Shipping Act 1970 (Commencement No. 1) Order 1971

726 (1) Surveyors of ships shall make such returns to the Board of Trade as that Board may require with respect to the build, dimensions, draught, burden, rate of sailing, room for fuel, and the nature and particulars of machinery and equipments of ships surveyed by them.

Returns by surveyors to Board of Trade.

(2) The owner, master, and engineer of any ship so surveyed shall, on demand, give to the surveyors all such information and assistance within his power as they require for the purpose of those returns.

(3) If any owner, master, or engineer, on being applied to for that purpose, fails without reasonable cause to give any such information or assistance, he shall for each offence be liable to a fine not exceeding five pounds.

Appointment of surveyors in colonies.

727 The governor of a British possession may appoint and remove surveyors of ships within the limits of the possession for any purposes of this Act to be carried into effect in that possession.

⚓ ⚓ ⚓ ⚓

Board of Trade Inspectors

Appointment of inspectors to report on accidents, &c.

728 The Board of Trade may as and when they think fit appoint any person as an inspector to report to them—

(*a*) upon the nature and causes of any accident or damage which any ship has sustained or caused or is alleged to have sustained or caused; or

(*b*) whether the provisions of this Act, or any regulations made under or by virtue of this Act, have been complied with; or

(*c*) whether the hull and machinery of any steamship are sufficient and in good condition.

COMMENTS.

Steamship.

For extension of this term, *see* section 743.

⚓ ⚓ ⚓ ⚓

Powers of inspectors.

729 (1) An inspector so appointed (in this Act referred to as a Board of Trade inspector) and any person having the powers of a Board of Trade inspector—

(*a*) may go on board any ship and inspect the same or any part thereof, or any of the machinery, boats, equipments, or articles on board thereof to which the provisions of this Act apply, not unnecessarily detaining or delaying her from proceeding on any voyage; and

(*b*) may enter and inspect any premises the entry or inspection of which appears to him to be requisite for the purpose of the report which he is directed to make; and

(*c*) may, by summons under his hand, require the attendance of all such persons as he thinks fit to call before him and examine for the purpose of his report, and may require answers or returns to any inquiries he thinks fit to make; and

(*d*) may require and enforce the production of all books, papers, or documents which he considers important for the purpose of his report; and (*e*) may administer oaths, or may, in lieu of requiring or administering an oath, require every person examined by him to make and subscribe a declaration of the truth of the statements made by him in his examination.

(2) Every witness summoned under this section shall be allowed such expenses as would be allowed to a witness attending on subpoena to give evidence before any court of record or if in Scotland to a witness attending on citation the Court of Justiciary; and in case of any dispute as to the amount of those expenses, the same shall be referred in England or Ireland to one of the masters or registrars of the High Court, and in Scotland to the Queen's and Lord Treasurer's Remembrancer, and the officer shall, on request made to him for that purpose under the hand of the inspector or person having the powers of an inspector, ascertain and certify the proper amount of those expenses.

(3) If any person refuses to attend as a witness before a Board of Trade inspector or before any person having the powers of a Board of Trade inspector, after having been required to do so in manner provided by this section and after having had a tender made to him of the expenses (if any) to which he is entitled under this section, or refuses or neglects to make any answer, or to give any return, or to produce any document in his possession, or to make or subscribe any declarations which an inspector or person having the powers of an inspector is hereby empowered to require, that person shall for each offence be liable to a fine not exceeding ten pounds.

COMMENTS.

B.O.T. Inspector.

See section 728 for appointment of inspectors.

Fine.

For summary prosecution of offences *see* section 680.

730 If any person wilfully impedes a Board of Trade inspector or any person having the powers of a Board of Trade inspector in the execution of his duty, whether on board a ship or elsewhere, that person shall for each offence be liable to a fine not exceeding ten pounds, and may be seized and detained by the inspector or person having the powers of an inspector, or by any person or persons whom

Penalty for obstructing inspectors in the execution of their duty.

that inspector or person may call to his assistance, until he can be conveniently taken before some justice of the peace or other officer having proper jurisdiction.

COMMENTS.

See comments to section 729.

⚓ ⚓ ⚓ ⚓

Exemption from Rates and Harbour Dues

Exemption from rates.

731 All lighthouses, buoys, beacons, and all light dues, and other rates, fees, or payments accruing to or forming part of the Mercantile Marine Fund, and all premises or property belonging to or occupied by any of the general lighthouse authorities or by the Board of Trade, which are used or applied for the purposes of any of the services for which those dues, rates, fees, and payments are received, and all instruments or writings used by or under the direction of any of the general lighthouse authorities or of the Board of Trade in carrying on those services, shall be exempted from all public, parochial, and local taxes, duties and rates of every kind.

COMMENTS.

This exemption does not apply to lighthouses under the control and management of local authorities. Mersey Docks and Harbour Board *v.* Llaneilian Overseers 1884,

and note that in accord with the Rating and Valuation Act 1961, section 12, sub-sections 1 and 3, that this section ceases to exempt from rates property belonging to or occupied by the Trinity House, with the exception of lighthouses, etc.

Mercantile Marine Fund.

Now the General Lighthouse Fund. *See* M.S. (Mercantile Marine Fund) Act 1898, section 1, sub-section 1 (*c*).

General Lighthouse Authorities.

See section 634.

Definitions.

'Lighthouse', 'buoys and beacons', *see* section 742.

⚓ ⚓ ⚓ ⚓

Exemption from harbour dues.

732 All vessels belonging to or used by any of the general lighthouse authorities or the Board of Trade shall be entitled to enter, resort to, and use any harbours, ports, docks, or piers in the United Kingdom without payment of any tolls, dues, or rates of any kind.

COMMENTS.

General Lighthouse Authority.

See section 634, sub-section 1.

⚓ ⚓ ⚓ ⚓

Private Signals

733 (1) If a shipowner desires to use for the purpose of a private code any rockets, lights, or other similar signals, he may register those signals with the Board of Trade, and that Board shall give public notice of the signals so registered in such manner as they think requisite for preventing those signals from being mistaken for signals of distress or signals for pilots.

Registration of private code of signals.

(2) The Board may refuse to register any signals which in their opinion cannot easily be distinguished from signals of distress or signals for pilots.

(3) Where a signal has been registered under this section, the use or display thereof by any person acting under the authority of the shipowner in whose name it is registered shall not subject any person to any fine or liability under this Act for using or displaying signals improperly.

COMMENTS.

Private Signals.

The use of a private signal, whether registered or not, which is liable to be mistaken for any distress signal, renders the master liable to a fine of fifty pounds. *See* the M.S. (Safety Convention) Act 1949, section 21, sub-section 3 (*b*).

Displaying Signals Improperly.

See section 667 of the Principal Act, also sections 42 and 43 of the Pilotage Act 1913.

⚓ ⚓ ⚓ ⚓

Application of Act to Foreign Ships by Order in Council

734 Where it has been made to appear to Her Majesty that the government of any foreign country is desirous that any of the provisions of this Act, or of any Act hereafter to be passed amending the same, which do not apply to the ships of that country, should so apply and there are no

Application by Order in Council of provisions of Merchant Shipping Acts to foreign ships.

special provisions in this Act for that application, Her Majesty in Council may order that such of those provisions as are in the Order specified shall (subject to the limitations, if any, contained therein) apply to the ships of that country, and to the owners, masters, seamen, and apprentices of those ships, when not locally within the jurisdiction of the government of that country, in the same manner in all respects as if those ships were British ships.

COMMENTS.

For extension effected by the Foreign Jurisdiction Acts of Part XIII of this Act, *see* comments to section 686.

For power to exempt foreign ships from certain provisions of the Merchant Shipping Acts, *see* the M.S. (Equivalent Provisions) Act 1925, section 1.

'There are . . . in this Act for that application.'

These words have been included to preserve the effect of such special provisions as contained in:—

section 84—tonnage regulations;
section 424—collision regulations;
section 545—salvage of life from foreign vessels.

Rules and Regulations.

See section 34 of the M.S. (Safety Convention) Act 1949.

Powers of Colonial Legislature

Power of colonial legislatures to alter provisions of Act.

735 (1) The legislature of any British possession may by any Act or Ordinance, confirmed by Her Majesty in Council, repeal, wholly or in part, any provisions of this Act (other than those of the Third Part thereof which relate to emigrant ships), relating to ships registered in that possession; but any such Act or Ordinance shall not take effect until the approval of Her Majesty has been proclaimed in the possession, or until such time thereafter as may be fixed by the Act or Ordinance for the purpose.

(2) Where any Act or Ordinance of the legislature of a British possession has repealed in whole or in part as respects that possession any provision of the Acts repealed by this Act, that Act or Ordinance shall have the same effect in relation to the corresponding provisions of this Act as it had in relation to the provision repealed by this Act.

COMMENTS.

British Possession.

This expression is defined by the Interpretation Act 1889, section 18, sub-section 2 as . . . any part of Her Majesty's dominions exclusive of the United Kingdom . . .

For the power of the Legislature of India and Pakistan to repeal or amend any Act, insofar as it is part of the law of the Dominion, *see* the India Independence Act 1947, section 6, sub-section 2.

This section and section 736 are to be construed as though reference therein to the legislature of a British possession did not include references to the Parliament of a Dominion. *See* Statute of Westminster 1931, section 5, and specifically:—

Parliament of Ceylon—
Ceylon Independence Act 1947, section 1 (3) and First Schedule, paragraph 3.

Parliament of Ghana—
Ghana Independence Act 1957, section 1, Schedule 1, paragraph 4.

Legislature of the Federation of Malaya—
Federation of Malaya Independence Act 1957, section 2 (1) Schedule 1, paragraph 9.

Legislation of the Republic of Cyprus—
Cyprus Act 1960, Schedule 1.

Legislation of Nigeria—
Nigerian Indepencence Act 1960, section 1 (2) (*b*), Schedule 1, paragraph 4.

Legislation of Sierra Leone—
Sierra Leone Independence Act 1961, section 1 (2), Schedule 11, paragraph 4.

Legislation of Tanganyika—
Tanganyika Independence Act 1961, section 1 (2), Schedule 1, paragraph 4.

Legislation of Jamaica—
Jamaica Independence Act 1962, section 1 (2), Schedule 1, paragraph 4.

Legislature of Trinidad and Tobago—
Trinidad and Tobago Independence Act 1962, section 1, sub-section 2, Schedule 1, paragraph 4.

Legislation of Uganda—
Uganda Independence Act 1962, section 1 (2), Schedule 1, paragraph 4.

Legislature of Kenya—

Kenya Independence Act 1963, section 1 (2), Schedule 1, paragraph 4.

Legislature of Malawi—

Malawi Independence Act 1964, section 1 (2), Schedule 1, paragraph 4.

Legislature of Malta—

Malta Independence Act 1964, section 1 (2), Schedule 1, paragraph 4 (*a*).

Legislation of Zanzibar—

Zanzibar Act 1963, section 1 (2), Schedule 1, paragraph 8 (1).

Ships Registered in British Possession.

For power to exempt British Ships registered out of the United Kingdom from certain provisions of the Merchant Shipping Acts, *see* the M.S. (Equivalent Provisions) Act 1925, section 2.

Orders in Council (under this section).

There have been several Orders in Council throughout the years confirming Dominion and Colonial legislation under this section.

Regulation of coasting trade by colonial legislature.

736 The legislature of a British possession, may by any Act or Ordinance, regulate the coasting trade of that British possession, subject in every case to the following conditions:—

(*a*) The Act or Ordinance shall contain a suspending clause providing that the Act or Ordinance shall not come into operation until Her Majesty's pleasure thereon has been publicly signified in the British possession in which it has been passed:

(*b*) The Act or Ordinance shall treat all British ships (including the ships of any other British possession) in exactly the same manner as ships of the British possession in which it is made:

(*c*) Where by treaty made before the passing of the Merchant Shipping (Colonial) Act 1869 (that is to say, before the thirteenth day of May eighteen hundred and sixty-nine), Her Majesty has agreed to grant to any ships of any foreign state any rights or privileges in respect of the coasting trade of any British possession, those rights and privileges shall be enjoyed by those ships for so long as Her Majesty has already agreed or may hereafter agree to grant the same, anything in the Act or Ordinance to the contrary notwithstanding.

COMMENTS.

Repeal.

The words underlined in this section—The M.S. (Colonial) Act 1869—repealed by section 745 and Twenty-second Schedule to this Act.

General.

Note comments to the preceding section, No. 735.

⚓ ⚓ ⚓ ⚓

Provision for Foreign Places where Her Majesty has Jurisdiction

737 Where under this Act anything is authorised to be done by to or before a British consular officer, and in any place outside Her Majesty's dominions in which Her Majesty has jurisdiction there is no such officer, such thing may be done in that place by to or before such officer as Her Majesty in Council may direct. Provision for foreign places where Her Majesty has jurisdiction.

COMMENTS.

There have been several Orders in Council promulgated over the years. Those up to the end of 1948 may be found in S.R. & O. and S.I. Rev. 1948 under 'Foreign Jurisdiction', and from the end of 1948 they are found in the annual volumes of S.I.'s under the title of 'Foreign Jurisdiction'.

⚓ ⚓ ⚓ ⚓

Orders in Council

738 (1) Where Her Majesty has power under this Act, or any Act hereafter to be passed amending the same, to make an Order in Council, Her Majesty may from time to time make that Order in Council and by Order in Council revoke, alter or add to any Order so made. Provision as to Orders in Council.

(2) Every such Order in Council shall be published in the *London Gazette*, and shall be laid before both Houses of Parliament within one month after it is made, if Parliament be then stitting, or if not, within one month after the then next meeting of Parliament.

(3) Subject to any special provisions of this Act, upon the publication of any such Order the Order shall as from the date of the publication or any later date mentioned in the Order, take effect as if it were enacted by Parliament.

COMMENTS.

Published in the 'London Gazette'.

See section 740 of this Act and comments thereto.

Laid before Parliament.

Orders are now subject to the Statutory Instruments Act 1946. Documents within the description in section 1, sub-section 2 of that Act are to be known as statutory instruments, section 4, sub-section 3 of that Act makes provisions for copies of instruments to be laid before Parliament normally before they come into operation.

As if it were enacted by Parliament.

For the competence of the court to question the authority of Orders in Council to which this provision applies, *see* Patent Agents Institute *v.* Lockwood 1894.

⚓ ⚓ ⚓ ⚓

Transmission and Publication of Documents

Notices, &c. to be in writing and provision as to sending by post.

739 (1) Where by this Act any notice, authority, order, direction, or other communication is required or authorised to be given or made by the Board of Trade, or the Commissioners of Customs, or the governor of a British possession, to any person not being an officer of such Board, or Commissioners, or governor, the same shall be given or made in writing.

(2) Where any notice or document is by this Act required or authorised to be transmitted or sent, the same may be transmitted or sent by post.

COMMENTS.

Commissioners of Customs.

Now the Commissioners of Customs and Excise.

⚓ ⚓ ⚓ ⚓

Publication in *London Gazette*. 56 & 57 Vict. c. 66.

740 Where a document is required by this Act to be published in the *London Gazette*, it shall be sufficient if notice thereof is published in accordance with the Rules Publication Act, 1893.

COMMENTS.

Repeal.

Rules Publication Act 1893, underlined above, repealed by the Statutory Instruments Act 1946.

Publication in the 'London Gazette'.

See, now, the Statutory Instruments Act 1946, section 12, sub-section 2.

⚓ ⚓ ⚓ ⚓

Exemption of Her Majesty's Ships

741 This Act shall not, except where specially provided, apply to ships belonging to Her Majesty. Exemption of Her Majesty's ships.

COMMENTS.

H.M. Ships.

See comments attached to section 557 of this Act.

For registration and application of the Merchant Shipping Acts to Government ships, *see* the Merchant Shipping Act 1906, section 80.

In regard to limitation of liability of an Australian Government ship, *see The River Loddon* 1955.

Where specially provided.

The following sections are applicable:

Section 73, sub-section 3—Seizing illegal colours.
Section 99—Certificates of service.
Sections 480 *et seq.*—Naval courts.
Section 516—Naval officer as receiver of wreck.
Section 557 *et seq.*—Salvage, *see* also section 8 of the Crown Proceedings Act 1947.
Sections 76 and 692—Detention of ships by naval officers.

⚓ ⚓ ⚓ ⚓

Definitions and Provisions as to Application of Act

742 In this Act, unless the context otherwise requires, the following expressions have the meanings hereby assigned to them; (that is to say,) Definitions.

'VESSEL' includes any ship or boat, or any other description of vessel used in navigation;

'SHIP' includes every description of vessel used in navigation not propelled by oars;

'FOREIGN-GOING SHIP' includes every ship employed in trading or going between some place or places in the United Kingdom, and some place or places situate beyond the following limits; that is to say, the coasts of the United Kingdom, the Channel Islands, and Isle of Man, and the continent of Europe between the River Elbe and Brest inclusive;

'HOME TRADE SHIP' includes every ship employed in trading or going within the following limits; that is to say, the United Kingdom, the Channel Islands, and Isle of Man, and the continent of Europe between the River Elbe and Brest inclusive;

'HOME TRADE PASSENGER SHIP' means every home trade ship employed in carrying passengers;

'MASTER' includes every person (except a pilot) having command or charge of any ship;

'SEAMAN' includes every person (except masters, pilots, and apprentices duly indentured and registered), employed or engaged in any capacity on board any ship;

'WAGES' includes emoluments;

'EFFECTS' includes clothes and documents;

'SALVOR' means, in the case of salvage services rendered by the officers or crew or part of the crew of any ship belonging to Her Majesty, the person in command of that ship;

'PILOT' means any person not belonging to a ship who has the conduct thereof;

'COURT' in relation to any proceeding includes any magistrate or justice having jurisdiction in the matter to which the proceeding relates;

'COLONIAL COURT OF ADMIRALTY' has the same meaning as in the Colonial Courts of Admiralty Act, 1890;

'A COMMISSIONER FOR OATHS' means a commissioner for oaths within the meaning of the Commissioners for Oaths Act, 1889;

'CHIEF OFFICER OF CUSTOMS' includes the collector, superintendent, principal coast officer, or other chief officer of customs at each port;

'SUPERINTENDENT' shall so far as respects a British possession, include any shipping master or other officer discharging in that possession the duties of a superintendent;

'CONSULAR OFFICER', when used in relation to a foreign country, means the officer recognised by Her Majesty as a consular officer of that foreign country;

'BANKRUPTCY' includes insolvency;

'REPRESENTATION' means probate, administration, confirmation, or other instrument constituting a person the executor, administrator, or other representative of a deceased person;

'LEGAL PERSONAL REPRESENTATIVE' means the person so constituted executor, administrator, or other representative, of a deceased person;

'NAME' includes a surname;

'PORT' includes place;

'HARBOURS' includes harbours properly so called, whether natural or artificial, estuaries, navigable rivers, piers, jetties, and other works in or at which ships can obtain shelter, or ship and unship goods or passengers;

'TIDAL WATER' means any part of the sea and any part of a river within the ebb and flow of the tide at ordinary spring tides, and not being a harbour;

'HARBOUR AUTHORITY' includes all persons or bodies of persons, corporate or unincorporate, being proprietors of, or intrusted with, the duty or invested with the power of constructing, improving, managing, regulating, maintaining, or lighting a harbour;

'CONSERVANCY AUTHORITY' includes all persons or bodies of persons, corporate or unincorporate, intrusted with the duty or invested with the power of conserving, maintaining, or improving the navigation of a tidal water;

'LIGHTHOUSE' shall in addition to the ordinary meaning of the word include any floating and other light exhibited for the guidance of ships, and also any sirens and any other description of fog signals, and also any addition to a lighthouse of any improved light, or any siren, or any description of fog signal;

'BUOYS AND BEACONS' includes all other marks and signs of the sea;

'THE TRINITY HOUSE' shall mean the master wardens and assistants of the guild, fraternity, or brotherhood of the most glorious and undivided Trinity and of St. Clement in the parish of Deptford Strond in the county of Kent, commonly called the corporation of the Trinity House of Deptford Strond;

'THE COMMISSIONERS OF IRISH LIGHTS' means the body incorporated by that name under the local Act of the session held in the thirtieth and thirty-first years of the reign of Her present Majesty, chapter eighty-one, intituled 'An Act to alter the constitution of the Corporation for preserving and improving the Port of

Dublin and for other purposes connected with that body and with the Port of Dublin Corporation,' and any Act amending the same;

'LIFEBOAT SERVICE' means the saving, or attempted saving of vessels, or of life, or property on board vessels, wrecked or aground or sunk, or in danger of being wrecked or getting aground or sinking.

Any reference to failure to do any act or thing shall include a reference to refusal to do that act or thing.

COMMENTS.

This Act.

Following Merchant Shipping Acts provide that they be 'construed as one' with earlier Merchant Shipping Acts.

Vessel.

It was held in Edwards *v.* Quickended and Forester 1939, that neither a skiff nor a rowing eight, in collision on the River Thames, was a vessel within the meaning of the Maritime Conventions Act 1911, and therefore, that Act did not apply. In other words, no vessel which is propelled by oars is within the definition of vessels. *See The St. Machar* 1939, where it was held that a vessel which has just been launched, though not capable of self-propulsion, is a vessel within the definition.

Ship.

The definition of ship given above has been extended by later Merchant Shipping Acts, q.v.: M.S. (Liability of Shipowners and Others) Act 1958, section 4, sub-section 1.

Merchant Shipping Act 1921, section 1.

Crown Proceedings Act 1947, section 5, sub-section 6, as amended by the M.S. (Liability of Shipowners and Others) Act 1958, section 8, sub-section 5.

Crown Proceedings Act 1947, section 30, sub-section 3.

The Harbours Act 1964, section 57, sub-section 1.

Decisions based upon the original definition as contained in section 742 of the Principal Act. It would appear that the purpose for which a vessel is being used at the material time is significant:—

Ex parte Ferguson and Hutchinson 1871: a coble having removable masts, which proceeded to sea, was held to be a ship, although she was fitted with oars for harbour movement.

A barge with no means of propulsion, not propelled by oars and towed by tugs, was held to be a ship. *The Mac* 1882; *The Mudlark* 1911; *The Harlow* 1922.

A vessel which had for four years been used as a coal hulk was held not to be a ship. The European and Australian R.M. Co. *v.* P. & O. Steam Navigation Co. 1864.

See Polpen Shipping Co. Ltd. *v.* Commercial Union Assurance Co. Ltd. 1943, where it was held that a flying-boat, which the insured vessel collided with, was not a 'ship or vessel'.

Particular note should be taken of Marine Craft Constructors Ltd. *v.* Erland Blomquist Engineers Ltd. 1953. (A pontoon stripped of its crane and used temporarily for carrying goods in tow of a tug.)

The foregoing represents a cross section of decided cases. A fuller treatment of the subject is contained in *Halsbury's Laws,* 3rd Edition, Vol. 35, Part 2, to which the reader is referred.

Home Trade ship. (Pilotage Act 1913.)

A ship is not exempted from pilotage if she calls first at a port within the limits in this section and then sails to a port outside these limits. Smith *v.* Van Der Veen 1965.

United Kingdom.

The term here includes the Republic of Ireland.

Home Trade Passenger Ship.

For definition of passenger, *see* section 267, which should be read in conjunction with section 26 of the M.S. (Safety Convention) Act 1949 and Merchant Shipping Act 1964, section 17, sub-section 2.

Seaman.

For persons included in this definition, *see* R. *v.* City of London Court Judge 1890, where it was stated per Lord Coleridge, C.J., that this definition would undoubtedly include such a person as a stevedore. For additional decided cases, the reader is referred to *Halsbury's Laws,* 3rd Edition, Vol. 35, Part 3.

Wages.

A steward's commission on bar receipts is part of his wages. Thompson *v.* H. & W. Nelson 1913.

A war bonus, entered in the ship's articles, is part of crew's wages. Shelford *v* Mosey 1917.

Victualling allowance included in wages, Kinley *v. Sierra Nevada* 1924.

See also the *Gee Whiz* 1951, National Insurance contributions included in wages where agreed to be paid by the owner.

See also, for additional decided cases, *Halsbury's Laws,* 3rd Edition, Vol. 35, Part 3.

Consular Officer.

See the Interpretation Act 1889, section 12, sub-section 20.

Lighthouses.

Certain additions to existing lighthouses may be treated as separate lighthouses.

Application of Act to ships propelled by electricity, &c.

743 Any provisions of this Act applying to steamers or steamships shall apply to ships propelled by electricity or other mechanical power with such modifications as the Board of Trade may prescribe for the purpose of adaptation.

⚓ ⚓ ⚓ ⚓

Application of Act to certain fishing vessels.

744 Ships engaged in the whale, seal, walrus, or Newfoundland cod fisheries shall be deemed to be foreign, going ships for the purpose of this Act, and not fishing boats-with the exception of ships engaged in the Newfoundland cod fisheries which belong to ports in Canada or Newfoundland, 'of ships engaged in the whale fisheries off the coast of Scotland and registered at ports in Scotland.'

COMMENTS.

The words 'whale, seal, or walrus fisheries' are substituted for the words underlined by the Merchant Shipping Acts 1950, section 4.

The words 'of ships engaged in the Newfoundland cod fisheries which belong to ports in Canada or Newfoundland' are omitted by the Merchant Shipping Acts 1950, section 4.

The words 'of ships engaged in the whale fisheries off the coast of Scotland and registered at ports in Scotland', have been added by section 83 of the Merchant Shipping Act 1906.

⚓ ⚓ ⚓ ⚓

Repeal and Savings

Repeal.

745 (1) The Acts mentioned in the Twenty-second Schedule to this Act are hereby repealed to the extent specified in the third column of that schedule

Provided that—

(*a*) Any Order in Council, licence, certificate, byelaw, rule, or regulation made or granted under any enactment hereby repealed shall continue in force as if it had been made or granted under this Act;

(*b*) Any officer appointed, any body elected or constituted, and any savings bank or office established, under any enactment hereby repealed shall continue and be deemed to have been appointed, elected, constituted, or established, as the case may be, under this Act;

(*c*) Any document referring to any Act or enactment hereby repealed shall be construed to refer to this Act, or to the corresponding enactment of this Act;

(*d*) Any penalty may be recovered, and any offence may be prosecuted, under any provision of the Merchant Shipping Acts, 1854 to 1892, which is not repealed by this Act, in the same manner as fines may be recovered and offences prosecuted under this Act;

(*e*) Ships registered under the Merchant Shipping Act, 1854, and the Acts amending the same, or duly registered before the passing of the Merchant Shipping Act, 1854, shall be deemed to have been registered under this Act;

(*f*) Nothing in this Act shall affect the Behring Sea Award Act, 1894, and that Act shall have effect as if this Act had not passed.

(2) The mention of particular matters in this section shall not be held to prejudice or affect the general application of section thirty-eight of the Interpretation Act, 1889, with regard to the effect of repeals.

(3) The tonnage of every ship not measured or remeasured in accordance with the Merchant Shipping Tonnage Act, 1889, shall be estimated for all purposes as if any deduction prohibited by the Merchant Shipping (Tonnage) Act, 1889, had not been made, and the particulars relating to the ship's tonnage in the registry book and in her certificate of registry shall be corrected accordingly.

COMMENTS.

Repeal.

'savings bank or.'

These words underlined repealed. The Merchant Shipping Act 1970 (Commencement No. 1) Order 1972.

Repealed as Spent.

The words underlined by doubled lines, from 'The Acts' to 'Provided that', repealed as spent by the Statute Law Revision Act 1908.

Merchant Shipping Tonnage Act 1889.

Repealed by this section and the Twenty-second Schedule to this Act.

Savings. 18 & 19 Vict. c. 104.

746 (1) Nothing in this Act shall affect the Chinese Passengers Act, 1855.

(2) Any local Act which repeals or affects any provisions of the Acts repealed by this Act shall have the same effect on the corresponding provisions of this Act as it had on the said provisions repealed by this Act.

(3) Nothing in this Act shall affect the rating of any seaman who was rated and served as A.B. before the second day of August one thousand eight hundred and eighty.

⚓ ⚓ ⚓ ⚓

Short Title and Commencement

Short title.

747 This Act may be cited as the Merchant Shipping Act, 1894.

⚓ ⚓ ⚓ ⚓

A.D. 1894.

Commencement.

748 This Act shall come into operation on the first day of January one thousand eight hundred and ninety-five.

COMMENTS.

Repeal.

This section was repealed as spent by the Statute Law Revision Act 1908.

⚓ ⚓ ⚓ ⚓

FIRST SCHEDULE

Form 'A', BILL OF SALE. Repealed M.S.A. 1965. The words 'Bill of Sale' to be added at the end of Part II of Schedule 1. *See* section 24, sub-section 2 of the Principal Act, as amended M.S.A. 1965, Schedule II.

Form 'B', MORTGAGE (1).

(Insert description of ship and particulars as in Bill of Sale.)

1. To Secure Principal Sum and Interest.

(*a*) the undersigned in consideration of this day lent to (*b*) by do hereby for (*c*) and (*d*) heirs, covenant with the said firstly that (*a*) or (*d*) heirs, executors, or administrators, will pay to the said the said sum of together with interest thereon at the rate of per cent per annum on the (*f*) day of next; and secondly, that if the said principal sum is not paid on the said day (*a*) or (*d*) heirs executors, or administrators will, during such time as the same or any part thereof remains unpaid, pay to the said interest on the whole or such part thereof as may for the time being remain unpaid, at the rate of per cent per annum, by equal half-yearly payments on the day of and day of in every year; and for better securing to the said the repayment in manner aforesaid of the said principal sum and interest (*a*) hereby mortgage to the said shares of which (*e*) the owner in the ship 1. above particularly described, and in her boats, guns, ammunition, small arms, and appurtenances 2. Lastly (*a*) for (*c*) and (*d*) heirs, covenant with the said and assigns that (*a*) has power to mortgage in manner aforesaid the above-mentioned shares, and that the same are free from encumbrances (*g*).

In witness whereof (*a*) has hereto subscribed (*d*) name and affixed (*d*) seal this day of One thousand eight hundred and .

Executed by the above named in the presence of .

(*a*) 'I' or 'we';

(*b*) 'Me' or 'us';

(*c*) 'Myself' or 'Ourselves'

(*d*) 'My' or 'Our'

(*e*) 'I am' or 'We are';

(*f*) Insert the day fixed for payment of principal as above;

(*g*) If any prior incumbrance add, 'save as appears by the registry of the said ship'.

NOTE—The prompt registration of a mortgage deed at the port of registry of the ship is essential to the security of the mortgagee, as a mortgage takes its priority from the date of production for registry, not from the date of the instrument.

2. To Secure Account Current, etc.

Whereas (*a*) .

Now (*b*) the undersigned in consideration of the premises for (*c*) and (*d*) heirs covenant with the said and (*e*) assigns, to pay to him or them the sums for the time being due on this security, whether by way of principal or interest, at the times and manner aforesaid. And for the purpose of better securing to the said the payment of such sums as last aforesaid (*b*) do hereby mortgage to the said shares, of which (*f*) the owner in the ship above particularly described, and in her boats, guns, ammunition, small arms, and appurtenances.

Lastly, (*b*) for (*c*) and (*d*) heirs covenant with the said and (*e*) assigns that (*b*) has power to mortgage in manner aforesaid the above-mentioned shares, and that the same are free from encumbrances (*g*) .

In witness whereof (*b*) has hereto subscribed (*d*) name and affixed (*d*) seal this day of One thousand eight hundred and .

Executed by the above named in the presence of .

(*a*) Here state by way of recital that there is an account current between the mortgagor (describing him) and the mortgagee (describing him); and describe the nature of the transaction so as to show how the amount of principal and interest due at any given time is to be ascertained, and the manner and time of payment.

(*b*) 'I' or 'we';

(*c*) 'Myself' or 'ourselves';

(*d*) 'My' or 'Our';

(*e*) 'His' or 'their';

(*f*) 'I am' or 'we are';

(*g*) If any prior encumbrance, add 'save as appears by the registry of the said ship'.

NOTE—The prompt registration of a mortgage deed at the port of registry of the said ship is essential to the security of the mortgagee, as a mortgage takes its priority from the date of production for registry, not from the date of the instrument.

Form 'C', TRANSFER OF MORTGAGE.

(To be indorsed on the original mortgage.)

(*a*) the within-mentioned in consideration of this day paid to (*b*) by hereby transfer to (*c*) the benefit of the within written security.

In witness whereof (*d*) has hereunto subscribed (*e*) name and affixed (*e*) seal , this day of One thousand eight hundred and .

Executed by the above named in the presence of .

(*a*) 'I' or 'we';

(*b*) 'Me' or 'us';

(*c*) 'Him' or 'them';

(*d*) 'I' or 'we';

(*e*) 'My' or 'our'.

PART II

Documents of which the Forms are to be Prescribed by the Commissioners of Customs* and Sanctioned by the (Minister of Transport)

Certificate of surveyor.

Declaration of ownership by the individual owner.

Declaration of ownership on behalf of a corporation as owner.

Certificate of registry.

Provisional certificate.

Declaration of ownership by individual transferee.

Declaration of ownership on behalf of a corporation as transferee.
Declaration of owner taking by transmission.
Declaration by mortgagee taking by transmission.
Certificate of mortgage.
Certificate of sale.
Revocation of certificate of sale or mortgage.
Bill of Sale.

*Now 'Commissioners of Customs and Excise' see Customs and Excise Act 1952, s.318 (1)

SECOND SCHEDULE

Repealed by M.S.A. 1965, Schedule 11

THIRD–FOURTH SCHEDULES

Repealed as from 19th November 1952
by the M.S. (Safety Convention) Act 1949
Section 37, sub-section 5, and Third Schedule

FIFTH SCHEDULE

REGULATIONS TO BE OBSERVED WITH RESPECT TO ANTI-SCORBUTICS.

Furnishing of Anti-Scorbutics.
Section 200.

(1) The anti-scorbutics to be furnished shall be lime or lemon juice, or such other anti-scorbutics (if any) of such quality, and composed of such materials, and packed and kept in such manner as Her Majesty by Order in Council may direct (i).

(2) No lime or lemon juice shall be deemed fit and proper to be taken on board ship, for the use of the crew or passengers thereof, unless it has been obtained from a bonded warehouse for and to be shipped as stores.

(3) Lime or lemon juice shall not be so obtained or delivered from a warehouse as aforesaid, unless—

(*a*) it is shown, by a certificate under the hand of an inspector appointed by the (Minister of Transport) to be proper for use on board ship, the certificate to be given upon inspection of a sample, after deposit of the lime or lemon juice in the warehouse; and (*b*) it contains fifteen per cent of proper and palatable proof spirit, to be approved by the inspector or by the proper officer of customs, and to be added before or immediately after the inspection thereof; and

(*c*) it is packed in such bottles at such time and in such manner and is labelled in such manner as the Commissioners of Customs may direct.

(4) If the lime or lemon juice is deposited in a bonded warehouse, and has been approved as aforesaid by the inspector, the spirit, or the amount of spirit necessary to make up fifteen per cent may be added in the warehouse, without payment of any duty thereon; and when any spirit has been added to any lime or lemon juice, and the lime or lemon juice has been labelled as aforesaid, it shall be deposited in the warehouse for delivery as ship's stores only, upon such terms and subject to such regulations of the Commissioners of Customs as are applicable to the delivery of ships' stores from the warehouse.

(5) The lime or lemon juice with which a ship is required by this Act to be provided shall be taken from the warehouse duly labelled as aforesaid, and the labels shall remain intact until twenty-four hours at least after the ship has left her port of departure on her foreign voyage.

Serving out of Anti-Scorbutics.

(6) The lime or lemon juice shall be served out with sugar (the sugar to be in addition to any sugar required by the agreement with the crew).

(7) The anti-scorbutics shall be served out to the crew so soon as they have been at sea for ten days; and during the remainder of the voyage, except during such time as they are in harbour and are there supplied with fresh provisions.

(8) The lime or lemon juice and sugar shall be served out daily at the rate of an ounce each day to each member of the crew, and shall be mixed with a due proportion of water before being served out.

(9) The other anti-scorbutics, if any, provided in pursuance of an Order in Council shall be served out at such times and in such quantities as the Order in Council directs.

SIXTH SCHEDULE

REGULATIONS TO BE OBSERVED WITH RESPECT TO ACCOMMODATION ON BOARD SHIPS.

Sections 79, 210.

(1) Every place in a ship occupied by seamen or apprentices, and appropriated to their use, shall be such as to make the space which it is required by the Second Part of this Act to contain available for the proper accommodation of the men who are to occupy it, and shall be

securely constructed, properly lighted and ventilated, properly protected from weather and sea, and as far as practicable, properly shut off and protected from effluvium which may be caused by cargo or bilge water.

Paragraphs 2–5 inclusive repealed M.S.A. 1965.

Paragraphs 6 and 7 Repealed by the M.S. (Safety Convention) Act 1949, section 37, sub-section 5, and Third Schedule.

(8) When the accommodation is inspected at the same time with the measurement of the tonnage, no separate fee shall be charged for the inspection.

SEVENTH SCHEDULE

Repealed by M.S.A. 1970
The M.S.A. 1970 (Commencement No. 1) Order 1972
As from 1st January 1973

EIGHTH SCHEDULE

Repealed by M.S.A. 1970
The M.S.A. 1970 (Commencement No. 1) Order 1972
As from 1st January 1973

NINTH SCHEDULE

Repealed as from the 19th November 1952
by the M.S. (Safety Convention) Act 1949, Section 37
sub-section 5 and Third Schedule

TENTH–FOURTEENTH SCHEDULES

Repealed M.S.A. 1906, Section 85, Schedule 11

FIFTEENTH SCHEDULE

Repealed by M.S.A. 1937

SIXTEENTH SCHEDULE

Repealed by M.S. (Safety Convention) Act 1949
Section 37, sub-section 5, and Third Schedule

SEVENTEENTH SCHEDULE

LIFE-SAVING APPLIANCES.

Constitution of the Committee.

(1) Three shipowners, selected by the Council of the Chamber of Shipping of the United Kingdom.

(2) One shipowner selected by the Shipowners Association of Glasgow and one shipowner selected by the Liverpool Steamship Owners Association, and the Liverpool Shipowners Association conjointly.

(3) Two shipbuilders selected by the Council of the Institution of Naval Architects.

(4) Three persons practically acquainted with the navigation of vessels selected by the shipmasters' societies recognised by the (Minister of Transport) for this purpose.

(5) Three persons being or having been able-bodied seamen, selected by seamens' societies recognised by the (Minister of Transport) for this purpose.

(6) Two persons selected conjointly by the Committee of Lloyd's the Committee of Lloyd's Register Society, and the Committee of the Institute of London Underwriters.

EIGHTEENTH SCHEDULE

Repealed by M.S. (Safety Convention) Act 1949
Section 37, sub-section 5, and Third Schedule

NINETEENTH SCHEDULE

PART I

STATEMENTS IN THE CASE OF SALVAGE BY HER MAJESTY'S SHIPS.

(1) Particulars to be stated both by the salvor and by the master or other person in charge of the vessel, cargo, and property saved:—

(*a*) the place, condition, and circumstances in which the vessel, cargo,or property was at the time when the services were rendered for which salvage is claimed.

(*b*) The nature and duration of the services rendered.

(2) Additional particulars to be stated by the Salvor:—

(*a*) the proportion of the value of the vessel, cargo, and property and of the freight which he claims for salvage, or the values at which he estimates the vessel, freight, cargo, and property respectively, and the several amounts that he claims for salvage in respect of the same.

(*b*) any other circumstances which he thinks relevant to the said claim.

(3) Additional particulars to be stated by the said master or other person in charge of the said vessel, cargo, or property:—

(*a*) a copy of the certificate of registry of the said vessel, and of the indorsements thereon, stating any change which (to his knowledge or belief) has occurred in the particulars contained in the certificate; and stating also to the best of his knowledge and belief, the state of the title to the vessel for the time being, and of the incumbrances and certificates of mortgage or sale, if any, affecting the same, and the names and places of business of the owners and incumbrancers:

(*b*) the name and place of business or residence of the freighter (if any) of the said vessel, and the freight to be paid for the voyage on which she then is:

(*c*) a general account of the quantity and nature of the cargo at the time the salvage services were rendered.

(*d*) the name and place of business or residence of the owner of the cargo and of the consignee thereof:

(*e*) the values at which the master or person making the statement estimates the vessel, cargo, and property, and the freight respectively, or if he thinks fit, in lieu of the estimated value of the cargo, a copy of the vessel's manifest.

(*f*) the amounts which the master thinks should be paid as salvage for the services rendered:

(*g*) an accurate list of the property saved in cases where the vessel is not saved:

(*h*) an account of the proceeds of the sale of the vessel, cargo, or property in cases where the same or any of them are sold at the port where the statement is made:

(*i*) the number, capacities, and condition of the crew of the vessel at the time when the services were rendered: and

(*k*) any other circumstances he thinks relevant to the matters in question.

PART II

SALVAGE FUND.

(*N.B.*—Any of the particulars not known or not required by reason of the Claim being only against the Cargo, etc., may be omitted.)

Whereas certain salvage services are alleged to have been rendered by the vessel (insert names of vessel and commander) commander to the merchant vessel (insert names of vessel and master) master, belonging to (name and place of business or residence of owner of vessel) freighted by (the name of the freighter) and to the cargo therein, consisting of (state very shortly the descriptions and quantities of the goods, and the names and addresses of their owners and consignees):

And whereas the said vessel and cargo have been brought into the port of (insert name and situation of port), and a statement of the salvage claim has been sent to (insert name of the consular officer or judge of the colonial court of admiralty or vice-admiralty court, and of the office he fills), and he has fixed the amount to be inserted in this bond at the sum of (state the sum).

Now I, the said (master's name) do hereby, in pursuance of the Merchant Shipping Act 1894, bind the several owners for the time being of the said vessel and of the cargo therein and of the freight payable in respect of that cargo and their respective heirs, executors, and administrators, to pay among them such sum not exceeding the said sum of (state the sum fixed) in such proportions and to such persons as (if the parties agree on any other court substitute the name of it here) the High Court in England shall adjudge to be payable as salvage services so alleged to have been rendered as aforesaid.

In the witness whereof I have hereunto set my hand and seal, this (insert the date) day of .

Signed, sealed, and delivered by the said (master's name)

(L.S.)

In the presence of (name of consular officer or judge of the colonial court of admiralty or vice-admiralty court, and of the office he fills).

TWENTIETH SCHEDULE
MAXIMUM FEES AND REMUNERATION OF RECEIVERS.

	£	s.	d.
For every examination on oath instituted by a receiver with respect to any vessel which may be or may have been in distress, a fee not exceeding	1	0	0
But so that in no case shall a larger fee than two pounds be charged for examinations taken in respect of the same vessel and the same occurrence, whatever may be the number of the deponents.			
For every report required to be sent by the receiver to the secretary of Lloyd's, in London, the sum of	0	10	0

For wreck taken by the receiver into his custody, a percentage of five per cent upon the value thereof.

But so that in no case shall the whole amount of percentage so payable exceed twenty pounds.

In cases where any services are rendered by a receiver in respect of any vessel in distress not being wreck, or in respect of the cargo or other articles belonging thereto, the following fees instead of a percentage; (that is to say),

If that vessel with her cargo equals or exceeds in value six hundred pounds, the sum of two pounds for the first, and the sum of one pound for every subsequent day during which the receiver is employed on that service, but if that vessel with her cargo is less in value than six hundred pounds, one moiety of the above-mentioned sum.

The Twentieth Schedule, so far as it specifies the amount or the maximum amount of any fees, was repealed as from 19th November 1952, by the M.S. (Safety Conventions) Act 1949, section 37, and Schedule 3.

The fees at present in force, are contained in part twelve of the Merchant Shipping (Fees) Regulations, 1975, in operation from 1st April, 1975, Viz:

Fees of Receivers of Wreck

1. The fees prescribed in this Part are payable under section 567 (1) of the principal act.

2. **Service**	**Fee:**
Every report required to be sent by the Receiver to the secretary of Lloyd's in London	£1·50
Wreck taken by the Receiver into his custody	a percentage of five per cent of the value thereof

Services rendered by a Receiver in respect of any vessel in distress, not being a wreck or in respect of the cargo or other articles belonging thereto.

(a) if the vessel with her cargo equalls or exceeds in value £5,000	£16·00 for the first and £8·00 for every subsequent day during which the Receiver is employed on that service.
(b) if the vessel with her cargo is less in value than £5,000.	One half of the fee under (a).

TWENTY-FIRST SCHEDULE

This Schedule Repealed by Pilotage Act 1913
Section 60, and Schedule 11
Note the saving in section 59 of the Pilotage Act 1913

TWENTY-SECOND SCHEDULE

Repealed as spent by the Statute Law Revision Act 1908

INDEX

INDEX